Hostis Humani Generis

Front Cover Images:

'Ballamy Salute' to the American Flag
ca. 1941
Symbol of the 'Theosophical Society', the Ouroboros: a
snake eating its own tail
ca. 1875

Rear Cover Images, from top left:

Richard T. Ely
Walter Lippmann
Washington Gladden
John Dewey
Francis Bellamy
Oliver Wendell Holmes Jr.
Franklin Delano Roosevelt
Woodrow Wilson

Hostis Humani Generis

The American Aeneid, and the Nature of Progressivism

Spencer D. Miles, PhD.

Tributary House Ltd.
Colorado
www.TributaryHouse.com

This work is a history built on critical analysis.

All analyses and criticisms are specific to the nature and quality of ideals.

Any perceived personal attacks or disparagement of living individuals are both subjective and unintended. Criticisms of the dead are legitimate opinions of an historian.

An ideal is not a man, and a man is not an ideal. What is true is indestructible; only what is false will feign offense.

If what I say is false, it will fail of its own weakness.

Tributary House Ltd.
Colorado
www.TributaryHouse.com

Paperback ISBN: 979-8-218-84764-7

Dedication

To the socially awkward outcast who daily lives the reality that 'it is no mark of sanity to be well-adjusted to a profoundly sick society.'

You are the sane man in the land of the mad.

Stay weird.

Table of Contents

Prologue: What Standard Without Measurement?.........1

Part I: The Design...11

    On Originalism...12

    On 'Liberty' or 'Freedom'.................................20

    Legitimacy...33

    Consent of the Governed................................44

    Popular Sovereignty.......................................51

    Limited Government.......................................57

    The Self-Governing Virtue.............................69

    The Yeoman..83

    The Design...97

Part II: The American Aeneid..............................103

    The Heresy of Perfectibility..........................103

    Auto-Apotheosis: The Elitism of the Expert Class. 147

    Freedom From Fear, Fear of Freedom.....................219

Epilogue: By Their Fruits....................................293

Coda...319

Select Bibliography..323

    Prologue...323

    Part I: The Design..324

    The Heresy of Perfectibility..........................336

    Auto-Apotheosis..344

    Freedom from Fear, Fear of Freedom.....................352

    Epilogue: By Their Fruits..............................364

    Historiographical Survey..............................369

Appendix to Part I...374

Historiographical Survey....................................377

About The Author..393

Who cannot or will not answer what I have said will seek instead to attack what they *think* I have said, or what they believe me to be…

That, or simply pretend I have said nothing at all.

Prologue: What Standard Without Measurement?

אֶהְיֶה אֲשֶׁר אֶהְיֶה[1]

- Exodus 3:14

Histoy does not, cannot repeat itself as though it were some actor with the capacity to do anything. History is the simple amalgamation of stories, interpretations, myths, lies, facts, views, and ideals ostensibly based on documentation or at least oral-retelling. History does not repeat itself but rather human beings do the same things for the same reasons as those in the past, thinking that this time it will render different results because they have ascended beyond the failings of their ancestors by virtue of their birth-date. History is the story of humanity, and the story of humanity is hubris.

---

1   "I AM WHO I AM" A grammatically untranslatable verb
    construction: the imperfect tense, a past, present, and future
    continuing action, something akin to an eternal gerund that remains a
    verb. God Was, Is, and Will Be – simultaneously; His attributes are
    inseparable from His essence; God is the Principle principle. Unless
    otherwise noted, all Bible references are taken from the King James
    Version, with or without Strong's Greek and Hebrew reference.

Let mystery be forestalled. The current power structure of the United States is illegitimate according to its own definition of the term. This illegitimacy is the inevitable product of a socio-intellectual contagion that drove the episode known as the Progressive Era. The contagion was the social gospel, and the manner by which it both combined with and facilitated solipsism. This solipsism is called many things, but reduces entirely to the overt attempt to dictate reality by those who would see themselves as gods. This fundamental usurpation has destroyed the ability to perceive of and apply the principles of the Founding, and this destruction has corroded the civilization built upon those principles. The whole essence of the matter amounts to a people who cannot be free.

As a debt that cannot be paid will not be paid, so too a people who cannot be free will not be free. The people of the United States of America, herein somewhat inappropriately called 'America', continue to conceive of themselves as the world's bastion of freedom. Arguments abound regarding liberty, equality, and justice – being more appropriate to late eighteenth century France, and *la règne de terreur*, than to America – yet these extend chiefly from the same collectivist worldviews making them arguments of semantics, rather than of substance.

The substance is not obscure. American independence orbits a document that represents the deliberate application of what is now called 'The Enlightenment' specifically in the form of so-called classical liberal individualism. The Declaration of Independence is applied Lockean thought and declares the legitimacy of a course of action based not only on the manifest nature of rights, but also on the fundamental principle of authority produced by those rights: the consent of the governed. This volume will seek to uncover the causes, nature, and effect of the governed having been rendered *incapable of consent*. The work is a socio-intellectual comparative analysis of American worldviews pivoting about the Progressive Era, researched and analyzed from a universal perspective. The subject of the analysis is two opposed and incompatible perspectives regarding the purpose and scope of authority.

The work is not necessarily chronological because the subject matter is not chronological. Terminology and semantics play a central role in the story because the data has dictated deeper understanding and connection among the apparently distinct, but wholly identical ideologies. Even between the ostensibly atheist, so-called 'humanism' of John Dewey and the perverse perfection theology of Richard Ely in the social gospel, deep and undeniable similarities have become apparent. In examining National Socialism, variations between that and Progressivism, or between Franklin Roosevelt and his German counterpart, become ever more distinctions without a difference. Whatever faces various camps might assume, there are only two sides.

John Locke was quite clear regarding how one who seeks to reduce the other under his will has set himself in a state of war against the one he seeks to so reduce. American civilization was wholly founded upon that fundamental principle expressed as Consent of the Governed in accordance with the Laws of Nature and of Nature's God. Without exception every 'collective,' 'democracy,' or 'social organism' variation has sought to reduce the individual under the 'will of the collective' being in practice, only the chosen few.

The Progressive Era wholly inverted the worldview upon which America was founded; from enlightened autonomous individualism to dependent technocratic collectivism; from classical liberalism to progressivism. The inversion regards worldview specific to the social arena, but was legally complete by the time of the unanimous Supreme Court decision rendered by Justice Robert Jackson in *Wickard v. Filburn* (1942).[2]

In setting this disastrous precedent, the Harlan Stone court manufactured an 'aggregation principle' as a means of punishing a man for growing his own feed, for his own animals, on his own land. This rationalization wholly abandoned the boundaries of limited government based on the inherently collectivist claim that, while Filburn's personal wheat was trivial, if other farmers also grew their own feed

---

2   Claude R. Wickard, Secretary of Agriculture, et al. v. Roscoe
        C. Filburn, 317 U.S. 111 (1942).

interstate commerce *might* be effected.[3] This decision served only to legitimize the illegitimate usurpations of 'administration.' By 1942, the concept of an autonomous, independent, and individual yeoman farmer was subordinated to the elitist technicism of Franklin Roosevelt's Empire. In current society, the very man whom Thomas Jefferson called "...the most valuable citizen...."[4] is now called a 'myth'[5] and libelously associated with 'whiteness'.[6] It is wholly clear that the gestalt worldview upon which America was founded has been inverted. This inversion invalidated the foundation of legitimate authority in America.

There exists no citizen of the United States who is able to comprehensively narrate or outline the *de facto* function of his government – whether local, state, or federal. There is neither police officer, lawyer, nor judge who may legitimately claim to have an exhaustive understanding of the law, either in word or in practice, yet the civilian remains under the implicit threat that 'ignorance of the law is no excuse'. Neither economist, MBA, nor accountant may reliably recite from memory what taxes and fees to which a citizen is daily subject. No man knows what the law will be tomorrow. Few citizens understand the ease and impunity with which a rival may send SWAT or CPS to their home – and fewer still question how or why such a thing is possible.[7] None, it would appear, are willing to recognize in concrete terms that the principles cited and celebrated *ad nauseam* for

---

3   "Wickard v. Filburn (1942)," *Institute for Justice*, n.d. Accessed July 24, 2024: https://ij.org/center-for-judicial-engagement/programs/victims-of-abdication/wickard-v-filburn-1942/.

4   Thomas Jefferson, Letter to John Jay, Paris, August 23, 1785. The Letters of Thomas Jefferson, Yale Law School, https://avalon.law.yale.edu/18th_century/let32.asp.

5   Richard Hofstadter, "The Myth of the Happy Yeoman," *American Heritage* 7 no. 3 (April 1956): https://www.americanheritage.com/myth-happy-yeoman; cf. Richard Hofstadter, *The Age of Reform: From Bryan to F.D.R.* (New York: Alfred A. Knopf, 1955).

6   Adam Calo, "The Yeoman Myth: A Troubling Foundation of the Beginning Farmer Movement," *Gastronomia: The Journal for Food Studies* 20, no. 2 (2020): 12 – 29.

7   CPS, Child Protective Services.

all practical purposes, mean less than nothing in the daily life-course of the American citizen. American liberty tastes a lie.

With disregard for current partisanship, propaganda, or political maneuvering, to objectively view American civilization today is to raise the question: How did a people so celebrated for their heritage of liberty lose their taste for freedom? The substance of current American civilization as compared against the intended image represents a clear upending or reversal. The belief, thinking, and behavior – the worldview – that characterized the Progressive Era is responsible for the reversal from the intended enlightened autonomous individualism to a monstrous dependent collectivism.

Adjunct to the Progressive Era, the ascendancy of materialism and post-modern solipsism from the mid-twentieth century has resulted in an academic climate with little regard for a universal approach to humanity. Most academic product appears obsessed with increasingly parochial arguments extending from economic status, ethnic stereotyping, or other delusional incidentals, ignoring the possibility of universal principles. This work rejects such a trend for two distinct reasons. The first reason is self-evident and inarguable. Mankind is one species; America is a 'nation' comprised of all nations. The differences among the American nations are apparent, important, and vast, but they remain superficial. Human is human and therefore America, being *e pluribus unum*, is best analyzed within a universal paradigm.

The second reason to adopt a universal perspective is a matter both of fact and of faith. The Bible is a universal history in its composition and scope; it overtly speaks to the course of all humanity. Whether taken as mere literature, read as history, or cited as both, the Bible is central to the story of America both for its primacy in this civilization and for the myriad of themes that it conveys. Universalism is inherent to a biblical worldview like that of the founding generations, without regard to epistemic claims regarding the Bible itself.

Suitable for the nature of the opaque themes and the flavor of American culture, one made use of Christian theology to cement the fields. Christianity declares overt positions regarding the nature, purpose, and future of humanity. This work presumed to analyze the intention (*telos*) of the founding compared against its reality (*anthropology*), and ventured to claim that the ideal of progress (*eschatology*) usurped the originally intended image. In essence, the Progressive Era was the cause for the effect seen in the current quality of the American civilization, whose "...foolish hearts were darkened."[8]

This 'darkening' is a *progressive* shift in the often unspoken and unmeasured expectations that collectively form the background of a given society. Due to this inherently gossamer quality, one perceived this process chiefly through court decisions, legislative acts, executive directives, and popular trends in publication. Taken collectively, these elements from legal and political history provided distinct and identifiable events to measure the change.

The shift to an engineered – technicist or technocratic– society and its resultant dependent citizenry is characterized by social activism targeting political reform. The Progressive Era represents the time-frame intended, *generally* within twenty to thirty years of 1900 but extended when necessary. Disregarding convoluted discussions, one employed the term 'political' to refer to any item that pertains to the application of power, specifically *force* because the defining quality of any political entity is the monopoly on the legitimate use of force within its domain. Given this understanding, the Progressive Era represents a period of time surrounding *fin de siècle* wherein a number of social elements undertook overt and concerted efforts to *force* a preferred image for society.

This preferred image was the product of a climate of scientific discovery, the proliferation of certain philosophical ideals, and the development of commercial industrialization from the nineteenth century. It represents a Faustian deal to exchange the essential character of American society for knowledge and comfort. The efforts were fueled by apotheotic delusions in the perfectibility of both man and the

---

8   Romans 1:22 NKJV; cf. Romans 1:16-32.

nation resulting from heretical doctrines of then concurrent American Christianity. This religiously fueled ambition to perfect the nation deeply resembles Aeneas' destiny to create an empire without end.[9]

Gaius Julius Octavian Caesar Augustus (63 BC – AD 14) became the first Roman Emperor by means of pragmatic – Machiavellian – exploitation of the pseudo-religious fantasy expressed in Virgil's *Aeneid*. Franklin Delano Roosevelt became the first American Emperor by means of the Machiavellian – pragmatic – exploitation of the delusional theology at the center of the social gospel. The parallels are clear and the agreement between details substantial. The history of power is the story by which men empower the most polished lunatic of any given age – the ceaseless rise of the demagogue; this is the story of how America gave her liberty to madmen.

The Progressive Era inverted the worldview upon which America was founded from classical liberalism to progressivism. The social perspective regarding legitimate authority reversed from consent of the governed to diktat of the expert; from critical thinking to 'trust the science'. This reversal invalidated the foundation of legitimate authority in America.

It is axiomatic that one cannot consent to that which one does not understand. This fundamental principle underlies such a plurality of social concepts so as to be nearly atomic: the deceived, the coerced, or the deluded cannot, by definition, enter into any rational agreement. Progressivism has so occluded government that consent is now impossible; authority was left bereft of legitimacy, and thusly was reduced to force and fraud.

To address the primary guiding inquiry, this work is divided into three parts.

Part I: The Design, Limited Government for the Sovereign Moral Yeoman addressed the 'heritage of liberty' as far as can be reasonably established. One consulted the earliest primary source documentation to address the question: what was the original vision for American

---

9   *Imperium sine fine* from Virgil's Aeneid, c. 19 BC.

civilization; upon what worldview was that society to be established? While one examined numerous chief actors from the founding, this inquiry focused on John Locke (1632 – 1704) due to his primacy in the thinking cited by the central documents in the creation of the United States. In addition to Locke, James Madison (1751 – 1836) worked to convey Enlightenment ideals directly into the concept of limited government, making practical the lofty principles contained in Jefferson's Declaration. Thomas Jefferson (1743 – 1826) left an extensive corpus of philosophical reasoning around liberty that expressed in a practical image of the romanticized yeoman farmer, but is most readily apparent in his insertion of Locke into the concept of government in America by means of the Declaration of Independence. John Adams (1735 – 1826) is chiefly consulted for his prolific writing aimed at the character of the Citizen in his new republic, most easily cited in his brief address to the Massachusetts Militia.[10]

Subsequent to establishing a rational basis for comparison, Part II: The American Aeneid began the assembly of an understanding of how historic currents weakened the individualist worldview in preparation for its inversion. "The Heresy of Perfectibility" addressed the religious underpinnings of social activism. This portion of the work analyzes the infiltration of Darwinism and 'higher criticism' into mainstream Protestantism, creating so-called 'liberal theology'. This mixture immediately lead to wholesale collectivism – the 'social organism' – which in turn facilitated nakedly racist eugenics, and social programs driven directly thereby.

"Auto-Apotheosis: the Elitism of the Expert Class" analyzed the intellectual basis for the inversion to 'progress'. This section demonstrates the manner by which critical thinking and the effective place of the common people were abdicated by delegation to an ever ascendant, self-affirmative expert 'elite'. This phenomena dissolved the fundamental ability of the governed to be capable of consent.

---

10   October 11, 1798,
        https://founders.archives.gov/documents/Adams/99-02-02-3102.

"Freedom from Fear, Fear of Freedom" demonstrates the effect of the combination of heretical zealotry and delusional philosophies on the practice and course of American civilization. This part of the story effectively narrates the total departure of American civilization from anything that might rationally be called a 'Republic' with any practicable level of accountability to the people it governs. In no uncertain terms, the concepts known as Progressivism, Socialism, Democracy, National Socialism, and Fascism completely lose differentiation under close scrutiny; they are all authoritarian collectivism based on the solipsism of Pragmatism, itself merely Historicism linked with Utilitarianism, fueled by the self-worshiping genocidal zealotry that is the 'social organism' application of the social gospel.

The question is "how did a people celebrated for their heritage of liberty lose their taste for freedom?" Part I: "The Design" examined the Founding as a means of deriving source-driven principles which may then compared to the dramatic turn of events between *roughly* 1880 and 1945. Part II: "The American Aeneid" narrates the growth of the 'social gospel' ("The Heresy of Perfectibility"), the rule of the 'expert class' ("Auto-Apotheosis"), and the total departure of American civilization from anything remotely resembling the founding ("Freedom from Fear, Fear of Freedom"). The Epilogue, "By Their Fruits" sought to make the contrast plain.

These divisions sought to answer questions directed at the socio-intellectual climate and produce of the Progressive Era that is so well reflected in the perverse reasoning displayed in *Wickard v. Filburn*. Taken collectively, this evidence served to answer the inquiry: what is the identifiable legacy of the various reforms? The analysis focused on the central tenet of legitimacy in American authority as extending from Locke through Jefferson: the consent of the governed.

The substance of current American civilization as compared against the intended image represents a clear reversal or degenerate inversion. The essential compromise that characterized the Progressive Era was responsible for the reversal from autonomous individualism, and therefore freedom, to a monstrous dependency and thereby covert despotic oligarchy.

The story of authority is the tale of the increasingly feverish search for the most polished sociopath of a given age, and heaping upon him exponentially more power to solve the problems created by his predecessors. Line upon line, precept upon precept, with brick for stone and pitch for mortar, a people builds a wall against fear until this cell they have constructed collapses under the weight of its own absurdity, only to begin again. This ceaseless exchange of the transcendent in favor of the transient has neither stopped nor slowed from the day Adam elected to doom the world, rather than to live on after his beloved Eve had died. The present story draws focus to the American civilization of the United States; the intention for this society compared to what it has become, and the manner by which fear conveyed into essential compromise. This compromise is the manner by which Americans have sought madmen for their leaders and in so doing, surrendered their ability to even conceive of liberty.

The legitimizing myth of the American Aeneid spurred a people to accept the satanic lie. Her soul having been sold, the Republic died but remains undead; her people in fear of conflict and impatient for paradise, contrived for themselves a counterfeit kingdom of God. What follows is the history of the manner by which America deceived *itself* during what is called the Progressive Era. How did a people with a heritage of liberty lose their taste for freedom? By swallowing the same ancient lie as did Eve: "ye shall be as gods."

Part I: The Design

Limited Government for the Sovereign Moral Yeoman

> Let no one irritate me further by saying,
> 'Moses did not mean what you say. He meant
> what I say.'…. They have no knowledge of
> the thoughts in his mind, but they are in love
> with their own opinions, not because they are
> true, but because they are their own.[11]

> – Augustine of Hippo, *Confessions*

W hat, precisely, is the heritage of liberty for which
America is ostensibly known? Late twentieth
century sociopolitical discourse has most
certainly tainted the reception of this operative inquiry,
though not nearly as much as the refined version: "What was
the original vision for American civilization; upon what
worldview was that society to be established?" Within this
inquiry, two words leave this author open to attack; such is
the gambit. The term 'original' invites rebuttal from current
perspectives regarding 'originalism,' and the concept of
'worldview' is a snare for the solipsist. The founding of the
United States, and the timbre of this argument derive from
first principles. Solipsism, whether masquerading as post-
modernism, materialism, historicism, pragmatism,
utilitarianism, or some other narcissistic sophistry, is without
a shadow of merit; if it is true, this author *imagines* it to be
false.

---

11   Augustine, *Confessions*, R.S. Pine-Coffin trans., (New York:
Dorset Press, 1961 [c. AD 398]), XII:25, 301 – 302.

Originalism, little better than an epithet in any case, serves as a retrospective heuristic to sidestep the labor in reason. Principles are primary; they may be correct or mistaken, complete or incomplete, accepted or rejected, but they of themselves do not change. The heritage, the 'original worldview' is a product of reasoning from principles; the thrust of originalism does not apply because one seeks to uncover and understand those principles and the reasoning based thereon. The question is not 'what did the founders mean', but rather whether or not their reasoning was – and is – valid.

On Originalism

Too many fall prey to the seduction of good intentions working from the literary aphorism "The Past is a foreign country: they do things differently there."[12] Many suggest a preference for, and even supremacy of context in the interpretation of historic documentation. This context invariably conveys a sleight of hand as the context of the interpretation itself evades scrutiny by authoritarian self-presentation. It is wholly certain that the pertinent men of the late eighteenth century lived and worked under the tyrant of the unexamined: the mores, expectations, and assumptions of 'their age' painted their whole person every bit as much as does that of today, 'the sixties', or the Progressive Era. Every foreign country has its own background radiation to color its climate, and Colonial America is no exception. This does not however privilege the present any more than it disadvantages the past. The inquiry 'what did the founders mean' is an unnecessary red-herring. Far better to ask from what axioms they argued, and whether or not (and why) one agrees with their conclusions.

The nature of power however demands a declaration in place of a perpetual dialectic. Herein lies the draw and the drawback of originalism. In his 1997 Pulitzer Prize winning *Original Meanings*, Jack N. Rakove devotes his introductory

---

12   L.P. Hartley, *The Go-Between* (London: Penguin Books, 1953), 7.

chapter to the concept.[13] Rakove notes that axioms are not enough to address the specific form that the new government would take. This subtlety in praxis – the conversion from theory to practice – lies at the root of the Constitutional Convention and, in Rakove's view, explains why analysis of the Enlightenment, from which the principles ostensibly descend, is an insufficient context for understanding the 'original meaning' of the Constitution. One does not agree.

Rakove highlighted the focus given to then recent controversies such as the Glorious Revolution or the Stamp Act as a means of contextualizing his argument and, owing to some superficially odd insertions in the Constitution (vis. the quartering of soldiers in the third amendment), this portion of his argument is self-evident. His argument suffers however from his almost exclusive focus on the drafting and ratification of the Constitution. By self-confessed necessity, he 'historicized' the fundamental metaphysics behind the the debates surrounding the convention, and he missed the inescapable pivot: the Constitution could have taken any form at all provided that the *principles* upon which it was written had remained intact.[14]

For example as a means of illustrating the weakness of the originalist strawman, Rakove employed an anemic view of the principle of popular sovereignty to assert that only the understanding of the ratifying men could be authoritative, with all others being "mere proposals."[15] The unstated assumption herein is the danger of veneration; one must cite some (usually long dead) authority to support one's argument. Rakove appears to argue that, if one insists upon an originalist interpretation, then only the opinions of the signatories can be valid. While Jefferson was not a signatory

---

13 "The Perils of Originalism" in Jack N. Rakove, *Original Meanings: Politics and Ideas in the Making of the Constitution*, (New York: Vintage Books, 2013 [1997]).

14 "...there is no form of Government but what may be a blessing to the people if well administered..." Benjamin Franklin, "Benjamin Franklin to the Federal Convention," September 17, 1787, in Max Farrand, ed., *The Records of the Federal Convention of 1787*, Revised ed., 4 vols. (London: Yale University Press, 1937), 2:641-643.

15 Rakove, *Original Meanings*, Chapter 1.

to the Constitution itself, one would be hard pressed to argue that he is not included in the 'Framers' and he most certainly had some applicable opinions in this matter.

> Some men look at Constitutions with sanctimonious reverence, & deem them, like the ark of the covenant, too sacred to be touched. They ascribe to the men of the preceding age a wisdom more than human, and suppose what they did to be beyond amendment. I knew that age well: I belonged to it, and labored with it.[16]

One can clearly hear the chortled snort in the aged Jefferson's use of 'sanctimonious' to describe those who *missed the point*. In what may be an historian's sin, one declares that Jefferson's philosophy included at least a portion of the principle of non-veneration; such is the nature of equality in creation. Inherent within this philosophical egalitarianism, Jefferson presaged the thought in a related statement in his letter to James Madison, from the autumn of 1789.

Jefferson declared that no generation can bind the next; that earth belongs exclusively to the living. "This principle that the earth belongs to the living, & not to the dead, is of very extensive application & consequences...."[17] Herein he declared his position to be a principle. This statement represents a mathematical method of reasoning as he stated the axiom, then sought to explore the implications of its application. The principle is set, its application and consequences are then analyzed and explored.

He again made the clear statement that he operated from the principle of non-veneration in his 1825 letter to

---

16   Thomas Jefferson, "Proposals to Revise the Virginia Constitution: I. Thomas Jefferson to "Henry Tompkinson" (Samuel Kercheval), 12 July 1816," *Founders Online*, National Archives, https://founders.archives.gov/documents/Jefferson/03-10-02-0128-0002.

17   Thomas Jefferson, "To James Madison from Thomas Jefferson, 6 September 1789," *Founders Online*, National Archives, https://founders.archives.gov/documents/Madison/01-12-02-0248.

Henry Lee. In this brief letter describing his intention in drafting the Declaration of Independence, he made it very plain that he did not seek to cite any authority, and none of his arguments were new. Quite the contrary, he viewed the document as merely a distillation of principles long established. The provenance of the 'sentiments' he sought to harmonize – Aristotle, Cicero, Locke – was not an appeal to authority, but rather evidence that he referenced a thread that continued through the ancients to the 'moderns' and *this* was evidence of its transcendence. In this, Jefferson intended to simply present the content of "the American mind" regarding the principles for which they sought the separation.[18]

To be certain, Jefferson had his heroes. The aforementioned thinkers would seem obvious, but he subordinated the Greek and the Roman to the more recent British Locke, Bacon, and Newton whom he claimed were "...the three greatest men that have ever lived, without exception... having laid the foundation of ...Physical and Moral sciences...."[19] Jefferson displayed an apparent and somewhat fanatical admiration of these men, in context speaking of an almost iconographic presentation. This certainly lays him open to a charge regarding the irrational admiration of the rational – yet one would suggest at least a partial pardon, as this does not appear to have overly colored his distillation of principles to application.

It is reasonable, owing to the previous, to suggest that Jefferson would have one set a principle, and follow that principle through application. Given the apparent ideal of at least a partial non-veneration, it would follow that any man or ideal is as subject to examination and scrutiny as is any other; such is a legitimate characterization of the alleged

---

18   Thomas Jefferson, "From Thomas Jefferson to Henry Lee, 8 May 1825," *Founders Online*, National Archives, https://founders.archives.gov/documents/Jefferson/98-01-02-5212. Note: Founder's Online disclaims this text as 'early access' and 'not an authoritative final version'. The irony of such a statement against the content of the text seems to be clear. What 'authority'? Is the text in doubt?

19   Thomas Jefferson, "From Thomas Jefferson to John Trumbull, 15 February 1789," *Founders Online*, National Archives, https://founders.archives.gov/documents/Jefferson/01-14-02-0321.

Enlightenment. Rakove certainly made such an attempt in his work, though his statement in an interview provoked a serious question.

In a 2020 interview for the *Stanford Report* regarding his work *Original Meanings*, Dr. Rakove declared that "When Jefferson wrote "all men are created equal" in the preamble to the Declaration, he was not talking about individual equality. What he really meant was that the American colonists, *as a people*, had the same rights of self-government as other peoples...."[20] This author was wholly surprised to see a collectivist rendition of equality in creation. Moreover, the phrasing "What he really meant..." in the context of a treatment of originalism, without any supporting evidence, necessitated contact.

On September 9, 2024, this author wrote to Dr. Rakove for clarification, specifically requesting some evidence or support – a citation – for such an interpretation. Very much to his credit, Dr. Rakove quickly responded. He referenced his earlier work on the Continental Congress[21] and "a few other essays"[22] on Thomas Jefferson, then clarified his argument thusly:

> The basic argument is that the form of equality the opening of the Declaration was concerned with was the collective right of the American people, having suffered a long train of abuses, to institute new governments, open relations with other nations, renounce their loyalty to the Crown (and G) etc. The delegates were not sitting around Philadelphia discussing theories of individual equality. Not

---

20   Melissa De Witte, "When Thomas Jefferson penned 'all men are created equal,' he did not mean individual equality, says Stanford scholar." *Stanford Report*, July 1, 2020. https://news.stanford.edu/stories/2020/07/meaning-declaration-independence-changed-time. Sic.

21   Jack N. Rakove, *The Beginnings of National Politics: An Interpretive History of the Continental Congress*, (New York: Knopf, 1979).

22   Jack N. Rakove, e-mail message to author, September 9, 2024.

that they were renouncing them either; only
that the context of political action had other,
more specific ends.[23]

One noted the lack of specific evidence, or rather the
conflation of *interpretation* for evidence – effectively the
essence of originalism against which Rakove argued in
Original Meanings. This author attempted to keep an open
dialogue with Dr. Rakove regarding some items in his
reasoning. He did make reference to some of his other works,
but then stated: "...what I was discussing is simply the
context within which the Declaration was written."[24] The
entire conversation is included in the appendix.

Rakove's statement to Melissa DeWitte does not
allow for this dissembling. He stated outright that
"[Jefferson] was not talking about individual equality"; this is
not a reference to context, this is not a claim that the concern
at Philadelphia was greater than individual rights. The
assertion that the rights listed in the second paragraph of the
Declaration of Independence were collective – *not* individual,
based upon the introduction of the first paragraph, is
specious. The first paragraph declares the intent to separate
as a people, and ends with the transition "...they should
declare the causes..."[25] The second paragraph declares those
causes, and is wholly Lockean in scope, intent, and content.
Jefferson himself subordinated collective rights to those of
the individual: "the rights of the whole can be no more than
the sum of the rights of the individuals."[26] That whole, being
comprised of and deriving its substance from the parts,
cannot wield a power that the parts to not have.[27] Gordon
Wood, whom Rakove consistently referenced, addressed the

---

23   Jack N. Rakove, e-mail message to author, September 9,
2024. Sic.
24   Jack N. Rakove, e-mail message to author, September 9,
2024.
25   The United States Declaration of Independence, 1776.
26   Jefferson to Madison, September 6, 1789.
27   Cf. John Locke, *Second Treatise of Government*. 1690.
Reprint, (London: A. Millar et. al., 1764), Project Gutenberg Ebook
#7370, X:132.

'meaning' behind the principle of equality in a 1995 speech given to the American Enterprise Institute.

Laying heavily into Jefferson's ideal of self-sufficiency as the *sine qua non* of independence and therefore liberty, Wood illustrated the concept of merit leading to a 'natural aristocracy'. The essence of his argument – that did indeed offer verifiable evidence – is a concept of equality in agreement with the Milton-and-Swift-citing definition given in Samuel Johnson's 1775 *Dictionary of the English Language*, noted by Monticello as having been in Jefferson's possession.[28] This definition, "the same degree of dignity" would appear to fit the context of the Declaration better than "likeness with regard to any quantities compared" or "evenness; uniformity; constant tenour; equability" also given, but none of the three admit to a collective interpretation.[29]

Whichever definition one wished to employ for what Jefferson 'really meant', it remains that "...this commandment… is not hidden from thee, neither is it far off."[30] Jefferson did not write in such a manner that requires an expert to explain. Indeed, he wrote outright that he merely distilled widely held concepts.[31] As Pauline Maier also noted in 1999, the clause beginning with the words "self-evident" are so aptly named, so common and unremarkable as to be considered almost "boilerplate."[32] More so, George Mason

---

28   "English Language Dictionaries", *The Jefferson Monticello*, Accessed September 9, 2024: https://www.monticello.org/research-education/thomas-jefferson-encyclopedia/english-language-dictionaries/#:~:text=Thomas%20Jefferson%20owned%20a%20number,Printed%20for%20Thomas%20Ewing%2C%201775.

29   "equality," *A Dictionary of the English Language*, by Samuel Johnson. 1755. Accessed September 9, 2024: https://johnsonsdictionaryonline.com/1755/equality_ns, Sic.

30   Deuteronomy 30:11.

31   Thomas Jefferson, "From Thomas Jefferson to Henry Lee, 8 May 1825.

32   Pauline Maier, "The Strange History of "All Men Are Created Equal"," *Washington and Lee Law Review* 56, issue 3 (Summer 6-1-1999): 877. Cf. Pauline Maier, *American Scripture: Making the Declaration of Independence*, (New York: Alfred A. Knopf, 1997).

(1725 – 1792) wrote in his 1776 *Virginia Declaration of Rights*, in his *first* clause, that natural rights are inherent, and crucially precede society to such an extent that no society can "...deprive or divest their posterity..." of these rights.[33] As is often noted, the Declaration of Independence and the *Virginia Declaration* are consanguineous in provenance, influence, scope, and intent.[34] The sentiments contained were not a product of Philadelphia, neither are they limited to the American continent. The principle of equality is self-evident, self-apparent, and self-explanatory; as Alexander Hamilton stated:

> The sacred rights of mankind are not to be
> rummaged for, among old parchments, or
> musty records. They are written, as with a sun
> beam, in the whole volume of human nature,
> by the hand of the divinity itself; and can
> never be erased or obscured by mortal
> power.[35]

Rakove and so many others have missed the point not for any deficiency of scholarship, but rather due to having been robbed of their birthright. No man ought to resign himself to being a footnote or a mere chronographer. All men being equal, he would be far better served to hazard embarrassment on the limb of an argument from principle, and to risk his own life, fortune, and sacred honor to test his convictions. Among equals, one neither studies nor writes the deeds of greater men; one takes his place alongside them. "State a moral case to a plowman and a professor. The former will decide it as well, and often better than the latter, because he has not been led astray by artificial rules."[36] The origin of

---

33   George Mason, "The Virginia Declaration of Rights." June 12, 1776, *National Archives: America's Founding Documents,* https://www.archives.gov/founding-docs/virginia-declaration-of-rights, Section 1.

34   Cf. Pauline Maier, "The Strange History", 878.

35   Alexander Hamilton, "*The Farmer Refuted*, &c., [23 February] 1775," *Founders Online*, National Archives, https://founders.archives.gov/documents/Hamilton/01-01-02-0057.

36   Thomas Jefferson, "From Thomas Jefferson to Peter Carr, with Enclosure, 10 August 1787," *Founders Online*, National

the 'artificial rules' and the failure to grasp the centrality of
principle are symptoms of the disease that is Progressivism;
one cannot consent to a superior any more than one can argue
with a fallacy.

Principles transcend, and are therefore independent of
time, place, and person; they are not subject to an elitist
interpretation of context. After the day the boy has learned
his letters, and found a dictionary, he has no further need for
one to explain to him what he has already known in his heart
from the day of his birth: "Therefore all things whatsoever ye
would that men should do to you, do ye even so to them: *for
this is the law and the prophets*."[37] Originalism is a red-
herring.

On 'Liberty' or 'Freedom'

Many have set upon the contrast or interoperability of
the terms 'liberty' and 'freedom'. This author would not be
so bold as to attempt a novel treatment. Disregarding the
semantics of 'originalism', one merely sought an appropriate
lexicographical foundation from which to make a definition
that then might be employed in understanding the frequent
references to the terms – not as items for quibbling, but rather
as principles from which to reason.

Liberty is a first principle among the most often
employed terms from the time and place in question. It is
wholly shameful that without doubt one can easily envision
the rebuttals that would precipitate should Patrick Henry
declare his boundary and resolve in some public forum
today:

Henry: "Forbid it, Almighty God! I know not
          what course others may take; but as for

Archives, https://founders.archives.gov/documents/Jefferson/01-12-
02-0021. Cf. Gordon Wood, "Thomas Jefferson and the Idea of
Equality", Speech, *American Enterprise Institute*, January 9, 1995.
https://www.aei.org/research-products/speech/thomas-jefferson-and-
the-idea-of-equality/.
37   Matthew 7:12, emphasis added.

me, give me liberty or give me death!"[38]

Interloper: "Actually, Mr. Henry, we live in a *society*, and your Christo-colonial-normative-toxic-masculine-extremist-individualism is oppressive; your violent narrative is a product of French misinformation and your hyper-focus on individual liberty is not only a white-supremacist dog-whistle, but exploitative of the proletariat and dangerous to our monarchy."

Henry: "What?"

Given the perfectly normal semantic shifting inherent in the course of language over centuries, it is already difficult enough to engage with somewhat distant primary sources. Adding layer upon layer of what amounts to little better than propaganda and fabrication for political or other dysfunctional purposes further frustrates dialogue across ages. It is reasonable therefore to seek out a grammar, such that one may employ at least the image of empirical communication.

Despite what misunderstandings may have resulted from the previous statements, context is important in understanding – it is not however a sovereign filter or ultimate arbiter of 'meaning'. Lexicography employs literary context to seek what has been conveyed in vocabulary as opposed to employing an imagined retrospective as a means of re-defining that vocabulary. Given such a distinction, one must seek some context for vocabulary, that being the vehicle

---

38   Patrick Henry, "Give me liberty or give me death", March 23, 1775, *Yale Law School,* https://avalon.law.yale.edu/18th_century/patrick.asp. Cf. Patrick Henry, "On the Resolution to Put the Commonwealth into a State of Defense," Virginia Convention, March 23, 1775, *The Constitution of the United States of America and Selected Writings of the Founding Fathers*, (New York: Barnes & Noble, 2012), 71.

through which principles convey. Vocabulary is physical, principles are *metaphysical*; though not of an ineffectual speculative variety.

The failure to grasp and to incorporate the Christian Bible in the analysis of Colonial America is as fundamentally corrosive to understanding as would be the total ignorance of Homer in the scrutiny of the Hellenic world. This is not a matter of post-modern imagined context, but rather a vital recognition that the Bible is the lexicon from which *most* eighteenth century American thought was derived. Few poignant men or documents fail to reference the central perspectives of the Bible, especially when addressing disagreements in particulars; even Hume and Voltaire knew their Bible, despise it though they did. Whether or not one agrees with the paradigm, biblical reference and criticism comprise an inarguable core to enlightenment thinking with which this entire analysis is concerned. Eighteenth century 'liberty' is therefore fundamentally grounded in the biblical concept, if not entire then most certainly in majority part.

By way of example for the above, the influence of John Witherspoon (1723 – 1794) over the events and meaning in question cannot be rationally dismissed, to say nothing of his paternity in influential scholarly paradigms within the new country. The sixth president of the College of New Jersey (Princeton), author of *Lectures on Moral Philosophy, and Eloquence* 1774 (required at the college), and signatory to the Declaration is frequently cited in the intellectual lineage of an impressive number of elevated names – delegates, senators, representatives, justices, and presidents. While the man deserves his own exclusive treatment, Witherspoon is herein cited due to his first-degree-antecedence in the life of James Madison.[39]

---

39   Highlights for Witherspoon referenced in George H. Nash, "John Witherspoon: Educating for Liberty", *Religion & Liberty* 34, no 1 (February 19, 2024), https://www.acton.org/religion-liberty/volume-34-number-1/john-witherspoon-educating-liberty#:~:text=Good%20Calvinist%20that%20he%20was,make%20man%20perfect%20or%20perfectible. A more complete biography, Cf. Jeffry H. Morrison, *John Witherspoon and the Founding of the American Republic*, (Indiana: University of Notre Dame Press, 2005).

When Madison arrived at Princeton in 1769, the entire faculty consisted of Witherspoon and three others.[40] The modesty of the institution belies the expansive influence it exerted; the Presbyterian Reverend Witherspoon conveyed the 'common sense' flavor of the Scottish Enlightenment directly to his students. His influence was such that both Madison and Hamilton would continue to seek out Witherspoon's advice during their public lives.[41] His 1774 "Thoughts on American Liberty" leaves no room for misunderstanding as he advised the Congress to declare to the Crown that they "...prefer war with all its horrors, and even extermination itself, to slavery rivetted on us and our posterity."[42] Liberty or death; liberty or... *extinction*.

The College of New Jersey was a far different institution under Witherspoon than might be expected by one in the early twenty-first century; indeed, all of the institutions extending from that time are now merely a crude mockery of their former selves. Despite what one might assume from the small size at the time, or from some modernist condescension regarding curriculum 'back then', the climate at the little school was of such vigor and extent as to utterly shame *any* of the extant so-called ivy league.[43] In addition to Moral Philosophy, Witherspoon taught French, Theology, History, Classics, and Hebrew.[44] Madison's study included classical languages (Greek and Latin) among mathematics, rhetoric, and the required Moral Philosophy. More poignantly however, Madison remained after his graduation in 1771 to

---

40   D. F. Thompson, "The Education of a Founding Father: The Reading List for John Witherspoon's Course in Political Theory, as Taken by James Madison", *Political Theory* 4, no. 4 (1976): 523.

41   Jefferey H. Morrison, "The Political Thought of John Witherspoon, 1768-1794," (PhD diss., Georgetown University, 1999), 247, 228.

42   John Witherspoon, "Thoughts on American Liberty," 1774, from *The Works of John Witherspoon*, 9 vols. Edinburgh, 1804, 9:73-77, Accessed September 11, 2024: https://www.njstatelib.org/wp-content/uploads/slic_files/imported/NJ_Information/Digital_Collections/NJInTheAmericanRevolution1763-1783/ThoughtsOnAmericanLiberty.pdf, 86. Sic.

43   Regarding the 'flavor' of early Princeton's intellectual climate, Cf. George Nash, "John Witherspoon," 2024.

44   D.F. Thompson, "The Education of a Founding Father," 523.

study Hebrew directly under Witherspoon.[45] The Greek and the Hebrew, with Witherspoon's preference for annihilation over *slavery* are of paramount importance in the understanding of what, precisely, the various men had in mind when they discussed liberty.

Given that the past is a foreign country, in this particular foreign country men knew their Bible – and that in the tongues of its composition. As John Hancock (1737 – 1793) thoroughly mixed his rhetoric for liberty with passages known so well he did not feel a need to cite them, it cannot be supported that biblical analysis is inapplicable to eighteenth century lexicography.[46] Biblical reference is most certainly appropriate to an eighteenth century definition for liberty, as Witherspoon declared, "If the Scripture is true, the discoveries of reason cannot be contrary to it; and therefore, it has nothing to fear from that quarter."[47]

In reference to both the Hebrew and the Greek, 'liberty' is the state of non-domination; the absence of being under another's dominion (i.e., not a slave or 'bondsman'). The translation of the former, דְּרוֹר — (*deror*), appears in Leviticus 25:10: "...proclaim liberty throughout all the land unto all the inhabitants thereof…" and alternately translates as 'release', especially from captivity or indenture, in reference to the Jubilee.[48] The latter, ἐλευθερία – (*eleutheria*), appearing first in Romans 8:21, refers specifically to a state of freedom from slavery (i.e., non-domination).[49]

---

45   "The Life of James Madison", *James Madison Montpelier*, n.d., Accessed September 10, 2024: https://www.montpelier.org/learn/the-life-of-james-madison/.

46   John Hancock, "The Boston Massacre," March 5, 1774, in *The Constitution of the United States of America*, 2012, 53; Cf. Habbakkuk 3:17, 18.

47   John Witherspoon, *Annotated Edition of Lectures on Moral Philosophy*, edited by Jack Scott. (Newark: University of Delaware Press, 1982), 64.

48   Cf. Isaiah 61:1; Luke 4:18; especially associated with 'deliverance': ἄφεσις – (*aphesis*), Strong's Greek 859.

49   "Liberty," Hebrew 1865; Greek 1657, *The Strongest Strong's Exhaustive Concordance of the Bible*, John R. Kohlenberger III and James A. Swanson eds. (Grand Rapids: Zondervan, 2001). Cf. II Corinthians 3:17; Galatians 5:1. Cf. "Free" Hebrew 2666 חָפַשׁ - (khaw-fash'): to be free, and derivative "freedom", 2668.

The state of non-domination is not difficult, it is that state in which one may do, or refrain from doing, what one wishes. Certainly there are limits on this freedom – liberty is not license. This caveat precedes the eighteenth century in John Locke's qualification:

> ...yet it is not a state of licence.... The state of nature has a law of nature to govern it... that being equal and independent, no one ought to harm another in his life, health, liberty, or possessions: for men being all the workmanship of one omnipotent, and infinitely wise maker....[50]

Earlier even than Locke, the concept of non-domination in liberty was connected to this inherently reflexive limitation in the first century James' "law of liberty" and the aforementioned concept of 'do unto others'.[51] Non-domination was considered to be all inclusive – neither dominate, nor be dominated. As is clear from Locke's reference to this being a natural product of the principle of equality (an individual, *not* collective equality), the equality itself is a product of the substance of mankind as having been created by the only One for whom dominion is no evil. Stated alternatively: "Locke based his entire approach to politics on an anthropology – a view of human nature – that drew its authority from the Bible, a book that most colonial Americans revered."[52] Lockean liberty was a product of self-evident creation with the 'same degree of dignity', and this is a product of Biblical – Christian – anthropology.

Given such a *context*, it is wholly unsurprising that both Johnson's and Webster's dictionaries from around the time, that Jefferson possessed, would not only offer an

---

[50]   John Locke, *Second Treatise of Government*, 1690. Reprint, (London: A. Millar et. al., 1764), Project Gutenberg Ebook #7370, II:6. Sic.

[51]   James 1:25; Cf. Romans 8:21; Matthew 7:12.

[52]   Joseph Laconte PhD, "1776: A Lockean Revolution," *The Heritage Foundation*, July 7, 2021 https://www.heritage.org/american-history/commentary/1776-lockean-revolution.

equivalent concept in the state of non-domination, but also cite both the Bible and Locke (among others including Shakespeare and Milton) as justification for their definitions.[53]

One need not reference the modern non-profit at Monticello to demonstrate that Jefferson had such a definition and provenance in mind in his understanding of both equality and of liberty. In his draft of the Declaration, he flatly stated as much. "We hold these truths to be sacred & undeniable; that all men are created equal & independant, that from that equal creation they derive rights inherent & inalienable, among which are the preservation of life, & liberty, & the pursuit of happiness...."[54] It is apparent also that even the span of four-decades, and two presidencies, did not shift his operative definition of liberty in the slightest. He wrote in 1819 that "...rightful liberty is unobstructed action according to our will, within the limits drawn around us by the equal rights of others."[55] This statement is, simply, the principle of bi-directional non-domination.

The bi-directionality of non-domination is of paramount importance in the comprehension of both 'liberty' and 'freedom' in the founding. The possibility of the 'golden rule' in operation is inseparable from the concept of self-government inherent in the limitations of non-domination. This image of self-government is encapsulated within the ideal of 'virtue' and, as Benjamin Franklin (1706 – 1790) stated succinctly in personal correspondence shortly before his death: "...only a virtuous people are capable of freedom.

---

53   "Liberty", *Webster's Revised*, 1913
         https://www.gutenberg.org/cache/epub/664/pg664-images.html;
         "Liberty", Samuel Johnson. *Dictionary of the English Language*,
         1755. *Johnson's Dictionary Online*.
         https://johnsonsdictionaryonline.com/.
54   *The Papers of Thomas Jefferson*, Vol. 1, 1760-1776. Ed.
         Julian P. Boyd. (Princeton: Princeton University Press, 1950), 243-
         247; Cf. "Jefferson's "Original Rough Draught" of the Declaration of
         Independence", *Library of Congress*, Accessed September 12, 2024:
         https://www.loc.gov/exhibits/declara/ruffdrft.html. Sic.
55   Thomas Jefferson, "Thomas Jefferson to Isaac H. Tiffany, 4
         April 1819," *Founders Online*, National Archives,
         https://founders.archives.gov/documents/Jefferson/03-14-02-0191.
         Cf. John Locke, *Second Treatise of Government*, 1690, II:4.

As nations become corrupt and vicious, they have more need of masters."[56] Where this author would offer only a tenuous, conceptual equivalence between freedom and liberty, four others would make this connection far more overt – and expand thereon.

In biblical translation, both the Greek and the Hebrew for 'liberty' and 'freedom' derive from the same words, with the same reference to non-domination.[57] Webster and Johnson also define 'freedom' as synonymous with 'liberty', but add the exemption from control, servitude, or power. These two also append the word 'independence' to their derived definitions, with Webster citing Milton yet again, and Johnson referencing the eminent Edmund Spenser (1552 – 1599).[58]

This latter addition – 'independence' – is of particular application. For this word, Samuel Johnson offered a definition of notable application in understanding Jefferson: "Freedom; exemption from reliance or control; state over which none has power."[59] Given such a clear connection, one re-examines Jefferson's position "...all men are created equal & independent...."[60]

To read Jefferson via Johnson, the words render thusly: 'all men are created with the same degree of dignity: with freedom, exemption from reliance or control, and into a

---

56   Benjamin Franklin, "To Messrs. The Abbés Chalut and Arnaud," April 17, 1787, in: Jared Sparks, ed., *The Works of Benjamin Franklin; containing several political and historical tracts not included in any former edition, and many letters official and private, not hitherto published; with notes and a life of the author*, Vol. X, (Boston: Hillard, Gray, 1840), 297.

57   Cf. "Liberty", Hebrew 1865; Greek 1657, "freedom", Hebrew 2668, and "free" 2666 in *The Strongest Strong's Exhaustive Concordance of the Bible*, 2001, above.

58   "Freedom", *Webster's Revised*, 1913: https://gutenberg.org/cache/epub/663/pg663-images.html; "Freedom", Samuel Johnson. *Dictionary of the English Language*, 1755. *Johnson's Dictionary Online*. https://johnsonsdictionaryonline.com/.

59   "Independence", *A Dictionary of the English Language*, by Samuel Johnson. 1773, https://johnsonsdictionaryonline.com/1773/independence_ns.

60   Jefferson's Draft Declaration.

state over which none has power.' For Jefferson at the very least, it is not remotely unreasonable to posit something of an inter-reinforcing 'civil trinity' regarding his anthropology with each deriving from the others: equality, liberty, and independence. One would here reiterate that while the vocabulary certainly required reference to literary context, it was a simple matter to derive *meaning* from Jefferson's writings and lexicon without the least whisper of 'historicizing context'; to state it yet again: principles transcend.

Liberty and freedom, both as terms and ideals, were interchangeable on the eighteenth century stage. They were not *limited* to mere synonyms as they carried differing shades for different emphases. This author would argue that 'liberty' is the umbra, the core of non-domination most delineated by the 'golden rule'[61], whereas 'freedom' is the penumbra. The ideal of 'independence' coalesces this 'region' into a cohesive whole by reference to both terms, yet the whole itself is but the 'shadow' cast by equality – itself the substance of creation. Where is a shadow cast without the light, and who indeed could it be who is "the Father of lights who illuminates our understandings?"[62] One would suggest that the image and argument are complete, but the tedious self-congratulations of modernity would beg to differ.

It is a mark of modernism to contrive absurd semantic sophistries from the incidental complexities of the English language. Owing to a certain Viking's great-great-grandson taking a boat ride in AD 1066, this mother tongue has repeated many concepts from both the Norman French, and the Saxon Germanic.

To be certain, the use of vocabulary in practice erodes the sharp distinctions or similarities between terms, yet the Old-English (the Anglish, or effectively Anglo-Saxon

---

61   Regarding the centrality of the 'golden rule' in equality, liberty, and Natural Law, Cf. Hooker in Locke, *Second Treatise of Government*, 1690, II:5., and again Locke II:7; IV:22.

62   Benjamin Franklin, "Constitutional Convention Address on Prayer," June 28, 1787, *American Rhetoric: Online Speech Bank*, Accessed September 12, 2024: https://www.americanrhetoric.com/speeches/benfranklin.htm.

tongue) *concept* that undergirded the word *"freodom"* was wholly identical to the Latin *"liber"* from whence descends 'liberty'.[63] Freedom and liberty are synonyms precisely for the same reason that the English phrase 'freedom and liberty' translates into the Dutch (Germanic) as *'vrijheid en vrijheid'* and into the Spanish (Romanic) as *'libertad y libertad'*. Differentiation in this regard is equivalent ridiculousness as the statement 'it's not a baby, it's a *fetus'* (offspring) – or 'it's not a baby, it's an *enfant'* (infant). While there are ill-defined shades deriving from the sanction of usage, they are and have always been merely arbitrary audible or written grunts or symbols employed to refer to *identical mental concepts*. Were this argument untrue, all inter-linguistic communication would therefore be impossible (as opposed to merely difficult). The act of translation presupposes, acts upon, and is enslaved within the self-evident *fact* that mental-concepts are the matter – the 'stuff' – of transcendent metaphysics, to which all functioning human minds have access.[64]

It is wholly fortunate that linguistics reflects universalism, as the fundamental similarity among human minds is not only that by which translation is facilitated between contemporaries, but also comprises the mechanic through which communication with the foreign past takes place. Were men wholly a product of their time, as the post-modernist would insist, the very compilation of history would be impossible (again, opposed to difficult) once a given age had passed. To be certain there are vast differences in particulars, but neither this argument nor the Declaration were confined to the temporary or particular. The temporal and particular are mere incidentals employed to indicate and to elucidate the transcendent, the essential, and the universal – whispers of the great beyond though they may be.

---

63   "Freedom," *Online Etymology Dictionary*, Accessed September 16, 2024: https://www.etymonline.com/word/freedom; "Liberty," *Online Etymology Dictionary*, Accessed September 16, 2024: https://www.etymonline.com/search?q=liberty.
64   For a more comprehensive treatment of language, including linguistics and semantics, cf. Mario Pei, *The Story of Language*, Revised ed., (New York: New American Library, 1984 [1949]).

Paul Eidelberg sought after this gossamer yet wholly present matter in the last volume of his trilogy addressing the political philosophy of the founding of the Republic. The third of the trilogy is his 1976 provocatively named *On the Silence of the Declaration of Independence*. This political scientist employed primary sources to illuminate the climate in which the Declaration was written – not as an historicized context, but as a thousand arrows pointing to the same elevated concepts. Without using the same terminology, Eidelberg demonstrated that the substance of bi-directional non-domination is inherent in the ephemeral concept of the oft-maligned Natural Law theory.

It was no theory to the eighteenth century. James Wilson (1742 – 1798), a self-made man, signer to both the Declaration and Constitution, tragic figure, profligate gambler, and Associate Justice on the first Supreme Court of the United States reflected on the universal essence of Natural Law while lecturing on law at the University of Pennsylvania shortly after the ratification of the Constitution.[65] Employing Cicero, Wilson argued not merely the omnipresence of this law – "given at all times and to all nations" – but also that the 'giver' of it was God "...the sole master and sovereign of mankind."[66] Eidelberg employed both Wilson and Cicero in this vein as yet further evidence of the equality of creation; not only that each man is made with the same dignity, but also that they have access to the same Law – transcending both time and demographics.[67]

This universal transcendence is the whole and inescapable grammar through which the vocabulary of the Declaration – and its attendant equality, liberty, and Laws of nature's God – *must* be understood. As Eidelberg argued, "...the pragmatic reason, uninformed by the metaphysical

65   USHistory.org, "James Wilson," *Independence Hall Association*, n.d., Accessed September 17, 2024: https://www.ushistory.org/declaration/signers/wilson.html.

66   *The Works of James Wilson*, ed. Robert G. McCloskey, 2 vols. (Cambridge, Mass.: Harvard University Press, 1967), 1: 145–46.

67   Paul Eidelberg, *On the Silence of the Declaration of Independence*, (Amherst: University of Massachusetts Press, 1976), 5. Cf. Cicero, *De Re Publica*, XXI, and XXXVII.

reason, tends to become preoccupied with immediate wants and transient interests."[68] He defined the 'pragmatic' as the expression of moral relativism, and forcefully demonstrated its wholly corrosive, destructive, and fatal nature. Let no mistake arise, the ethics of solipsism are not merely self-corrosive. Where Eidelberg would speak of moral relativism, this author prefers a far more appropriate terminology: self-reinforcing delusional narcissism.[69] It is not a matter of insult.

The repudiation of the universal, the insatiable insistence upon the immediate and transient, initiates a recursive, harmonic, and *progressive* decay from man to beast. The recognition of the universal by the power of reason is that detail that separates human from sub-human.[70] Absent the universal perspective, one is rendered not only incapable of comprehending the very words liberty or equality, but one embraces intellectual, psychological, and moral decay. Without the universal, liberty, equality, and *humanity* become impossible; this is the festering mass at the center of pustulant boil that is the Progressive Era.

In seeking his 'original meaning', Rakove focused on the Constitution. This myopia failed to grasp and incorporate the universal principles upon which it was written – those contained in the Declaration. Rakove's failure is a product of a lack of recognition for the universal and deep meaning behind the 'Blessings of Liberty' for which the Constitution was written.[71] As reflected in his conversation with this author, Rakove relied on an *interpretation* of context to make a wholly false statement regarding what Jefferson "really meant." While his scholarship of that context is likely to be impeccable, lest the Pulitzer itself come under suspicion, he appears to have been ignorant of the grammar under which that context operated, and so makes an absurd statement.

Ironic that Rakove, seeking a context divorced of the spiritual provenance and wholistic intellectual *climate* from

---

68   Eidelberg, *On the Silence*, 37.
69   "The Declaration Applied: Relativism versus Universalism," Chapter 3 in Eidelberg, *On the Silence*, 27 – 52.
70   Cf. Eidelberg, *On the Silence*, 51.
71   Preamble to the Constitution of the United States of America, 1787.

which the principles derive, should miss the point entirely. It is clear then that not only are moral questions impeded by artificial rules, but also the substance of words themselves. This trend – to subsume bastardized principles divorced of their spiritual, metaphysical, provenance – is the essence of the ersatz moralism that drove the Progressive Era, and characterizes the depravity of today.

Interpretation, as it is so promiscuously employed in modern parlance, is unnecessary. As Hamilton, Wilson, Madison, Jefferson, and so many others wrote so often regarding the inescapable reality, the plain meaning of principles and their application are written in the very flesh of one's heart. This is the whole substance: what one wishes, or does not wish to be done to them, one will do or refrain from doing to another. It is by no means more complex or subject to interpretation than this. It may be called 'natural law theory' or termed as simply 'common decency'. It may be couched in non-domination, non-veneration, or some other snooty terminology, but the principle remains and it is indifferent to both time and place.

The 'heritage of liberty' is so entirely simplistic that any functioning human mind can both grasp and apply it in daily life. This simplicity is so thorough that the failure to comprehend it is the mark of a derelict mind, and the failure to apply it is the very image of criminal. As Locke said so clearly: "...he who attempts to get another man into his absolute power, does thereby put himself into a state of war with him...."[72] The whole of American civilization extends from this and Jefferson's 'trinity': equality, liberty, and independence. The importance thereof is made plain in Adams' words to his beloved:

> ...But a Constitution of Government once changed from Freedom, can never be restored. Liberty once lost is lost forever. When the People once surrender their share in the Legislature, and their Right of defending the Limitations upon the Government, and of

---

72   Locke, *Second Treatise*, III:17.

resisting every Encroachment upon them, they
can never regain it.[73]

Legitimacy

The inalienable rights listed in the ratified Declaration
comprise merely a *part* of the transcendent, universal, and
wholly apparent 'truths' so held. The second paragraph of the
Declaration is a massive run-on sentence, and what beauty
that it is so. Each of the many points are introduced with the
demonstrative 'that', and all of them fall under the same "We
hold these truths to be self-evident…" which constitute the
"causes which impel them to the separation". Two of these
causes/clauses are of primary importance in addressing the
application of the worldview under which the American
civilization was built – that being equality, liberty, and
independence *under God*, as a result of His act in creation.

The preceding pages have already analyzed, and one
would hope utterly proved the introductory premise "That all
men are created equal". In perfect Lockean reasoning, the
next clause flows directly from the first: "they are endowed
by their Creator with certain unalienable rights"[74]. The first
principle of the legitimacy of American government is the
absolute and unqualified fact that God Himself is the Author,
Origin, and Master of humanity and human rights; *no human
power has claim to originate rights.*[75] As Adams phrased the
principle very early in his career: "…liberties are not the
grants of princes or parliaments, but original rights,
conditions of original contracts, coequal with prerogative and
coeval with government."[76] The contracts are conditioned

---

73   John Adams, "John Adams to Abigail Adams, 7 July
1775," *Founders Online*, National Archives,
https://founders.archives.gov/documents/Adams/04-01-02-0160.

74   Locke, *Second Treatise*, II:6, 7; IV:22

75   Cf. Thomas Jefferson, "A Summary View if the Rights of
British America," 1774, *Yale Law School*, Accessed September 17,
2024: https://avalon.law.yale.edu/18th_century/jeffsumm.asp; Cf.
Alexander Hamilton, "*The Farmer Refuted*, &c," 1775.

76   John Adams, "VI. "A Dissertation on the Canon and the
Feudal Law," No. 4, 21 October 1765," F*ounders Online*, National

upon the rights; rights being prior, the concept of the contract itself and its derivative society are subordinate and conditional to those rights. No rights would mean no contract as the origin and character of rights descend directly from the hand of God to every living human being. Rights therefore stand abreast any possible human authority, by no means subordinate. Again *ad nauseam*, natural rights are prior and superior to authority.

Given such an elevated origin, it is clear that authority itself cannot exceed – being derived of the same substance.[77] The phrasing 'that among these', arguably the eighteenth century rendition of the modern contract-legalese "including, but not limited to", introduces the famous trilogy, but this brief list serves to introduce the second principle of legitimacy in American government: "that, to secure these rights, governments are instituted among men, deriving their just powers from the consent of the governed".[78]

The rights of one are the rights of all, those of all are of the one, and these are given from God by virtue of creation and not from governments by deign or design.[79] Government exists solely and wholly as a means to provide guards for those rights' security; the *entire raison d'être* for American government is to *secure rights*, not to 'grant' them – and most certainly not to encroach thereupon. Of the many 'powers' (impositions of will – force) that government may exercise, only those derived of consent are just; without

Archives, https://founders.archives.gov/documents/Adams/06-01-02-0052-0007.

77   Lock, *Second Treatise*, X:132.
78   Cf. Locke, *Second Treatise*, III:17, and throughout; Cf. "As the people are the only legitimate fountain of power....", James Madison, "Method of Guarding Against the Encroachments of Any One Department of Government by Appealing to the People Through a Convention," Federalist no. 49, February 5, 1788. Accessed September 18, 2024: https://guides.loc.gov/federalist-papers/text-41-50.
79   Cf. Jefferson to Madison, September 6, 1789; George Mason, "The Virginia Declaration of Rights." June 12, 1776; John Adams, "VI. "A Dissertation on the Canon and the Feudal Law," No. 4, 21 October 1765," *Founders Online*, National Archives, https://founders.archives.gov/documents/Adams/06-01-02-0052-0007.

consent, a power is inherently unjust. Not merely unjust, Locke makes it clear that despite any rationalization, dressing, or regalia with which such despotism might conceal its actions, to act outside of consent is to not only forfeit authority, but to be reduced to nothing more than a common thief.[80]

Owing to the perversity in recent parlance, one must define the term 'rights', lest the unscrupulous make overt demands on another's property based in a delusional claim to have a 'right' thereto. Declining further than merely poorly rationalized theft, many employ a dishonest inversion of 'rights' to presume to dictate the words, thinking, and even *belief* of another extending entirely from psychotic claims regarding 'identity' or a 'right to feel'. Supreme among this patently depraved sophistry, many have descended so far as to legitimize *infanticide* under the sickly delusional euphemism of 'a woman's right to choose'. These clearly juvenile arguments hold no validity in reference to reality itself, let alone to the founding worldview.

Johnson's *Dictionary* categorizes a 'right' as an adjective, adverb, interjection, noun and verb in both the 1755 and 1773 editions. Aside from the expected image of 'correct', as in 'not erroneous' or 'not wrong', the concept is intimately linked to 'justice', especially as 'a just claim' and thereby a power or prerogative.[81] The verb form of the concept refers entirely to bringing about such things. The use of the word 'just' offers a much more expansive concept. As an adjective, Johnson painted that image as that which is upright, incorrupt, proper, accurate, virtuous, innocent, pure, true, honest, complete, and without defect.[82] In both definitions, Johnson cited Richard Hooker (as did Locke), Alexander Pope, Shakespeare, and most extensively from the

---

80   Locke, *Second Treatise*, XVIII:202.
81   "right" *A Dictionary of the English Language*, by Samuel Johnson. 1755. Accessed September 17, 2024: https://johnsonsdictionaryonline.com/1755/right_ns..
82   "just" *A Dictionary of the English Language*, by Samuel Johnson. 1773. Accessed September 17, 2024: https://johnsonsdictionaryonline.com/1773/just_adj.

Bible; specific to 'right', the definitions offered rely heavily
on the Bible and Locke.

The intimacy between 'right' and 'just' is far more
vital than merely 'not wrong' as it is both an epistemic and a
moral claim. Literally, to claim a 'right' is to claim that it is
morally or ethically wrong to oppose that claim. To assert a
right is to presume the highest pedestal from which to make a
claim; to claim right is to claim moral supremacy.

As has already been demonstrated, moral authority
for the eighteenth century is inextricable from the Bible. In
the parable of the workers Jesus speaks of a landowner who
performs an 'unfair' act of paying an equal wage to a number
of workers who have labored for different times.[83]
Specifically, those who had "...borne the burden and heat of
the day" were upset that they were paid the same as those
who had only worked an hour. The landowner responds with
two points that assume two principles inherent in the concept
of rights. First, the workers had *agreed* to the pay they were
given and second, the money itself was the private property
of the landowner. Jesus renders these concepts thusly: "Didst
thou not agree with me for a penny? ... Is it not lawful for me
to do what I will with that which is mine?"[84]

The parable contains a principle regarding envy ("evil
eye"[85]) that is wholly integral to the perverse image of
'rights' as a demand upon another, yet within the story one
finds a clear reference to consent in agreement. This consent
was bi-directional in an employment contract, informal and
brief though it may be, and cannot operate without the
principle of private property. The 'penny' – a denarius,
δηνάριον (dēnarion)[86] – belonged to the landowner, the labor
to the worker; consent was in the exchange precisely because
each could do with their property as they saw fit. Such a
scene as Jesus paints, while somewhat irritating for the
superficial 'unfairness', presents a clear moral position:
property is primary. The idea that one's rights could have any

---

83   Matthew 20:1-16.
84   Matthew 20:13,15.
85   "...Is thine eye evil, because I am good?" Matthew 20:15b;
    Cf. Proverbs 28:22.
86   Strong's Greek, 1220.

claim against another's property in absence of or contrary to that one's consent is utterly absurd.

While one cannot well argue that Jefferson thought of this parable in particular, though it is wholly reasonable to assume he was familiar therewith, in remarking on the implications of a treaty with France he stated that "...if performance becomes self-destructive to the party [to the treaty, agreement], the law of self-preservation overrules the laws of obligation to others."[87] In this document, Jefferson equates contracts between nations to contracts between men – individuals – predicated upon "Moral duties" extending from Locke's state of nature, and adding yet again to the individual derivation of rights.

Not merely repeating the fact that the rights of the whole are derived from the rights of the individual, Jefferson declared that the evidence of the truth of "these principles" is in "the head and heart of every rational and honest man [where] Nature has written her Moral laws, and where every man may read them for himself."[88] Again, it is merely an application of the sublime simplicity in the 'golden rule' – one immediately knows an act to be wrong when he is the target of such an act.

Not to be limited to Jefferson, Franklin spoke regarding the causality of poor social policy. While he began with a reference to Britain, Franklin shifted to a clearly universalist lens with the utterly common "History affords us many instances..." of the causes of ruin. Among those causes, "[t]he ordaining of laws in favor of one part of the nation, to the prejudice and oppression of another, is certainly the most erroneous and mistaken policy. An equal dispensation of protection, rights, privileges, and advantages, is what every part is entitled to, and ought to enjoy."[89] His

87   Thomas Jefferson, "IV. Opinion on the Treaties with France, 28 April 1793," *Founders Online*, National Archives, https://founders.archives.gov/documents/Jefferson/01-25-02-0562-0005.
88   Thomas Jefferson, "Opinion on the Treaties", 1793.
89   Benjamin Franklin, "DXCI. The Result of England's Persistence in her Policy Towards the Colonies Illustrated", in *The Complete Works of Benjamin Franklin*, Vol. V, 1772-1775, John Bigelow, ed. (New Yok: G.P. Putnam's Sons, 1887), 417.

statement, and the principle of equality from which it clearly derives, does not allow for one group – say women – to have a 'right' – 'choice' – that is not evenly afforded to every other group – men. To state succinctly, if a 'right' is not universal, it is no 'right' at all. It is hardly improper to reason that the right to one's property, specifically against its seizure for 'redistribution' to another group, is also wholly included in this protection. To rob the rich and pay the poor is still robbery, even when done by policy.[90]

Such reasoning was mirrored nearly a century later in Justice Thomas Stanley Matthews' (1824 – 1889) unanimous opinion in *Yick Wo v. Hopkins*. Crucially, Justice Matthews made an identical equation of the concept of 'freedom' with that of non-domination, and hearkens even further back to Locke's position that "Natural liberty... [is] not to be subject to the inconstant, uncertain, unknown, arbitrary will of another man...."[91] Additionally, Matthews clearly knew his Locke in equating property to life itself.[92]

> For the very idea that one man may be compelled to hold his life, *or the means of living*, or any material right essential to the enjoyment of life, at the mere will of another, seems to be intolerable in any country where freedom prevails, as being the essence of slavery itself.[93]

It is clear that rights descend from God, and are prior and superior to society and governments. As the concept of an agreement derives from rights according to Jefferson, then any agreement is also subordinate to the rights of the parties to that agreement. Far from an obligation upon another, or entitlement to somebody's stuff, rights are limitations such that the violation of a right obviates obligations, and even authority itself.[94] As Hamilton wrote: "If the representatives of the people betray their constituents, there is then no

---

90   Cf. Locke, *Second Treaties*, XI:138; XXVIII:202.
91   Locke, *Second Treatise*, IV:22.
92   Locke, *Second Treatise*, V:25, 35; IX:124.
93   *Yick Wo v. Hopkins,* 118 U.S. 356 (1886); emphasis added.
94   Locke, *Second Treatise*, XVIII:202.

resource left but in the exertion of that original right of self-defense which is paramount to all positive forms of government."[95] In this case Hamilton spoke of the "original right of self-defense", that being inherent in life itself, and it is superior to all authority.

To argue that one has a 'right' to have some thing provided to them by another is a ridiculous non-sequitur. Such an assertion is the moral claim to command an obligation and simply, "to be commanded we do not consent".[96] Rights are limitations, neither wages nor entitlements; specifically a right is a line that it is morally repugnant for another to cross and it would be self-destructive to that line should a 'right' entitle one to obligate another. Rights descend from God, obligations derive from consent – and these are perpetually subject to the preservation of rights. All have a right to speak, none the 'right to be called' as such would obligate another's words. All have a right to live, none the 'right to choose' murder – whether or not the living are called child or *fetus*.

Furthermore, in his 1819 letter to Isaac Tiffany, Jefferson made it plain that the circumscription of liberty is naturally produced by the individual equality of others.[97] It is hardly to be considered a difficult matter to state that one who claims a 'right' to *force* an act or acquiescence makes a clear and notorious attack upon the liberty of another, to say nothing of infanticide being an attack on the first right itself. The presumption of 'right' as 'entitlement' is self-destructive; to make this claim is identical to the fundamental *stupidity* in all solipsism – it is to saw the branch upon which one sits.

---

95   Alexander Hamilton [Attributed], "The Same Subject Continued: The Idea of Restraining the Legislative Authority in Regard to the Common Defense Considered," *Federalist No. 28*, 1787, *Library of Congress*, Accessed September 19: https://guides.loc.gov/federalist-papers/text-21-30#s-lg-box-wrapper-25493341.

96   John Adams, "III. Reply of the House to Hutchinson's Second Message, 2 March 1773," *Founders Online*, National Archives, https://founders.archives.gov/documents/Adams/06-01-02-0097-0004.

97   Thomas Jefferson, "Thomas Jefferson to Isaac H. Tiffany, 4 April 1819.

Given a clear understanding of the origin and nature of rights, one returns again to the purpose and legitimacy of government – to *secure* these rights with authority deriving from the consent of the governed.

Locke selected as epigraph for his *Second Treatise* the Ciceronian maxim: *salus populi suprema lex esto* from *De Legibus.*[98] A simple translation is as follows: "the safety [lit. 'health'] of the people is the highest law." In yet another historian's sin, one would present such a statement as indicative of an 'organic law', or a law that comprises a foundation of a government. Were Rome a non-profit institution, one might assert this as its mission statement, ignored though it was. Locke's reason for selecting this reference cannot be employed in a collective or corporate sense – Spock's claims regarding the needs of the many outweighing the needs of the few cannot be shoehorned into Locke[99]. The many are comprised of the few, or the one, the needs of the collective derive from the needs of the individual:

> But though men, when they enter into society, give up the equality, liberty, and executive power they had in the state of nature, into the hands of the society, to be so far disposed of by the legislative, as the good of the society shall require; *yet it being only with an intention in every one the better to preserve himself, his liberty and property; (for no rational creature can be supposed to change his condition with an intention to be worse)* the power of the society, or legislative constituted by them, can never be supposed to extend farther, than the common good; *but is obliged to secure every one's property….*[100]

---

98   Book 3, III:8.
99   Leonard Nimoy as Spock in *The Wrath of Khan*, 1982.
100   Locke, *Second Treatise*, IX:131; emphasis added. Cf. Jefferson to Madison, September 6, 1789.

And yet again, according to Locke, the purpose of civil or political society is the preservation of property.[101] This position statement was again reiterated by Madison's suggestion on amending the Constitution to include "[t]hat government is instituted, and ought to be exercised for the benefit of the people; which consists in the enjoyment of life and liberty, with the right of acquiring and using property, and generally of pursuing and obtaining happiness and safety."[102] Given that this specific suggestion was not incorporated into the amendments that would become the Bill of Rights, there would appear to be weasel-room to disagree with the purpose of American government. Such is entirely impossible.

The Constitution is subordinate to the Declaration. It would be wholly delusional to assert that sentiments completely changed in the brief years between these two documents. Owing to Madison's introduction in his thoughts on possible amendments, and the ensuing premises he outlined, one may rationally claim that he saw the latter document as pursuing or enacting the principles outlined in the former. He was certainly not alone in this perspective.

The previously mentioned prodigal framer James Wilson – who was party to both documents – stated the provenance directly. After reciting the second paragraph of the Declaration, he declared: "This is the broad basis on which our independence was placed: on the same certain and solid foundation this [constitutional] system is erected."[103] It is wholly poignant that one of the first Associate Justices (appointed by Washington, 1789) spoke of the foundation upon which the Constitution was built.[104]

---

101   Locke, *Second Treatise*, IX:124.
102   James Madison, "Amendments to the Constitution, [8 June] 1789," *Founders Online*, National Archives, https://founders.archives.gov/documents/Madison/01-12-02-0126.
103   James Wilson, "Remarks of James Wilson in the Pennsylvania Convention to Ratify the Constitution of the United States, 1787," in *Collected Works of James Wilson*, Vol. 1, Eds. Kermit L. Hall and Mark David Hall. (Indianapolis: Liberty Fund, 2007).
104   "Justice James Wilson," *Justia, U.S. Supreme Court*. Accessed September 23, 2024:

As previously mentioned, organic laws comprise the foundations of governments. Justice David Josiah Brewer (1837 – 1910), citing *Yick Wo*, spoke of the 'force of organic law'. While he stated that the principles within the Declaration did not have such force, he qualified by saying that "...it is always safe to read the letter of the Constitution in the spirit of the Declaration of Independence." In the court's opinion as late as 1897, the Constitution was merely "...but the body and the letter of which [the Declaration] is the thought and the spirit...." Thusly it is clear that even at this late date, the essential purpose – 'spirit' – animating the various provisions of the Constitution extended directly from the Declaration; the Constitution was merely "intended to secure that equality of rights which is the foundation of free government."[105] Justice Brewer's use of 'force of organic law' in his statement is however incorrect.

The 43rd Congress (1873 – 1875) commissioned George S. Boutwell (1818 – 1905) to codify the first official United States Code. He noted in his 1878 preface that he was "directed also to include... the Declaration of our National Independence...." as the "Organic Laws of the United States of America".[106] While it can be disingenuously dismissed as a nicety of tradition holding no legitimate basis for argument, this convention in United States law has extended through every edition of the revised statues; indeed, 1 U.S.C. § 1 (2012) is the Declaration of Independence. Factually speaking, 'rule number one' of the United States Government is, and always has been, the Declaration of Independence – the Constitution is rule *number four*.[107]

It is, and has been clear that the Declaration serves *ad fontes* for the Constitution. The 'meaning' and purpose for the Constitution is not found therein; as Eidelberg stated "The Constitution is not a political treatise. Its philosophic

---

https://supreme.justia.com/justices/james-wilson/.

105   *Gulf, Colorado & Santa Fe Railway Co. v. Ellis*, 165 U.S. 150 (1897).

106   *U.S. Statutes at Large*, Volume 18 (1873-1875): 43rd Congress; Revised Statutes in Force, Accessed September 20, 2024: https://www.loc.gov/resource/llsalvol.llsal_018a/?sp=19&st=text, Preface V: image 6; 1: image 19.

107   *U.S. Statutes at Large*, 17: image 33.

principles are not evident, its key terms are not defined."[108] Justice Brewer clarified 'rule number one' succinctly: "The first official action of this nation declared the foundation of government in these words: "We hold these truths to be self-evident...."""[109] The Declaration is to the Constitution what Johnson's lexicon is to American English of the eighteenth century; to understand or to 'interpret' the Constitution's introductory "We the People of the United States...", one need only to consult the principles of the Declaration.

The whole legitimacy of the United States government, from its conception and inception, is rooted in and wholly enslaved by God's abundantly clear act of creation-with-the-same-degree-of-dignity, from which is derived the concept of universal, individual rights – upon which depends the authentic veracity of an agreement freely entered: the consent of the governed. As Madison would have put it: "That all power is originally vested in, and consequently derived from the people."[110] For a closed argument, Johnson defined 'legitimacy' in only two manners: the lawfulness of birth, and genuine, as opposed to spurious.[111]

As simply as may be stated, to spurn or repudiate the Declaration – specifically the self-evident principles therein cited – is to abandon legitimacy. To abandon legitimacy in questions of power is to forego the very image of authority, to reduce government to nothing more sophisticated or justifiable than brutal, bestial, criminal force. This repudiation may be the most clear and damning characterization of the Progressive Era – as will be made wholly clear.

---

108   Paul Eidelberg, "The Philosophy of the American Constitution" PhD Diss., 12.
109   *Gulf, Colorado & Santa Fe Railway Co. v. Ellis*, 165 U.S. 150 (1897), citing the Declaration, referencing *Yick Wo*.
110   James Madison, "Amendments to the Constitution, [8 June] 1789".
111   "legitimacy," *A Dictionary of the English Language*, by Samuel Johnson, 1773, https://johnsonsdictionaryonline.com/1773/legitimacy_ns.

Consent of the Governed

God Himself asked for consent prior to issuing the once revered ten words.[112] This is not simply an impotent homiletic to be forgotten in time for 'Monday night football'. As has been exhaustively demonstrated, Locke set Creation as the basis for his anthropology; both preceding and descending from this basis, he also sets God as the Supreme Judge to whom all, including civil authorities, must answer.[113] This aspect of Locke's philosophy is not only crucial to understanding the eighteenth century worldview, it constitutes the essential thesis of the Declaration – to separate from Britain based on an appeal "...to the Supreme Judge of the world...."[114]

This appeal to God, by and for the people, was a direct citation from Locke. Notably, Locke introduced his concept of the 'appeal to heaven' in his third chapter "State of War". This warfare is exemplified by one's attempted usurpation over another, and is to be answered by this appeal when there is no other appropriate venue. For a precedent, Lock cited Jephtha's similar claim against the Ammonites in the book of Judges and concluded that in absence of an established arbiter one is left with no other recourse.[115] Yet again, in the Declaration's phrasing "...evinces a design to reduce them under absolute despotism..."[116] it is abundantly clear that the signatories believed that George III had placed *himself* into a state of war against the colonies and, as there was no human court over both he and them, the colonies were left with only one recourse. As Locke stated: "And where the body of the people, *or any single man*, is deprived of their right, or is under the exercise of a power without right, and have no appeal on earth, then they have a liberty to appeal to heaven, whenever they judge the cause of sufficient moment."[117]

---

112   Exodus 19:5.
113   Locke, *Second Treatise*, XIX:241; Cf. II:13.
114   Declaration of Independence, closing paragraph.
115   Locke, *Second Treatise*, III:17, 20, 21. Cf. Judges 11:27.
116   Declaration of Independence, second paragraph.
117   Locke, *Second Treatise*, XIV: 168; emphasis added.

This 'appeal to heaven' or the resort to God appears in such a body of eighteenth century product so as to suggest that it was a phrase in common parlance.[118] Recent illiterately delusional controversies regarding the slogan contemptuously dismissed, the phrase itself may be the original motto of the revolution itself as evidenced by the abundance of 'appeal to heaven' flags and other paraphernalia from the period.

This detail, being sufficiently established, demonstrates yet another evidence of the supreme place of both the Bible and John Locke in eighteenth century colonial American thought. The meaning behind its use cannot be misunderstood – the colonists made their argument directly to God as according to Locke, the mad king George III had proven himself the enemy of the people by repeatedly acting contrary to right without their consent. Certainly if even God seeks consent, what man could be more insane that to believe such things to be beneath his station?

As James Wilson stated in 1774, "...no one has a right to any authority over another without his consent: all lawful government is founded on the consent of those who are subject to it...."[119] Fourteen years later Madison repeated the concept when he rebutted some of the anti-federalist arguments stating that his opponents must remember that "...the ultimate authority, wherever the derivative may be found, resides in the people alone..."[120] And yet again, Locke's anthropology led his argument to the very same

118   Cf: Patrick Henry, "On the Resolution to Put the Commonwealth into a State of Defense," Virginia Convention, March 23, 1775 in *Constitution*, 2012, 70; "A Declaration by the Representatives of the United Colonies of North America, Setting For the the Causes and Necessity of Their Taking Up Arms", Congress July 5, 1775, in Charles C. Tansil ed., *Documents Illustrative of the Formation of the Union of the American States*, (Washington: Government Printing Office, 1927), 10.

119   James Wilson, "Considerations on the Nature and Extent of the Legislative Authority of the British Parliament, 1774," in *Collected Works of James Wilson*, Vol. 1, Eds. Kermit L. Hall and Mark David Hall, (Indianapolis: Liberty Fund, 2007).

120   James Madison [Attributed], "The Influence of the State and Federal Governments Compared," *Federalist No. 46*, 1788, in *Constitution*, 2012, 463.

ideal: "The liberty of man, in society, is to be under no other legislative power, but that established, by consent, in the commonwealth...."[121] Given the clear Lockean-literacy among the pertinent men, this statement is self-evidently directly connected to the Constitution's "blessings of liberty", if one cannot see it in the clearly delineated "We the People".

Consent, as previously seen in the parable of the workers, is intimately linked with the whole image of rights, life, property, liberty, and equality as others have noted.[122] This ideal – that one who seeks power in absence or in spite of consent is a criminal – is fundamental to the whole of legitimate government, not merely in America but universally. It would be reasonable then, as well as internally consistent, to consult with Johnson regarding the definition for such a term.

The eighteenth century term 'consent' encapsulated a bit more than that of the twenty-first. For the noun, Johnson cited some unexpected though not inappropriate literature (indeed, lexicography is thoroughly promiscuous in sources). From Charles I (1600 – 1649) and John Dryden (1631 – 1700) Johnson derived 'the act of yielding or consenting'; from Abraham Crowley (1618 – 1667) he drew 'concord, agreement, accord, unity of opinion'; from Milton, 'coherence with, relation to, correspondence'; and from Alexander Pope (1688 – 1744) 'tendency to one point, joint operation'.[123] One may therefore suggest a combined concept of a mutual, coherent agreement or accord; a unified perspective extending from *an act* of concession. The term 'mutual' is placed for 'joint operation', 'perspective' for 'opinion', and 'concession' for 'yielding'. Emphasis is given to the active nature of the term; as it is abundantly clear that there is, and can be no passivity in the concept. Consent is an active verb masquerading as a noun.

---

121   Locke, *Second Treatise*, IV: 22.
122   Jeremy Waldron, *God, Locke, and Equality: Christian Foundations in Locke's Political Thought*, (Cambridge: Cambridge University Press, 2002), 136.
123   "consent," *A Dictionary of the English Language*, by Samuel Johnson, 1773, Accessed September 23, 2024: https://johnsonsdictionaryonline.com/1773/consent_ns.

While the term 'yield' does indeed allow for 'resignation' or 'surrender', these are Johnson's eighth and ninth definitions respectively.[124] It would be a masterwork of sophistry indeed to shoehorn the idea of 'resigned surrender' into anything that Locke, Jefferson, or Madison wrote regarding the legitimacy of authority, though one does leave the possibility for such an argument. Consent is presented by the men in question as an axiom and, should one set this axiom in the martial sense of the surrender of the defeated, one has much larger problems to solve than the argument presented herein.

To explore such a possibility, one need only examine Locke's argument regarding the state of slavery – the perfect inversion of freedom as previously demonstrated. Locke introduced his reasoning on slavery with his definition of 'natural liberty' as being only constrained by the law of nature, from which consent for authority derives.[125] He then reasoned from the substance of this definition to argue that one cannot give what one does not possess, and as no man has power over his own life, he cannot place himself under the 'absolute, arbitrary power of another'; one cannot consent to be enslaved. This power, according to Locke, is the nature of slavery – to kill on a whim.[126] While his reasoning may be dismissed as somewhat ontological, it is by no means an 'academic' question.

Yet again in reference to contemporary tedium, this concept of 'slavery' is different for Locke than for the moderns. It is not merely ownership, but rather 'absolute, arbitrary power' – specifically the ability to murder the slave without any repercussion. Slavery, for Locke, is the equivalence of another's life being entirely reduced to nothing, and it is a rational impossibility outside of the state of war. As Locke argued, if there is any level of agreement between captive and captor, consent applies thereby ending

---

124   "yield," *A Dictionary of the English Language*, by Samuel Johnson. 1773. Accessed September 23, 2024: https://johnsonsdictionaryonline.com/1773/yield_va.

125   Locke, *Second Treatise*, IV:22.

126   Locke, *Second Treatise*, IV:23.

the states of war and slavery.[127] Most importantly, Locke answered the charge so often leveled against Christianity by addressing indenture among the Jews and others extending from passages in the Bible. Citing Exodus, Locke noted that even in cases of *voluntary* servitude – that amounts to something like a highly distasteful employment contract – the master is wholly forbidden from murder, and proscribed from maiming and other rough treatment. Locke also noted that the duration of this contract was restricted.[128] The concept of indenture or bond-slavery in the Bible is not 'absolute, arbitrary power' and thusly, according to Locke, does not fall within the state of slavery – and thereby the state of war.

Johnson, citing Shakespeare, Milton, Dryden and others, substantially agreed with Locke's rendition. A slave refers to the *lowest state of life*, it is one who has *lost the power to resist*, who is not free and is thereby *dependent*.[129] The emphases herein are added to make plain the foreshadow. To meddle with consent is not merely a fraud; its nature speaks to the festering fetid evil at the center of despotism itself. To the eighteenth century mind, liberty was life and slavery was death. Freedom was the essence, the substance of what it was to be human; slavery in submission to the absolute arbitrary power of another was the putrid, degenerate decomposition of humanity itself. To meddle with consent was to reduce to slavery; the reduction to slavery was the revocation of human dignity. It is therefore no wonder at all that those men would prefer death and even extinction.[130]

One would suggest therefore that consent is the expression of human dignity; that dignity deriving from the

---

127   Locke, *Second Treatise*, IV:24.
128   Exodus Chapter 21, Cf. Locke, *Second Treatise*, IV:24. The author notes that there is cause to disagree with Locke's argument based on Ex. 21:21, "...he is his money", translated as "property" in other versions.
129   "slave," *A Dictionary of the English Language*, by Samuel Johnson. 1773. Accessed September 24, 2024: https://johnsonsdictionaryonline.com/1773/slave_ns.
130   Cf. "A Declaration by the Representatives of the United Colonies of North America, Setting For the the Causes and Necessity of Their Taking Up Arms", Congress July 5, 1775, in Tansil, *Documents Illustrative*, 1927, 15; Cf. Witherspoon above.

substance of the Creation as the inherent gift given by God to every human being. Again, the One who has no need of asking anything of anyone yet asked for consent in His various covenants. He did not attempt to force, trick, or bamboozle Noah, Abraham or Moses; He both asked, and made his laws apparent, easily accessible and clear to anyone who would deign to look.[131] Disagreements cast aside with contempt, Natural Law is the the echo of God's "Let there be light" reverberating within the being of every living soul, and *any* attempt to sidestep the direct appeal to this dignity by means of voluntary agreement is, by its nature, attempted murder of the soul. This is hardly rhetorical – it is the essence of the state of war, and the force behind the precious value in liberty.

Without consent given freely, no authority can arise. One *cannot* honestly examine the Bible, Locke, Jefferson, Madison, or Wilson without recognizing this inescapable and unassailable fact. Creation is the essence of anthropology, consent is the basis of authority. This concept offers yet another connection between the Declaration and the Constitution, again as seen in the imagery contained within the 'blessings of liberty' that 'We the people' sought to secure.

This principle continued wholly unabated from 1776 to 1787. It formed and informed the reasoning, and is wholly referenced in the unnecessarily occluded term 'ratify'. In writing on the various measures taken for the Senate as a means to argue for the ratification, Madison appealed to the vital importance of stable order in government. While speaking on stability, he based the pivot of his argument on the importance of voluntary *informed* consent:

> The internal effects of a mutable policy are
> still more calamitous. *It poisons the blessing
> of liberty itself.* It will be of little avail to the
> people that the laws are made by men of their
> own choice, *if the laws be so voluminous that*

---

131   Cf. Deuteronomy 30; Romans 10; Matthew 7; Luke 6; Thomas Jefferson, "Opinion on the Treaties",1793; Alexander Hamilton, "*The Farmer Refuted*, 1775; Locke, *Second Treatise*, II:6.

they cannot be read, or so incoherent that they
cannot be understood; if they be repealed or
revised before they are promulgated, or
undergo such incessant changes that no man
who knows what the law is today can guess
what it will be tomorrow. Law is defined to be
a rule of action; but how can that be a rule,
which is little known and less fixed?[132]

And again, as late as 1835 Madison stressed the
necessity of informed consent in his discourse regarding the
nature of sovereignty in the federal system: "...all power in
just & free Govts. Is derived from Compact, that where the
parties to the Compact are *competent to make it*...."[133] One
herein assumes that another understands that 'compact' is
synonymous with 'agreement', and that to be competent to
make an agreement by definition demands a full
comprehension of the terms of that agreement.

Let it be stated again, often, widely, and *forcefully*:
the substance of humanity is equality in creation; the essence
of society is defined as either consensual or *criminal*; without
understanding of that to which one consents, the interaction
becomes inherently evil and wholly destructive. This is the
entirety of legitimacy, and legitimacy is the entirety of
authority. This is the wellspring of just power in the United
States of America; these are the ends for which independence
was declared, and the core of the Cause against Britain.
Without voluntary, informed consent by definition,
"government becomes destructive of these ends." Just powers
deriving from the consent of the governed, in the absence of
consent, there can be only *criminal* justice.

---

132   James Madison [Attributed], "The Senate," *Federalist no.
62*, 1788, in *Constitution*, 2012, 534; Emphasis added.
133   James Madison, "Essay on Sovereignty" December, 1835,
Founders Early Access, Accessed September 25, 2024:
https://rotunda.upress.virginia.edu/founders/default.xqy?
keys=FOEA-print-02-02-02-3188, Emphasis added, minor
compositional edits. Rotunda notes that this is early access, derived
from raw transcription, and the URL used for access is not
permanent.

Popular Sovereignty

Deriving from the consent of the governed, or as the Declaration put it "...in the name and by the authority of the good people of these colonies..."[134], the seat of supremacy within the United States was 'the people'. To be certain, the terminology used – popular sovereignty – is anachronistic to the eighteenth century, but the *concept* of ultimate authority being vested in the people is most certainly not.[135]

Chief Justice John Jay (1745 – 1829), in his opinion on the first substantial question put before the very new Supreme Court of the United States – *Chisholm v. Georgia* – wrote in 1793 that "In Europe, the sovereignty is generally ascribed to the Prince; here, it rests with the people... our Governors are the agents of the people, and, at most, stand in the same relation to their sovereign in which regents in Europe stand to their sovereigns."[136] While *Chisholm* is a pivotal case due to its part in having precipitated the eleventh amendment, it is not herein cited for that common reason.[137]

Chief Justice Jay was integral to the revolution before his brief term on the court. In addition to serving in both the first and second Continental Congresses, and as President of the Congress under the Articles of Confederation, he is one

---

134   Closing paragraph; Cf. *The Virginia Declaration of Rights*, Section 2.

135   The term per se is associated with nineteenth century debates regarding the institution of race-based slavery in the territories; Cf. Ushistory.org, "Popular Sovereignty," *U.S. History Online Textbook*, n.d., Accessed September 25, 2024: https://www.ushistory.org/us/30b.asp; also Nicole Etcheson, "'A Living, Creeping Lie': Abraham Lincoln on Popular Sovereignty," *Journal of the Abraham Lincoln Association* 29, no. 2 (2008): 1–25. The origin of the phrasing is not germane to the topic, but only the concept to which it refers; Cf. *Virginia Declaration*, Section 2.

136   Jay Opinion, *Chisholm v. Georgia*, 2 U.S. 419 (1793); Cf. *Virginia Declaration*, Section 2.

137   Cf. Bradford R. Clark and Vicki C. Jackson, "The Eleventh Amendment," *National Constitution Center*, Accessed September 25, 2024: https://constitutioncenter.org/the-constitution/amendments/amendment-xi/interpretations/133.

of the three men – along with Madison and Hamilton – to which *The Federalist Papers* are attributed.[138] Given that this present argument seeks and relies upon principles, it is reasonable to suggest that Jay's subordination of government authorities to mere regents rests upon the principle of popular sovereignty.

Johnson defined 'sovereignty' as "Supremacy; highest place; supreme power; highest degree of excellence"[139] To be certain, one is unaware if Chief Justice Jay possessed a copy of Johnson's lexicon, but it would be unreasonable to suggest that he held an alternative view in light of his comparison between the people of the United States and the royals of Europe. The image of the people holding the 'highest place' and 'supreme power' is clearly consistent with the myriad of renditions expressed in the various official documents. From Locke and Jefferson, to Jay and Madison, they over whom power is exercised retain the penultimate position of authority – being the source of legitimacy itself – only God Himself holds a greater prerogative.

Again in addressing some concerns and objections to the new Constitution, Madison suggested the verbiage "[t]hat the people have an indubitable, unalienable, and indefeasible right to reform or change their government, whenever it be found adverse or inadequate to the purposes of its institution."[140] Even should one object that those words were not included in the document, they were included nearly verbatim in Mason's *Virginia Declaration*.[141] Additionally, it is clear that this concept reflects an identical principle to the *casus belli* in both the Declaration, and its antecedent (and aptly named) "Declaration of the causes and necessity of taking up arms" from July 6, 1775. It is not necessary however to make appeal solely to principle in understanding

---

138   "Jon Jay, 1789-1795," *Supreme Court Historical Society*, n.d., Accessed September 25, 2024: https://supremecourthistory.org/chief-justices/john-jay-1789-1795/.

139   "sovereignty," *A Dictionary of the English Language*, by Samuel Johnson. 1773. Accessed September 25, 2024:. https://johnsonsdictionaryonline.com/1773/sovereignty_ns.

140   James Madison, "Amendments to the Constitution, 1789."

141   *Virginia Declaration*, Section 3.

the elevated place of the people in the mind of the colonials. As with so many things, Franklin made this principle both plain and pithy – circumspect though he famously was.

As has been consistent with each of the principles herein identified, it is apparent that they operate at a 'deeper level' in the reasoning, such that these foundations of reason appear in some of the most superficially unrelated topics. At the convention in mid 1787, Franklin weighed in on a debate regarding the prohibition on re-election of the presidency. In discussing the office of the executive, he set possibly the best definition for parameters in the relationship between 'civilian' and 'official' in the new nation: "In free Governments the rulers are the servants, and the people their superiors & sovereigns. For the former therefore to return among the latter was not to *degrade* but to *promote* them...."[142] Again, this was not merely flowery rhetoric, subject to a wink and a smirk. The men to whom he said these words had very recently *survived* a ruinous and horrific armed conflict – in which many had lost nearly all, in beloved persons as well as property. One has not found any record of objection to Franklin's statement regarding this relationship. While the lack of evidence is not the evidence of lack, one stands entirely confident that such a sentiment guided much of the conversation regarding the parceling of power – even or especially among those whose only aim in ratification was self preservation or aggrandizement.

Certainly it would be naive, anachronistic, dishonest, and *stupid* to paint these men, events, and documents with "sanctimonious reverence."[143] These were not saints by any delusional measure of the term, and their documents are by no means holy. The *substance* upon which they reasoned however is superior both to them and their words; the principles or metaphysical *Forms* to which they appealed, and that they sought to distill into vocabulary and policy – these are beyond reproach. Whether or not he was a

---

142   Benjamin Franklin, *The Political Thought of Benjamin Franklin*, ed. Ralph Ketchum, (Indianapolis: Hackett Publishing Company, 1965), 398; Cf. *Virginia Declaration*, Section 2.
143   Thomas Jefferson, "Proposals to Revise the Virginia Constitution," 1816.

philandering syphilitic is immaterial, Franklin's words
substantially echo those in Matthew: "...rulers of the Gentiles
lord it over them, and those who are great exercise authority
over them. Yet it shall not be so among you; but whoever
desires to become great among you, let him be your
servant."[144] Equality leads to consent, consent comprises
legitimacy; these combine into popular sovereignty, but they
all operate upon a greater, a deeper principle.

The essence of popular sovereignty is that in all
questions of permission, the people do not ask the
government, but rather that the government must ask the
people. To be certain, *salus populi suprema lex esto*, but this
concept admits no condescension. There is no room in
popular sovereignty for the 'moral busybody'; authority
cannot be employed *against* the people with the hollow
justification that it is 'for their own good.' This is the
principle, extending yet again from equality, of non-elitism.

As Chief Justice Jay stated in *Chisholm* "at the
Revolution, the sovereignty devolved on the people, and they
are truly the sovereigns of the country, but they are
sovereigns without subjects, and have none to govern but
themselves".[145] The individual man himself holds the highest
place in, and supreme power over himself, answerable only
to God. This sovereignty is discrete. A man is master of
himself; as Locke repeatedly pointed out, one cannot grant
what one does not have and thusly, the mere agglomeration
of men into groups does not grant any more authority than is
already possessed by the one. An individual man, of whom
groups are composed, is master of himself *and only of
himself*.

In addressing the concept and scope of sovereignty,
Madison addressed the pitifully bastardized ideal of 'majority
rules'. It is by no means so simple as such a rendition
implies:

> What ever be the hypothesis, of the origin of
> the *lex majoris partis*, it is evident that it
> operates as a plenary substitute of the will of

---

144   Matthew 20:25,26 NKJV.
145   Jay Opinion, *Chisholm v. Georgia*, 2 U.S. 419 (1793).

the majority of the Society, for the will of the
whole Society; and that the Sovereignty of the
Society as vested in & exerciseable by the
majority, may do any thing that could
be <u>rightfully</u> done, by the unanimous
concurrence of the members; the reserved
rights of individuals (of Conscience for
example), in becoming parties to the original
compact, being beyond the legitimate reach of
Sovereignty, wherever vested or however
viewed.[146]

Again, as Locke rendered it, "[n]o body can give
more power than he has himself…."[147], and this fact does not
change as a result of the quantity of men. Madison's *lex
majoris partis* certainly translates as the law of the majority,
but only so far as an individual within that majority might do:
*sovereignty also ends at the inalienable rights of the
individual*. Locke subordinated the "will and determination
of the majority" to "being only the consent of the individuals
of it…."[148] Being that the sovereignty of the many derives
from the sovereignty of the one; "no one can be put out of
this estate, and subjected to the political power of another,
without his own consent."[149] Those things that may be
"rightfully" done by a group cannot impose upon the
"reserved rights of individuals" any more than one individual
might impose upon another. Having been repeated three
ways, let a fourth be added such that the point is made as
aggressively as text will allow: even were the 99 to vote to
kill the one, it remains murder as murder is still and always
murder; the majority is not more entitled to act than is the
one, neither is the one less entitled to act than is the majority.

---

146   James Madison, "Essay on Sovereignty", December, 1835,
       Founders Early Access, Accessed September 25, 2024:
       https://rotunda.upress.virginia.edu/founders/default.xqy?
       keys=FOEA-print-02-02-02-3188. Edited for minor composition;
       underline emphasis in original.
147   Locke, *Second Treatise*, IV:23.
148   Locke, *Second Treatise*, VIII:96.
149   Locke, *Second Treatise*, VIII:95.

The majority derives of individual consent; consent derives of equality, and equality of Creation. Creation itself contains within it the Natural Law that encompasses the natural liberty to which all are entitled as a product of the "one omnipotent and infinitely wise maker."[150] Popular sovereignty is merely an expression of all these combined, and does not constitute a legitimate excuse for infringement or abuse. Bad government is always bad government, even if it is 'democratic', and bad government is self-dissolving: "Where there is no longer the administration of justice, for the securing of men's rights… there certainly is no government left."[151] Who would ask what is bad government need only to consult his own head and heart to find whether he would have it done to him.[152]

Such a humble, 'blue-collar' appeal to the substance of Natural Law that limits all legitimate power is the highest possible demonstration of its validity. It is immaterial whether some academic jargon such as 'popular sovereignty' is applied, and it is by no means a matter of political theory. In remarking on the decidedly *practical* bent of the American colonial, Jeffrey Morrison related (third-hand) a first-hand account of at least one soldier's reason for fighting in the Revolution. While ignorant of John Locke or any other storied commentary on political theory, this man decided to hazard his blood on the most appropriate and reasonable definition of 'popular sovereignty' that one has ever found: "Young Man, what we meant in going for those red-coats was this: we always had governed ourselves and we always meant to. They didn't mean we should."[153] While one could find little else on Captain Levi Prescott of Danvers Massachusetts, it is clear that the principle behind his independent spirit is reflected in the more philosophical rendition as related by Jefferson: "…what country can

---

150   Locke, *Second Treatise*, II:6.
151   Locke, *Second Treatise*, XIX:219.
152   Cf. Thomas Jefferson, "Opinion on the Treaties",1793.
153   Capt. Levi Prescott of Danvers Massachusetts in 1837 to Mellen Chaimberlain, in Charles Warren, *The Making of the Constitution*, (Boston: Little Brown and Co., 1937), 4; in Jeffrey Morrison, "Political Thought of John Witherspoon," 1999, 243.

preserve it's liberties if their rulers are not warned from time to time that their people preserve the spirit of resistance?"[154]

Popular sovereignty is simply a rendition of individual liberty writ large, and it does not concede any oversight greater than that inherent in Natural Law. Neither does popular sovereignty presume to encroach upon that from which it is derived; it cannot by some sorcery conjure a power or right, or excuse some abuse of authority. Popular sovereignty is not a magical legitimacy for infringement for the 'good of the many', but rather a hard limit that no legitimate government may pass. This analysis of the concept is foreshadowed by Mason's Declaration; individual rights precede and create society, they are not subordinate thereto.[155]

Limited Government

One may assume at this point that it has been wholly proved that to the eighteenth century thinking man, there was an unavoidable and wholly settled image of the Newtonian universe not merely in the measures of electromagnetism or gravitation, but also in the measures of conduct. Whether or not any given thinker's understanding of the cogs and levers of right conduct was correct or complete, each of the men herein cited operated entirely from the foundation that there existed transcendent, immutable, and universal standards – principles – to which every man had access should they but look. As demonstrated, the Author of this Standard was that same Being from whom descended Euclid's or Newton's laws; the substance of this image or *Form* toward which proper, right, or just conduct tends is wholly encapsulated in the term 'Natural Law.'

It would expand the size and scope of this argument by orders of magnitude to attempt even the weakest presentation of the nearly four-thousand year old concept of

---

154   Thomas Jefferson, "From Thomas Jefferson to William Stephens Smith, 13 November 1787," *Founders Online*, National Archives, https://founders.archives.gov/documents/Jefferson/01-12-02-0348.

155   George Mason, "The Virginia Declaration of Rights," 1776.

Natural Law theory; such is therefore left to other far more ambitious philosophers and historians. This concept is now herein cited because it is and has been the thread running through and behind each item thus far demonstrated. The essential *anima* of Natural Law is that it is not merely the 'spark of the divine' in the soul, but that it is the *standard*. That which resembles the Natural Law is good or just in proportion to its alignment; what does not – or what is contrary – is by definition bad, unjust, or *evil*. Every characterization of conduct employing some form of 'good' or 'bad' relies *entirely* upon this comparison; any argument to the contrary is absurd. Natural Law is *the* standard.

  The cosmology of the colonial took this statement at face value to such an extent that to fail to incorporate its implications would be as corrosive to understanding as attempting to read their literature without a working knowledge of English. The existence and supremacy of Natural Law is to the founding as visible light is to the sunrise. To measure rights or justice, to examine legitimacy or liberty is fundamentally to make comparison between the conduct of power against the immovable precepts of Natural Law. This is the substance and scope of limited government.

  Yet another man of his time James Otis (1725 – 1783) wrote in 1764: "Should an act of Parliament be against any of *his* natural laws, which are *immutably* true, *their* declaration would be contrary to eternal truth, equity, and justice, and consequently void."[156] The natural laws are inherently higher than those of men, and take precedence. Remarkably, the manifestly Newtonian nature of Natural Law was known even to at least one progressive. Henry Commager, in seeking to reduce the ideal of Natural Law to little better than a mythic ploy, stated that to the colonials "[t]he principles of law were like the axioms of Euclid...."[157]

---

156 James Otis, *Rights of the British Colonies Asserted and Proved*, 1763, in *The American Republic: Primary Sources*, ed. Bruce Frohnen, (Indianapolis: Liberty Fund, 2002), sic.

157 Henry Steel Commager, "Constitutional History and the Higher Law," in *The Search for a Usable Past, and Other Essays in Historiography*, (New York: Alfred A. Knopf, 1967), 31; Cf. Henry Steel Commager, "Constitutional History and the Higher Law," in *The Constitution Reconsidered* (New York: Columbia University

In keeping with the progressive failure to grasp the point however, Commager defines Natural Law as deriving "from an *a priori* or intuitive rather than experimental" basis.[158]

Poppycock, Commager himself performed extensive experimentation into the veracity of Natural Law when as a toddler he threw a tantrum when one took from him his cookie, thereby demonstrating that he knew theft to be wrong. As Wilson rendered the concept in reference to introspection on right conduct, "God has not left himself without a witness, nor us without a guide."[159]

Whatever sophistry might have been contrived to escape, or as Commager put it "the philosophy which justifies it has been repudiated now for three quarters of a century", the founding of the United States cannot be divorced of the absolute supremacy of Natural Law.[160] This law was not a matter of theory nor some mystical appeal, as Jefferey Morrison demonstrated, "...those universal ideas and rights were instantiated in concrete and particular circumstances... no patriot, least of all an American patriot, has ever fought for a mere theory."[161]

As demonstrated, rights precede authority. Because authority cannot attain in the absence of prior rights due to the substance of consent, rights are not granted within either the Constitution or the Declaration. The Bill of Rights does not 'grant' one single right – it proscribes the powers of government in encroaching or infringing upon those antecedent rights. Where the Declaration presents principles and the Constitution assembles mechanisms, the Bill of Rights states unequivocally what government *may not do* (abridge speech, ban weapons, torture) even and especially in instances wherein it declares what government *must do* (provide a jury, show probable cause, publish proceedings).

Press, 1938), 225 – 246.

158   Commager, *The Search*, 30.

159   James Wilson, *Collected Works*, 506.

160   Commager, *The Search*, 30; Commager cites Morris Cohen, "Jus Naturale Redivivum," *Philosophical Review*, XXV, 761: "To defend a doctrine of natural rights today requires insensibility to the world's progress or else considerable courage in the face of it".

161   Morrison, "The Political Thought of John Witherspoon, 1768 – 1794," 243.

The Organic Laws of the United States, previously analyzed, operate entirely on the premise of constraining power under the concept of Natural Law.

The purpose of the Organic Laws in Adams' view was to base the new society on "[t]he noblest principles and most generous affections in our nature...." Adams argued that these 'noblest of principles' were written in, among many, Milton and Locke to create – Adams citing Cicero's *De Re Publica* – "an empire of laws, and not of men."[162] Not to be limited to the so recently dead, Adams also cited Aristotle: "a government where the laws alone should prevail, would be the kingdom of God."[163] It is wholly clear that in America, the government *especially* was subject to law. Whether or not Adams cited the particular portion of Locke's *Second Treatise* or not, his reference to the latter's "principles and reasonings" appropriately connected this government of law with the original law as defined:

> The law, that was to govern Adam, was the same that was to govern all his posterity, the law of reason. .... So that, however it may be mistaken, the end of law is not to abolish or restrain, but to *preserve and enlarge freedom...* therein not to be subject to the arbitrary will of another, but freely follow his own.[164]

Locke spoke of the 'law of reason'. This rendition is so synonymous with Natural Law that Commager also made many of the same citations as those contained within this argument.[165] These concepts exercise simultaneously within Adams' and Cicero's definition of the government of law. As previously beaten pulpy, liberty necessitates freedom from the "arbitrary will of another", and Locke made it plain that

---

162   John Adams, "Thoughts on Government," in *Constitution*, 2012, 174.
163   Adams, *Works of John Adams, Second President of the United States: with a Life of the Author, Notes and Illustrations*, Edited by Charles Francis Adams, 10 vols, (Boston: Little, Brown and Co., 1850 – 1856), IV:403.
164   Locke, *Second Treatise*, VI:57; Emphasis added.
165   The Declaration, Otis, and Hamilton.

Natural Law serves to "preserve and enlarge freedom"; a government of men (capricious laws made by unscrupulous men) would be indistinguishable from subjugation to arbitrary will. The republic is not merely a limited government, it is a government *subjugated* by Natural Law, not a people subjugated by capricious men.[166]

The image of authority as inherently limited by Natural Law is neither new in the eighteenth century, nor limited to the American continent. Chief Justice Sir Edward Coke (1552 – 1634) of the English Court of Common Pleas wrote in 1610 that "when an act of Parliament is against common right and reason, or repugnant, or impossible to be performed, the common law will controul it, and adjudge such Act to be void."[167] To hold a legislative act as null, void, or of no effect when "against common right and reason, or repugnant" reflects the supremacy of Natural Law over government. This principle is so central in American constitutionalism that it ran through the earliest application of Article III.

In 1803, Chief Justice John Marshall (1755 – 1835) referenced both Hamilton's *Federalist 78*[168] and Adams' *Thoughts on Government* in his unanimous opinion that "...an act of the legislature, repugnant to the constitution, is void."[169] The legacy of the case, as with all things regarding government, has been perverted from its origins. In *Marbury*, the law so repugnant was section 13 of the Judiciary Act of 1789 granting the Supreme Court more power than that allowed for in Article III of the Constitution.[170] This case is enshrined for having established the practice of 'judicial review' wherein the Judiciary established its co-equal power with the Executive and Legislative branches, yet in this very early and very pivotal exercise of 'checks and balances', the exercise of that judicial authority was to *reduce* the authority of the Judiciary, viewing section 13 as beyond its

---

166   Cf. Locke, *Second Treatise*, II:13; IV:22.
167   *Thomas Bonham v. College of Physicians* (1610), sic.
168   In *Constitution*, 2012, 604.
169   *Marbury v. Madison*, 5 U.S. (1 Cranch) 137 (1803).
170   September 24, 1789, ch. 20, 1 Stat. 73.

constitutional prerogative. What irony in light of 21st century judicial practice, rationalized by this opposed opinion.

The Madison referenced in *Marbury* is James Madison who, acting under then President Jefferson, appeared to have been engaging in the ancient practice of political shenanigans against Adams, Hamilton, et al.[171] To be certain, this peculiar detail could, and likely does serve as the impetus for a soap-opera-like retelling of this very early disagreement in the application of constitutionalism, or at the very least a treatment of Chief Justice Marshall's *realpolitik*, on account of the tense political climate between four of the men so consistently cited in this argument.[172] The power-drama between these men however serves as evidence of the centrality of principle in their work; it was an instance wherein the preacher was called to practice.

A paltry sixteen years prior – while in the process of writing and ratifying the document under which he was judged in 1803, Madison declared that "[t]he truth was that all men having power ought to be distrusted to a certain degree."[173] And Jefferson, in opposition to the the Alien and Sedition Acts signed by Adams in 1798 shortly before *Marbury*, made a substantially similar declaration – agreeing with Adams' government of law: "In questions of power, then, let no more be heard of confidence in man, but bind him down from mischief by the chains of the Constitution."[174] Not to be confined to an oblique

---

171   Cf. "Marbury v. Madison: Primary Documents in American History," *Library of Congress*, Accessed October 1, 2024: https://guides.loc.gov/marbury-v-madison#:~:text=The%20U.S.%20Supreme%20Court%20case,by%20Chief%20Justice%20John%20Marshall.

172   Cf. Joseph Fawbush, "Marbury v. Madison Case Summary: What You Need to Know," *FindLaw*, March 24, 2023, Accessed October 1, 2024: https://supreme.findlaw.com/supreme-court-insights/marbury-v—madison-case-summary--what-you-need-to-know.html.

173   James Madison, Notes, "Madison Debates," July 11, 1787, *Yale Law School* Accessed September 14, 2024: https://avalon.law.yale.edu/18th_century/debates_711.asp.

174   Thomas Jefferson, "Resolutions Relative to the Alien and Sedition Acts," November 10, 1798, In "The Founders' Constitution" Volume 1, Chapter 8, Document 41, *The University of Chicago Press*,

interpretation, Jefferson presaged Chief Justice Marshall's words in that – the very beginning of the disagreements that would eventually lead to *Marbury*:

> "... whensoever the General Government assumes undelegated powers, its acts are unauthoritative, *void*, and of no force: that to this compact each State acceded as a State... that the government created by this compact was not made the exclusive or final judge of the extent of the powers delegated to itself; since that would have made its discretion, and not the Constitution, the measure of its powers...."[175]

Yet again, principles transcend not only time and place, but even the disagreements, arguments, and political shenanigans between the very men who sought to commit them to paper; as Jefferson stated in his first inaugural address, "...every difference of opinion is not a difference of principle."[176] Germane to this particular event, Chief Justice Marshall stated that "...the Constitution of the United States confirms and strengthens *the principle*, supposed to be essential to all written Constitutions, that a law repugnant to the Constitution is void...."[177] One would propose something of a chain of command in this principle. This law was created by a legislature, that being created by the Constitution and so is subject thereto. Marshall most certainly agrees with this. One has herein argued that the Constitution in turn is subordinate to the Declaration as the former was created to make practical the principles outlined in the latter; these

Accessed October 1, 2024: http://press-pubs.uchicago.edu/founders/documents/v1ch8s41.html. Cf. *The Writings of Thomas Jefferson*. Edited by Andrew A. Lipscomb and Albert Ellery Bergh. 20 vols. Washington: Thomas Jefferson Memorial Association, 1905, 17:379 – 80, 385 – 91.

175   Thomas Jefferson, "Resolutions Relative to the Alien and Sedition Acts," November 10, 1798; emphasis added.

176   Thomas Jefferson, "First Inaugural Address," in *Constitution*, 2012, 786.

177   *Marbury v. Madison*, 5 U.S. (1 Cranch) 137 (1803), emphasis added.

principles in-turn descend from rights. These rights are the
equal gift of the Creator, as set forward in the form and
substance of Natural Law. The whole of American authority
is therefore subordinate to Natural Law, by design.

Locke stated that the scope and end of this natural law
was, in a word, freedom.[178] Hearkening back to the earlier
analysis of that term, Jefferson employed the principle
defined as bi-directional non-domination, but such non-
domination was by no means limited to conduct between
individuals. This is to be expected from the ideal that because
the group is comprised of individuals, and no man may give
what he does not have[179], the group does not magically
possess more right to act than does the individual:

> of Liberty then I would say that, in the whole
> plenitude of it's extent, it is unobstructed
> action according to our will: but rightful
> liberty is unobstructed action according to our
> will, within the limits drawn around us by the
> equal rights of others. *I do not add 'within the
> limits of the law'; because law is often but the
> tyrant's will, and always so when it violates
> the right of an individual.*[180]

Let it be made plain to answer what one has
anticipated to be an objection to the argument up to this
point. Between Adams, Madison, Locke, and Jefferson – to
say nothing of Hamilton, Otis, Wilson, or the many others –
there is an inter-reinforcing consistency displayed in the
simultaneity of their overlapping principles. That four of
these men (at least) would run through a ridiculous
disagreement over certain applications has no power to
diminish the principles which they sought to uncover and
apply. Adams, Hamilton, and the Federalists may well have
played the tyrant in the Alien and Sedition Acts, but no more
so than the petty and dishonest machinations in which
Jefferson, Madison, and the 'democratic-republicans'

---

178   Locke, *Second Treatise*, VI:57.
179   Cf. Locke, *Second Treatise*, IV:23.
180   Thomas Jefferson, "Thomas Jefferson to Isaac H. Tiffany, 4
   April 1819." Emphasis added.

engaged while meddling with the Judiciary.[181] The supremacy of God-given rights remain the source and well-spring of legitimacy in authority, and also as the fundamental limits placed upon that authority.[182] The *Forms* of good that were and are the target of all these thoughts do not merely transcend, they are simultaneous.

The transcendent simultaneity – or simultaneous transcendence depending on one's pleasure – of the principles has been recognized by many as well as missed by many. With delightfully careful diplomacy, Hans Eicholz addressed many of the historiographic ghosts to haunt the understanding of the founding in his 2001 well-named *Harmonizing Sentiments*.[183] Pleasantly, he recognized at least sub-textually that the obsession with academic categorization and its inherent presentist retrospection has lead to 'confusion' when addressing the founding. Whether they were 'Whig,' 'liberal,' 'republican,' 'liberal-republican,' or some other worthless distinction, there was a solid and identifiable thread running throughout the colonials' sentiments. Modern – Progressive – scholarship is obsessed with power dynamics and oppressive 'structures', and so cannot conceive of a society distinct from government, to say nothing of a government subject to society. Progressivism wholly denies God in any actionable sense, and so cannot conceive of supreme natural law beyond Darwinism. Simply, for the vast majority of modern scholarship, and *all* of Progressive sophistry, it all boils down to *force*.

This was not so for the colonials, or for the government they conceived. For whatever dishonest resort may be made to the 'total depravity' doctrine of the Puritans, the colonials had a higher opinion of humanity than that inherent in the twisted self-worship of elitism. As Eicholz

---

181   Cf. Jerry W. Knudson, "The Jeffersonian Assault on the Federalist Judiciary, 1802-1805; Political Forces and Press Reaction," *The American Journal of Legal History* 14, no. 1 (1970): 55–75.

182   Cf. Locke, *Second Treatise*, XVIII:202.

183   Cf. Thomas Jefferson, "From Thomas Jefferson to Henry Lee, 8 May 1825."

explained, to the colonials and founders, men were neither angels *nor demons*:

> They believed in natural rights, but they did
> not rely on government *alone* to secure them.
> They wanted to limit government, to keep it
> from invading the rights of society, and to
> ensure that it would confine itself to
> protecting property…. where the meaning of
> self-government was much more than
> democratic politics…. If the order of society is
> principally political, then there is no appeal to
> any authority beyond power, and that is
> precisely what the Declaration was designed
> to reject.[184]

The substance of limited government is deeper than constitutionalism or judicial review – far deeper. Consciousness of Natural Law, yet again as stated in the golden rule, is an inescapable reality operating on an individual, not a collective basis. As Jefferson stated regarding worship, "legitimate powers of government reach actions only, & not opinions…."[185] so too Justice David J. Brewer (1837 – 1910), one of the last surviving impediments to the Progressive destruction of America, wrote in his dissent of *Budd v. New York* that "[t]he paternal theory of government is to me odious."[186] The interactions of men with men, as men, or that which is encompassed in the term 'society' does not derive from government or political power (i.e., *death threats*). Locke went even further to argue that

---

184   Hans L. Eicholz, *Harmonizing Sentiments: The Declaration of Independence and the Jeffersonian Idea of Self-Government*, Masterworks in the Western Tradition, Nicholas Capaldi and Stuard D. Warner eds., vol. 4, (New York: Peter Lang, 2001), 148 – 150. Emphasis added; Cf. Locke, *Second Treatise*, XI:138.

185   Thomas Jefferson, "V. To the Danbury Baptist Association, 1 January 1802," *Founders Online*, National Archives, Accessed October 2, 2024: https://founders.archives.gov/documents/Jefferson/01-36-02-0152-0006.

186   *Budd v. New York* 143 U.S. 517 (1892).

these interactions precede even society itself.[187] Madison however added a level of poetry to the concept as he argued that he would have rejected the Convention had it been against the happiness of the people:

> We have heard of the impious doctrine in the
> old world, that the people were made for
> kings, not kings for the people. Is the same
> doctrine to be revived in the new, in another
> shape – that the solid happiness of the people
> is to be sacrificed to the views of political
> institutions of a different form?[188]

Finally, in his 1779 draft bill regarding religious liberty, Jefferson again referenced Locke to make it plain that there are regions into which government shall not tread. He declared yet again that God made men free, with the insightfully self-evident addition that the mind is created so inherently free and "...altogether insusceptible of restraint; that all attempts to influence it by temporal punishments, or burthens, or by civil incapacitations, tend only to beget habits of hypocrisy and meanness....". So thorough was this freedom that even God Almighty, though He could, did not attempt coercion but rather sought to influence "reason alone". Jefferson declared "...that the opinions of men are not the object of civil government, nor under its jurisdiction...." He justified this position with the same principle that Witherspoon gave regarding the Bible's fearlessness of reason: "...truth is great and will prevail if left to herself... and has nothing to fear from the conflict...."[189]

---

187   Locke, *Second Treatise*, II:14.
188   James Madison [Attributed], "The Alleged Danger from the Powers of the Union to the State Governments," *Federalist 45*, 1788, in *Constitution*, 2012, 458, 459.
189   Thomas Jefferson, "82. A Bill for Establishing Religious Freedom, 18 June 1779," *Founders Online*, National Archives, https://founders.archives.gov/documents/Jefferson/01-02-02-0132-0004-0082, sic; Cf. Witherspoon, *Annotated Edition of Lectures on Moral Philosophy*; Belief cannot be compelled, John Locke, *A Letter Concerning Toleration*, ed. J. Brook, (Yorkshire: Huddersfield, 1796 [1689]), 12-13.

One would think that Jefferson's principles are clear, but let it be made more plain. Attempting to force a thought, belief, or opinion is at best always a failure – an act of gross imbecility. What one thinks, opines, or believes is *none of governments' business*. Even God does not try to encroach upon the freedom of opinion or sovereignty of conscience – it is an act of supreme delusion to assault the fortress of the mind's liberty. This fact alone perfectly describes the insanity of post-Progressive America; the founding world-view was not so insane.

The government exists for the people, not the people for the government. It is inarguable that the origin and purpose of legitimate government is to secure rights at the behest of the people, and that this is an outgrowth of Natural Law. It is also inarguable that the violation of Natural Law, by individuals *and* by governments is a criminal act. It is therefore impossible that any legitimate government would have even the faintest whisper of a claim against Natural Law. The concept of limited government is not so small as to say that there are rules, or that authority can only do what the majority wants. The concept of limited government is the hard and obstinate *command* that government must tend only to those things to which it is suited, and *nothing else* – as that would be by definition a tyranny.

As God said to the sea, so too does Natural Law say to power "Hitherto shalt thou come, but no further"[190] whereas Adams said "...every individual has his rights, of which the nation cannot deprive him, except by violence and an unlawful use of the general power."[191] Government is not limited by the Constitution, *legitimate* government is limited by its inherent foundations because poor government is self-dissolving – of which arbitrary or limitless government is most certainly a part.[192] Simply, to the eighteenth century American, a government that exceeds or overrides its limits is fundamentally illegitimate and nothing more sophisticated than a common thief. Let one remember that the people are not made for the 'king' as one references the total usurpation

---

190   Job 38:11.
191   John Adams, *Works*, IV:401-402.
192   Locke, *Second Treatise*, XIX:219.

of legitimacy in the despicably psychotic concept of *rex non potest peccare* – 'sovereign immunity' – that obviated the entirety of the rule of law, to say nothing of its horrific arrogance. Natural Law limits authority so completely that if government is not limited it is not government, it is evil.

The Self-Governing Virtue

If legitimate government may not tread into certain arenas, how was American society to maintain cohesion and good order in light of its liberty? Few things are so simple, and few principles enjoy such a plurality of substantial agreement among the many men as that of individual virtue. In the most unequivocal of terms, it appears that to *most* of the pertinent men, this quality was the single most vital ingredient to the construction and maintenance of American civilization. It is by no means an overstatement to declare that the majority of these men saw this necessity as so complete that its lack would utterly vitiate the whole of their creation. Virtue, specifically a public, collective outgrowth *produced by* a private, individual quality, is the necessary and sufficient condition of liberty – that which extends from the essential nature of creation.

Let the previous terminology be examined such that the uninitiated might grasp the importance of the concept. It is a delight that the tapestry of humanity dictates that few men are philosophers – a glut of philosophers would be a despicably tedious and impotent state of affairs. That which is a 'necessary and sufficient condition' is a mathematical proposition; the *sine qua non* – 'without which, nothing' – of an observation. Without the sun, earth has no life; without the Son, there can be no life in the soul. In the case of the necessary and sufficient condition, the factor examined can be true *if and only if* that condition is met. Liberty in a society, any society; under a government, any government, can exist *if and only if* a critical mass of its people conduct themselves with a self-imposed, voluntary, consistent, internalized virtue. Liberty can only exist among a people who control *themselves*.

Men are neither angels nor demons, but they are most certainly devious. More than merely devious, men on the whole are admirably creative in their ways of skirting, flouting, escaping, and loop-holing their way around external barriers to their wishes. For every rule, code, or law ever put to words, there are ten-thousand manners of affirming the letter, and castrating the spirit of that law, rendering it of no effect.[193] Adding to Jefferson's observation regarding the nature of the human mind, one would expand the concept to state that neither opinion nor behavior can ever truly be externally controlled; authoritarian constraints lead only to a little perfunctory compliance, and a lot of secret deviance.[194]

Benjamin Rush (1746 – 1813), yet another of the names found affixed to the Declaration, is the youngest known Princeton graduate at age 14, and may have influenced Witherspoon's move from Scotland.[195] He rendered the above in a far less verbose distillation: "Without Virtue there can be no liberty."[196] George Washington (1732 – 1799), who need not be summarized here, substantially agreed in his 1788 letter to the Marquis De Lafayette wherein he subordinated the assurance of human rights to the presence of a "virtuous people."[197] Adams and Jefferson both, who had much to say on the topic, invalidated any argument regarding a separation between individual and collective morality – they are reciprocal.

---

193   Cf. Mark 7:9-13.

194   Thomas Jefferson, "82. A Bill for Establishing Religious Freedom, 18 June 1779."; Cf. Spencer D. Miles, "Path To Pardon: Ending the Abuse of Perpetual Criminal Sanctions", Article Preprint: http://dx.doi.org/10.13140/RG.2.2.33957.22249, 21.

195   Brief summary of Benjamin Rush, Class of 1760 at the College of New Jersey (Princeton): "Benjamin Rush," *Princeton University, Art Museum*, n.d., Accessed October 8, 2024: https://artmuseum.princeton.edu/collections/objects/45169.

196   Benjamin Rush, *Thoughts Upon The Mode of Education Proper in a Republic* (1786), in *Essays, Literary, Moral and Philosophical*, (Philadelphia: Thomas and William Bradford, 1806), 8.

197   George Washington, "Washington to Marquis De Lafayette, February 7, 1788," in John C. Fitzpatrick, ed., *The Writings of George Washington*, (Washington D. C.: U. S. Government Printing Office, 1939), 29:410.

Jefferson cited Quintus Horatius Flaccus (Horace, 65 – 8 BC) *hic niger est, hunc tu Romane caveto* to demonstrate that there is absolutely no difference between individual and collective virtue, deriving of "...but one code of morality...."[198] Adams defined "public virtue" as a function of "private virtue" and set it as "the only Foundation of Republics."[199] Going further than merely acting as the only foundation of a Republic, Adams made the expansive claim that "[a]ll sober inquirers after truth" set virtue as the source of both happiness and dignity.[200] Friend of both Adams and Jefferson, Franklin stated in 1787 that "...only a virtuous people are capable of freedom" as previously cited, but expanded the statement later that same year at the Federal Convention where he declared that vice – 'corruption' – necessitates despotism, as a corrupted people is incapable of a well administered government.[201]

Second cousin to John Adams, Samuel (1722 – 1803), also a signatory to the Declaration, adds even more agreement in the statement that "Neither the wisest constitution nor the wisest laws will secure the liberty and happiness of a people whose manners are universally corrupt."[202] Madison employed a more poetic manner of description, and agreed with Samuel Adams' connection of

---

198   Thomas Jefferson, "From Thomas Jefferson to James Madison, 28 August 1789," *Founders Online*, National Archives, https://founders.archives.gov/documents/Jefferson/01-15-02-0354. Citing Horace's *Satires*, I:1.37: 'This man is black of heart; beware of him, good Roman.'

199   John Adams, "John Adams to Mercy Otis Warren, April 16, 1776," A. Koch and W. Peden, eds., *The Selected Writings of John and John Quincy Adams,* (New York: Knopf, 1946), 57.

200   John Adams, "Thoughts on Government," 1776, in *Constitution*, 2012, 173.

201   Benjamin Franklin, "To Messrs. The Abbés Chalut and Arnaud," April 17, 1787, in: Sparks, 1840, 297; Benjamin Franklin, "Benjamin Franklin to the Federal Convention," September 17, 1787, in Max Farrand, ed., *The Records of the Federal Convention of 1787*, Revised ed., 4 vols. (London: Yale University Press, 1937), 2:641-643..

202   William V. Wells, *The Life and Public Service of Samuel Adams*, (Boston: Little, Brown, & Co., 1865), 1:22.

public virtue directly to the practical functionality of the Constitution:

> Is there no virtue among us? If there be not,
> we are in a wretched situation. No theoretical
> checks—no form of government can render us
> secure. To suppose that any form of
> government will secure liberty or happiness
> without any virtue in the people, is a
> chimerical idea. If there be sufficient virtue
> and intelligence in the community, it will be
> exercised in the selection of these men. So
> that we do not depend on *their* virtue, or put
> confidence in our rulers, but *in the people
> who are to choose them.*[203]

If it were ever appropriate to employ the word 'plethora', it would be here. Perhaps only the concepts of 'liberty' or 'rights' enjoy more ink than the image and importance of virtue in the quality and function of the new Republic. There is an absolute excess of discourse regarding this central principle, and while it is expanded and employed to various shades among the men, appropriate to the instances in which they made the reference, they are all in substantial agreement. The lack of widespread virtue, as a product of individual morality, is inarguably and inherently fatal to the perpetuation of the natural freedom as enumerated in the Declaration, and the function of legitimate authority as presented in the Constitution. It is, therefore, obviously reasonable to examine the term in far more detail.

Johnson defined 'virtue' in his first two definitions as "moral goodness: opposed to *vice*" and as "[a] particular

---

203   James Madison, "Judicial Powers of the National
Government, [20 June] 1788," *Founders Online*, National Archives,
https://founders.archives.gov/documents/Madison/01-11-02-0101; cf.
Saul K. Padover, ed., *The Complete Madison*, (New York: Harper &
Brothers, 1953), 49; Emphasis added; Cf. *Speech* in
the *Virginia Ratifying Convention, June 20, 1788*. Jonathan
Elliot, *The Debates in the Several State Conventions on the Adoption
of the Federal Constitution* (J. B. Lippincott Company, Philadelphia,
1891) 3:536.

moral excellence"; he also noted in his fifth definition that the term may reference 'efficacy' or 'power', in agreement with the translation of δύναμιν (*dynamin*) from Luke 8:46.[204] The etymology of the English term descends from the expected Latin via French, first attested around 1200 AD referencing "moral life and conduct; a particular moral excellence" but deriving from the earlier Latin *virtus* that speaks to "moral strength, high character, goodness; manliness; valor, bravery, courage (in war); excellence, worth." Curiously, the root of the word, *vir,* is the Latin 'man'.[205] If nothing else, this provenance adds a high level of legitimacy to the contemporary English 'be a man' or 'man-up' in reference to worth deriving from expected moral performance, especially that requiring courage.

Whatever inherently masculine traits might be understood from the derivation of the term, the thrice repeated reference to 'moral excellence' draws the attention, specifically for its placement in the ancient etymology of another term. The term translated as 'virtue' in the King James Bible is the Greek ἀρετὴ (*aretē*), and is curiously a grammatical feminine.[206] Again, disregarding the Y or X 'chromosome' of the vocabulary lest one be lost in the absurd, the translation of ἀρετὴ is of particular importance whether examining biblical exegesis, the founding, or philosophy.

Among the sentiments that Jefferson sought to harmonize, Aristotle is prominent.[207] Adams also placed Aristotle first in his list of influences, along with Cicero and Locke, but added that among these men one finds "...what are

---

204   "virtue," *A Dictionary of the English Language,* by Samuel Johnson. 1773. Accessed October 7, 2024: https://johnsonsdictionaryonline.com/1773/virtue_ns; Cf. "And Jesus said, Somebody hath touched me: for I perceive that virtue is gone out of me." Luke 8:46; use of virtue for power is considered archaic English, though poetic.

205   "virtue," *Online Etymology Dictionary,* Accessed October 8, 2024: https://www.etymonline.com/word/virtue.

206   Phillippians 4:8, 2 Peter 1:3, 5 Strong's 703. Note that the same word is translated as 'praises' in 1 Peter 2:9.

207   Thomas Jefferson, "From Thomas Jefferson to Henry Lee, 8 May 1825."

called revolution principles…. The principles of nature and eternal reason. The principles on which the whole government over us, now stands."[208] Additionally, the curious Justice Wilson frequently cited Aristotle in his discourse on the philosophical basis of many of his positions.[209]

The branch of Ethics deriving from Aristotle's *Nicomachean Ethics* is termed 'Virtue Ethics' for the frequent use of ἀρετὴ in the text.[210] Aristotle's use of ἀρετὴ (Latinized as arete – *are–eh–TAY*) is not nearly as simplistic as translation directly to 'virtue' might imply. As argued by James Opie Urmson (1915 – 2012), something of an authority regarding Aristotle, arete is "excellence or goodness of any kind. It is an abstract noun connected with *aristos*, excellent."[211] One would suppose that the derivative of *aristos* is obvious – especially were one to consider Jefferson's natural *aristocracy*.[212] For Aristotle, "human good turns out to be activity of soul [Ψυχῆς (*psyche*), essential animating quality, the *anima*] in accordance with virtue [arete, excellence]…."[213] Simply, the 'good' is that expression of the *anima* in its most excellent example.

To find this excellence, the Philosopher offered the concept of the 'mean', or what is poorly referenced in the

---

208   John, Adams, "Addressed to the Inhabitants of the Colony of Massachusetts Bay," January 23, 1775, in *Novanglus, and Massachusetts; or Political Essays*, (Boston: Hews & Goss, 1819 [1775]), Gutenberg Ebook #45205, 12.
209   Cf. Especially James Wilson, "Of the General Principles of Law and Obligation," *Collected Works*, 2007, Chapter II.
210   Aristotle, *The Basic Works of Aristotle*, Edited by Richard McKeon, (New York: The Modern Library, 2001 [1941]).
211   J.O. Urmson, *The Greek Philosophical Vocabulary*, (Great Britain: Duckworth, 2001 [1990]), 30, 31; Cf. "Professor J.O. Urmson," Obituary, March 16, 2012, *The Times,* Accessed October 9, 2024: https://www.thetimes.com/article/professor-j-o-urmson-lq5c8wwtt3h.
212   Cf. Locke, *Second Treatise*, VII:94; Gordon wood, "Thomas Jefferson and the Idea of Equality", 1995; generally rule of the best, greatest, noblest, cf. "aristocracy," *A Dictionary of the English Language*, by Samuel Johnson, 1773, Accessed October 9, 2024: https://johnsonsdictionaryonline.com/1773/aristocracy_ns.
213   Aristotle, "Nichomachean Ethics" in *Basic Works*, 1098a:17, 943.

contemporary 'happy medium', "...virtue [arete] is a kind of mean, since... it aims at what is intermediate.... A state of character concerned with choice... determined by a rational principle...."[214] Arete is therefore a product of character produced by rationally informed decision in favor of balance. Aristotle made it clear that reason must inform the choice "...since reason more than anything else *is* man" because "[t]his life therefore is also the happiest."[215] And neither is the choice a 'one and done' proposition, it is a product of consistency in *character* because "moral virtue comes about as a result of habit, whence also its name *ethike* is one that is formed by a slight variation from the word *ethos* (habit)."[216]

Samuel Adams mirrored the ongoing necessity of habituation, ethics, or of having an *ethos* of virtue, "[Men] will be free no longer than while they remain virtuous."[217] Adams connected this habituation to "...government productive of human happiness"[218] where Jefferson focused on the importance of balance, in addition to habituation.[219]

Arete is therefore not merely a translation of 'virtue' or of 'excellence', and the definition of virtue is not limited to 'moral excellence', these are all synonymous with the consistently conscious decision to govern one's self according to balance within one's purpose, and thereby to live freely. It would increase tedium far too much to summarize yet another of Aristotle's operative terms – that

---

214   Aristotle, "Nichomachean Ethics" in *Basic Works*, 1106b:27-28; 1107a, 958, 959.
215   Aristotle, "Nicomachean Ethics," in *Basic Works*, 1178a:7-9.
216   Aristotle, "Nicomachean Ethics," in *Basic Works*, 1103a:16-18, 952.
217   Samuel Adams, "Letter to John Scollay (Dec. 30, 1780)", in Wells, *The Life and Public Service of Samuel Adams*, Volume III, 115.
218   Adams, "Thoughts on Government," in *Constitution*, 2012, 174; Cf. Adams, *Works*, IV:194-195.
219   Thomas Jefferson, "From Thomas Jefferson to Chastellux, with Enclosure, 2 September 1785," *Founders Online*, National Archives, https://founders.archives.gov/documents/Jefferson/01-08-02-0362; Cf. Thomas Jefferson, "Thomas Jefferson to John Adams, 10 December 1819," *Founders Online*, National Archives, https://founders.archives.gov/documents/Jefferson/03-15-02-0240.

being *telos* or roughly, purpose – therefore, let Jefferson outline the application of the above:

> The practice of morality being necessary for the well-being of society, He [God] has taken care to impress it's precepts so indelibly on our hearts that they shall not be effaced by the subtleties of our brain. We all agree in the obligation of the moral precepts of Jesus, & no where will they be found delivered in greater purity than in his discourses.[220]

And yet again as though by design, one is lead back to the principle-principle, the undeniable and innate summation of the "moral precepts of Jesus" of which all are aware: "Therefore all things whatsoever ye would that men should do to you, do ye even so to them: for this is the law and the prophets."[221] Additionally, hearkening back to Adams' description of virtue as the wellspring of dignity, and the previously demonstrated centrality of consent, deriving from equality – that being the same degree of dignity – one finds yet another self-reinforcing and reflexive principle operating within this difficult examination of moral excellence.[222]

Human dignity is inherent also in creation, and the virtue of which Adams spoke leads directly to that dignity. For the eighteenth century mind, virtue was the essential ingredient in the whole image of human flourishing as well as for Aristotle; in excellence one finds one's happiness.[223] Dignity speaks directly to this excellence, as Johnson defined 'dignity' as a rank of elevation, grandeur of mien, elevation of aspect, advancement, preferment, or high place.[224]

---

220   Thomas Jefferson, "Thomas Jefferson to James Fishback (Final State), 27 September 1809," *Founders Online*, National Archives, https://founders.archives.gov/documents/Jefferson/03-01-02-0437-0003; edited for convention.
221   Matthew 7:12; Cf. Luke 6:31.
222   John Adams, "Thoughts on Government," 1776, in *Constitution*, 2012, 173.
223   Aristotle, "Nicomachean Ethics," in *Basic Works*, 1178a:7-9.
224   "dignity," *A Dictionary of the English Language*, by Samuel Johnson. 1773. Accessed October 9, 2024:

One would posit that among the plethora of writers on virtue in the founding, the antonym of virtue, moral excellence, or dignity would be corruption, corrosion, or the reduction of man to beast.[225] This is not confined to either individual depravity or to collective decay, but rather an expression in both. The simplest manner of example for the interaction between individual and collective virtue would be the oft repeated nature of 'compact' – agreement, contract, promise.

Locke analyzed virtue with an example argument for upholding one's end of a compact from three paradigms – Christian, Hobbesian, and from that of the 'old philosophers'. According to Locke, the latter of these would state that one must keep one's agreements as it is "dishonest, below the dignity of man, and opposite to virtue, the highest perfection of human nature, to do otherwise." The Christian would do it fearing hell because God has commanded it, and the Hobbesian because the State (the "Leviathan") would punish him if he did otherwise. In any case, Locke argued that God had made "an inseparable connexion" between virtue and the public happiness, such that the latter cannot exist without the former, to such an extent that even though the "great principle of morality, "to do as one would be done to," is more commended than practiced," still the ultimate self-interest of the individual actors would motivate compliance.[226]

To be certain, Locke departs in some ways from much that is inherent in this argument's reasoning around the eighteenth century, as he goes on to argue that conscience is merely the product of external conditioning, specifically that the consciousness of virtue is not "written on their hearts".[227] Herein, one expects the greater objection to one's argument to be based on Locke's *tabula rasa*. Such is yet another

---

https://johnsonsdictionaryonline.com/1773/dignity_ns.

225   Did not one say that 'plethora' would be applicable?

226   John Locke, *An Essay Concerning Human Understanding*, in *Great Books of the Western World*, Vol. 35, Edited by Robert Maynard Hutchins, (Chicago: Encyclopædia Britannica, Inc., 1952 [1689]), I:2.5-7,105.

227   Locke, *An Essay Concerning Human Understanding*, I:2.9-13 and further, 106 – 107.

product of depraved reasoning – not on the part of Locke, but on that of his much later interlopers.

Locke's 'white paper' (not *tabula rasa*) is directly in reference to knowledge and ideas – not the structures employed to form them.[228] The structures themselves operate at a 'deeper level' than mere knowledge, as Locke stated there is "[n]o knowledge without discernment."[229] It is clear that, while knowledge and ideas are written upon that paper, the nature of humanity as created *is the paper itself.* While that paper may be made beautiful by virtue or marred with vice, it does not change that "God has stamped certain characters upon men's minds."[230] This coincides well with the "inseparable connexion" between virtue and happiness that Locke identified, and so the 'white paper' is in no way contradictory of Jefferson's rendition:

> He has formed us moral agents... that we may promote the happiness of those with whom he has placed us in society, by acting honestly towards all, benevolently to those who fall within our way, respecting sacredly their rights bodily and mental, and cherishing especially their freedom of conscience, as we value our own.[231]

One would emphasize Jefferson's "by acting honestly towards all…" as a means of promoting happiness. This

---

228   Locke, *An Essay Concerning Human Understanding*, II:1.2, 121.

229   Locke, *An Essay Concerning Human Understanding*, II:11.1, 143.

230   In Robert Duschinsky, "'Tabula Rasa' and Human Nature." *Philosophy* 87, no. 342 (2012): 517, 518; Citing John Locke, *Some Thoughts Concerning Education, and Of the Conduct of the Understanding*, Ruth W. Grant & Nathan Narcov, eds. (London: Clarendon Press, 1996 [1693]), 44, 161. Duschinsky gives an extensive discussion regarding the poor understanding of Locke's reasoning, based mostly on later 'caricatures' of the concept of *tabula rasa.*

231   Thomas Jefferson, "Thomas Jefferson to Miles King, 26 September 1814," *Founders Online*, National Archives, https://founders.archives.gov/documents/Jefferson/03-07-02-0495.

happiness is quite likely a deliberate invocation of Aristotle's virtue, and the whole of Jefferson's prescriptions of conduct, deriving from the creation as "moral agents" speaks directly to the same degree of dignity with which all are created. The later words "...as we value our own" is wholly a rendition of the golden rule.

This detail contains within it an inherently outward thrust. Private virtue may well involve goodness towards one's self, but it is chiefly a quality of one's conduct towards others, not as a measure of the other, but as an expression of one's self. Akin to James' rendition of visible faith, so too is one's personal moral excellence demonstrated primarily by how one conducts one's self regarding other people.[232] Virtue qua virtue does not allow for atomization.

Eidelberg, citing Madison's previously mentioned "chimerical idea" noted that "Without virtue in the people a pluralistic society may for a time avoid the worst of political evils, but only to exist as a discordant assemblage of self seeking collectivities."[233] This atomization is at the heart of what appears to be Patrick Deneen's operative definition of 'liberalism' that subordinates personal virtue to something resembling the habituation of the individual into "extensive social norms in the form of custom."[234]

Oddly, Deneen correctly identified liberty within the realm of self-government via virtue, but then claimed that 'liberalism' saw liberty as freedom from all externals, including social customs, and that the only legitimate restraint ought to be law. He then correctly went on to demonstrate that as the individual is left uncontrolled, the State expands to fill the gap "with an ever-enlarging sphere of state control."[235] Simply, one is confused at Deneen's definition of 'liberalism'; as virtue is moral excellence most especially demonstrated within the 'precepts of Jesus', or what can be seen as reflexive self-interest. While social

---

232   James 2:14-20.
233   Eidelberg, PhD Diss., 74.
234   Patrick J. Deneen, *Why Liberalism Failed*, 1st ed, (New Haven: Yale University Press, 2018), xiii.
235   Deneen, *Why Liberalism Failed*, xiii, xiv.

custom may mirror the golden rule, it is absurd to attempt to reduce the sublime simplicity therein to mere custom.

Wherever Deneen may speak correctly or mistaken regarding 'liberalism', the substance of his argument appears to be limited by the parochialism of terminology. It is for this reason that Deneen cites liberalism's 'individualism', what is really hedonism in practice, as the seeds of its own failure. Deneen does however correctly identify the irreconcilability of progressivism with the founding, but unfortunately cast it under wholly inapplicable and therefore misleading terminology – liberal v. conservative, neither of which have any application to the founding world-view.[236] In either case, the terminology is anachronistic, and yet another example of the impediment to understanding represented by aggressive superficial taxa. Jargon castrates understanding.

Moral excellence is seen primarily, though not wholly, in one's conduct towards others and this conduct proceeds from what one wishes others to do to him; it is nothing so small or transient as 'custom'. Custom may reflect Jesus' maxim, wherein "the law and the prophets" are encapsulated – but this is a spiritual, metaphysical proposition most visible in the voluntary expression of religion.

Washington made clear that, in his view, there could be no isolated, atheistic morality.[237] It was his position that the morality derived of religion was the greatest of supports "which lead to political prosperity."[238] If such a citation is insufficient to break Deneen's claim that 'liberalism' refused any constraint beyond law, let the well-worn words of Adams demonstrate how the 'classical liberals' felt about the matter:

> ...We have no Government armed with Power capable of contending with human Passions unbridled by morality and Religion. Avarice, Ambition, Revenge or Galantry, would break

---

236   Deneen, *Why Liberalism Failed*, 45.
237   George Washington, "Farewell Address", in *Constitution*, 2012, 775.
238   George Washington, "Farewell Address", in *Constitution*, 2012, 774.

the strongest Cords of our Constitution as a
Whale goes through a Net. Our Constitution
was made only for a moral and religious
People. It is wholly inadequate to the
government of any other[239]

No law, code, or regulation externally applied is able
to control, or even appreciably limit the appetites of
humanity. Only the internalized, voluntary pursuit of moral
excellence – virtue – is sufficient to temper the conduct of a
man. If, uncontrolled, the man seeks to employ his 'liberty'
as license to disregard and abuse the equivalent rights of
another, that one's rights so usurped are to be secured and
championed by government; if however, the uncontrolled
employ government itself in the usurpation, then there is no
government any longer, as previously demonstrated. Human
law is wholly impotent in the greater realm of humanity: in
these regions virtue reigns. Where virtue does not reign,
liberty is dead.

The substance of legitimate authority is the consent of
the governed, this deriving from the equality of the
individuals due to creation under Natural Law. Again,
deriving from these, there are many arenas where authority is
inherently illegitimate – such as the sovereign conscience.
Eicholz noted that to the colonial, government was distinct
from society; Locke argued that even society itself was
subordinate to the inherent natural rights of the individual,

239   John Adams, "From John Adams to Massachusetts Militia,
11 October 1798," *Founders Online*, National Archives,
https://founders.archives.gov/documents/Adams/99-02-02-3102. Not
ed by the National Archives as an 'early access' and 'non
authoritative' transcription; editorial remarks from source removed;
Cf. John Adams, October 11, 1798, "Letter to the officers of the First
Brigade of the Third Division of the Militia of Massachusetts,"
Charles Francis Adams, ed., *The Works of John Adams, Second
President of the United States*, (Boston: Little, Brown, and Co.,
1854), 9:229; Cf. Compendium of Jefferson's many claims regarding
the place of morality in government: "Thomas Jefferson on Politics
and Government, 3. Moral Principles," n.d., *Family Guardian
Fellowship*, Accessed October 8, 2024:
https://famguardian.org/Subjects/Politics/ThomasJefferson/jeff0200.h
tm.

and this is wholly encapsulated in the Declaration's phrasing
"...that to secure these rights, governments are instituted
among men...". The conduct of the individual is, therefore,
not subordinate to government, but rather the government is
subordinate to the rights of the individual. The worth of the
individual *exceeds* the worth of government.

As Madison noted that the government is for the
people, not the people for the government, and Jefferson that
the law is so often merely the expression of the tyrant's will,
it is clear that the ideal of government as an agent of *control*
is wholly illegitimate to the American founding. As stated
before, the people do not ask of government but rather the
government must ask of the people; the attempt for
government to control, rather than to merely protect, is a
usurpation – an act that dissolves legitimacy. The only
legitimate measure of control among a free people is *self-*
control. Any attempt by government to control the people is
inherently tyrannical – full stop.

Self-control is the expression of virtue, of moral
excellence, of the consistent deliberate voluntary rational
decision to seek balance, of the pursuit of one's purpose. In
essence, the only legitimate control in a free society is the
practicable individual cognizance of Natural Law as it
applies to the self. To state this *via negativa*: "The fool hath
said in his heart, There is no God. They are corrupt, they
have done abominable works, there is none that doeth
good."[240]

A government by the people will reflect that people;
virtue is so far elevated above the mundane concept of a
'code of rules' that it does not ask 'what should I do', but
rather contemplates 'what sort of man am I becoming?'. A
written code of laws is vital to avoid arbitrary acts of power,
but to write it is to make it static, confined solely to
anticipated situations; *character* however is infinitely
adaptable. Where the habit – *ethos* – of moral excellence
flexes to apply itself to anything that life might contrive,
external laws are rigid and multiply without bound until
every act one might perform is unlawful somewhere – and

---

240   Psalm 14:1; 53:1.

one must consult a lawyer before taking any steps. That one who must ask another 'is this legal' cannot be free; who asks 'is this right' is close, but freest of all is the one who asks 'is this what a good man would do?'. License is vice; vice is servitude.

> What then? shall we sin, because we are not
> under the law, but under grace? God
> forbid. Know ye not, that to whom ye yield
> yourselves servants to obey, his servants ye
> are to whom ye obey; whether of sin unto
> death, or of obedience unto
> righteousness? But God be thanked, that ye
> were the servants of sin, but ye have obeyed
> *from the heart* that form of doctrine which
> was delivered you. Being then made free from
> sin, ye became the servants of
> righteousness.[241]

If authority bereft of consent is reduced to force, and government in opposition to Natural Law is a self-dissolving evil, then the individual mind divorced of reason best displayed by virtue in conduct, ceases to be human.[242] Without virtue liberty is impossible because without it men become beasts; a beast cannot be free.

The Yeoman

Reflecting back on Morrison's statement regarding practicality, and Rakove's observation regarding the necessity of conveying theory into practice, it would follow that one might find some identifiable image of the daily-lived, practical life for the free and virtuous citizen in this new civilization.[243] Overlaying the far earlier James – who illuminates the obvious to show that one's belief is demonstrated in his behavior – it is clear that the individual

---

241   Romans 6:15-18; emphasis added.
242   Aristotle, "Nicomachean Ethics," in *Basic Works*, 1178a:7-9.
243   Morrison, "The Political Thought of John Witherspoon, 1768 – 1794," 243; "The Perils of Originalism" in Jack N. Rakove, *Original Meanings*, 2013.

virtue so advocated bore no resemblance to the
sanctimonious kill-joy with which the ideal of a 'moral
citizen' may be associated in contemporary assumption.

Virtue primarily concerns its own behavior over the
intrusion upon that of others.[244] It is obvious, one would
hope, that sloth, dereliction, or parasitism are contrary to the
principle of virtue as much as are addiction to 'workahol' or
industrialized, self-righteous, aggressive anhedonia, let alone
the self-appointed grand-social-inquisitor. Again, one's rights
are proscriptions not entitlements to another's stuff; one may
pursue happiness not demand it.

A contemporary may object to such a connection, but
each of the principles thus far analyzed lead in simultaneity
to this image, as put by Adams, "[l]iberty can no more exist
without virtue and independence, than the body can live and
move without a soul."[245] It is no accident that Adams would
select these words; movement is animation, and the soul is
the *anima* previously mentioned.[246] Again referencing
Jefferson's original draft Declaration and Mason's Virginia
Declaration, men were created free *and independent*. As one
given to vice is a slave to fickle passion, so too is an
employee beholden to his employer.

Let it be made plain in eighteenth century thought.
Johnson's dictionary does not contain the word 'employee',
but it does include the term 'employer': "one that uses or
causes to be used."[247] Employment is *use*. While there is a
spectrum of semantic shading *employed* in the term, such that
one who employs one's resources towards business is the

---

244 James 2:18; Cf. Matthew 7:3-5, John 7:5-11.

245 John Adams, "To the Inhabitants of the Colony of
Massachusetts-Bay," in *Papers of John Adams Volume 2, December
1773 – April 1775*, (Cambridge: Harvard University Press, 1977),
245.

246 'anima' is employed in it its *actual* meaning of 'wind,
breath, life, soul' as in Aristotle's *De Anima*, not in either the Jungian
or Freudian, popular-psychological use of the term; Cf. "anima,"
Cassell's Latin English Dictionary, (Boston: Houghton, Mifflin,
Harcourt, 2002).

247 "employer," *A Dictionary of the English Language*, by
Samuel Johnson. 1773. Accessed October 15, 2024:
https://johnsonsdictionaryonline.com/1773/employer_ns.

employer, it is inescapable that to substitute a human-being as a resource is to *use* a human-being. While, in a conscionable contract, the man so reduced to a resource may be 'free' to decline a directive, he cannot do so without risk to his employment at the arbitrary will of his user. Certainly there is an element of consent in such an arrangement, yet should one's food, water, or shelter be subject to continued acquiescence, the *context* of coercion fundamentally invalidates the possibility of a 'no', thereby rendering the 'yes' meaningless.[248] Human resources may operate with the colors of consent, but it is impossible to banish the stench of indenture.

What then? Should it be that all the meaning behind the principle of liberty deriving from equality in creation be rendered impotent merely by the necessity of a life lived in service to one's boss? Certainly not. Is this side-wind assault on liberty mitigated by labor-regulations or 'collective bargaining'? Not remotely, as such would merely trade the master from the regular boss to the union boss, or to the Department of Labor's boss. In either case, one's subsistence is subordinated to the arbitrary will of another; independence is not outsourced. The connection between freedom and independence is inseparable and unmistakable, as Jefferson stated a bit poetically "I think our governments will remain virtuous for many centuries; as long as they are chiefly agricultural.... When they get piled upon one another in large cities, as in Europe, they will become corrupt as in Europe."[249]

To be certain, Jefferson makes use of the term 'emploiment' in his 1785 letter to John Jay that clarifies his romantic view of agrarianism.[250] This is however, in accord with Johnson, merely the use of one's own time in the act of

---

248   Cf. *Yick Wo v. Hopkins,* 118 U.S. 356 (1886).
249   Thomas Jefferson, "To James Madison from Thomas Jefferson, 20 December 1787," *Founders Online*, National Archives, https://founders.archives.gov/documents/Madison/01-10-02-0210.
250   Thomas Jefferson, "From Thomas Jefferson to John Jay, 23 August 1785," *Founders Online*, National Archives, https://founders.archives.gov/documents/Jefferson/01-08-02-0333.

"business; object of industry; object of labor."[251] There were most certainly employees, laborers, servants, and slaves inherent in the employment of cultivation at the time, but this is not the defining detail of the image that Jefferson painted. "Cultivators of the earth are the most valuable citizens. They are the most vigorous, the most independant, the most virtuous, and they are tied to their country and wedded to it's liberty and interests by the most lasting bands."[252] One can fixate on the failures of the founders, or one can seek the principles they attempted to achieve; who would prefer the former can by no means be convinced.

Disregarding, yet again, the useless adolescent libel aimed at the 'rich old white man' Jefferson, there is one who takes more issue with Jefferson's Lockean property rights inherent in his agrarianism, than with his status as a slaveholder.

Lisi Krall wrote in 2002 of Jefferson's inability to anticipate the shifting concept of property rights primarily as a result of the industrial revolution. Krall's concern chiefly orbits disagreements regarding capitalism as it applies to property, with heavy emphasis on Jefferson's substantial agreement with Adam Smith (1723 – 1790). Of Jefferson, she correctly stated that "...the intellectual roots that guided Jefferson in his effort to create the institutional framework for the unfolding of his vision are found in the tradition of natural law and economic liberalism which he wholeheartedly supported."[253]

Krall however employed a diminutive caricature of industry, claiming that, in Jefferson's view, it was "...a mostly self-sufficient independent farmer tinkering with a little nail manufacturing on the side."[254] From this straw-man, Krall eventually arrived at the same notion – that private property

251   "employment," *A Dictionary of the English Language*, by Samuel Johnson. 1773. Accessed October 15, 2024: https://johnsonsdictionaryonline.com/1773/employment_ns.
252   Thomas Jefferson, "From Thomas Jefferson to John Jay, 23 August 1785." Sic.
253   Lisi Krall, "Thomas Jefferson's Agrarian Vision and the Changing Nature of Property," *Journal of Economic Issues* 36, no. 1 (2002), 132.
254   Krall, "Agrarian Vision," 146.

is an 'institution' that must be changed. Beneath the useless jargon inherent in her 'framework' or 'institution', Krall missed the point of independence – the most certain safeguard of future liberty – in her failure to recognize the vital necessity of self-sufficiency without regard to what toys or tools technology might supply, or vices these might facilitate. It would seem, sub-textually, that Krall is either more irritated that Jefferson was a capitalist, or that she sought to pile on the reasons to dismiss his inarguable principles with the perverse charge that he was a 'capitalist' in addition to having owned slaves.

Whatever Krall's view of Jefferson's 'economics' she, like so many, failed to recognize and incorporate simultaneous principles. Independence is freedom is virtue is self-government is limited government is Natural Law is self-control is liberty is equality is dignity. Virtue does not admit to robber-baron-greedy-capitalist-worker-exploitation any more so than it does to lazy-dependent-socialist-parasitism. Jefferson's 'vision' that Krall denigrated was not 'tinkering', and it was not that one should seek a lucrative position in the C-suite, his vision was independence in *productive land-ownership* as Gordon Wood summarized:

> Equality for Jefferson was related to the personal independence of each citizen, which was essential for Republicanism.... Men should be equal in that no one of them should be dependent on the will of another, and property made this independence possible. Hence, his proposal in 1776 that every Virginian be given at least fifty acres of land.[255]

For Jefferson, the foundation for a society in which liberty-in-equality is the chief concern is that each man has his own parcel – not only to take shelter, but from which to derive his own living, raise his family, and in general do as he wanted without interference – and without interfering. In what passes for 'domestic policy' in the Jefferson

---

'administration', it could not be made any more plain than his statement "… encouragement of agriculture, and of commerce as its handmaid."[256] The convolutions regarding Jefferson's agrarianism represent yet another example of that moral case better put to the plowman than to the professor.[257]

The point is independence; spiritualism, flowery poetics, shades of transcendentalism or primitivism are incidental and unimportant. The same Jefferson who may be dismissed for the *schmaltzy* claim that "[t]hose who labor in the earth are the chosen people of God…" also clarified in the same breath that "[d]ependence begets subservience and venality, suffocates the germ of virtue, and prepares fit tools for the designs of ambition."[258] Made ever more plain, rural landowners who produce their own life necessities are *hard to oppress* whereas urban wage-earning-renters are *hard to free*. Who works to produce for his own subsistence is pressed towards dignity by necessity, and his independence safeguards his freedom from coercion; who works for a *wage* without security of ownership exchanges things of far more value than merely labor. One would posit that this may be one reason that God cursed the ground – *for your sake.*[259]

To answer yet another complaint or criticism of Jefferson, deriving from his earlier opinions regarding manufacture and artisanry as inferior to agriculture, one would state that Jefferson merely outgrew that limited and mistaken perspective[260]:

256   Jefferson's First Inaugural Address in Krall, "Agrarian Vision," 140; Cf. Thomas Jefferson, "First Inaugural Address," in *Constitution*, 2012, 787.

257   Thomas Jefferson, "From Thomas Jefferson to Peter Carr, with Enclosure, 10 August 1787," *Founders Online*, National Archives, https://founders.archives.gov/documents/Jefferson/01-12-02-0021. Cf. Gordon Wood, "Thomas Jefferson and the Idea of Equality", Speech, *American Enterprise Institute*. January 9, 1995. https://www.aei.org/research-products/speech/thomas-jefferson-and-the-idea-of-equality/.

258   Thomas Jefferson, *Notes on The State of Virginia: Annotated Edition*, (New Haven: Yale University Press, 2022 [1785]), 252, 253.

259   Cf. Genesis 3:17.

260   Cf. Thomas Jefferson, "From Thomas Jefferson to John Jay, 23 August 1785"; Thomas Jefferson, *Notes on the State of Virginia*, 252 – 253.

...to be independant for the comforts of life we
must fabricate them ourselves. We must now
place the manufacturer by the side of the
agriculturist. ...shall we make our own
comforts, or go without them, at the will of a
foreign nation? He therefore who is now
against domestic manufacture must be for
reducing us either to dependance on that
foreign nation, or to be clothed in skins, & to
live like wild beasts in dens & caverns. I am
not one of these. Experience has taught me
that manufactures are now as necessary to our
independance as to our comfort[261]

It is readily apparent here that Jefferson's *principle* of
independence exceeded his previous *position* regarding
manufacture on both a national as well as individual level.
Far from his limited view of artisanry being a criticism,
Jefferson's later recognition of 'value-added goods' being
integral to independence due to experience, and subsequent
revision to place "the manufacturer by the side of the
agriculturist" is the mark of an internal logical consistency –
a precise example of applied virtue.

Independence as a practice, naturally extending from
a principle, did not merely change one of Jefferson's
positions, it underlies the first right – that of life itself. As
Locke argued, the first possession or property is one's own
self, one's body. Labor derives directly from the body
therefore one's labor is one's property. The origin of property
is, by this means, derived of nature by the mingling of
labor.[262] Not to be limited to the abstraction of 'property',
Locke directly connects this derivation to the substance of
so-called 'real' property – land:

As much land as a man tills, plants, improves,
cultivates, and can use the product of, so much

261   Thomas Jefferson, "Thomas Jefferson to Benjamin Austin, 9
January 1816," *Founders Online*, National Archives,
https://founders.archives.gov/documents/Jefferson/03-09-02-0213;
Edited for punctuation.
262   Locke, *Second Treaties*, V:27.

> is his property. He by his labor does, as it
> were, inclose it from the common…. God,
> when he gave the world in common to all
> mankind, commanded man also to labour, and
> the penury of his condition required it of
> him.[263]

One will note the latter part of the citation - "…the penury of his condition required it of him." Penury is poverty; the condition of man is poverty. Any guffaw in retort notwithstanding, to place a naked man in nature, even Eden as it were, is objectively to place him in a state of poverty; the man must labor or he quickly becomes a corpse. Such an inescapable reality immediately washes as an icy wave over anyone who ever finds himself lost in the wilderness. This forms the basis of a number of contemporary 'reality shows' – whether genuine or fraudulently contrived. Labor, and land upon which to labor, are inherent in the very essence of life itself; the ability for one to have such things under his own competence is the essential, the necessary and sufficient condition of independence. The absence of independence is dependence, dependence is substantially synonymous with *slavery*.[264] The landowner is free – or at least can be; the renter or tenant is a slave – beholden to another for the maintenance of his very first right to live.

Jefferson may well have fetishized the bucolic, but he understood whence men obtain their bread – far better than the alarming number of moderns who appear in practice to believe that it simply materializes on aisle twelve. The starving do not debate well the practice of Natural Law with those who offer bread in exchange for their soul. Whatever condescension may result from an overly artistic ideal of the farmer, the power inherent in the hands that harvest completely devastates the moronic claim in Richard Hofstadter's 1955 *Age of Reform* that Jefferson's yeoman is a national fiction: "[t]he agrarian myth represents a kind of homage that Americans have paid to the fancied innocence of

---

263   Locke, *Second Treaties*, V:32, sic.
264   Cf. "slave," *A Dictionary of the English Language*, by
Samuel Johnson. 1773.

their origins."[265] Unfortunately, Hofstadter's viscosity in such a claim would become the *mos maiorum* of elitist retrospection subsequent to the Progressive inversion – when Americans forgot the source of their liberty, and of their power.

The source of this power, the ability to effect one's will, was well addressed by Noah Webster in 1787. Webster (1758 – 1843) certainly deserves his own full treatment for many reasons beyond his 1806 namesake dictionary – which Jefferson also possessed.[266] In his *Examination into the Leading Principles of the Federal Constitution*, Webster spoke with unmistakable force in favor of "...an agricultural country, a general possession of land in fee simple...." He declared that "[a]n equality of property... is the very *soul of a republic* – [w]hile this continues, the people will inevitably possess both *power* and *freedom*; when this is lost, power departs, liberty expires, and a commonwealth will inevitably assume some other form."[267]

Webster held the widespread, private ownership of real property without subordination (in fee simple) so highly that he placed this factor above the "palladia of freedom", or the free press, the jury, and Habeas Corpus. So precious is this principle, that he even took Montesquieu (1689 – 1755) to task, declaring that the word 'virtue' in his 1748 *The Sprit of Law* must be replaced with "property or lands in fee simple." He took the argument even further than this: "*Virtue, patriotism, or love of country, never was and never will be, till mens' natures are changed, a fixed, permanent principle in support of government.*"[268]

It is fortunate that Webster employed footnotes, uncharacteristic but not unheard in eighteenth century literature, lest one's previous argument for virtue be undone by this one declaration. Webster clarified that in

---

265   Richard Hofstadter, *The Age of Reform: From Bryan to F.D.R.*, (New York: Alfred A. Knopf 1955), 24.
266   "English Language Dictionaries", *The Jefferson Monticello*.
267   Noah Webster, "An Examination into the Leading Principles of the Federal Constitution," in *Constitution*, 2012, 689; emphasis in original.
268   Noah Webster, "An Examination," in *Constitution*, 2012, 689; emphasis in original.

Montesquieu's use, deriving of a Greco-Roman analysis "...this *virtue* consisted in pride, contempt of strangers and a martial enthusiasm which sometimes displayed itself in defense of their country. These principles are never permanent – they decay..."[269] One cannot speculate on Webster's use of arete or balance in this analysis, yet two items are clear. English, especially as a result of translation, has consistently lead to divergent understanding from the same term even among lexicographers; and Adams, Jefferson, Wilson, Locke, and Aristotle most certainly did not speak of self-inflated, warlike chauvinism in reference to balanced moral excellence. One would posit that the chief difference herein lies in the aforementioned derivation of 'virtue' through the French. Montesquieu, via Webster, appears to emphasize the 'manliness' aspect more closely related to the *virile* branch of *vir*, rather than the concept extending from Aristotle's *ethike*.[270]

In either case, moral excellence and private, real-property ownership act as simultaneous wellsprings to the concept of American freedom. The point here is practical lived independence – not to be held in hock, subordinate and subject to the 'rentier'. Webster calls this ideal "the *basis* of the freedom of the American yeomanry...."[271]

The word itself – yeoman – is of a curious lineage. It is unattested in Old English, appearing to spring into existence, fully understood and in wide use, some time in the fourteenth century in reference to an "attendant in a noble household". It has some martial uses, including the current 'clerk' or 'secretary' in the United States Navy, along with placement in chivalric codes or the strata of nobility – of which there is none in America. Its use to mean a "commoner [not noble] who cultivates his [own] land" from the founding extends from the sixteenth century.[272] Johnson defined it as "a

269   Noah Webster, "An Examination," Note 16 in *Constitution*, 2012, 696; emphasis in original.
270   Cf. "virile," *Online Etymology Dictionary*, Accessed October 16, 2024: https://www.etymonline.com/word/virile.
271   Noah Webster, "An Examination," in *Constitution*, 2012, 689; emphasis in original.
272   "yeoman," *Online Etymology Dictionary*, Accessed October 16, 2024: https://www.etymonline.com/word/yeoman; This author

man of a small estate in land; a farmer; a gentleman farmer", though additional definitions include military ceremony, the concept of a commoner 'freeholder', and a reference to a "gentleman servant".[273] In addition to the artistic whispers of 'simple country folk' – that 'modern' scholars hold in such derision – there *appears* to be the ghost of a reference to Lucuis Quinctius Cincinnatus (c. 519 – 430 BC), if for no other reason than the image of the man who left his plow for absolute power then, task completed, quickly returned back to his plow.[274]

Of the many obscure terms in the English lexicon, 'yeoman' may be the more difficult to pin. Post-Progressive inverted thinking from a wholly dependent urban view appears incapable of conceiving of a self-sufficient farmer as anything beyond a bare-foot, uneducated peasant reeking of animal excrement, outmoded morality and vestigial romanticism. Among the throng who think of government as an omnipotent 'daddy' mandated to provide goodies on demand, or of the individual as nothing better than a minor organelle in the grand behemoth of 'society', the image of one who eats by the sweat of his brow is not only incomprehensible, but boorish, unevolved and apparently (somehow) racist. Among the terribly sophisticated – meaning full of sophistry – Keynesians, any reference to economics means policy, interest, banking, wages, inflation, or exchange markets; such was not the case among the founders.

> Finally, there seem to be but three Ways for a
> Nation to acquire Wealth. The first is by War

---

once served in the United States Navy; Yeoman is a 'rate', a job, of clerical duty.

273   "yeoman," *A Dictionary of the English Language*, by Samuel Johnson. 1773. Accessed October 14, 2024: https://johnsonsdictionaryonline.com/1773/yeoman_ns.

274   The story of Cincinnatus is far beyond this argument, but serves as a cultural archetype of specific kind of civic-virtue in addition to 'yeomanish' humility of an almost puritanical work ethic. Detractors of Jefferson's – or perhaps Washington's – agrarianism would do better to criticize this image, as Cincinnatus was a patrician who opposed plebeian causes; Cf. Livy, *History of Rome*, c. 27 BC.

as the Romans did in plundering their
conquered Neighbours. This is Robbery. The
second by Commerce which is generally
Cheating. The third by Agriculture the only
honest Way; wherein Man receives a real
Increase of the Seed thrown into the Ground,
in a kind of continual Miracle wrought by the
Hand of God in his favour, as a Reward for his
innocent Life, and virtuous Industry.[275]

Whether or not what amounts to retail arbitrage is
"generally cheating" is certainly a curious question regarding
Franklin's view of political economy or, time-appropriately
œconomy, being a reference to *household* management.[276] It
is certainly clear that many of the pertinent men respected the
anachronistic 'primary economic sector' – resource
extraction – as superior or preferable to other 'sectors'.

Though Jefferson modified his previous view of the
secondary sector – manufacture – as noted, he did not shift
his view that the earth belongs to the living. In speaking of
republican virtues, he placed "economy" at the top. One
would assume it is clear that the use of the term herein is of a
wholly different flavor than current use; Jefferson does not
speak of *the* economy, but of *economy* being a virtue. This
use directly precedes the statement that "...public debt... [is]
greatest of the dangers to be feared." The substance of this
letter is clear enough – public debt resulting from profligacy
amounts to rule by the dead, and acts as a cancer what
consumes such that "...the feesimple [real-property
ownership] ... transferred to the public creditors....".[277]

---

275   Benjamin Franklin, "Positions to be Examined, 4 April
        1769," *Founders Online*, National Archives,
        https://founders.archives.gov/documents/Franklin/01-16-02-0048,
        sic; cf. Charles Pinckney, "America's Unique Structure of Freedom,"
        1788, in *Constitution*, 2012, 701.
276   "economy," *Online Etymology Dictionary*, Accessed
        October 17, 2024: https://www.etymonline.com/word/economy.
277   Thomas Jefferson, "Thomas Jefferson to William Plumer, 21
        July 1816," *Founders Online*, National Archives,
        https://founders.archives.gov/documents/Jefferson/03-10-02-0152.

The inherent differences between economy as a virtue and '*the* economy' as a talking-point can hardly be overstated, especially in comparison to debt. Johnson's dictionary simply does not contain a sense of the term that would admit to its current use; in all of its variations it speaks directly to frugality, arrangement, and generally rational management – specifically of a family, meaning government of a household.[278] The word 'economy' means, in effect, the good and decent stewardship of resources. One laments that a twenty-first century American is likely incapable of truly grasping that this *has nothing to do with an industrial average, or even the price of gasoline*, to say nothing of an imaginary GDP or wholly fabricated third-quarter-jobs-report. Economy is a virtue, it means good management.

This understanding is crucial to the thrust of eighteenth century yeomanry. Public debt invariably results from corrupt squandering by the grandfathers. Attempting to meet the maintenance of this note, the fathers must resort to taxation; this taxation does not ask for representation, yet amounts to such a drain that real-property – the fountain head of independence and therefore surest guard of liberty – is stolen from the sons, by their dead grandfathers. Debt is fundamentally antonymous to economy. Clearly the Keynesian requires some vocabulary lessons.

The far more appropriate term for what current vacuous-talking-heads mean when they say 'economy' is commerce, that being simply trade: "exchange of one thing for another"[279] As already demonstrated, the proper place for trade in Jefferson's view was as the 'handmaid' of agriculture.[280] Franklin defined agriculture as "virtuous industry", a term that Johnson, in turn, defined as "diligence; assiduity; habitual or actual laboriousness."[281] Wonderfully, where Aristotle would place habituation in excellence, and

---

278   "economy," *A Dictionary of the English Language*, by Samuel Johnson, 1773, Accessed October 17, 2024: https://johnsonsdictionaryonline.com/1773/economy_ns.
279   "commerce," *A Dictionary of the English Language*, by Samuel Johnson, 1773, Accessed October 17, 2024: https://johnsonsdictionaryonline.com/1773/commerce_ns.
280   Thomas Jefferson, "First Inaugural Address," in *Constitution*, 2012, 787.

Franklin would connect this excellence to diligence, so Johnson returns it back to habituation in 'laboriousness'. Industry is diligence; it is not 'smoke-stacks and factories', nor even a collection of proprietors or legal-entities all performing substantially the same economic activity.

Another may argue that this may have been the case in the eighteenth century, but the semantics have shifted. Semantics are not principles, American civilization was founded on principles not semantics. Without unnecessarily multiplying the page count of this argument, in examination of eighteenth century agrarianism a curious detail became clear. It is a reasonably safe position to declare that the overwhelming majority of the founders were not statesmen; these were what is called 'renaissance men'. Certainly militarism and statecraft were among their interests as much as were the various sciences, linguistics, mathematics, history, or theology. Among the majority however, farming as both a discipline – agronomy – and as a practice was quite widespread, from Jefferson and Franklin, to Washington, Adams, and Madison.[282] From these, America has Monticello, Mount Vernon, Peacefield, and Montpelier among others not so easily identified; framers they may have been, but farmers they always will remain.

The central importance, the practicable realistic importance of yeomanry in the creation of American civilization cannot be overstated. The lived empirical independence of self-sufficient land-ownership was not limited to the individual, nor abstracted to the collective. This wholly clear variable was the central factor of not simply personal, but enduring national freedom. 'Small-business' or 'self-employment' are by no means the 'backbone' of the American economy, but rather *economy* and *industry* of the *yeomanry* are the fountainhead of American commerce,

---

281   Benjamin Franklin, "Positions to be Examined, 4 April 1769"; "industry," *A Dictionary of the English Language*, by Samuel Johnson, 1773, Accessed October 17, 2024: https://johnsonsdictionaryonline.com/1773/industry_ns.

282   "The Founders, Farms, and Facts," n.d. *The Lehrman Institute*, Accessed October 16, 2024: https://lehrmaninstitute.org/history/founders-farms-facts.html.

independence, freedom, security, and prosperity. To denigrate Jefferson's 'agrarianism', even if it may be somewhat saccharine, is fundamentally a repudiation of the very mode of life that begets freedom-birthing-independence. The American citizen *is* the yeoman; the independent, self-supporting, land-owning free man.

The Design

As demonstrated, America was founded upon principles and these principles transcend; they are not subject to time or place, or to the failings of the men by whom they were committed to paper. In reflecting on one of these principles, rendered in the Declaration as a "decent respect to the opinions of mankind", one finds a highly distasteful necessity in addressing some of the charges leveled against some of the names.

Jefferson, Washington, Witherspoon and others having owned slaves does not invalidate the substance of the principles these men sought. To make such a claim betrays the self-destruction inherent in solipsism: one employs the principle of equality descending from these men to dismiss that same principle, based on a retrospective assessment of their adherence to the current image of the principle. To make this point more clearly, one employs the ancient and well honored practice of sarcasm.

Washington and Jefferson were slaveholders, clearly everything they believed regarding equality, limited government, and freedom are invalid – obviously equality does not exist, government is limitless, and freedom is just a word. Adams and Hamilton's conduct in the *Alien and Sedition Acts* does not invalidate the substance of the principles these men sought. These men passed laws onerous to the Constitution, obviously therefore authority can do anything it likes and rights are more like informal guidelines at best. The plurality of these men having been wealthy (at least *before* the war) does not invalidate the substance of the principles these men sought. Clearly, because many of their farms were enormous, and worked by slaves, no humble citizen ought to possess and work his own small freehold. One could continue, but the point is made.

Over and again in the course of seeking primary sources, one has encountered hollow adolescent moralism invariably seeking to 'discredit' the various men on charges ranging from hypocrisy and white-supremacy to colonialism, 'capitalist exploitation', and sexual perversion. All of these charges are summarily dismissed for two specific reasons.

First, the validity of a principle is found in its application and empirical validity in a plurality over time – not in the limited view of a man's character as so anemically attested by documentation. A man is not properly condemned by the key-hole view offered by sources analyzed centuries and millennia after his death and even if he were, what is true remains true even when identified as true by the most rapacious sociopath. Principles are so far beyond humanity that they remain inviolate in even the most despicable of mouths. The failures of the founders are irrelevant.

Second, deriving of the first, the retrospective moralism employed in attacking these men is little better than simplistic reactive iconoclasm. Disregarding the inherent hypocrisy in employing juvenile presentism to cast the charge of hypocrisy, as well as the absurdity in all *ad hominem*, had these men not been lionized it is unlikely they would be such a target. This author's opinion is that it is *always* foolhardy to cut the image of a man in stone. From Washington and Jefferson to Aristotle and Moses, veneration of a man is not only inherently *stupid*, but counterproductive. The great danger in carving gilt statuary is that when time causes the gilding to flake, men will see the stone beneath and think it to be a flaw. The irreverent iconoclasm that many 'conservatives' find so abhorrent is a natural product of these same persons having venerated those men. It is wholly simple and self-evident: there are no great men.

From a certain perspective, American civilization was founded *via negativa*; she is not defined so much by what she is, as by what she *is not*. American civilization is not an empire of men, thusly to make statues of her men is at best a

waste of good stone.[283] Good government is summarized by
what it *does not* rather than by what it does, thusly to look to
government in most cases is to miss the point entirely.[284]
Rights deriving of Natural Law do not say to the people 'you
may', but declare to authority – *all* authority – 'you shall
not!', thusly the very act of asking the Supreme Court to
define rather than to *recognize and secure* the inalienable is a
repudiation of the very concept of rights itself.[285] That which
is given or granted may as easily be revoked by the one who
grants, thusly dependent subsistence is fundamentally
antithetical to even the whisper of liberty.[286]

In addressing the heritage of liberty, many are quickly
lost in useless arguments regarding 'originalism', inevitably
to suffer elitist obscurantism and vacuous rationalizations. It
is demonstrated that not only was the founding world-view
one of transcendent, 'Newtonian' principles, but that these
principles are apparent to any functioning human mind. More
than this, the principles are simple – better observed by the
humble man than perverted and occluded by the
intelligentsia; state one's case to the plowman and he will
offer a *usable* verdict.

The principles are not merely simple and eminently
approachable, but are intrinsic to human-nature (for lack of a
more appropriate term). Liberty and freedom are
substantially the same concepts, speaking to bi-directional
non-domination and the exemption from the arbitrary will or
limitations of another. This exemption is not a matter of law,
it is a matter of creation; to exist is to be entitled to freedom.

Owing to the substantial basis of liberty inherent in
the creation, all are simultaneously free – none being by
nature worthy of a greater dignity than any other. This
simultaneity is manifest in the bi-directionality of non-
domination, such that one's liberty is limited only by the very

---

283   Cf. Adams, "Thoughts on Government," in *Constitution*,
    2012, 174.
284   Cf. Jefferson, "First Inaugural," in *Constitution*, 2012, 787.
285   Cf. James Wilson, "Remarks of James Wilson," in *Collected
    Works of James Wilson*, Vol. 1, 2007.
286   Cf. Noah Webster, "An Examination," in *Constitution*, 2012,
    689.

same limits that protect him – that of rights. Equality in creation is coeval with the proscriptions of rights, being the substance of liberty. This concept is the gravitic kernel of the Declaration of Independence, in both drafts, as well as other consanguineous documents. The individual dignity of each man, an inherent property of God's first gift, is the *anima* of legitimate government in the United States – written *first* in the Declaration, and only later expanded in procedure by the Constitution. Rights are a matter of nature, merely to be reflected in procedure.

This procedure displays in the inescapable foundation for cooperation – whether among friends or strangers, neighborhoods or nation-states. Consent is the sole legitimate basis for interaction, the whole adhesive of society, and the entire litmus of authority. Absent consent, authority is by definition illegitimate and therefore tyranny. Consent in practice is the antonym of enslavement, and the application of human dignity. Following directly from this principle, the people do not ask the government, but rather the government must ask the people. This is not anthropic omnipotence; even the people as a whole cannot command any more than might any one man of their number. The collective, made of individuals, cannot be greater than the individual.

This is not to say that collectives cannot do great things, but rather that by design the whole of American authority is subordinate to Natural Law; this far, and no farther. Were the ninety-nine to elect to kill the one-hundredth, it is still murder. Even in unanimity, there are many regions wherein it would be fundamentally wrong for authority to tread. America is a republic, *not* a democracy, for this reason alone: an empire of laws, a nation of *principles*.

Stated yet again, these principles are fundamental, primary, transcendent, and simultaneous. Every functioning human being is aware of them – forever evidenced by their outrage when they have been the target of a violation. Legislation is simply far too coarse a tool, and authority far too impotent to approach the seat of belief and behavior; laws cannot approach the practice of liberty, only virtue can do this. The voluntary consistent rational pursuit of balanced moral excellence in seeking one's purpose is the essential quality that allows for a man to be free. Whether free from his own passions or from those of others, liberty is only possible among those who choose to control themselves.

Finally, all of these simultaneous principles combine to approach the identifiable image of practicable liberty: independence. It is both self-evident and undeniable that one who's subsistence must wait on the pleasure of another is dependent upon that one's will. Who is dependent looses his dignity, cannot exercise his consent, is not equal, and cannot be free. The substance of the Declaration of Independence – equality leading to liberty by God's design – is enacted by independence derived of private, productive land-ownership. Only the independent are able to consent, and thusly only the yeoman is truly free.

These are the principles upon which the foundation was lain for civilization in America. It is readily apparent in the consistent genetics of the simultaneous principles that equality of creation underlies, supports, begets, and sustains the whole of the world-view upon which American civilization was founded. Failings or shortcomings do nothing to change the target; the principles are the standard of measure. The whole of the matter is the dignity of the man.

Part II: The American Aeneid

The Heresy of Perfectibility

How art thou fallen from heaven, O Lucifer,
son of the morning! How art thou cut down to
the ground, which didst weaken the nations!
For thou has said in thine heart, I will ascend
into heaven, I will exalt my throne above the
stars of God: I will sit also upon the mount of
the congregation, in the sides of the north: I
will ascend above the heights of the clouds; *I
will be like the most High*. Yet thou shalt be
brought down to hell, to the sides of the pit.

– Isaiah 14:12-14; Emphasis added.

T he whole of the matter is the dignity of the man. The individual dignity of each man, an inherent property of God's first gift, is the *anima* of authority in the United States. This authority is predicated on consent, the antonym of enslavement and the application of human dignity. This image is realized only by independence because the dependent man has no dignity, cannot consent, is not equal, and cannot be free. It is inherent in the nature of dignity that such a thing cannot be forced; it would be supremely paradoxical to command another in this regard – as a lie cannot beget honesty, so a command cannot beget equality: who obeys is subordinate to who commands. The mechanisms of American civilization were created to safeguard dignity, not to provide or to produce what had already been given by the act of Creation.

Preeminent among sentiments in eighteenth century writings, one finds consistent warnings against the many factors that would corrode God's liberty, rather than a preference for utopian fantasies. To be certain, many have characterized Jefferson as a 'utopian', most especially in his views on education, yet there is a sharp contrast.[287] Between Moore's satirical and utterly totalitarian *Insula Utopia* (1516) or other renditions of 'enlightened' despotism inherent in the genre, and Jefferson's natural freedom, there can be no comparison. The previously mentioned men wrote so thoroughly and consistently regarding the ease of falling into despotism that they have created their own distinct genre.

These warnings, interspersed among discussions around the various procedures being created, appear nearly item for item to have been ignored. Washington warned against 'usurpations', especially those operating from good intentions because "...it is the customary weapon by which free governments are destroyed."[288] Madison clearly noted the importance of *simplicity* of law among a free people, noting that convoluted laws poison "the blessing of liberty itself."[289] Franklin made 'equal protection' clear long before the Fourteenth Amendment when he spoke of "[t]he ordaining of laws in favor of one part of the nation, to the prejudice and oppression of another..."[290] The list continues to such an extent that one suggests that this genre of founding literature be classified as admonition.

Most poignant from these admonitions, one clearly recognizes a poetic refusal to heed the warnings. "There is nothing which I dread so much as a division of the republic into two great parties.... This, in my humble apprehension, is to be dreaded as the greatest political evil under our

---

287   Cf. M. Andrew Holowchak, *Thomas Jefferson's Philosophy of Education: A Utopian Dream*, (London: Routledge, 2014).

288   Washington, "Farewell Address", in *Constitution*, 2012, 774.

289   James Madison [Attributed], "The Senate," *Federalist no. 62*, 1788, in *Constitution*, 2012, 534.

290   Benjamin Franklin, "DXCI. The Result of England's Persistence in her Policy Towards the Colonies Illustrated", in *The Complete Works of Benjamin Franklin*, Vol. V, 1772-1775, John Bigelow, ed. (New Yok: G.P. Putnam's Sons, 1887), 417.

constitution."[291] Owing to the current season during which this argument is written (autumn, 2024), one is drawn to the tragedy in Alexander Hamilton's prophesy: "...every vital interest of the state will be merged in the all-absorbing question of who shall be the next president."[292] And, by way of foreshadow, Jefferson not only warned, but accurately predicted: "...by what road it will pass to destruction... consolidation first, and then corruption.... The engine of consolidation will be the federal judiciary; the two other branches the corrupting and corrupted instruments."[293] While the obstinate refusal to heed the myriad of cautions, or indeed wantonly oppose them directly, is clearly an aspect of the "...love of power and proneness to abuse it which predominate in the human heart...", it is seen most clearly in the production of a founding mythopoeic contriving its own *telos* for American civilization.[294]

John Winthrop (1558 – 1649) spoke in Southampton aboard the Arbella, 1630 to the soon-to-be-Bostonians.[295] Setting aside the fertile detail that one of the first poignant American speeches took place in Britain, Winthrop's exhortation to his puritan flock is often referenced as the source of the ideal called 'American exceptionalism' due to a *perversion* of his reference to Matthew 5:14 – the 'city on the hill'.[296]

---

291   John Adams, "From John Adams to Boston Patriot, 4 August 1809," *Founders Online*, National Archives, https://founders.archives.gov/documents/Adams/99-02-02-5405; noted as 'early access' and 'not authoritative'.
292   Max Farrand, ed., *The Records of the Federal Convention of 1787*, vol. 3, (New Haven: Yale University Press, 1911), 410-411, Cf. Eidelberg Dissertation, 182.
293   Thomas Jefferson, "Thomas Jefferson to Nathaniel Macon, 23 November 1821," *Founders Online*, National Archives, https://founders.archives.gov/documents/Jefferson/03-17-02-0549.
294   Washington, "Farewell Address", in *Constitution*, 2012, 774.
295   John Winthrop, "A Model of Christian Charity," 1630, *Gilder Lehrman Institute of American History*, 2012, Accessed November 6, 2024: https://www.gilderlehrman.org/sites/default/files/inline-pdfs/A%20M odel%20of%20Christian%20Charity_Full%20Text.pdf.
296   This detail is beyond the scope of the current argument. Regarding 'American exceptionalism' and civil religion, cf. Perry

Winthrop's speech falls decidedly into the genre of admonition. Where a Kennedy, Reagan, or an Obama might invoke the shining city as an example or *casus belli* – the 'good child' or legitimizing myth in a manner of speaking, Winthrop offered it as a warning.[297] The portion of this short sermon that contains the contentious verbiage is introduced with the easily understood sentence: "Now the only way to avoid this shipwreck, and to provide for our posterity, is to follow the counsel of Micah, to do justly, to love mercy, to walk humbly with our God."[298] Simply, Winthrop gave a rather dire warning to his intrepid band that would be well rendered today as 'if we fail everyone will see it, and blaspheme God because of us.' The city on the hill of which Jesus spoke was one that "cannot be hid", while it is clearly a 'light' to shine for God's glory, it is also a very visible opportunity for failure. Winthrop cannot be misunderstood in his use; he encouraged his followers to be careful for their visibility, by no means did he intend for Boston to become some sickly rendition of the Borg.[299] Due place given for 'exceptionalism', Winthrop is not a legitimate source for expansionism – ideological or otherwise.

A second particle in the growth of the fraudulent American *telos* could be President Madison's second cousin Bishop James Madison (1749 – 1812). A credentialed member of the founding generation, if not canonized as a Founder, Bishop Madison clearly held strong views regarding the 'destiny' (manifest or otherwise) of the new republic.

A clearly enthusiastic man given to what strikes as overly exuberant prose, Bishop Madison saw the Revolution as the unfolding of a divine plan for the "...universal redemption of the human race from domination and

---

Miller, *Errand into the Wilderness*, (Cambridge: Belknap Press of Harvard University Press, 1956), and especially Abram C. Van Engen, *City on a Hill: A History of American Exceptionalism*, (New Haven: Yale University Press, 2020).

297   Regarding the political use of this interpretation, cf. Abram C. Van Engen, "Models," Part V in *City on a Hill*, 199 – 285.

298   Winthrop, "A Model of Christian Charity," 1630.

299   Fictional race from *Star Trek* science fiction, known for intractable genocidal collectivism in the pursuit of 'perfection'.

oppression..."[300] Charles Crowe argued in 1964 that, in Bishop Madison's opinion, "it was America's mission to end the tyrannical agonies of history by making the world forever republican."[301]

While Crowe consistently employed the term 'manifest destiny' in relation to Bishop Madison, his use of the term is anachronistic if reasonably applicable.[302] It is noteworthy that both this term and 'popular sovereignty' were coined by democrats as a retrospective in favor of annexation and slavery in the mid nineteenth century.[303] Whether under applicable terminology or not, Bishop Madison had a clear image of America's 'calling', but something crucial remains absent from that view.

Arising from clear agreement with Jefferson and others on the sovereignty of conscience in pursuit of truth, Bishop Madison held the position that, in Crowe's view, "Christ had championed republican principles and rational piety in opposition to… social coercion…." He lay the faults of tyranny at the attempts to force belief or opinion, going as far as to advocate a near universal tolerance for even subversive opinions, so as to "…demonstrate the power of truth in a free society."[304] Consistent with this magnanimity, Bishop Madison disavowed any hint of the infinite perfectibility of man, stating that the millennium and the

---

300   Bishop James Madison, *Manifestations of the Beneficence of Divine Providence Towards America; a Discourse, Delivered on Thursday the 19th of February, 1795, Being the Day Recommended by the President of the United States, for General Thank giving and Prayer*, (Richmond: Thomas Nicolson, 1795), Accessed November 6, 2024: https://quod.lib.umich.edu/e/evans/N22012.0001.001/1:2?rgn=div1;view=fulltext, 8.

301   Charles Crowe, "Bishop James Madison and the Republic of Virtue," *The Journal of Southern History* 30, no. 1 (1964), 70.

302   The term is almost universally ascribed to John O'Sullivan, specific to annexation of territory (Texas, California, Oregon, and even Canada) from *Democratic Review*, July-August, 1845. Cf. Julius W. Pratt, "The Origin of 'Manifest Destiny,'" *The American Historical Review* 32, no. 4 (1927): 795–98.

303   Cf. Nicole Etcheson, "'A Living, Creeping Lie': Abraham Lincoln on Popular Sovereignty," *Journal of the Abraham Lincoln Association* 29, no. 2 (2008): 1–25.

304   Crowe, "Republic of Virtue", 60.

"...Epoch of infinite perfectibility" were asymptotic in their conjunction.[305] Bishop Madison, among many things, shared Locke and Jefferson's anthropology – men are neither angels nor demons.

Though many held grand ideals regarding the universality or positive future of the principles of the new nation, equating it with a clearly apparent purpose for America, in the founding and preceding generations this detail reads as an optimistic hope thoroughly mingled with admonition to stay the course, rather than as a legitimizing mythos for the projection of power.

Certainly in Winthrop's Puritanism, but also in Madison's Episcopalianism, the inescapable core reality of human nature remained. Even in the *cautious* optimism resulting from the martial triumph of Jefferson's sentiments, man's capacity for evil remained thoroughly understood. In remarking on this primary concern, Ronald Pestritto invoked the President Madison in demonstrating a continuity in this understanding. "America's Founders thought it folly to conceive of government as something perfectible, or to think that human government could ever be capable of solving every human problem."[306] This wisdom however was lost in the nineteenth century.

The idea, termed 'Christian Perfection Theology' was certainly known much earlier; to Jefferson and Bishop Madison at the very least.[307] The origins and theological nuances however are not vital to the current argument, but rather its nature and infestation of American society in the closing decades of the nineteenth century. A sufficient

---

305   Lit. "...two approaching geometrical lines which... never meet."; Bishop Madison 1786, in Crowe, "Republic of Virtue", 63.

306   Citing *Federalist* 51, "If men were angels…. If angels were to govern….", Ronald J. Pestritto, "Making the State into a God: American Progressivism and the Social Gospel." In *Progressive Challenges to the American Constitution: A New Republic.* edited by Bradley C. S. Watson, (Cambridge: Cambridge University Press, 2017), 144–59, 153.

307   Cf. Thomas Jefferson, "From Thomas Jefferson to Bishop James Madison, 31 January 1800," *Founders Online*, National Archives, https://founders.archives.gov/documents/Jefferson/01-31-02-0297.

quantity of twenty and twenty-first century scholars have analyzed the naissance (though not the legacy) of this virulent pathogen, necessitating only a brief narration.

Alan Heimert (1928 – 1999) argued that there was a crucial shift in Puritanism resulting from a schism between the 'revivalists' and the 'anti-revivalists', itself a product of the 'great awakening' of the days just prior to the Revolution. This change in Puritan belief established the beginnings of perfection theology by a rejection of the old view of 'total depravity'[308] in favor of a human ability to forward the progress of history to bring about paradise.[309]

Continuing in this shift, Daniel Howe analyzed the so-called 'second great awakening' defined by the public ministries of Lyman Beecher (1775 – 1863) and Charles Finney (1792 – 1875). Howe credits Beecher with the idea of social-salvation (as opposed to individual), and Finney with pioneering perfection theology. This episode saw the combination of exuberant and ecumenical evangelicalism with social activism in the form of abolitionism, prohibition, suffrage, prison and education reforms, and trade-unions.[310] Crucially, by the mid-nineteenth century the image of *causing* the millennium by means of government intervention and Christian perfectionism, especially as combined with technological development, was already a mainstream ideal.[311]

James Moorhead, in both his 1978 *American Apocalypse* (that Howe references) and 1984 "Between Progress and Apocalypse"[312] demonstrated the expansion of

308   A core tenet of Calvinism regarding the 'fallen nature' of man, or the total dependence upon Christ for salvation.
309   Alan Heimert, *Religion and the American Mind: From the Great Awakening to the Revolution*, (London: Oxford University Press, 1966).
310   Daniel Walker Howe, *What Hath God Wrought: the Transformation of America, 1815-1848*, (New York: Oxford University Press, 2007).
311   Cf. Howe, citing "The Magnetic Telegraph," *Ladies' Repository* 10 (1850) in *What Hath God Wrought*, 2007, 3; Cf. James H. Moorhead, *American Apocalypse: Yankee Protestants and the Civil War, 1860-1869.* (New Haven: Yale University Press, 1978), 6.
312   James H. Moorhead, "Between Progress and Apocalypse: A Reassessment of Millennialism in American Religious Thought,

'postmillennialism', or the belief of history as a gradual improvement rather than punctuated by a divine cataclysmic finale.[313] This view, combined with the perception of revivalism as a 'new age dawning', gave the image of the American Civil War as something of an apocalypse. This in turn lead to a concept of the 'kingdom' being the result of gradual conversion of the world in direct opposition to Matthew 24:12, 21-27.[314] By this means, in Moorhead's view, the Union victory gave cause to equate the American Republic with the *actual* Kingdom of God, and therefore the eschatological fulfillment of Christ's Return. His argument is ultimately that these currents combined to view the American industrial revolution as the literal millennial reign of Christ foretold in John's Revelation.[315]

By the closing years of Reconstruction, a new *telos* had taken root in American society. Where before a cautious optimism based on centuries of understanding sought to preserve and safeguard the individual dignity of Creation, now a 'civil religion' had mingled the idea of God's Kingdom with the American Republic. Christian theology was no longer constrained to the individual and his relation to God, but now had been expanded to cover the whole of society. Some Americans began to view their religion as a duty to usher in a literal kingdom of God using social reform, and government *force* as the means to that end.

The *zeitgeist* of Reconstruction to the Progressive Era may be more appropriately classified as the age of 'auto-apotheosis.' In this 'age,' not only the individual but also

---

1800-1880." *The Journal of American History* 71, no. 3 (1984): 524–42.

313   The differences between 'post-millennialism' and 'a-millennialism' are the matter of theological pedantry, heavily dependent upon context. Moorehead probably ought to have used 'amillennialism', but it is not a matter of significance; neither perspective can be supported *sola escritura*.

314   Cf. II Thessalonians 2:1-3.

315   Regarding 'millennialism' and the Civil War/Reconstruction, Cf. Grant R. Brodrecht, *Our Country: Northern Evangelicals and the Union during the Civil War Era*, (New York: Fordham University Press, 2018); and George C. Rable, *God's Almost Chosen Peoples: a Religious History of the American Civil War*, (Chapel Hill: University of North Carolina Press, 2010); Revelation 20:4 – 6.

society could become so perfect as to be equivalent to the reign of Christ on earth, should they but find the right policy. If the insertion is forgiven, in the latter decades of the nineteenth century, a lie took hold of American Christendom: "...Ye shall not surely die: for God doth know that in the day ye eat thereof, then your eyes shall be opened, and ye shall be as gods, knowing good and evil."[316]

At its core, perfection theology represents a delusional attempt to rationalize self-deification. When applied to society as a whole, it constitutes a legitimizing mythos substantially similar to another Republic who changed to something other. Publius Vergilius Maro – Virgil (70 BC – 19 BC) – wrote the Epic of Aeneas, the Trojan progenitor of Rome via Romulus. Central to this epic, Jupiter calms his troubled daughter Venus as she asks after the troublesome fate that beset the refugee Aeneas. Promising future glory, Jupiter declares "Thence shall Romulus... take up their line, and name them Romans after his own name. I appoint to these neither period nor boundary of empire: I have given them dominion without end."[317]

The 'dominion without end' is of particular importance. Rendered as *imperium sine fine*, the etymological connection to 'imperial' or 'empire' is obvious.[318] This line was written within two-to-eleven years of the Battle of Actium (31 BC), whereupon Gaius Octavian Caesar Augustus (63 BC – AD 14) secured his rise to power, and the end of the Republic. Primarily due to this line, the *Aeneid* is generally received as having given a foundation to Augustus' government: "The Aeneid reinforces that idea Augustus, as the telos of Roman history and as the ultimate head of the secular authority, signifies the gods' will."[319]

---

316   Genesis 3:4,5.

317   Lit. "*his ego nec metas rerum nec tempora pono; imperium sine fine dedi*"; Virgil, *The Aeneid of Virgil*, trans. J.W. Mackail, (London: Macmillan and Co., 1885 [c. 25 BC]), Project Gutenberg Ebook #22456, I:276-279.

318   Cf. "imperial," *Online Etymology Dictionary*, Accessed November 11, 2024: https://www.etymonline.com/search?q=imperium.

319   Sabine Grebe, "Augustus' Divine Authority and Vergil's "Aeneid"", *Vergilius* 50, (2004): 35 – 62, 46, sic; Cf. 49.

Not to be limited to a vague image of an immortal empire, Jupiter also gives an ultimate, and clearly disproved prediction of Rome's future: "Then shall war cease, and the iron ages soften."[320] As summarized by Sabine Grebe, "Authority in Roman times was derived from mythico-historical origins that carried divine pretensions."[321]

It has already been wholly demonstrated that authority in America is derived of consent of the governed, as a natural product of the dignity of Creation. Divine pretensions are notably absent from this provenance as the aforementioned dignity is an inherent property of *all*, not *some*. A "firm reliance on the protection of divine Providence" does not equate to empire by divine right, even as a collective.[322] While the American experiment was as visible – in success or failure – as a city on a hill, and the principles of her founding carry inherently universal traits, among the admonitions of that founding the concept of *imperium* is conspicuously absent. Such is not the case in the expanded application of perfection theology upon society – one primary driver of the Progressive Era known as 'The Social Gospel'.

Washington Gladden (1836 – 1918) – a Puritan schismatic, Congregationalist minister is consistently credited with having been the 'father' or a 'prophet' of the Social Gospel.[323] In his autobiography, speaking of Henry Ward Beecher (1813 – 1887, son of Lyman Beecher), Gladden credits his calling to ministry as being attracted by his "...religion that laid hold upon life, and proposed first and foremost, to realize the Kingdom of God *in this world*."[324]

---

320   Virgil, *Aeneid*, I:295.
321   Griebe, "Augustus' Divine Authority," 61, sic.
322   United States Declaration of Independence.
323   Cf. Jacob Henry Dorn, *Washington Gladden: Prophet of the Social Gospel*, (Columbus: Ohio State University Press, 1967); Paul Boyer, "An Ohio Leader of the Social Gospel Movement: Reassessing Washington Gladden." *Ohio History* 116, no. 1 (2009): 88-100; Robert R. Roberts, "The Social Gospel and the Trust-Busters," *Church History* 25, no. 3 (1956): 239–57. The theological schisms between Puritans and Congregationalists are beyond the scope of this argument.

The reference to the younger Beecher, among other names, is of remarkable significance in the development of the social gospel perspective. The younger Beecher appears to have exceeded the influence of his father to become "...the most popular preacher in America."[325] In the years surrounding the Civil War and Reconstruction, this man's proximity to both power and culture certainly qualifies him under the very recent (and retch inducing) term 'influencer'.[326]

From what began as a somewhat Freudian rejection of his father's 'brimstone' approach, Beecher developed a view of Christianity as a tool for human improvement, rather than as news of salvation from condemnation.[327] Rejecting the elder Beecher's theology, the younger cited Apostle Paul's conversion from Acts 8:9, "a Pharisee of the Pharisees" in his general repudiation of rational inquiry in favor of emotive, rhetorical homiletics.[328] Some credit him with creating a new theology, "...a Christianity that catered to the progressive... American audience that did not want to believe that their cultural, artistic, and material interests excluded them from the Kingdom of Heaven."[329] Beecher's focus on appeals to emotion gave way to a promiscuity that would ultimately embrace the rank misanthropy of Herbert Spencer (1820 – 1903) and Charles Darwin (1809 – 1882).

Shortly before his death, the younger Beecher published *Evolution and Religion*.[330] In this work, he credits Spencer as having "...given to the world more truth in one

---

324   Washington Gladden, *Recollections*, (London: Houghton Mifflin Company, 1909), 63, emphasis added.

325   Clifford E. Clark, "The Changing Nature of Protestantism in Mid-Nineteenth Century America: Henry Ward Beecher's Seven Lectures to Young Men," *The Journal of American History* 57, no. 4 (1971): 832–46, 832.

326   Cf. Lincoln soliciting Beecher's council in Michael Souders, "'Truthing It in Love': Henry Ward Beecher's Homiletic Theories of Truth, Beauty, Love, and the Christian Faith," *Rhetoric Society Quarterly* 41, no. 4 (2011): 316–39, 319.

327   Souders, "'Truthing It in Love'", 325.

328   Beecher in Souders, "'Truthing It in Love'," 332.

329   Souders, "'Truthing It in Love'," 335.

330   Henry Ward Beecher, *Evolution and Religion*, (London: James Clarke & Co., 1885).

lifetime than any other man that has lived...."[331] This, the
man who brought the concept of "survival of the fittest" not
only into pseudoscientific parlance, but as an approach to
society.[332] Beecher equates evolutionary arguments with the
Bible, calling it one of "The Two Revelations" in his chapter
with the same name. This chapter relies heavily on argument
from authority and elitism.[333] Ultimately, three observations
arise from Beecher's *Evolution and Religion*, and from
Gladden's citation of his influence.

First, Beecher's claim "...the creation of this earth
was not accomplished in six days...."[334] and his statement
that evolution "...postulates as a theory of the Divine method
of creation..."[335] demonstrate that he knew very little of either
evolution or the Bible. The Genesis narrative can by no
means be combined with natural selection over great ages, to
say nothing of Christ's citation of creation "from the
beginning."[336] Evolution absolutely excludes any reference to
the Divine – this being the substance of the entire paradigm,
that it rejects the possibility of the supernatural or the
metaphysical Origin. All attempts to reconcile the two are
ridiculously, *prima facie* absurd; these are mutually exclusive
and wholly incompatible.

Second, Beecher's praise of "...the great doctrine of
Evolution"[337] and Herbert Spencer, combined with his grand
influence in American Protestantism represents a clearly
integral connection between Darwinism/Lamarckism[338] and
the Social Gospel via Gladden. Due recognition of differing

331   Beecher, *Evolution and Religion*, 126.
332   Cf. discussions between Spencer, Darwin, and Huxley
regarding the term: I. W. Howerth, "Natural Selection and the
Survival of the Fittest," *The Scientific Monthly* 5, no. 3 (1917): 253–
57.
333   "...Evolution is accepted as *the method* of creation by the
whole scientific world", sic, 50; "This science of Evolution is taught
in all advanced academies....", sic, 51; "Evolution is substantially
held by men of profound Christian faith....", 51; "...a layman should
not meddle with that which can be judged by only scientific
experts....", 47.
334   Beecher, *Evolution and Religion*, 49.
335   Beecher, *Evolution and Religion*, 3.
336   Mark 10:6.
337   Beecher, *Evolution and Religion*, 3.

interpretations between Spencer and Darwin, the ideal of a naturalistic origin and improvement relying on the death or reproductive failure of the unfit or maladapted was an integral part of progress to a literal 'heaven on earth' from its very beginning.

Third, Beecher's preference for emotional rhetoric over rational inquiry gave place to softer, uncritical allegorical interpretation of the Bible that ultimately resulted in the total repudiation of the basic foundations of Christianity *within mainstream Protestantism*. This latter detail is well demonstrated in Gladden's 1891 work *Who Wrote the Bible?* and evokes consideration of Paul's concern for leaven and the fellowship between righteousness and unrighteousness.[339]

Like Beecher's attempt to mix oil and water in 'two revelations', Gladden begins his criticism of the Bible with an appeal to authority. In the first sentence of the first chapter, Gladden commits the consensus fallacy "...the principal facts upon which scholars are now generally agreed concerning the literary history of the Bible."[340] One would gently highlight the later developments of that field, namely the Scrolls of Qumran (1947, 1956), in addition to the *highly* speculative and inherently unfalsifiable nature of textual criticism – especially Biblical criticism – as a practice; consensus fallacy invariably ignores dissent. Setting this aside, one immediately perceives the lens through which Gladden conceived of his argument.

Gladden references 1868 "On a Piece of Chalk" calling it "a delightful treatise," and *The Crayfish* in the his opening.[341] Both of these works were written by Thomas

---

338   The nuances between these perspectives amount to very little when applied as a world-view.

339   Cf. I Corinthians 5:6; II Corinthians 6:14.

340   Washington Gladden, *Who Wrote the Bible?: A Book for the People*, (Boston: Houghton, Mifflin, & Company, 1891), Project Gutenberg Ebook #6928, Chapter I. Note, this edition does not contain page numbers.

341   Gladden, *Who Wrote the Bible?*, Chapter I; Thomas Huxley, "On a Piece of Chalk," *Macmillan's Magazine*, (1868), Accessed November 12, 2024: http://aleph0.clarku.edu/huxley/CE8/Chalk.html; Thomas Huxley,

Huxley (1825 – 1895) – "Darwin's Bulldog".[342] This
reference is quite out of place, being used as a comparison of
sorts, asking that biblical scholars aspire to or "repay our
study" in like manner.[343] From this, Gladden extols the field
that he terms "Higher Criticism", a term that one would
submit is in-and-of-itself indicative of a modernist, rather
condescending approach. Leaving this aside, though it does
reinforce the previously made connection, Gladden's 1891
work lays out a direct and clear image of his estimation
regarding the Bible as a text. "The book is not infallible
historically….. It is not infallible scientifically…. It is not
infallible morally"[344]

It is exceedingly apparent that Gladden's 'higher'
criticism amounted to little more than vacuous claims
regarding solipsistic 'truths' that are as easily contrived as
they are dismissed. In essence, his position is that the Bible is
effectively a lie, but somehow still good. Gladden claims that
the Bible describes a development, a "progress from a lower
to a higher morality", that "the standards of the earlier time
are therefore inadequate or misleading in these later limes"[345]
One would wonder if this 'lower morality' encapsulated in
the command "Ye shall not steal; neither deal falsely, neither
lie one to another" is inadequate or misleading today.[346] More
than this, one would ask how to reconcile Gladden's weak
interpretation of 'truths' if the book that commands honesty
is itself a fabrication.

Theological epistemology aside, Gladden's view of
the Bible is self-serving. His summation reads as a maxim for
his post-millennial solipsism: "The Bible is the record of the

---

The Crayfish: An Introduction to the Study of Zoology, (London: C. Kegan Paul & Co., 1880).

342   The historicity of this 'sobriquet' is known, and dubious – as all such things usually are. Cf. John van Wyhe, "Why there was no 'Darwin's bulldog,'" *The Linnean Society of London*, July 1, 2019, Accessed November 12, 2024: https://www.linnean.org/news/2019/07/01/1st-july-2019-why-there-was-no-darwins-bulldog.

343   Gladden, *Who Wrote the Bible?*, Chapter I.
344   Gladden, *Who Wrote the Bible?*, Chapter XIII.
345   Gladden, *Who Wrote the Bible?*, Chapter XIII.
346   Leviticus 19:11.

development of the kingdom of righteousness in the world....the record of this moral progress...."[347] A refutation of this statement is unnecessary to the current argument; he clearly held a view of history as a gradual improvement and the past as inferior or somehow deficient – obvious presentism; ideological patricide. What is most poignant however is how easily his argument condenses into an introduction for the previous insertion. "Now the serpent was more cunning than any beast of the field which the LORD God had made. And he said to the woman, "Has God indeed said, 'You shall not eat from any tree of the garden'?""[348] Has God not said "let there be light" – in Gladden's view, no.

Lest one make the claim that this author has made unrealistic connections, this argument is not the only place where one might find these statements. In his biography of Gladden, Jacob Henry Dorn (1939 – 2017) summarizes the 'liberal theology' behind the social gospel. He briefly discusses the 'reconstruction' of "the historical origins of the biblical writings" and implies an historicist attempt to convey the Bible into 'social' perspectives.[349] Additionally, Dorn highlights the "incorporation of evolutionary theory [which] lead naturally to a doctrine of progress that presupposed the melioration of both the social organism and its environment."[350]

The 'Social Organism' extends from Herbert Spencer in 1860.[351] Giving due place to the complex nuance of Spencer's views – he was apparently "...one of the most extreme defenders of liberalism, [and] individualism...." – it remains that he advocated Social Darwinism as a scientific *and* a legislative paradigm.[352] For any mitigating argument that may be offered on his behalf, "Spencer argued that the process of evolution spontaneously led to social

---

347   Gladden, *Who Wrote the Bible?*, Chapter XIII.
348   Genesis 3:1.
349   Dorn, *Washington Gladden*, 1967, 183.
350   Dorn, *Washington Gladden*, 1967, 184.
351   Walter M. Simon, "Herbert Spencer and the 'Social Organism,'" *Journal of the History of Ideas* 21, no. 2 (1960): 294–99, 296.
352   Simon, "The Social Organism," 294, 297.

betterment...."[353] Gladden used Spencer to view the Bible as indistinguishable from a fable, society as a single organism, and the past as fundamentally inferior.

Gladden made it abundantly clear that he viewed society as a single organism.[354] Speaking of poverty by means of unemployment Gladden stated "[t]here is a certain important work to be done which no voluntary organization can succeed in doing, – a work which requires the exercise of the power of the sate."[355] He outlined a government mandated work program, based on a 'work test', for those willing to work, and "workhouses" for those unwilling as they have "by their unsocial conduct [forfeited] their freedom."[356] It is notable that he insists that these institutions should be primarily for education, but that "...the sentence to the workhouse should be indeterminate, and the discipline should not be relaxed...."[357] He then goes on to recommend a "penal farm colony... as much under restraint as if they were in prison" for whom he terms the "deadbeat crowd."[358]

Tellingly from this plan, Gladden moves into the 'social organism' as a means of advocating for "...the free use of the knife – the excision of the diseased parts of the body."[359] While he quickly follows this with softer language centered on "curative treatment", the odor of the seeds of eugenics – for the good of the social organism – surrounds the thought, especially as he concludes this portion of his argument.

> They ["criminal classes"] are rightly regarded
> as diseased social tissue, and we isolate them
> that we may make them whole... And the
> same treatment must be given to the class

353   Simon, "The Social Organism", 297.
354   Washington Gladden, *The Church and the Kingdom*, (New York: Fleming H. Revell Co., 1894), 6, and throughout – Gladden cites Huxley directly for his conception of the social organism.
355   Washington Gladden, *Social Salvation*, (Boston: Houghton Mifflin, 1902), 61.
356   Gladden, *Social Salvation*, 82.
357   Gladden, *Social Salvation*, 83.
358   Gladden, *Social Salvation*, 84.
359   Gladden, *Social Salvation*, 86.

which is sinking into penury and pauperism.
Chronic mendicants must be separated from
society and the sexes from each other, so that
the race of "ne'er-do-weels" shall not be
propagated, and so that those segregated may
be reclaimed and fitted for social service.....

...It involves a measure of compulsion which
only the state can exercise. And the state can
never do it as it ought to be done until it gets a
new conception of its function as the
representative of the divine power and the
divine goodness.[360]

Giving recognition to Gladden's ideal of the
'fatherhood of God' leading to a connection to human
dignity, and to his consistent philanthropic terminology
throughout his works, it remains clear that Gladden's concept
of the social gospel was a *radical* expansion of state power,
especially as expressed by assessment, arrest, and
confinement.[361] He does not appear to consider the intricacies
of how his 'work test' would be administered, and what
would be done in cases of popular refusal to engage with
such an overbearing system. While he does not overtly
advocate for eugenics or authoritarian society, his image of a
'christian' society – where government represents 'divine
power' and 'divine goodness' – certainly relies on the same
concepts and the same terminology.

Gladden's anthropology is as disjointed as his
bibliology. Dorn describes his "optimism concerning human
nature,"[362] and many of his writings can be construed in this
manner, yet even amid his humanitarian language he decries
"...a comment on our intelligence that Massachusetts should

360   Gladden, *Social Salvation*, 87, 88, sic.
361   Washington Gladden, *The Christian Way: Whither it Leads
and How to Go On*, (New York: Dodd, Mead & Company, 1877); Cf.
Washington Gladden, *The Lord's Prayer: Seven Homilies*, (Boston:
Houghton Mifflin & Co, 1880), 25 – 27 in Dorn, *Washington
Gladden*, 1967, 187.
362   Dorn, *Washington Gladden*, 1967, 189.

allow 8000 feeble-minded girls to be loose in the community breeding their kind, instead of humanely and kindly shutting them up."[363] Gladden believed that being 'loose' or 'breeding' are subject to a State overseen IQ test, and that the inherent right to liberty is subject to sufficient 'social service', in the estimation of… someone.

All philanthropic, humanitarian, or 'christian' verbiage aside, Gladden's ideals and anchor-less theology lead him to the precipice of authoritarian and eugenic arguments for the good of the 'organism' indicative of the very usurpations against which Washington warned; the cobbles on the road to hell.[364] Gladden's conception of society is monstrous, and extends directly from his 'liberal theology' fed, evolution-induced claim that "The kingdom of heaven is the entire social organism in its ideal perfection…."[365] His anthropology, whether intentionally or not, repudiates individual dignity; subsumes it under and subordinates it to a wholly collectivist paradigm. If it is indeed an 'organism', it certainly fits the image of The Blob.

In departing Gladden, one further detail is worthy of inclusion. In his claim that the Bible is not infallible morally, he clarifies that earlier ethical portions were "an imperfect morality". He states that "[m]any things are here commanded which it would be wrong for us to do."[366] Which things specifically, and why would it be wrong to do them? What is the standard of comparison to make such a claim, and what or who, precisely, is the source or authority for this other standard? Is this other standard written, such that it is freely available to any literate, and inured against the gaslighting inevitably employed by one who would seek to reduce others under his arbitrary will? Gladden does not address what seem obvious questions, but rather introduces a solipsistic ethic wholly subordinated to the meaningless placement in time – yet again modernism or presentism.

---

363   Gladden, *Social Salvation*, 85, emphasis added.

364   Washington, "Farewell Address", in *Constitution*, 2012, 774.

365   Washington Gladden, *The Church and the Kingdom*. (New York: Fleming H. Revell Co., 1894), 11-12.

366   Gladden, *Who Wrote the Bible?*, Chapter XIII.

In essence, Gladden divorces biblical ethics from any foundation, and in so doing introduces fertile ground for the development of the ersatz moralism that would come to dominate American civilization – where one will declare 'the right thing to do' or that some thing is 'wrong' without any measurable or verifiable means of determining such claims apart from the arbitrary will of the speaker. He argues for a process of development, stating that "there were many truths which they [the ancients] could not receive, which to us are as plain as the daylight."[367] He does not address what these are, why or how these have been made so plain, or why the ancients were somehow retarded; the Sermon on the Mount that Gladden prefers over say, Leviticus, is hardly a complex treatise.

In all of Gladden's self-serving, baseless moralizing to support his progressive preconception, he never addresses the simplest, and most obvious argument: "Jesus Christ the same yesterday, and to day, and for ever."[368] What he does however is deify the 'social organism' to such an extent that anything – anything at all – is permissible if it can be rationalized by the words 'for the good of the State' or more recently, 'a compelling state interest'. The god that he describes in his repudiation of the Bible is an incompetent buffoon, requiring eons of trial-and-error for both creation and ethics; the god he describes in *Social Salvation* and elsewhere is simply the State.

Another has already distilled the essence of Gladden's version of the social gospel, especially as outlined in his idea regarding unemployment, far more eloquently and concisely than this author. Again, despite Gladden's claims around the brotherhood of men, his policies and view of society constitute the root and stem of something far more insidious.

> My contention is that good men (not bad men) consistently acting upon that position [the humanitarian theory of punishment] would act as cruelly and unjustly as the greatest tyrants. They might in some respects act even worse.

367   Gladden, *Who Wrote the Bible?*, Chapter XIII.
368   Hebrews 13:8.

> Of all tyrannies a tyranny sincerely exercised
> for the good of its victims may be the most
> oppressive. It may be better to live under
> robber barons than under omnipotent moral
> busybodies. The robber baron's cruelty may
> sometimes sleep, his cupidity may at some
> point be satiated; but those who torment us for
> our own good will torment us without end for
> they do so with the approval of their own
> conscience. They may be more likely to go to
> Heaven yet at the same time likelier to make a
> Hell of earth. Their very kindness stings with
> intolerable insult. To be 'cured' against one's
> will and cured of states which we may not
> regard as disease is to be put on a level with
> those who have not yet reached the age of
> reason or those who never will; to be classed
> with infants, imbeciles, and domestic animals.
> But to be punished, however severely, because
> we have deserved it, because we 'ought to
> have known better', is to be treated as a human
> person made in God's image.[369]

Inarguably as stated, it is inherent in the nature of dignity that such a thing cannot be forced; it is supremely paradoxical to command another to be equal. Gladden's concept of a social organism immediately and quickly led him to revoke the humanity of the individual as mere 'organs' of the greater organism – subject to excision or amputation without the slightest deference to their consent, independence, or dignity. The reduction of the individual to a mere appendage of the State, the revocation of humanity – *evil* – is baked into the social gospel from its very inception.

Where Gladden's conception of society was monstrous, another prominent 'social gospeler' was simply put, a monster. Richard Ely (1854 – 1943) embraced and

---

369   C.S. Lewis, "The Humanitarian Theory of Punishment" in *God in the Dock: Essays on Theology and Ethics*, Edited by Walter Hooper, (Grand Rapids: William B. Eerdmans Publishing Company, 1970), 324.

expanded Gladden's socialized christianity far beyond poorly considered acts with 'the best of intentions'; he did not limit his deification of the State to sub-textual references. In his version of the social gospel, Ely overtly contrived a theocracy to exhume the corpse of divine right by means of rigidly brutal, authoritarian eugenics. Simply, this man took *Deus Vult* to levels never imagined by even the most unscrupulous crusader.

In matters of authority, a simple question presents itself: which came first, the man or the State? It has already been thoroughly demonstrated that to the eighteenth century founders, this was a settled matter; Ely inverted that perspective. Operating from what he termed the 'ethical school', Ely declared that it "...places society above the individual.... Individual sacrifices should be demanded for the good of others. The end and purpose of economic life are held to be the greatest good of the greatest number, or of society as a whole."[370] In Ely's anthropology, the individual human being *has no value* apart from what he might offer the State.[371] Neither does the individual posses any natural rights, but rather only privileges that the State might deign to offer: "...there is no limit to the right of the State, the sovereign power, save its ability to do good."[372]

Ely, in his often celebrated capacity as one of the organizers of the American Economics Association (AEA), worked closely with Gladden who served on the committee to draft its statement of principles, that notably included a "...recognition of the state as a positive agent in human progress [and]... the united effort of church, state, and

---

370   Richard T. Ely, *Social Aspects of Christianity, and Other Essays*, (New York: Thomas Y. Crowell & Company, 1889), 128.

371   Cf. "The State has been described as a continuous, conscious organism.... It is not the product of the will of man.... the State is the natural condition of men."; Richard T. Ely, *The Social Law of Service*, (New York: Eaton & Mains, 1896), 167.

372   Richard Ely, *Introduction to Political Economy*, (New York: Chautauqua Press, 1889), 92, in Tiffany Jones Miller, "Richard T. Ely, The German Historical School of Economics, And the "Socio-Teleological" Aspiration of the New Deal Planners," *Social Philosophy & Policy* 38, no. 1 (Summer, 2021): 52-84, 60.

science" in reaching their policy objectives.[373] This radical
triumvirate relied upon the same collectivist 'organism'
championed by Gladden and others. It is noteworthy that,
while he is normally cited or otherwise cast as an economist,
Ely is far more appropriately defined as something of a
pseudo-religious ideologue, as he *employed* economics,
science, or religion as mechanisms to achieve his
preconceived ideal of a perfected society: "Religion is a
social tie; it unites men; it is a necessary element in the social
organism if its members are to work harmoniously
together...."[374]

The ideal perfected society was the social organism, a
"moral person" or a "moral personality" in Ely's view.[375] It
appears certain that he and Gladden's cooperation extended
beyond the founding of the AEA. The latter spoke of the
focus on individual rights, deriving from the Declaration, as
"...a radical defect in the habitual thinking of the average
American – a wrong conception of what is fundamental in his
relation to that government...."[376] The 'wrong conception'
was that government existed to secure rights. Ely reiterated
this extreme departure from the founding world-view in a
nearly verbatim claim that "...we especially need... emphasis
on duties rather than rights. This is a first condition of civic
regeneration."[377] This is also a first condition of
authoritarianism – Fascism, National-Socialism, and
Communism being at the forefront.

Gladden and Ely most certainly conceived of a
wholly different *raison d'être* for American government, as

---

373   Robert R. Roberts, "The Social Gospel and the Trust-
Busters," *Church History* 25, no. 3 (1956): 239–57, 248, 249.
374   Ely, *Social Aspects*, 144. Cf. Richard T. Ely, *Property and
Contract in their Relations to the Distribution of Wealth*, Vol. I
(Dallas: Kennikat Publishing Co., 1971 [1914]), 87, 88, in Miller,
"Richard T. Ely, The German Historical School," 54.
375   Ely in Thomas C. Leonard, *Illiberal Reformers: Race,
Eugenics, and American Economics in the Progressive Era*,
(Princeton: Princeton University Press, 2016), 24; Cf. Ely, *Political
Economy*, 92.; Ely, *The Social Law*, 167.
376   Washington Gladden, *The New Idolatry: and Other
Discussions*, (New York: McClure, Phillips & Co., 1905), 195, 198 –
199.
377   Ely, *The Social Law*, 175.

the head of an 'organism', and Ely particularly intended for that head to encapsulate – to absorb – the 'church'. Referencing who he calls "the Lutheran Rothe", presumably Richard Rothe (1799 – 1867), he affirms the latter's claim that "the State in idea is the Church, and… the perfect State… will be the Church."[378] He reinforces this agreement with the statement that all proper laws are 'religious', and the "main purpose of the State is the religious purpose." By this, he clarifies, he does not mean the requirement of a given sect or denomination, but rather "laws designed to promote the good life", after which he lists several traditionally Progressive talking points centering on regulations and public works.[379] Ely's stated goal is to have the Church "strengthen and purify the State… to change the constitution in so far as this may stand in the way of righteousness. [to the end that] The nation must be recognized fully as a Christian nation."[380]

When Ely speaks of this 'christian' nation, he speaks of his ideal perfected social organism, and nothing of the worship or emulation of Christ. There can be no doubt of Ely's view, this 'organism' was no metaphor or rhetorical device, it was "strictly and literally true."[381] He clarifies elsewhere that "Christianity is *primarily* concerned with this world, and it is the mission of Christianity to bring to pass here a kingdom of righteousness and to rescue from the evil one and redeem all our social relations."[382] In his version of the social gospel as the road to perfection, it is abundantly clear that Ely wholly missed the concept in Christ's words that "My kingdom is not of this world."[383]

Disregard for biblical gestalt characterizes 'liberal theology' in general and social gospel thinking in particular. It is readily apparent that the Bible or 'christian' imagery are recruited entirely as legitimizing mechanisms in a naked lust

---

378   Ely, *The Social Law*, 172.
379   Ely, *The Social Law*, 173.
380   Ely, *The Social Law*, 173 – 174.
381   Richard T. Ely, *The Past and the Present of Political Economy*, (Baltimore: N. Murray, 1884), 49; Cf. Leonard, *Illiberal Reformers*, 2016, 101.
382   Ely, *Social Aspects*, 53, emphasis added.
383   John 18:36.

for power. Appealing to the ancient practice of 'God agrees with me', Ely cast opposition to his policy objectives as deliberate attempts to "hinder the kingdom of God."[384] Aside from this obvious rendition of *Deus Vult*, complete with shades of the inquisitor, Ely argued a clear conception of the State in the development of his ideal society. "God works through the state in carrying out His purposes more universally than through any other institution.... [I]t takes the first place among his instrumentalities."[385] Social gospel proponents consistently support this position with reference to Paul's words "[l]et every soul be subject unto the higher powers..."[386] yet it is clear that Ely did not have the meek and compliant peacemaker in mind, but rather a *deified* State.

Ely makes a direct equivalence between law and morality "...even the most degraded usually realize that what is illegal is wrong."[387] In essence, he places the law in the position of speaking *ex cathedra*, making the State the new 'vicar' of God – *vox leges, vox Dei*. Under such a scheme, it is impossible for one to make a claim that a law itself is wrong as did Jefferson's discourse regarding liberty wherein he stated "I do not add 'within the limits of the law'; because law is often but the tyrant's will, and always so when it violates the right of an individual."[388] Indeed, this peculiar *ordo cognoscendi* would render impossible Peter and the other apostles' response to an overt act of religious censorship: "...we ought to obey God rather than men."[389]

In his discourse regarding the supremacy of law over 'right and wrong', Ely claimed that "[m]anly character, free and independent, can be developed only in countries where law, suitably enforced, establishes secure conditions of social life."[390] He did not appear to recognize that such a statement is absurd – if this character can only proceed from law, from whence does such law descend? He justified the view with

---

384   Ely, *The Social Law*, 179.
385   Ely, *The Social Law*, 162 – 163, sic.
386   Romans 11:1 – 7; Cf. I Peter 2:13 – 25.
387   Ely, *The Social Law*, 180.
388   Jefferson, "Thomas Jefferson to Isaac H. Tiffany, 4 April 1819."
389   Acts 5:29.
390   Ely, *The Social Law*, 182.

the claim that "Reformatory institutions... have shown their power to reform and improve the morally defective classes...." and goes on to reference the Elmira Reformatory of New York that apparently claimed to have "permanently reformed" eighty percent. Ely gives no effort to expand upon the basis for such a dubious claim – neither what 'permanently reformed' means, nor how such a massive percentage was calculated – but he used the 'statistic' as a retort against the claim that "you cannot make men good by law."[391] While Ely of course cannot be held to account for later developments, it is clear that if penal reformatories are the variable, and recidivism the measure, the law has consistently proven to be worse than utterly useless regarding the improvement of morality.[392]

Like Gladden, Ely equated poverty with crime and disease in his grand 'organism'.[393] In his assortment of causes, two elements remain constant: the deification of the State, and simply bizarre interpolations into biblical passages. Ronald Pestritto stated that "Ely urged the church to take up the abolition of poverty as a central element of its earthly mission to establish a general social welfare."[394] In Ely's words this was because "...there runs through all the Bible... a distinct aim of God's purpose for Israel the abolition of poverty, and the establishment of general social welfare...." This diaphanous thread was "beyond controversy" in Ely's estimation, and was "a part of the law of God which Christ came to fulfil."[395]

Two factors are immediately apparent in this wholly fabricated interpretation of the god-given *telos* for Israel.

---

391   Ely, *The Social Law*, 186 – 187.
392   High imprisonment and recidivism rates in the United States are almost legendary, but beyond the scope of this argument. Cf. Bureau of Justice Statistics, "Recidivism of Prisoners Released in 24 States in 2008: A 10-Year Follow-Up Period (2008 – 2018)," *U.S. Department of Justice, Office of Justice Progarams*, September 2021. Accessed November 19, 2024: https://bjs.ojp.gov/sites/g/files/xyckuh236/files/media/document/rpr2 4s0810yfup0818 _sum.pdf.
393   Ely, *Social Aspects*, 23, 89.
394   Pestritto in Watson, *Progressive Challenges*, 149.
395   Ely, *Social Aspects*, 155, sic.

First, Ely did not appear to understand that Christ stated outright that the abolition of poverty was impossible: "For ye have the poor always with you...."[396] Second, Ely intended for this abolition to be accomplished by means of philanthropy – but not simply voluntary donations or charity. He stated that "Philanthropy must be grounded in profound sociological studies" and crucially, that it must also be "coercive", by which he intends "insane asylums", "reformatories", and the "penal code" – in part "to purify politics".[397] While Ely was certainly correct in his literal definition that "[l]ove to man is philanthropy"[398] he did not seem to understand, nor care if he did, that while God is qualified to command love, the attempt to *force* such a thing is not merely beyond the scope of rational government, it is an act of *insanity*.[399]

Not merely is the idea of 'coercive philanthropy' a ridiculous *non-sequitur* – the use of threats or force to compel the love of man[400] – indicative of severe delusion, it is also wholly against, and entirely destructive to the concept of limited government *as established*.

> If Congress can employ money indefinitely, for the general welfare, and are the sole and supreme judges of the general welfare, they may take the care of religion into their own

---

396   Matthew 26:11.
397   Ely, *Social Aspects*, 88, 89 – 92.
398   Ely, *Social Aspects*, 86.
399   Cf. Thomas Jefferson, "V. To the Danbury Baptist Association, 1 January 1802," *Founders Online*, National Archives, Accessed October 2, 2024: https://founders.archives.gov/documents/Jefferson/01-36-02-0152-0006; Thomas Jefferson,"82. A Bill for Establishing Religious Freedom, 18 June 1779," *Founders Online*, National Archives, https://founders.archives.gov/documents/Jefferson/01-02-02-0132-0004-0082, sic.
400   Cf. 18 USC § 1591(e)(2): "The term "coercion" means – (A) threats of serious harm to or physical restraint against any person; (B) any scheme, plan, or pattern intended to cause a person to believe that failure to perform an act would result in serious harm to or physical restraint against any person; or (C) the abuse or threatened abuse of law or the legal process."

hands; they may appoint teachers in every state, county, and parish, and pay them out of the public treasury; they may take into their own hands the education of children, the establishing in like manner schools throughout the union; they may assume the provision of the poor.... Were the power of Congress to be established in the latitude contended for, it would subvert the very foundations, and transmute the very nature of the limited government established by the people of America.[401]

It would appear that either Ely was unaware that his twisted theocracy was wholly incompatible with the concept of authority in the United States or more likely, that he simply did not care. If it was the latter, as seems to be the case due to his declaration against the Constitution, Ely was not merely an ideologue, he was a *seditious* ideologue.[402] In his drive to 'redeem' humanity and replace the Republic with a counterfeit *theocracy*, Ely did not stop at co-opting the Bible in his version of the Church-State, but also for his 'scientific' world-view.

Going further with his perverse attempt to recruit Christ to his crusade, Ely subsumes the concept of 'love your neighbor as yourself' under his pseudoscientific paradigm "[T]he second commandment...in its elaboration, becomes social science or sociology."[403] As mentioned, he placed this 'second commandment' under the guise of 'coercive philanthropy' and demanded the broad application of

401   James Madison, "The Cod Fishery Bill, February 7, 1792," in Jonathan Elliott, ed. *The debates in the several state conventions on the adoption of the federal Constitution, as recommended by the general convention at Philadelphia, in 1787. Together with the Journal of the federal convention, Luther Martin's letter, Yates's minutes, Congressional opinions, Virginia and Kentucky resolutions of '98-'99, and other illustrations of the Constitution ... 2d ed., with considerable additions. Collected and rev. from contemporary publications,* (Washington: 1836), Vol. IV, 429.
402   "...to change the constitution in so far as this may stand in the way of righteousness..." Ely, *The Social Law,* 173 – 174.
403   Ely, *Social Aspects,* 9; Cf. Matthew 22:37 – 40.

sociological studies for its application. Lest there be room for mistake, by 'social science', Ely meant specifically the then-widely-fashionable 'science' of eugenics.

Where drives for a theocratic, coercively philanthropic 'christian' nation might be dismissed as religious rhetoric, not unlike any evangelical homily from the various 'awakenings' in America's story, Ely's discourse regarding the 'health' of his social organism leaves absolutely no room for misunderstanding. His philanthropic-misanthropy is not limited to the criminal or impoverished 'classes'. For him, it was a matter of blood and good-breeding. Ely's goal was, and is, indistinguishable from the old bugaboo the *übermensch*.

Late in his career, Ely turned his attention to the specific problem of developing leadership suitable for the Great War. By this point his perspective had wholly crystallized and with deep irony, consistently pivots about vocabulary that would be received with horror by his intellectual descendants. Referencing the concept of 'human resources' from earlier in this argument, that a reader may have assumed to be disjoint, Ely conceived of society-at-large as a resource pool of sorts.

Launching from his preference for military service – that amounts to a *very* 'Prussian' or Spartan ideal of an authoritarian-regimented society – Ely speaks of an ancillary benefit from "this service to native land… that it will bring all our human resources into view and uncover defects of every sort."[404] He speaks of 'human resources' in the same manner as of "farm animals" and "soil surveys", then declares:

> As a part of the preparation of our human
> material we shall give increasing attention to
> eugenics…. We have got far enough to
> recognize that there are certain human beings
> who are absolutely unfit and who should be
> prevented from a continuation of their kind.
> We do know it is important that a superior

---

404   Richard T. Ely, *The World War and Leadership in a Democracy*, (New York: Macmillan Co. 1918), 114.

stock should not be swallowed up and lost by
a more rapid increase of the inferior stock.[405]

From this, Ely goes on to quote, at considerable
length, from Michael F. Guyer (1874 – 1959) 1916 *Being
Well-Born: An Introduction to Eugenics*, introducing the
pages of citation with the advice that the reader give the
words "the most careful consideration." The citation is
peppered with terminology from "strata", "class", and
"overbreeding", to "a larger percentage of sedimentation
made up of the worthless and inferior stocks" who
"...threaten our very existence as a race."[406]
Any attempt to minimize or to dismiss the abundantly
clear perspective displayed in such horrifically misanthropic
language is entirely dishonest. A clear progression to this
depravity is apparent in Ely's thinking. In his 1901
contribution to *The Cosmopolitan*, the very same periodical
known as 'Cosmo' today, Ely wrote at length on the topic he
dubbed "Social Progress".[407] In this article, Ely moves from
evolutionary, biologically-based 'social altruism' to state that
"Pure individualism is... a scientific absurdity... the
conditions of social progress are largely capable of social
determination... under social control. The great word is no
longer natural selection, but social selection."[408] From this
foundation, Ely again returns to religion as the agent of his
progress, from which he launches into his Progressive
platform against monopolism, and in favor of wealth-
distribution and labor legislation.
Ely's "social selection" can by no delusional stretch
be cast as 'altruistic'. Two years after his rather softly worded

405   Ely, *The World War*, 115.
406   Childhood and Youth Series, Edited by M.V. O'Shea,
(Indianapolis: The Bobbs-Merrill Company, 1916); Ely, *The World
War*, 115 – 118.
407   The history of "Cosmo" (Cosmopolitan) is beyond the scope
of this argument, but it is clear that it has been a pivotal, trend-setting
periodical in America from the late nineteenth century – later market
focus notwithstanding. Cf. Algernon Tassin, "The Magazine in
America," *The Bookman*, Vol 42, (September, 1915 – February,
1916): 396 – 412.
408   Richard T. Ely, "Social Progress," *The Cosmopolitan* 31(1),
(1901): 61– 64, 62; Cf. Leonard, *Illiberal Reformers*, 2016, 104.

article in *The Cosmopolitan*, he speaks of the "human rubbish heap of the competitive system." He observes that "There are those who are not able to live in its strenuous atmosphere." Most tellingly, he shifts his analysis from what might be called a 'rigged system' to murderous plots. "The sad fact, however, is not that of competition, but the existence of these feeble persons.... If the weakest are favored and their reproduction encouraged, we must have social degeneration."[409]

Ely's version of 'altruism' is best displayed in his summation of this section of the work. "The socially rejected [those not 'selected'] must be cared for and given as happy an existence as possible, provided only that we do not encourage the increase of those who belong to this sad human rubbish-heap."[410] Ely grounds his conception of 'competition' in agricultural metaphor, noting that "[w]eeds are just as fit for survival" as desirable crops, and speaks of how man "assists nature, and removes and destroys as completely and as rapidly as possible those species and individuals which are not adapted to his purposes...."[411] For Ely, competition – especially economic competition – "is an essential constituent of that social evolution which is producing the ideal man."[412] It is from this elitist paradigm that he derives his policy objectives; it is wholly clear that his 'altruism' or 'philanthropy' are *not* expressions of a kind soul towards the dignity of another man, but rather the *condescension* of a farmer *to his crops*. As Ely summarized, "[t]he problem is to keep the most unfit from reproduction, and to encourage the reproduction of those who are really the superior members of society."[413]

Much of Ely's rank elitism is merely a repetition of Gladden's. "Let us next take up the degenerate classes, and ask whether any effort is being made to prevent their

---

409   Richard T. Ely, *Studies in the Evolution of Industrial Society*, (New York: Chautauqua Press, 1903), 163.
410   Ely, *Studies in the Evolution*, 163.
411   Ely, *Studies in the Evolution*, 142 – 143.
412   Ely, *Studies in the Evolution*, 148.
413   Ely, *Studies in the Evolution*, 139.

reproduction."[414] Ely offers his list of deplorables: criminals, paupers and the feeble-minded before eulogizing a list of legislation aimed at the regulation of marriage to prevent the "vicious progeny" of "idiotic pauper women."[415] His social-welfare policy proposal, again as a product of his utterly baseless theology, is nearly identical to Gladden's: "We must give to the most hopeless classes left behind in our social progress custodial care with the highest possible development and with segregation of sexes and confinement to prevent reproduction."[416]

Where Gladden would take his perverse theology to the edge of eugenics and authoritarianism, Ely employed his twisted ideal of altruism to extend his regimented eugenic society directly to the edge of genocide. Ely's 'social science' which he attached directly to Christianity amounts to the captivity of anyone deemed 'unfit,' with expressed and overt demands that they be prevented from furthering their 'kind'. *Tu quoque* references to the various genocides of the Canaanites from Deuteronomy and Joshua simply cannot justify or excuse this level of overbearing tyranny. Cast as 'philanthropy', extending from a flatly degenerate and supremely arrogant interpretation of the Bible, Richard T. Ely assembled both license and manual for the entire image and purpose of the *concentration camp*. It would be simple to dismiss such an obvious sociopath – such men exist in every age – were it not for his placement in first-degree antecedence in not just social gospel thinking and economics, but American sociology, politics, and academia at large.

Put as succinctly as possible, "...Richard T. Ely was one of the most important architects, perhaps the most important architect, of the administrative welfare state in the

414   Ely, *Studies in the Evolution*, 173; Cf. Gladden, *Social Salvation*, 84.
415   Ely, *Studies in the Evolution*, 174 – 175; Cf. Gladden, *Social Salvation*, 85.
416   Richard T. Ely, "The Price of Progress." *Administration* 3(6) (1922): 657-663, 662 in Thies, Clifford F. and Ryan Daza. "Richard T. Ely: The Confederate Flag of the AEA?" *Econ Journal Watch* 8, no. 2 (May, 2011): 147 – 156. Note, Ely's "Price of Progress" could not be located for confirmation of the citation or context in which it was composed. Cf. Gladden, *Social Salvation*, 87, 88.

United States."[417] Ely brought German historicism from
Heidelberg to John's Hopkins, and from there to the AEA.[418]
While at Hopkins, Ely's students included the journalist
Albert Shaw (1857 – 1947), the exceedingly influential
faceless bureaucrat M.L. Wilson (1885 – 1969), eminent
busybody John R. Commons (1862 – 1945), and the arch
traitor Woodrow Wilson (1856 – 1924).[419] In his drive to
bring about "perfection"[420], to *coerce* the kingdom of god into
existence, Ely more than most any other, it would seem, is
directly responsible for the metastasization of collectivism
over American civilization. In no uncertain terms, in the
plague that is the baseless self-affirming solipsism of
historicism, the lethal contagion of the omnipotent State at
the expense of individual dignity, Richard T. Ely is Typhoid
Mary and his most successful vector was the apotheotic
heresy of perfectibility at the heart of the social gospel.

The final man to be treated in the development of this
grandiose megalomania was once honored as the social
gospel's "most "brilliant and satisfying exponent."[421] Walter
Rauschenbusch (1861 – 1918) thoroughly assimilated
Gladden's 'higher criticism' and Ely's eugenic social
selection in his comprehensive outlook. His work
demonstrates a clear progression from his early adoption of
German historicism to a repudiation of Biblical authority in
his theology. After his education, he interpreted the squalor
he witnessed in 1880's Hell's Kitchen as *casus belli* for his

---

417   Miller, "Richard T. Ely, The German Historical School," 53.
418   Miller, "Richard T. Ely, The German Historical School," 55
– 56.
419   Cf. Miller, "Richard T. Ely, The German Historical School"
and Clifford F. Thies, and Gary M. Pecquet, "The Shaping of a
Future President's Economic Thought: Richard T. Ely and Woodrow
Wilson at "the Hopkins"," *The Independent Review* 15, no. 2 (Fall,
2010): 257-77.
420   Ely cites Schäffle, presumably Albert Schäffle (1831 - 1903)
ideal of economic progress "that distribution of income which brings
society as a whole, and in all its subdivisions, nearest to perfection.";
Ely, *Introduction to Political Economy*, 87.
421   Howard E. Jensen, "The Social Gospel in America, 1870 –
1920: Washington Gladden, Richard T. Ely, and Walter
Rauschenbusch, Edited by Robert T. Handy," Review in *Social
Forces*, 45, no. 4 (June, 1967): 612.

ideal of theocratic reform.[422] Most poignantly,
Rauschenbusch capped his career with the creation of a
systematic theology of the social gospel specifically aimed at
creating the Kingdom of God on earth.

    Rauschenbusch's manner of thinking is well
demonstrated in his frequent references to the 'social
organism'. These references appear in each of his four most
well-known works, and he consistently employs them in a
manner that suggests that to him the matter was utterly
proved. He does not employ the same manner of discussion
as Gladden or Ely, but rather speaks of the social organism in
the same manner that one might of gravity or sunshine.
Additionally, his historicist Biblical interpretation is as
abundantly apparent in his work as is his clear enthusiasm for
the evolution-fueled, eugenics-facilitated 'new era'
modernism. The primary detail of Rauschenbusch's career to
differentiate him from Gladden or Ely is that where the latter
men sought to build or compile their worldview,
Rauschenbusch had already swallowed it whole, and worked
merely to systematize it. Rauschenbusch finalized the
doctrine of the social gospel into a sophisticated, infernal
paradigm.

    As Thomas C. Leonard would summarize,
"Rauschenbusch, the most influential social gospel
theologian of the twentieth century, described the social
gospel as a translation of evolutionary theory into religious
faith, and he placed heredity at the center of economic
reform."[423] In cooperative agreement with Gladden and the
younger Beecher, Rauschenbusch spoke of the positive
influence of evolutionary thought on religion.

    It has opened a vast historical outlook… and
    trained us in bold conceptions of the upward
    climb of the race…. it has prepared us for
    understanding the idea of a Reign of God
    toward which all creation is moving. Translate

---

422   Rauschenbusch spent "some time as a student in Germany"
before "…Rochester where he began to question the infallibility of the
Bible…": Pestritto, in Watson, *Progressive Challenges*, 151.
423   Leonard, *Illiberal Reformers*, 2016, 125.

the evolutionary theories into religious faith,
and you have the doctrine of the Kingdom of
God.[424]

This 'race' of which he spoke was exactly as it
appears to contemporary readers, and is not appended to the
broadly inclusive qualifier 'human' as will be analyzed. In
any interpretation however, Rauschenbusch does not address
how, precisely, a feckless deity having little to no
involvement with ages upon ages of accidental death,
adaptation, mutation, or survival of animated, presumptuous
amino-acid-chains leads to an ideal Kingdom of God. What
he did say however betrays the same horrific hubris that
inevitably proceeds from all such reasoning – the claim to
'take control of our own evolution': "We now have such
scientific knowledge of social laws and forces, of economics,
of history that we can intelligently mold and guide the
evolution in which we take part."[425]
Expanding Beecher's irrational corelation of
evolution and religion, and operating from Gladden's higher
criticism, Rauschenbusch concludes that religion's
"combination with scientific evolutionary thought has freed
the Kingdom ideal of its catastrophic setting ... and so
adapted it to the climate of the modern world."[426] The
reference to the 'catastrophic setting' demonstrates the same
soft interpretation of biblical narrative that lead Gladden to
the gradualist perspective. Rauschenbusch however takes this
paradigm to an extreme to contrive a distillation of
amillennialism.
He contrives a view of Jewish history, utterly
dominant in today's biblical criticism, that apocalypticism
was little more than exilic prose written to cope with foreign
oppression or 'status anxiety', and contained not a whisper of
divine inspiration or prediction. He employs this view to
dismiss an enormous portion of the Bible with the clam that
"...the apocalyptic hope was a debased form of the prophetic

---

424   Walter Rauschenbusch, *Christianizing the Social Order*,
        (New York: The Macmillan Company, 1912), 90.
425   Rauschenbusch, *The Social Order*, 41.
426   Rauschenbusch, *The Social Order*, 90.

hope.... The whole scheme of the future in the apocalyptical literature is artificial, unreal, unhistorical, and mechanical. Jesus turned away from it and emphasized the law of organic development...."[427] One would hope that it is unnecessary to point out that one of the most well-known and often (mis)quoted pieces of apocalyptic literature is Jesus' own words in Matthew twenty-four, or its parallel in Luke twenty-one. Rauschenbusch's claim regarding Jesus having 'turned away' from apocalypticism is patently absurd, but no more so than Rauschenbusch's confused and unqualified claim that the Gnostics were the "evolutionary philosophers of that age."[428]

The imaginary world of historicism is especially apparent in this section of Rauschenbusch's work. Comparing his almost libelous characterization of the 'Jewish' hope with flat-out false-attribution-plagiarism of Jesus, Rauschenbusch paints an image of the early church that he claimed had a "high sense of an historical mission, but combined it with a saner and more philosophical outlook on the world." In his estimation and praise, this fantasy which he created "...was evolutionary, while apocalypticism was catastrophic."[429]

While he is certainly correct in a sense, that the apocalypse *will be* catastrophic – this being effectively the definition of the term – he did not use the term 'catastrophic' in such a manner. He employs the term as the nemesis of gradualism, his preferred cosmology without which neither eugenics nor evolution can be supported. Previously cited, Rauschenbusch fabricated an image of Jesus as gradualist, claiming that He had "emphasized the law of organic development," but his manufacture does not end here.

Entirely without supporting evidence or analysis, Rauschenbusch claimed that "Jesus... never viewed the human individual apart from human society...." and later that "Jesus always stood for an ethical and social outcome of

427   Walter Rauschenbusch, *Christianity and the Social Crisis*, (New York: The Macmillan Company, 1907), 112.
428   Rauschenbusch, *The Social Crisis*, 112.
429   Rauschenbusch, *The Social Crisis*, 112.

religion...."[430] Honestly, one is at a loss to comprehend how Rauschenbusch was able to make such a leap. The Gospels record dozens of instances wherein Jesus discusses the individual, inclusive of his responsibility, prerogatives, and relation to God but none are more clear, one would think, than Jesus' words to Peter regarding John: "... If I will that he tarry till I come, what is that to thee? Follow thou me."[431] It is ironic that Rauschenbusch repudiated the Old Testament apocalyptics as he did or he might have recalled the prophesy that utterly rejects his image of collectivism: "But every one shall die for his own iniquity."[432]

It is apparent, however he prevaricated, that Rauschenbusch's Christology was *useful* to his purposes. The silhouette of Jesus that he fabricated appears to have been tailored to lend the vapors of authority to his rendition of the social organism. He claimed that Jesus "...was socially minded and... the Kingdom of God as a right social organism was the really vital thing to him."[433] Rauschenbusch most certainly contrived this socially-minded 'Jesus' to support the construction of his theology. He defined the social gospel as "the old message of salvation, but enlarged and intensified" and declared that it "seeks to bring men under repentance for their *collective sins* and to create a more sensitive and more modern conscience."[434] Setting aside the obvious presentism of the 'more modern conscience', one is reminded that to 'enlarge and intensify the old message' may qualify as having added "unto these things" – an act against which John warned, being the final words of the Bible.[435]

The collective sins of which Rauschenbusch spoke played a central role in his conception of the social gospel – being that collectivism is the whole of the matter. He goes further than mere references to 'national sin' as the Book of

---

430   Rauschenbusch, *The Social Crisis*, 65 – 66; Walter
       Rauschenbusch, *The Social Principles of Jesus*, (New York: Grosset
       & Dunlap, 1916), 193.
431   John 21:22.
432   Jeremiah 31:29 – 30.
433   *The Social Principles*, 193.
434   Walter Rauschenbusch, *A Theology for the Social Gospel*,
       (New York: The Macmillan Company, 1917), 5, emphasis added.
435   Cf. Revelation 22:18.

Jonah or others might suggest; the collectivist paradigm was, to him, far superior to the concept of an individual. "The kingdom of God is still a collective conception, involving the whole social life of man. *It is not a matter of saving human atoms*, but of saving the social organism. It is not a matter of getting individuals to heaven, but of transforming the life on earth into the harmony of heaven."[436] Such a claim might suggest that any given individual – the one in the one-hundred so-to-speak[437] – is meaningless when compared to the grandiloquent 'organism' in Rauschenbusch's kingdom. He repeats this revocation of an individual's dignity, or indeed value to God, in favor of the grand collective: "The new life of the individual is mediated by the social organism which is already in possession of that life."[438]

Again, Rauschenbusch combines his evolutionary gradualism with his higher-criticism-induced Borg-like collective, and reduces even the power of God Himself under his world-view. "The Kingdom of God is not a concept or an ideal merely, but an historical force.... *Its capacity to save the social order depends on its pervasive presence* within the social organism."[439] This 'historical force' was a product of his version of the early church, from which he substituted his own *telos*: "the essential purpose of Christianity was to transform human society into the kingdom of God by regenerating all human relations and reconstituting them in accordance with the will of God."[440] The goal was, in his view "...the redemption of the social organism...."[441] Given that this man reduced even the power of God under his own conception of the social organism – an arena which it appears even Gladden and Ely did not tread – it is necessary to understand the specific characteristics of that organism, that he so clearly equated with the kingdom.

---

436   Rauschenbusch, *The Social Crisis*, 65, emphasis added; Cf. Rauschenbusch repudiates individualism in Old Testament prophetic morality, claiming that it was "the public morality on which national life is founded." *The Social Crisis*, 8.

437   Matthew 18:12.

438   Rauschenbusch, *A Theology*, 125.

439   Rauschenbusch, *A Theology*, 165, emphasis added.

440   Rauschenbusch, *The Social Crisis*, xiii.

441   Rauschenbusch, *A Theology*, 24.

His organism was Teutonic or Aryan. To be clear, his use of these terms were every bit as overloaded as one in the early twenty-first century might suspect. It is wholly apparent that Rauschenbusch's rather promiscuous use of history was not confined to biblical criticism. In addition to carefully crafting an image of Jewish and Christian history most suitable to his purposes, he paints a romantic and supremely malodorous tableau of the origins of his preferred 'stock'. He claims: "[w]henever historical investigation has uncovered the the early history of the Aryan race, we see communities of free men in organized fraternity of life."[442]

> Thus the essentials of a righteous social life, justice, property, democracy, equality, coöperation, were embodied in the rude and simple conditions of these communities. Here *the social supremacy of the Aryan race* manifested itself and got its evolutionary start. Here the traditions of democracy and justice were dyed into the fiber of *our breed* so that they outlasted ages of despotism and reasserted themselves whenever the grip of tyranny slackened.[443]

Regarding the redemption or preservation of this *race*, the chief danger was economic. The 'capitalist' was to be opposed for his deplorable habit of importing the undesirable, the unfit – Chinese, Catholics, and "...an undigested mass of alien people…." He speaks of the "...private interests [who] have…. Checked the propagation of the Teutonic Stock; they have radically altered the racial future of our nation…."[444] Speaking of this propagation, Rauschenbusch decries the effects of the commercial system as he saw it. "The shiftless, and all those with whom natural passion is least restrained, will breed most freely…. Thus the reproduction of the race is left to the poor and ignorant….

---

442   Rauschenbusch, *The Social Order*, 375.
443   Rauschenbusch, *The Social Order*, 376, emphasis added, vocabulary sic.
444   Rauschenbusch, *The Social Order*, 277 – 278.

Our social system causes an unnatural selection of the weak for breeding, and the result is the survival of the unfittest."[445]

Rauschenbusch's eugenics were far more understated than Ely's, yet in his polemic against capitalism he espouses ideals and attitudes deeply reminiscent of Ely's social selection.[446] Additionally, Rauschenbusch's consistent use of nakedly racist ideology evokes clear parallels with each of the previously analyzed men. It is abundantly clear that among those things that characterize the social gospel, Darwinism, statism, and historicism are common themes in which all enjoy substantial agreement – even when diverging in particulars.

Rauschenbusch saw historicism and evolution as having sparked or introduced a 'new era' or a 'social revolution' that stood as the culmination of previous religious, political, and intellectual revolutions "of the past five centuries."[447] His goal is well-defined as a theocratic order, a drive towards the realization of God's Kingdom on earth. To be certain, the man saw himself, in his time, as historically momentous: "The present revival of the Kingdom idea is due to the combined influence of the historical study of the Bible and of the social gospel."[448]

Rauschenbusch's perception of his present and his prescriptions for the future were an inevitable product of his clearly self-affirmative fantasy view of the past. He saw his work as a mandate "...to get rid of laws, customs, maxims, and philosophies inherited from an evil and despotic past...." This past, in his view, was less-than because where "[o]ur fathers cowered before the lightning; we have subdued it to our will." While it is unclear from his prolific writing whether or not he included the Declaration within these 'evil philosophies', his core belief that truth itself is historically constructed would suggest that he held little admiration for the concept of universal principles like those espoused in the creation of the United States. He declared that "[f]ormer generations were swept along more or less blindly toward a

---

445   Rauschenbusch, *The Social Crisis*, 274 – 275, sic.
446   Ely, "Social Progress," 62.
447   Rauschenbusch, *The Social Crisis*, Introduction throughout.
448   Rauschenbusch, *A Theology*, 133.

hidden destiny; we have reached the point where we can make history make us."[449]

Historicism and evolution were and are wholly central to the idea that society might be 'redeemed', or otherwise converted into a glorious heaven-on-earth. Rauschenbusch's words above especially reinforce this central fact. As Ronald Pestritto would render it: "For both the Social Gospel and progressivism generally, the evolutionary power of history had brought a sea change in what was possible both in human nature and in human government."[450] This 'sea change' obviated the need for caution and circumspection regarding issues of power and authority to such an extent, that in Gladden and Ely's views, government – the omnipotent State – could, and ought to be the agent by which perfection would be achieved. Rauschenbusch's view of perfection itself was somewhat more nuanced than that of his confreres.

When laying out his plan to 'christianize' society, Rauschenbusch offered a weak disclaimer. "We shall demand perfection and never expect to get it."[451] His belief was such that the very demand would produce pressure in the right direction. While this portion of his argument certainly rings the tones of reasonable consideration for the facts of human nature, his constant references to his imagined 'kingdom ideal', and the inherently authoritarian system necessitated by the 'order' which he advocates adds the discordant tones of posturing. He may well have not believed in perfection *qua* perfection, but he most certainly advocated for the perfectibility of society – again, provided the right policies were discovered and *enforced*.

Given the Teutons for Troy, 'Jesus' for Jupiter, the 'kingdom of god' for *imperium sine fine,* and the imaginary ascent of historicist-evolution in place of an epic, these four men among countless others contrived their own mythopoeic. From this self-deifying world-view, an inverted anthropology arose to rationalize the image of omnipotent man – provided he descends from the right breeding. Having recruited a

---

449   Rauschenbusch, *Social Order*, 41.
450   Pestritto in Watson, *Progressive Challenges*, 156.
451   Rauschenbusch, *The Social Order*, 126.

decrepit simulacrum of Jesus to their cause, each man enjoyed his own version and level of broad public and popular influence as previously demonstrated. The net result of the social gospel is that American Christians appear to have accepted the ideal that they could, under their own auspices, cause or create the Kingdom of God. By this means the first and most robust bulwark against tyranny was pulled down in the creation of the American Aeneid to legitimize this counterfeit kingdom.

Whether classed as a social organism, social progress, social selection, or the social gospel, the whole of the matter is the repudiation of individual value – dignity – in favor of an imagined, divinely omnipotent State. It seems only a mere convenience that those who advocated for such a thing just so happened to be among the ascendant rather than the 'degenerate classes'. There can be no effective legerdemain to excuse the currently-received-as-unsavory aspects of the social gospel; Beecher, Gladden, Ely, and Rauschenbusch – among so many others – most certainly conceived of themselves as a superior race or a better breed, and to varying degrees and for varying motives, they assumed a sickly condescending mantle of benevolent, genocidal despotism in relation to all those they considered to be unfit. This was not adjunct to their time or incidental to their paradigm, it was central to, the fountainhead of their world-view.

Reflecting the founding admonitions, the curmudgeonly Socratic of his time H.L. Mencken (1880 – 1956) distilled the heart of the social gospel in its truest and most essential form. "The urge to save humanity is almost always only a false-face for the urge to rule it. Power is what all messiahs really seek: not the chance to serve."[452] One will note that in their grandiosity, these did not reduce the power of the bogies – the 'robber barons' or monopolies – but rather only sought to increase their own power via the State, ostensibly under the mantle of 'philanthropy'.

In place of admonition, these self-proclaimed gods would speak only of their own power to bring about the kingdom, should society but heed their gospel. As a direct

---

452   H.L. Mencken, *Minority Report: H.L. Mencken's Notebooks*, (New York: Alfred A. Knopf, 1956), 247.

product of the inescapable hubris that comprises the entire core of historicism or evolution as applied to 'history' and 'truth' – that is self-obsessed solipsism – the social gospel utterly rejects the inarguably consistent duality of humanity. Simply, these failed to recognize that ignorance of the universal capacity for evil, especially among those who purport to aim at the good, is the very means by which evil frequently arises. In agreement with C. S. Lewis' position regarding the 'omnipotent moral busybodies', the one who thinks himself a god – or at the least a 'god-seed' – commits evil far more insidious than mere base greed, dishonesty, or aggression.

The criminal, the enemy attacks the body, the property, and can be resisted; the self-appointed 'apostle' or 'philanthropist' attacks the mind and the soul, he presumes upon the substance of reality itself. It is vital to recognize the historicism and evolutionary solipsism at the heart of the social gospel; repudiation of Biblical authority did not merely allow for wholesale fabrication of a self-affirming world-view, but as Ronald Pestritto phrased it represents "...a fusion of liberal Protestantism and Hegelianism."[453]

This connection is neither political, philosophical, nor epistemic. Where the whole matter of the creation of American civilization was the dignity of the individual man, Hegel (1770 – 1831) usurped the whole *substantial, metaphysical* worth of the individual, to subordinate it to his Borg. "All the worth which the human being possesses, *all spiritual reality*, he possesses only through the State."[454] Whether influenced by Hegel or not, the direct line of central European cosmology to Gladden, Ely, and Rauschenbusch is well established. The social gospel sought the State as god, the omnipotent collective, the apotheosis of the *right* 'stock'. These merely couched their delusional, rapacious power-lust in 'christian' terminology; "and no marvel; for Satan himself is transformed into an angel of light."[455]

---

453   Pestritto, in Watson, *Progressive Challenges*, 147.
454   Georg Wilhelm Friedrich Hegel, *The Philosophy of History*, trans. J. Sibree (New York: Dover Publications, Inc., 1956), 39, emphasis added.
455   II Corinthians 11:14.

As the unmistakable lightning slashes the sky from
the east to the west, so too are the apocalypse and
millennium.[456] One may accept or one may disregard the
many clear irritants of Biblical eschatology, but to shoehorn
an imaginary or 'spiritual return', to equate *any* human
government with the Reign of Christ, to fabricate an image of
gradualism from obvious biblical catastrophism necessitates
a level of dishonesty or *insanity* only found among
sociopaths and their supremely ignorant fodder. There is *no*
Gospel in the social gospel.

Returning again to the anxieties of the Civil War and
Reconstruction whence the soil for this demonic seed was
tilled, the previously mentioned misquoted words of Jesus
appear to have fallen on completely deaf ears. The Civil War
was no apocalypse, the 'industrial revolution' no millennium,
and the American Republic is most *certainly not* the
Kingdom of God – no human government can be. Conflict
will happen entirely without apocalyptic significance, but the
actual end will be *wholly* unmistakable.

> For many shall come in my name, saying, I
> am Christ; and shall deceive many. And ye
> shall hear of wars and rumours of wars: *see*
> *that ye be not troubled: for all these things*
> *must come to pass, but the end is not yet.* For
> nation shall rise against nation, and kingdom
> against kingdom: and there shall be famines,
> and pestilences, and earthquakes, in diverse
> places. All these are the beginning of sorrows.
> Then shall they deliver you up to be afflicted,
> and shall kill you: *and ye shall be hated of all*
> *nations for my name's sake.*
>
> … For then shall be great tribulation, such as
> was not since the beginning of the world to
> this time, no, nor ever shall be. And except
> those days should be shortened, there should
> *no flesh be saved*….[457]

---

456   Cf. Matthew 24:27.
457   Matthew 24: 5 – 9, 21, 22a; emphasis added, spelling sic.

Where the substance of the foundation of the United States was individual dignity, a *gift* from God given freely to all – even agnostics, atheists, 'infidels', doubters, 'deists', and 'the unfit' – the heresy of perfectibility prompted and permitted Americans to honestly believe that they could, and would, be as gods. While the greater influence of the social gospel on American Christendom as a whole is a debatable point, one suggests that the summation of that matter is that the social gospel effectively rendered American Protestantism completely apostate. The Divine act of Creation being the anchor cut, the ship of State was cast adrift.

This apostasy facilitated the zealotry that lies at the heart of the *cult* that came to conquer America: technicist elitism and the rule of the expert class. Aeneas having run his course, the way is paved for Romulus and his promised heir, Augustus. The counterfeit kingdom arose.

Auto-Apotheosis: The Elitism of the Expert Class

> When an unclean spirit goes out of a man, he
> goes through dry places, seeking rest, and
> finds none. Then he says, 'I will return to my
> house from which I came.' And when he
> comes, he finds it empty, swept, and put in
> order. Then he goes and takes with him seven
> other spirits more wicked than himself, and
> they enter and dwell there; and the last state of
> that man is worse than the first. So shall it also
> be with this wicked generation.[458]
>
> – Jesus, *The Gospel of Matthew*

Having cast off the burden of the mad king George III, the rush to become as gods lead American civilization to adopt the vicious burden of the ascended master expert. The truest characterization of the Progressive Era, and measure of its impact, is the conversion of government's purpose from safeguarding the principles of the Declaration, to universalizing the peevish proclivities of the professor and enforcing the policy objectives of the self-ascended moralist. Elitism is self-evidently fundamental to the vacuous schemes of historicism – especially 'higher' criticism – and the inescapably murderous implications of the evolutionary world-view.

---

458   Matthew 12: 43 – 45.

Historicism is abusive condescension, most especially as an expression of argument from authority. The act of presuming to elucidate what any writer 'really meant', of undertaking to 'explain' why clear statements indicate something other than what they say; or of 'defining truth' as anything more complicated than "the contrary to falsehood; conformity of notions to things" is an act of gaslighting.[459]

Evolutionary arguments are integral, not proximal, to collectivist analysis of human beings, that being nothing more complex than naked bigotry. The attitude that humanity evolved lead directly and *immediately* to calls for mutilation, imprisonment, and murder of individuals for the preservation and progress of the 'social organism'. Again it must be stated: eugenics and collectivism are and always have been wholly central to the entire paradigm. It is not coincidental that the various champions of the perspective – activists, academics, administrators – were fortunately part of the 'evolved' or 'desirable' classes, but rather it is demonstrative of the true nature of the world-view: rationalized sociopathy. The notion of 'progress' is adopted by those who will to be as God, and these immediately went about benevolently condescending to the vestigial mortals; to re-make society and humanity according to their own divine plan.

To be certain, progressivism was not universally commingled with 'gospel' iconography but, the more rhetorically atheistic renditions serve only to make the self-worship, ideological patricide, and absurdity more readily apparent. One characterizes certain renditions as 'rhetorically atheistic' because each inevitably substitutes a belief in God or the supernatural with the slavish self-veneration of the 'present', 'modern democracy', and 'modern science'; those who disclaim God inevitably worship themselves or some other man-made construct. Among these, Irish historian and philologist at Cambridge, John Bagnell (J.B.) Bury (1861 – 1927), quite in opposition to the window dressing of the 'social gospel', conflated the whole of Christian belief with *Roman* Catholicism in a transparently prejudiced attempt to

---

459   "truth," *A Dictionary of the English Language*, by Samuel Johnson. 1773. https://johnsonsdictionaryonline.com/1773/truth_ns.

cast Christianity as the antithesis of freedom in his 1913 *A History of the Freedom of Thought*.

Writing from a similarly contrived historical perspective as did Rauschenbusch, Bury arrived at an equal, opposite, and substantially identical conclusion. He insinuated both a degenerate morality and mental oppression at work in the 'Jewish' Bible. He stated that "the Jewish writings... reflect the ideas of a low stage of civilization...." and cast the Bible as "...an obstacle to moral and intellectual progress...."[460] He did this overtly as a means of supporting his claim that Christianity imprisoned 'reason' for over a thousand years. Curiously, though he edited one full printing of Gibbon's *Decline and Fall*, he appears to have missed one particularly important (and contentious) item in Gibbon's thesis.[461]

Bury claimed that the view that "...religious belief is voluntary and not a thing which can be enforced" was abandoned when "...faith became the predominant creed and had the power of the State behind it...."[462] It appears that Bury viewed the first Church as something like a conspiracy, merely lying-in-wait for their chance to wreck stuff. Gibbon on the other hand, in his overly loquacious eighteenth century pen, spoke with a more reasonable tone of the "primitive and apostolic model" that "[t]he hostile disputants of Rome, of Paris, of Oxford, and of Geneva [sought] to reduce... to the respective standards of their own policy."[463] While both presented their own claims based in 'Jewish' or 'Mosaic' tradition (Bury, a fable; Gibbon: zealotry), the elder may be interpreted as having demonstrated how *political* maneuvering used, perverted, and corrupted the essential nature of Christianity to become Catholicism whereas the

---

460   J.B. Bury, *A History of Freedom of Thought*, (Cambridge: Henry Holt and Company, 1913), Project Gutenberg Ebook #10684, Chapter III. Note, this Ebook does not contain page numbers.
461   Edward Gibbon, *The History of the Decline and Fall of the Roman Empire*, ed. J.B. Bury with an Introduction by W.E.H. Lecky, in 12 vols, (New York: Fred de Fau and Co., 1906 [1776]).
462   Bury, *Thought*, III.
463   Edward Gibbon, *The Decline and Fall of the Roman Empire: An Abridgement by D.M. Low*, (New York: Harcourt Brace and Company, 1960), 170.

younger argued that Christianity (being Roman Catholicism in his whole treatment) is itself violently opposed to critical thought and scientific inquiry altogether – an exceedingly common attitude.

Gibbon, being only proximate to the point, may or may not have been aware of the process of usurpation that he narrated; Bury however clearly lost the plot. Conveying Christianity into a political sphere – *any* political sphere – destroys its essential nature as not of this world.[464] It matters very little if one was crucified by Diocletian, or burnt at the stake by Theodosius I; the murdered care not for motives. This factor illuminates the meaning behind Paul's attitude regarding leaven – essentially in the context that rules do not make for righteousness.[465] Whether the unholy marriage of 'christianity' with Roman bureaucracy, or the iron and clay of evolution and the 'gospel', "Evil company corrupts good habits."[466] Both of these attitudes towards God – Rauschenbusch and his comrades, or Bury and his ilk, rely on fundamentally and transparently false interpretations of the Bible and Christianity as the rationalization for their world-view. It is no marvel that these would arrive at the same destination via alternate routes; all roads and Rome as it were.

Bury stated that Darwin's work (both *Origin*, 1859 and *Descent*, 1871) hammered "[a]nother nail … into the coffin of Creation and the Fall of Adam…" such that "...the doctrine of redemption could only be rescued by making it independent of the Jewish fable on which it was founded."[467] This statement invokes both the younger Beecher's *Evolution and Religion* and Gladden's *Who Wrote the Bible?*. First as previously mentioned, Beecher cast evolution as "the Divine method of creation…."[468] Whether aware of this view or not – being British, one does not expect him to know anything of 'America's most popular preacher' – Bury categorically denied such an absurd correlation. The reference to 'Jewish

---

464   Cf. John 18:36.
465   Galatians 5:9. Cf. I Corinthians 6.
466   I Corinthians 15:33, NKJV.
467   Bury, *Thought*, VII.
468   Beecher, *Evolution and Religion*, 3.

fables', aside from the darkly 'Aryan' semantic overtones, recalls Gladden's 'higher criticism' in a far less flattering light. Crucially however, Bury stated that "We must remember that, according to the humane doctrine of the Christians, pagan, that is, merely human, virtues were vices."[469] This *assertion* reflects Gladdens claim that the Bible commanded things "which it would be wrong for us to do" – in an equally unqualified and uncritical manner.[470] Not to interrogate the dead yet again, one really must ask of his tomb: what pagan/human virtues were vices? Bury did not attempt to explain this statement, but rather launched a libel on all Christian belief based solely on the persecution of heretics by some few 'christians' – that is, unscrupulous men with an excuse, as though that excuse mattered.

Humorously enough, Bury betrayed his own hubris in a patently ignorant attempt at deifying evolution. Much as this author criticized Rauschenbusch's appeal to evolution as requiring a feckless deity having little to no involvement with ages upon ages of accidental death, Bury also made a similar observation. "If intelligence had anything to do with this bungling process [ages of selection via death], it would be an intelligence infinitely low. And the finished product, if regarded as a work of design, points to incompetence in the designer."[471] One simply declares that Bury's 'modern science' was hardly modern to take such an arrogant view of biological structures and systems. The best intelligence of man has found only layer upon layer of increasing complexity, that continues to confound him, in the century from that pompous declaration. His logic rendered the statement even less effective; Bury's 'bungling process' is a false premise – he used his conclusion as the premise for his conclusion.

There is no intelligence in nature, says the haughty one, claiming respect for the intelligence presumed by the claim. The self-sawed branch does not end there, and connects this exceedingly weak philosophy to the greater theme of the American Aeneid. Much of Bury's worldview

469   Bury, *Thought*, III.
470   Gladden, *Who Wrote the Bible?*, Chapter XIII.
471   Bury, *Thought*, VII.

was effectively Newtonian; he stated that "[t]he phenomena of nature are a system of things which co-exist and follow each other according to invariable laws."[472] He dropped dozens of names to support his perspective – Copernicus, Linnaeus, Buffon, Lyell, Mill, Compte, and Spencer, *ad nauseam* – but ironically criticized Hegel for having failed to "take into account the probability of further development in the future" (much like life being much more well-designed than understood in the early twentieth century).[473] Ultimately however, employing the very same 'higher criticism' (that he termed 'modern') as Gladden, making identical appeals to authority, unfalsifiable and later-disproved claims, and consistent conflation of interpretation with fact, Bury based his paradigm on his view of natural laws. Contrasting with the eighteenth century however, where Jefferson's Natural Law is the design of the Creator, Bury's natural laws amount to law bereft of a lawgiver – concealing his vacuous cosmology with the old legerdemain 'it's turtles all the way down'. Though he called this "the progress of rationalism", it is more rationally termed the progress of *rationalization*.[474]

All things arise as a product of laws, except the laws themselves. What then, if no lawgiver? Universal, transcendent principles to which one might appeal no longer exist; the very concept of what is right, or what is evil, is subordinated to the shifting emotional state of the mob. The veracity of a given claim depends not on the "...conformity of notions to things", but rather upon a given interpretation of the 'time' or 'age' in which the claim was made.[475] Admonition to carefully guard against the repetitious turpitude of all men, any man, with power can only be thought of as quaint, backward, not in keeping with the times. One would note that Bury's position significantly agreed with this author's in one vital detail: progressivism is and always has been wholly incompatible with Christianity. Not merely Christianity, but also the eighteenth century

---

472   Bury, *Thought*, VII.
473   Bury, *Thought*, VII.
474   Bury, *Thought*, Title of Chapter VII.
475   Cf. "truth", Samuel Johnson, 1773 above.

transcendent 'Newtonian' principles from which *legitimate* American authority derives.

> Now the idea of the progress of the human race must, I think, be held largely answerable for this change of attitude [in the nineteenth century]. It must, I think, be held to have operated powerfully as *a solvent of theological beliefs*.... It inspired the English Utilitarian philosophers... who preached the *greatest happiness of the greatest number as the supreme object of action and the basis of morality*. This ideal was powerfully reinforced by the doctrine of historical progress... the *organic principle of history*.... science endorsed it; it has been associated with, though it is not necessarily implied in, the scientific theory of evolution; and it is perhaps fair to say that it has been the guiding spiritual force of the nineteenth century. ...it has *dissolved the blighting doctrine of the radical corruption of man.*[476]

Lest the argument be made that one has inserted a meaning beyond 'the blighting doctrine', Bury offered his view of the supremacy of his time. "It may be doubted whether what Lord Acton wrote in 1877 would be true now: "There are in our day many educated men who think it right to persecute.""[477] In the age of eugenics, to say nothing of other currents in 1913, Bury took the position that a mere 46 years had erased the ancient and self-evident habitual alignment between power, dominant narratives, bigotry, and elitism. It would seem that either Bury was unaware of the substance of the ideologies that were growing directly towards the Great War, its sequel, and the dramatic explosion of democide that characterized the twentieth century – or that he considered these ideologies to be leading towards greater happiness for the greater number, without regard to what it

---

476   Bury, *Thought*, VII. Emphasis added.
477   Bury, *Thought*, VII.

exacted of the lesser. He cannot be discounted for not knowing the future, but an historian and philologist is most certainly vulnerable to criticism for failing, in 1913, to discern the face of the sky.

He could not have anticipated, one may retort. Not so; he directly cited these very currents. Bury stated that during the 'second period' of progress' history, roughly the 1860's, "[the idea of progress] harmonized with the notion of "development"... Socialists and other political reformers appealed to it as a gospel.... The ORIGIN OF SPECIES led to the THIRD stage of the fortunes of the idea of Progress.... the decisive fact which has established the reign of the idea of Progress."[478] Auto-apotheosis was integral to both evolutionary thinking and political agitation *from the beginning*. Bury cited Darwin's faith in his own claims: "...as natural selection works solely by and for the good of each being, all corporeal and mental environments will tend to progress towards perfection."[479] He placed this in the context of analyzing whether evolution was fundamentally optimistic or not; to its most visible name it most certainly was.

There has always been an equation between evolution, perfection, 'gospel', 'reform', and progressivism, but not only these. Bury highlighted the concept of perfectibility as endorsed by Spencer, based on the claim "that the constancy of human nature... is a fallacy.... If then humanity is indefinitely variable, perfectibility is possible."[480] But Spencer did not stop here as Bury noted:

> The ultimate purpose of creation, he asserts, is to produce the *greatest amount of happiness*, and to fulfil this aim it is necessary that each member of the race should possess faculties enabling him to experience the highest enjoyment of life, yet in such a way as not to diminish the power of others to receive like

---

478   J.B. Bury, *The Idea of Progress: An Inquiry into its Origin and Growth*, (London: 1920), Project Gutenberg Ebook #4557, Chapter 19: "Progress in the Light of Evolution": 1. Sic. Note, this Ebook does not contain page numbers.

479   Darwin in Bury, *Progress*, XIX:2.

480   Spencer in Bury, *Progress*, XIX:2.

satisfaction. Beings thus constituted cannot multiply in a world tenanted by inferior creatures; these, therefore, must be dispossessed to make room....[481]

In explaining his meaning behind 'survival of the fittest', Spencer narrated a concept that would be shortly adopted under the term *Lebensraum*. In one breath Spencer softened his utility with a vague caveat 'not to diminish the power of others;' in the next, he spoke of the integral necessity of displacement and genocide in the 'development' of the fittest. Inverse teleology, perverse anthropology, did not merely justify perfectibility, it lead immediately to genocidal arguments. To miss this in 1913 may be forgivable; to eulogize it in 1920 is inexcusable.

Despite the overall dismissal of anything that might be called individuality, and the irrationally adolescent equation of Darwin with Galileo in his 1920 *Idea of Progress*, Bury made at least one other point with which this author stands in substantial agreement. He claimed that by the closing decades of the nineteenth century, "[t]he majority... received [optimistic evolutionary progress] in a vague sense as a comfortable addition to their convictions. But it became a part of the general mental outlook of educated people."[482] This, it would seem, is at least *mostly* true – there being no monoliths, nothing ever applies to everything.

Where emotional homiletics and frankly bad theology had rendered American Protestantism apostate and impotent to its purpose, irrational 'science' and solipsistic 'history' had lead the academy to inhumanity. Where the one contrived a theocracy, the other conceived an oligarchy. Whether toward an imagined 'kingdom of god', or vague appeals to the ostensibly atheistic-but-divine future of man, both avenues lead to self-deification and from here, deliberate and largely successful attempts to force their worldview upon a once-free people.

---

481   Bury, *Progress*, XIX:2. Emphasis added, spelling sic.
482   J.B. Bury, *The Idea of Progress*, XIX:4.

As previously stated, it would be simple to dismiss one or all of the various men as mere kooks or crackpots, to assert that any given belief-statement or policy objective was nothing more than an opinion of the time or at worst, a small group of relatively non-influential men. Simple to claim though it may be, it is inarguably false. Even were one to dismiss the prestige of Bury as confined to the relative obscurity of his respective fields, his sentiments and conclusions aligned with the social gospel, being derived of much the same substance. These sentiments ran from man to man, from ideology to proposal, and to policy and law – from which current the American worldview derives via the perversity of public 'education.'

One such lineage ran from Richard Ely through Bury's American contemporary the aforementioned 'eminent busybody' John R. Commons (1862 – 1945). Commons conveyed Ely's perverse cosmology directly into policy by means of his influence over an ever increasing pool of acolytes. As Paul J. McNulty (1931 – 1988; of Columbia University, not the United States Deputy Attorney General of the same name) claimed, no other scholar had "...turned as many graduate students in the direction of labor studies as did Commons."[483] In a eulogistic, and carefully curated biography, John Chasse an opponent to this argument, impressed upon his readers the extent of Commons' influence:

> ...it would be hard to find a teacher whose students exercised as much influence on public policy. John B. Andrews, the executive secretary of the American Association for Labor Legislation, oversaw the intellectual dialogue that became the "seedbed" for most labor and social legislation between 1907 and 1940. Edwin Witte and Arthur Altmeyer worked on the design of the Social Security Act, and Altmeyer served as commissioner of

---

483   Paul J. McNulty, *The Origins and Development of Labor Economics: A Chapter in the History of Social Thought*, (Cambridge: The MIT Press, 1980), 151. Cf. Chasse, *A Worker's Economist*, 11.

Social Security until 1950. Wilbur Cohen
under Presidents Kennedy and Johnson,
oversaw the creation and implementation of
Medicare, the Elementary and Secondary
Education Act, the Civil Rights Act, and a host
of Social Security amendments.[484]

Where Ely brought central European historicism to
America, Commons spread it wide and directly into public
policy. In addition to his prolific writing, extensive teaching
career, and political machinations, Commons was elected
President of the American Economics Association (AEA),
1917 – a position created by both his mentor Ely, and by
Gladden.[485] Lest the charge be lain that this is mere guilt by
association, the intellectual alignment between Gladden, Ely,
Commons, and even Rauschenbusch is substantial, and by no
means limited to simple membership in the AEA. One may
be forgiven for sensing the vapors of conspiracy around these
men, if for no reason other than the extent of alignment
between them.

In a manner reflecting the impotent 'debate' between
Darwinism and Lamarckism, or Lippmann against Dewey to
be addressed later, both Commons and Ely took umbrage
with Spencer's somewhat 'non-interventionalist' and
optimistic rendition of evolution by means of competition,
yet both relied entirely on his concept of the social
organism.[486] Commons believed that "...competition has no
respect for superior races. The race with lowest necessities
displaces others."[487] He expressed anxiety that "A new race

---

484   John Dennis Chasse, *A Worker's Economist: John R.
Commons and His Legacy from Progressivism to the War on Poverty*,
(New York: Taylor & Francis Group, 2018), 11.
485   American Economics Association, "Past Presidents",
Accessed January 22, 2025:
https://www.aeaweb.org/about-aea/leadership/officers/past-officers/
presidents.
486   Cf. Bury, *Progress*, XIX.
487   John R. Commons, *Races and Immigrants in America*,
(London: The Macmillan Company, 1907), 151. Cf. Thomas C.
Leonard, ""More Merciful and Not Less Effective": Eugenics and
American Economics in the Progressive Era", *History of Political
Economy*, 35 no. 4, 701.

of men is being created with the inherited traits of physical and moral degeneracy...."[488], and again that a "race of vagabonds is being brought up in our midst."[489] Ely voiced a warning: "[w]e do know it is important that a superior stock should not be swallowed up and lost by a more rapid increase of the inferior stock."[490] In Commons' view, this deplorable state was a product of 'natural' selection, as he stated that "[w]e cannot placidly rely on natural selection to wipe out crime and intemperance.... Evolution is not always development upwards."[491] Ely's alternative to this frightening prospect was intervention by means of "[not] natural selection, but social selection."[492]

Both Ely and Commons stood in substantial agreement with Gladden regarding the answer – the means of 'social selection' – as State mandated work programs. These are not mechanisms to assist the willing to improve their economic station, but rather *penal* institutions relying expressly on *force* to achieve eugenic, utilitarian ends for the benefit of the social organism.

Commons made yet another statement to illuminate the insidious nature of 'employment' and 'human resources'. He declared outright that "The man without an employer is a vagabond and an outlaw."[493] He did not say that a man without a job is a burden; he did not say that one who will not work shall not eat.[494] It would seem obvious, one would think, that such an equation necessarily subordinates all men – to say nothing of the yeomanry – under what amounts to a neo-feudal arrangement. This is not merely a moralistic condemnation of the unemployed, it is an overt 'either-or' proposition: either one has a *boss*, or one is an *outlaw*.

---

488   John R. Commons, *Social Reform and The Church, With an Introduction by Prof. Richard T. Ely*, (New York: Thomas Y. Crowell & Company, 1894), 7.

489   Commons, *Social Reform*, 78 – 79.

490   Ely, *The World War*, 115.

491   Commons, *Social Reform*, 6.

492   Richard T. Ely, "Social Progress," *The Cosmopolitan* 31 no. 1, (1901): 61– 64, 62.

493   Commons, *Social Reform*, 5 – 6.

494   Cf. Thessalonians 3:10.

An outlaw is neither Robin Hood nor a mere criminal; it is "one *excluded from the benefit of the law*."[495] It may be argued that Commons did not intend to claim that someone who is not used by another (employed) is no longer entitled to the benefit of law – civilly dead – but such a claim is vacuous.[496] Images of the social organism, relying on majoritarian-utility as the measure of right and wrong, lead directly to the idea that one who does not know and keep to their place regarding the social organism is, in Gladden's words, a member of the "deadbeat crowd" whose "unsocial conduct [has forfeited] their freedom."[497] Such an image is a far cry from the simple causality of reaping (or not) what one sows as so easily portrayed in the old children's fable "The Little Red Hen".[498]

According to Gladden, this ideal of one who will not perform as directed, for the good of the greater part, required "a measure of compulsion which only the state can exercise."[499] In Common's rendition, this was because "[g]overnment is the only supreme authority among men. It is the only institution which can make its plans comprehensive."[500] In his view however, the applicable use of force was not limited to Gladden or Ely's workhouses. After citing Gladden's position regarding the need for government to 'christianize', Commons continued: "[s]o it is with temperance reform. There is no Christian work which needs more thoughtful and scientific treatment. But nothing can be

---

495 "outlaw," *A Dictionary of the English Language*, by Samuel Johnson. 1773. Accessed January 23, 2025: https://johnsonsdictionaryonline.com/1773/outlaw_ns. Emphasis added.
496 The concepts of 'outlawry' and 'civil death' are both ancient and current. In basic terms, it references one who is, for a variety of reasons, outside of the benefits, privileges, protections, and rights of civil society. Cf. Harry David Saunders, "Civil Death – A New Look at an Ancient Doctrine," *William & Mary Law Review* 11, no. 4, (May 1970): 898 – 1003.
497 Gladden, *Social Salvation*, 82 – 84.
498 Frequently re-told nineteenth century American child's fable attributed to Mary Mapes Dodge, "The Story of the Little Red Hen," *St. Nicholas*, Vol. 1, Part 2, (1874), 680 – 681.
499 Gladden, *Social Salvation*, 87, 88, sic.
500 Commons, *Social Reform*, 77.

done without proper legislation."[501] Only the use of *force*, at
the direction of 'educated men' was sufficient to remake
society as he wished.[502]

    Commons adopted and expanded Ely's contention
that "...there is no limit to the right of the State...."[503] In
Common's estimation rights are not the free gift given by the
Creator to all men, but rather fickle grants of the
legislature.[504] He rejected the concept of natural (and
therefore inalienable) rights, and elevated what he called
'legal rights'. "It is easy to show that "natural rights" are a
myth, but they are a fact of history."[505] That latter portion,
that they are a fact of history, was a rendition of his
historicist 'product of their time' paradigm. Commons
derided natural rights as "idealism" and cast them as nothing
more than a ploy against legal rights made by Republican
homesteaders wishing to squat on another's land.[506]

    Commons' estimation of natural versus legal rights
developed directly from his origins in social gospel
evolutionary historicism. Where his claim that natural rights
were a myth was written in 1913, his 1894 *Social Reform
and the Church* contrived a straw-man to defend his creation
of a right to employment. Commons, quite correctly, spoke of
"wage-slavery" which he defined as "the dependence of one
man upon the arbitrary will of another for the opportunity to
earn a living."[507] It must be stated that this concept is
fundamentally and absolutely true; subsistence derived of
wage labor is functionally indistinguishable from the state of
slavery – save only for the ability to depart one employer in
favor of another; this being the whole animating substance of
the independent, and therefore free yeoman.

    Commons sought to address the greater reality that is
normally ignored in what passes for free-market-

---

501   Commons, *Social Reform*, 79.
502   Cf. Commons, *Social Reform*, 53 – 56.
503   Richard Ely, *Introduction to Political Economy*, (New York:
Chautauqua Press, 1889), 92.
504   Commons, *Social Reform*, 78.
505   John R. Commons, *Labor and Administration*, (New York:
The Macmillan Company, 1913), 50.
506   Commons, *Labor*, 50.
507   Commons, *Social Reform*, 34.

employment-debate today. Monopolism, whether by actual collusion or as a simple reflection of free-market wage-leveling in a given region, by necessity invalidates the possibility of wage-seeking practice. When most jobs pay about the same, making similar demands on the wage-earner, there is little 'freedom' in seeking a new one. Given that the non-yeoman is beholden to wage and currency for *subsistence* not luxury, this is a very serious charge. Commons however, in the ancient practice of bait-and-switch, did not recognize the obvious value of independent yeomanry as an answer to this predicament. He addressed the sad state of the laborer by contriving a 'right to employment' that he placed on equal footing with Jefferson's famous list. He claimed that employment was an inalienable right, stating this was the *only* solution, and defended himself against the charge that he was an 'innovator and disturber' by appeal to the wicked past when men "...recognized neither the right to life nor to liberty."[508] Commons did not address the inescapable detail in all such 'rights' – that the conjuring of a 'right' in this manner contrives an *obligation* upon another, with little regard for either consent or the cost exacted by that obligation.

As a contrived past is a fixture in Progressive ideology, so authoritarian collectivism is the inevitable mission statement. Historicism's solipsism vitiated any appeal to transcendent universals; evolution by necessity exalted control of the social organism by means of the educated elite.

True to his social gospel origins, Commons reasoned from a collective paradigm. He declared that "[t]he Church should not content herself with saving individuals.... *Society* is the subject of redemption."[509] Obviously this stood in agreement with Gladden's position that "[t]he kingdom of heaven is the entire social organism...." as well as Rauschenbusch's contention that "[i]t is not a matter of saving human atoms, but of saving the social organism."[510]

---

508   Commons, *Social Reform*, 35.
509   Commons, *Social Reform*, 71, Sic.
510   Washington Gladden, *The Church and the Kingdom*, 11-12; Rauschenbusch, *The Social Crisis*, 65.

These were expanded and defined by Ely's magnification of sociology as the application of 'love thy neighbor'.[511]

According to Commons, "The sociologist studies the individual man not as a separate particle, but as an organ intimately bound up in the social organism."[512] He sought to address the many illnesses of that organism by means of materialistic reformation: "...in society a large part of the question of reform is not how to reform, but how to *displace*, the baser elements.... The only remedy is to reform the surroundings, – and this means to reform society from top to bottom."[513] From the top down meaning by means of condescension. This was not a call to elect wise representatives to faithfully pursue the principles of the Declaration through the structures of the Constitution, it was the creation of the Administrative State, enacted and enforced by means of judicial oligarchy.

In his posthumously published *The Economics of Collective Action*, 1951, Commons directly applied his worldview to a number of pivotal events. While written much later than the traditional Progressive Era, this work gives deep insight into Commons' vision of the social organism as it demonstrated the manner by which he analyzed and approved of overt acts of force undertaken in large part as a result of his influence.[514] His final work demonstrates his attempt to rationalize his worldview in light of the several events of the first half of the twentieth century. With due regard for his work as "...a participant and investigator for sixty years...", the logic of the work is a curious exercise in the *non sequitur*.[515]

Commons characterized this work as pivoting around the administration of credit, agriculture, and capital-labor,

---

511   Ely, *Social Aspects*, 9.
512   Commons, *Social Reform*, 3.
513   Commons, *Social Reform*, 73 – 74, Sic.
514   The last chapter "Valuations" was written in 1944. Kenneth H. Parsons "Editor's Preface" in John R. Commons, *The Economics of Collective Action*, (New York: The Macmillan Company, 1951) vii. Commons' influence previously detailed.
515   Commons, *Collective Action*, 285.

"three economic features" that he defined as "strategic and decisive"[516] He summarized his analysis thusly:

> The science of political economy [which had]
> the purpose of liberating the inventive genius
> of individuals from the restrains of
> feudalism... has become... an investigation of
> how to prevent the former military restraints
> from suppressing again the freedom of
> individuals.[517]

He decried the increase of "administrative commissions or boards [that] could easily become a large step toward complete fascism, socialism, or communism" in his conclusion, yet appears to have been unaware that he had affirmed the basis for all such authoritarian collectivism in his previous examination.[518]

The bulk of his tripartite analysis is contained in Part IV of the work, "Public Administration in Economic Affairs". By way of example, he offered a 'case study' regarding one portion of the "New Deal", analyzing the Agricultural Adjustment Act of 1933. This act, when placed in practice, precipitated one of the more pivotal – yet ultimately impotent – Supreme Court decisions regarding the appropriate limitations on the authority of Congress in the life of an individual, especially as justified by utilitarian – that is collectivist – rationale.[519]

United States v. Butler (1936) was among the last defenses against wholesale collectivism prior to its direct

---

516   Commons, *Collective Action*, 285.
517   Commons, *Collective Action*, 286.
518   Commons, *Collective Action*, 289.
519   *United States v. Butler* became moot with the passage of the Agricultural Adjustment Act of 1938 and the elevation of Harlan Stone to Chief Justice in 1941, leading directly to *Wickard v. Filburn*. The broader shift in Supreme Court acquiescence towards 'New Deal' legislation around this time is certainly proximate to the argument, but not keeping with the socio-intellectual thrust of this thesis. Cf. James A. Henretta, "Charles Evans Hughes and the Strange Death of Liberal America," *Law and History Review* 24, no. 1 (2006): 115–71.

successor *Wickard v. Filburn*.[520] The substance of the 1933
Agricultural Adjustment Act was the implementation of a tax
on the processing of agricultural product with the proceeds of
that tax to be distributed to farmers, contingent upon their
willingness to deliberately reduce production. The ostensible
purpose of the Act was "...to relieve the existing national
economic emergency by increasing agricultural purchasing
power..." meaning simply, supply-side market manipulation
by means of artificial scarcity, or "...the Secretary of
Agriculture shall have power (1) To provide for reduction in
the acreage or reduction in the production for market, or
both, of any basic agricultural commodity...."[521] The Hughes
Court (1930 – 1941) struck down the Act on the grounds that
the Act amounted to a tax that was "but [a] means to an
unconstitutional end". Justice Owen Roberts' (1875 – 1955)
majority opinion held that agricultural production was
beyond federal power, being a matter for the States.[522]

Commons side-stepped the constitutional substance
of the ruling. In his perspective, Roberts reasoned from the
extreme whereas the minority opinion – authored by at-the-
time-Associate Justice Harlan Stone (1872 – 1946) –
reasoned from "an actual case statistically located
somewhere between the extremes."[523] The central issue, in
Commons' view, was whether or not it was appropriate for
Congress to employ economic coercion in addition to the
traditional application of physical force; he opined in the
affirmative.

Commons noted that the facts of this case represented
something "entirely new, the restriction of food supply,
symbolized by the extreme case of the slaughter of six

---

520   United States Solicitor General v. William M. Butler et al.,
297 U.S. 1 (1936).
521   "Agricultural Adjustment," 73d Congress, Session I, Chapter
25, May 12, 1933, Part 2, Section 8. Pub. L. 73-10. Accessed January
27, 2025:
https://govtrackus.s3.amazonaws.com/legislink/pdf/stat/48/STATUT
E-48-Pg31.pdf. The Agricultural Adjustment Act of 1933 was signed
into law by Franklin D. Roosevelt May 12, 1933.
522   "United States v. Butler," *Oyez.org*, Accessed January 27,
2025: https://www.oyez.org/cases/1900-1940/297us1.
523   Commons, *Collective Action*, 214.

million pigs by administrative process... in order to maintain the price of hogs."[524] Though he referenced the threat of totalitarianism citing Roberts, Commons dismissed these concerns as merely "[a]n emotional result of reasoning from extremes."[525] To state the matter succinctly, Commons excused the deliberate creation of *food scarcity* as a way of deliberately increasing food prices during a period of high unemployment, with an appeal to "a credit emergency."[526] He justified his dismissal of Roberts' opinion and agreement with Stone's by using the claim that "Collectivism and individualism are not incompatible except when reasoning from extremes at either end...."[527] In Commons' view, *artificial food scarcity* induced to increase prices during a period of *extreme unemployment and starvation*, to address a 'credit emergency', was not related to the appropriate authority of government in the lives of individuals, but rather "...is the problem of administrative economics in actual cases rather than unconstitutionality in all cases."[528]

Commons claimed that his 'administrative economics' lay the foundation for the "fourth branch of American government" – that is, the Administrative State – and bestowed this administration with precedence over independence.[529] "An administrative department alone can meet promptly the "adjustments" needed to ward off inflations and deflations of prices, or bring relief promptly in time of deflation."[530] In his view, the political process was too unwieldy or took too long to respond to market forces; he did not address why or if addressing market forces is a legitimate function of government under the principles of the Declaration.

By this late stage in both Commons' life and Progressive reforms, the *de facto* practice of government presumed that meddling with markets was entirely within

524 Commons, *Collective Action*, 219 – 220.
525 Commons, *Collective Action*, 220.
526 Commons, *Collective Action*, 228 – 229.
527 Commons, *Collective Action*, 237.
528 Commons, *Collective Action*, 237 – 238.
529 Commons, *Collective Action*, 236.
530 Commons, *Collective Action*, 231. Sic.

legitimate authority, in large part due to Woodrow Wilson who is addressed much later. Commons clearly approved of this presumption but more than this, he also included a corollary. In the same manner that he and Ely both spoke of sociology, Commons elevated statistics to something like a moral compass regarding his administrative State. "It is only by the use of statistics that the essential distinctions in economic investigations can be made for the guidance of administrative action."[531]

Again reflecting Ely, Commons substantially agreed with Stone's assertion that "...the court, having the last word in affirming or preventing the use of physical force....is limited only by its own sense of self-restraint.[532] In his view, not only was there no limit to the rights of the State, but the only limit to the court was the court itself. Combining this wholly unaccountable rendition of *anti-Constitutionalism* with his irrational infatuation with statistics, Commons constructed his own 'organic act' to rationalize the power of the Administrative State: "Justice Stone's opinion lays the legal foundations for this regulation of private collective action by administrative departments... while the modern statistical science lays the economic foundations."[533]

It is reasonable to insert that the concept of statistics is inherently collective in its scope and application. Were the 'average' person to be encountered, it is likely that one would wonder after that person's health. The 'average' person has slightly less than two eyes, an ovary, a testicle, and slightly less than four limbs. The 'average' American is the parent of one whole child, and ninety-four percent of a second child.[534] The 'average' is an often inconvenient convenience, little more than a numerical ghost that reduces particulars into generalities at the cost of detail, nuance, and specificity – the illegitimate universalization of generality. Simply put, where

---

531   Commons, *Collective Action*, 233.
532   Commons, *Collective Action*, 223.
533   Commons, *Collective Action*, 238.
534   "Average number of own children under 18 in families with children in the United States from 1960 to 2023," *Statista*, Accessed January 27, 2025:
https://www.statista.com/statistics/718084/average-number-of-own-children-per-family/.

statistics may characterize a collective it says nothing of an individual, and less of the true state of things. As Mark Twain and others would remind, statistics is the third of three lies. Statistics is, however, exceedingly useful in rationalizing a preferred ideal – such as abusive acts against individuals that objectively amount to seizure of property, artificial inflation of necessities' pricing, and arbitrary diktat of the *Politburo*.

In keeping with all renditions of expert-worshiping elitism governed by decree of the ascended, Commons engaged in the practice of 'retroactive continuity', colloquially known as the 'retcon' but far more appropriately defined as gaslighting. He stated that a complete policy reversal in later years, wherein the Department of Agriculture demanded greater production after having *forced* less, was neither a "reversal nor a confession". He excused it as merely a "...consistent policy of "adjustment" to the credit cycle...by means of administrative process...."[535]

Such a privilege claimed for experts is prescient of Nixon's total usurpation of the rule of law in his famous statement that "when the president does it... that means that it is not illegal" or, *rex non potest peccare*.[536] Commons made no effort in this work to address the long term effects of *unpredictability* on markets, credit, and contracts, to say nothing of law and liberty. It is apparent that he did not consider the perspective of the individual farmer who is fined one year for producing too much, then fined the next for not producing enough; any practicable freedom in such a climate is impossible as Madison foretold.[537] He defended this arbitrary application of coercion as 'administrative process' but crucially described the manner by which such usurpations

---

535   Commons, *Collective Action*, 230.
536   Lit. "The King can do no wrong;" Congress.Gov, "Transcript of David Frost's Interview with Richard Nixon, 1977," *Teaching American History*, Accessed January 28, 2025: https://www.congress.gov/116/meeting/house/110331/documents/H MKP-116-JU00-20191211-SD408.pdf.
537   Cf. "The internal effects of a mutable policy are still more calamitous. It poisons the blessing of liberty itself." James Madison [Attributed], "The Senate," *Federalist no. 62*, 1788, in *Constitution*, 2012, 534.

fade to background radiation or, those practices that are perpetuated as 'just the way it is'.

His described his process as 'administrative law' based on the presumption that the courts will not interfere with the inherent coercion of any given policy. He expanded his analysis of this factor, which he termed 'custom', by extolling its virtues as "...the modern development on the legal side of the American separation of powers."[538]

> If, in addition, [administrative law] has discretion in issuing orders to individuals, the reason why the latter do not challenge the orders by appeal to the Court for review and reversal is because they and their lawyers expect that the courts will decide as they had formerly decided. In this respect the administrative "orders" are analogous to the force of custom.[539]

One interprets the above as a somewhat pedantic manner for defending the force exercised by a wholly unaccountable, inscrutable, and functionally unassailable unelected legislative body. Simply, he gave leave for any act at all because a crime unchallenged becomes legal; a dramatic expansion of the power in *stare decisis*. The decrees of the fourth-branch cannot be challenged in court and, there being no other legal mechanism of redress beyond the impotent petition, are therefore the arbiters of custom. This custom has the force of law as evidenced by both *United States v. Butler* and *Wickard v. Filburn*; the faceless 'experts' are imbued with the power to utterly devastate a man's life on a whim by *control over his food*, and Commons justified this power with a simplistic appeal to 'statistics'.

It must be stated as forcefully as possible that this arrangement utterly revokes the possibility of consent of the governed. Unknown bodies of men were given unknowable license to exercise inscrutable, self-contradictory, and unchallengeable power over arbitrary numbers of individuals,

---

538   Commons, *Collective Action*, 228.
539   Commons, *Collective Action*, 225.

justified with a hand-wave of 'statistics' and 'emergency'. In essence, by the middle twentieth century, American civilization had traded one tyrant for one thousand. Commons derided opposition to this arrangement with the claim that "...the method of extreme cases creates absurdities...."[540] He did not appear to allow for the reality that *all* acts of force, that being the only real tool of government as even Commons attested, are definitively extreme cases.[541]

Whether temporarily prohibited by *United States v. Butler*, or disastrously enshrined into precedent – custom – by *Wickard v. Filburn*, it is a supreme act of elitist disregard to tell the victim of government-enforced-robbery that his complaints are mere absurdities. This is the inescapable nature of utilitarianism as a worldview – one who complains against the administrators is of the lesser part, it is good that he should suffer for the 'happiness' of the greater.[542]

The mechanisms as exemplified in Commons' analysis of *United States v. Butler*, the manner by which decisions are made and enacted, amount to nothing more complex than unaccountable and arbitrary judicial oligarchy. This paradigm is by no means limited to agriculture, but expands through economic control to encompass the entirety of the State. In Abram L. Harris' 1952 summation, published shortly after Commons' final work, the arbitrary nature of this oligarchy was made plain.

> In Commons' welfare state the enterprise system operating by means of relatively free markets tends to be supplanted by a capitalism regulated by administrative bureaucracy. ...While nominally retaining a separation of powers, this state is in fact based upon judicial supremacy, since the courts are made the final arbiters of what is reasonable in conflicts. But what, one is prone to ask, are

---

540   Commons, *Collective Action*, 232.

541   Cf. Commons, *Social Reform*, 54.

542   Cf. "Individual sacrifices should be demanded for the good of others." Richard T. Ely, *Social Aspects of Christianity*, 128.

> the economic principle courts should employ
> in arriving at a judgment of reasonable in
> specific value cases? Commons offers no such
> principles. Reasonable value is what the
> courts say it is[543]

Commons did not offer principles because the social organism, a product of evolution and historicism, rejects the entire concept of principles; utility has only the 'happiness' of the greater part – as arbitrarily determined by the expert. Principles as exhaustively demonstrated are transcendent, universal, and wholly unchanging; the imaginary world of solipsism is in so many ways a complete and polar opposite to this idea. In application, social organism thinking necessitates the rule of the expert; in the administration that Commons conceived, created, and analyzed this expresses simply as the very judicial oligarchy against which so many warned.[544]

Returning again to Commons' earlier career illuminates the reasoning and worldview that informed the calculus that he used to justify the abuses of the Administrative State. Like Ely, Gladden, Rauschenbusch, et al, anything at all is possible and equitable if it can be credited to the good of the social organism; all for the greater good, the cost is no object.

Commons' 1913 *Labor and Administration* is a collection of some of his earliest articles collated into chapters. His introduction provides a clear insight into his worldview, most especially the repetition of his earlier position that rights are products of legislatures, not given by

---

543   Abram L. Harris, "John R. Commons and the Welfare State.", *Southern Economic Journal*, 19 no. 2 (1952): 233.

544   Jefferson on the road to destruction: Consolidation then corruption via the federal judiciary; Thomas Jefferson, "Thomas Jefferson to Nathaniel Macon, 23 November 1821," *Founders Online,* National Archives, https://founders.archives.gov/documents/Jefferson/03-17-02-0549. Cf. Aaron N. Coleman, "Anti-Federalists and the Roots of Judicial Oligarchy," *Law and Liberty*, August 5, 2020, https://lawliberty.org/anti-federalists-and-the-roots-of-judicial-oligarchy/.

the Creator. Here, in the context of 'labor laws', he stated that
"[a] law creates an abstract right – an empty ideal", and
declared that the history of labor law is a field for "the
utilitarian idealist, who sees [questions arising in the field] as
they are…. His constructive problem is not so much the law
and its abstract rights, as administration and its concrete
results…."[545]

 Commons reflected on his own paradigm, what he
saw as the unifying sentiments across his various articles.
"Through them run the notions of utilitarian idealism... a
programme of progressive labor within social
organization."[546] His estimation of social organization
presumed the oversight of a committee or administration –
the 'community organizer' before the term came in vogue.
This organization operates on the same views espoused by
both Gladden's claim that government's *raison d'être*
according to the Declaration is "...a radical defect in the
habitual thinking of the average American..." and Ely's
position that duty to the State exceeds the value of
inalienable rights.[547] Commons rendered this superiority of
the social organism as "the ethics of utilitarian idealism"; he
contrived a duty for the individual to "...make and sell a
product of more value to society and more cost to himself
than the price he gets for it."[548]

 Despite his claimed advocacy on the part of labor,
Commons appeared to be either unaware of or unconcerned
with the fundamental nature of labor. Labor is to give one's
most precious resource – time, and to expend one's most
limited capacity – health. In Commons' paradigm one ought
to give these things over, not for his own subsistence or to
improve the lot of his children, but rather for the nebulous
benefit of the social organism. One ought not only to prefer
society over himself as determined by 'the administration',
but one ought to be diminished by the sacrifice. While all
illustrations of the social organism amount to the Borg,

---

545 Commons, *Labor and Administration*, v.
546 Commons, *Labor and Administration*, vi. Sic.
547 Gladden, *The New Idolatry*, 195, 198 – 199; Ely, *The Social Law*, 175.
548 Commons, *Labor and Administration*, 4.

Commons' in particular reduces men further. In his anthropology, men become more like ants than organs; should some of them drown to float the colony it is not unfortunate, it is ideal.

While each of the men thus far analyzed fit well within Thomas Leonard's distillation of social organism thinking, few were as directly influential in its application in such a clear manner.

> The Progressive intellectual commitments were (1) a belief in the power of scientific social inquiry; (2) a belief in the legitimacy of social control, which derives from a conception of society as an organism prior to and more important than its constituent individuals; and (3) a belief in the efficacy of social control via state scientific management…. The idea is that benignly motivated experts should interpose themselves, in the name of the greater good, to better represent the interests of the industrial poor, for whom many reformers felt contempt as much as pity.[549]

Commons' particular variation of this contempt was clearly manifest in his 1907 *Race and Immigrants* in which he applied his anthropology to the concept of human resources. He based his argument in the same fetid ground as Ely: "Race differences are established in the very blood and physical constitution."[550] The work is wholly collectivist in scope, analysis, and purpose. Repeating yet again Gladden's position regarding unsocial conduct, Commons declared that when individuals "sink below the level of joint participation" they must be recognized as "belonging to a defective or criminal or pauper class" and social programs aimed at these

---

549   Thomas C. Leonard, ""More Merciful and Not Less Effective": Eugenics and American Economics in the Progressive Era," *History of Political Economy*, 35 no. 4, (2003), 706.

550   John R. Commons, *Races and Immigrants in America*, (London: The Macmillan Company, 1907), 7.

classes are "not on the basis of their rights, but on... charity or punishment."[551]

Presaging Rakove, Commons introduced his work with the same elitist trick regarding what Jefferson 'really meant'. ""All men are created equal." So wrote Thomas Jefferson, and so agreed with him the delegates from the American Colonies. But we must not press them too closely nor insist on the literal interpretation of their words."[552] Later, in addressing 'the negro question', Commons argued that slavery had selected, via hardship and survival, the most "docile and hardy", to claim that while "[o]ther races of immigrants... have been civilized – the negro has only been domesticated." He lamented that the Civil War, wherein he claimed 'the negro' had not participated, had unleashed this unsuitable race upon American society. Commons placed the blame for what he called the "fallacies of self-government" on the "dogmatism" of "a theory of abstract equality and inalienable rights".[553] True to form, Commons' advocated greater government meddling in society, in place of inalienable rights:

> Therefore, if [tropical] races are to adopt that industrious life which is a second nature to races of the temperate zones, it is only through some form of compulsion. The negro could not possibly have found a place in American industry had he come as a free man....[554]

John Chasse, in his rush to present Commons as "A Worker's Economist", found himself playing the role of the crisis manager rather than historian. The charge of racism consistently meets commentary such as the above; indeed a great majority of work from Commons' time may be dismissed with this simplistic epithet, yet Chasse took a far weaker escape. To excuse this highly embarrassing work, he simply declared that "the book is out of date" for no reason other than having been based on discredited ideas, and he

---

551   Commons, *Race and Immigrants*, 2.
552   Commons, *Race and Immigrants*, 1.
553   Commons, *Races and Immigration*, 40 – 43.
554   Commons, *Races and Immigration*, 136, 141.

dismissed the reasoning therein by claiming that it "plays no role in the development of Commons's thought."[555] Chasse does not address the inescapable reality that Commons' work and policy-activism *derived* from these 'discredited ideas'; it is hardly reasonable to dismiss one branch, champion another, and condemn the root-stock.

Chasse adopted this response because, other than his obvious ideological alignment with Commons, he responded to something like a straw-man. Chasse did not cite the "writers" who apparently decried Commons' racial theses, but rather attempted to explain away the rather clear condescension that runs throughout the work. Benevolent or not, Commons most assuredly viewed certain classes and races as inferior to his preferred Anglo-Saxons, and this work advocates for top-down policies *on that basis*. To undertake to 'civilize the inferior races' is hardly more humanitarian than to advocate their sterilization or imprisonment. It may be debatable whether or not Commons was a 'racist' in the twenty-first century overloaded sense, but it remains clear that he most assuredly held elitist views throughout his career; Chasse's facile attempt to gaslight his readers notwithstanding. While Chasse did make some vague references to Commons' connection to Ely, Rauschenbusch, and the Social Gospel, he did not appear to recognize the deep connection between that worldview and eugenics – if more understated in Commons than the others. To state that *Races and Immigration* played no role in the development of Commons' thought is a misdirection; it did not play a role in his thought, *it was an integral expression of it*.

Commons rejected the substance of the Declaration and wholeheartedly embraced the paradigm of the social organism. While he frequently made references to freedom and the individual, his reasoning and policy proposals consistently advocated collectivism – both in measurement and practice – and administration, always administration. As previously stated, much of his work is an exercise in the *non sequitur*, and this arose as a direct and inescapable product of his historicist, evolutionary worldview. Where he made

---

555   Chasse, *A Worker's Economist*, 92. Sic.

numerous valid observations – wage-slavery being chief among them – his answer was invariably more regulation, more administration, more collectivization, more power in the hands of the beneficent, enlightened, expert few. Though he gave lip service to the danger of totalitarianism, his incoherent philosophy in practice is ultimately indistinguishable from it. It is no surprise; one who views rights as nothing more than grants of government and the State as supreme, becomes unable to recognize the inverse relationship of virtue and power – grand democratic claims notwithstanding.[556] This is the worldview that Commons bequeathed to his students who would go on to dictate and direct the substance of American Civilization throughout the twentieth century.

Commons' influence was certainly not limited to the various bureaucracies that his students would both create and staff. His ideals regarding the expert administrator appear to have resonated – among the expert administrators, one cynically interjects – and are mirrored in a plurality of thinkers both from his and from subsequent generations. One such comrade-in-worldview carried portions of Commons' cosmology outside of academia, social agitations, and politics, and into the realms of *haute couture* ('society') in addition to the the arena of people versus government: mass-media and journalism.

Pulitzer prize laureate, and 1964 Presidential Medal of Freedom recipient Walter Lippmann (1889 – 1974) may be only surpassed in grand influence by names like Henry Kissinger (1923 – 2023) or Walter Cronkite (1916 – 2009). Variously dubbed "the most influential American journalist of the 20th century"; "the father of modern journalism"; and "a guru on nearly every public issue," Lippmann's influence extended beyond journalism through presidential speech and policy writing.[557] As Ronald Steel would state quite

---

556   Cf. Benjamin Franklin, "To Messrs. The Abbés Chalut and Arnaud," April 17, 1787.

557   Sidney Blumenthal, "Walter Lippmann and American Journalism Today," *Open Democracy*, October 31, 2007, Accessed February 3, 2025: https://www.opendemocracy.net/en/ walter_lippmann_and_american_journalism_today/, sic; Manhattan

succinctly in his 1980 biography, "Walter Lippmann had left his fingerprints on, and even helped mold, almost every major issue in American life over six decades."[558]

A highly relatable cynic – altogether the pragmatist – Lippmann was mentored at Harvard by both William James (1842 – 1910) and Graham Wallas (1858 – 1932).[559] James was yet another 'father' – of American psychology – whereas Wallas was deeply influential in the creation of political psychology, in large part due to Darwin's influence, as well as having "had a profound impact" on Charles Merriam, briefly addressed later.[560] Lippmann credited both James and Wallas as having "illustrate[d] the changing focus of political thought" via psychology, and his work betrays Wallas' thinking in psychology, itself borrowing from James' estimation of pragmatism.[561] Wallas' *The Great Society*, 1914 was dedicated to Lippmann and the term "The Great Society" frequently appeared in Lippmann's work, including his 1924 title *The Good Society*.

The somewhat credulous James, a member of the lunatic Blavatsky's Theosophical Society from 1891, wrote

---

Rare Book Company, "Lippmann, Walter. Public Opinion," Accessed February 3, 2025: https://www.manhattanrarebooks.com/pages/books/2869/walter-lippmann/public-opinion; Ronald Steel, *Walter Lippmann and the American Century*, (Boston: Little Brown, 1980), xii.

558   Steel, *Walter Lippmann*, xii.

559   Lippmann was also famously mentored by George Santayana (1863 – 1952) who is generally omitted for brevity. Cf. Steel, *Walter Lippmann*, 1980; John Patrick Diggins, "From Pragmatism to Natural Law: Walter Lippmann's Quest for the Foundations of Legitimacy," *Political Theory* 19, no. 4 (1991): 519 – 538.

560   Bekah Dillon, "Psyography: William James," Archive accessed February 2, 2025: https://web.archive.org/web/20141124184737/http://faculty.frostburg.edu/mbradley/psyography/williamjames.html; William F. Stone, and David C. Smith. "Human Nature in Politics: Graham Wallas and the Fabians." *Political Psychology* 4, no. 4 (1983): 694.

561   Walter Lippmann, *A Preface to Politics*, (New York: Mitchell Kennerley, 1913), 83; Stone and Smith, "Human Nature", 697 – 699. Cf. Tom Arnold-Forster, "Walter Lippmann and Public Opinion." *American Journalism* 40, no. 1 (2023): 53.

The Meaning of Truth in 1909.[562] This curious work, that frequently referenced John Dewey, claimed that pragmatism "...is *compatible* with solipsism" though it denied any "special affinity" with the perspective.[563] The working definition, the answer to the implied titular question as far as can be understood from such a meandering work, was that "[t]he truth of an idea will then mean only its workings, or that in it which by ordinary psychological laws sets up those workings...."[564] This rendition is compatible with the *pragmatick* definition of pragmatism, and is most certainly apparent in Lippmann's work.[565] As Steel noted, "James provided an intellectual justification" for what he claimed was Lippmann's affinity for iconoclasm.[566] Lippmann's 1913 *Preface to Politics* clearly reflected the promiscuous, utilitarian estimation of truth, especially as applied: "No moral judgment can decide the value of life. No ethical theory can announce any intrinsic good. The whole speculation about morality is an effort to find a way of living which men who live it will instinctively feel is good."[567]

The phrasing around 'instinct' is neither rhetorical nor incidental. Graham Wallas' 1908 *Human Nature in Politics* pivots about the concept. Stone and Smith noted in 1983 that "[t]he primary psychological mechanism that follows from the theory of natural selection is the instinct."[568] Wallas' treatment of this instinct was to place it first among all factors in human decision making, especially regarding

---

562   Jason Ānanda Josephson Storm, "A Theosophical Discipline: Revisiting the History of Religious Studies," *Journal of the American Academy of Religion* 89, no. 4, (December 2021): 1153; Helena Blavatsky (1831 – 1891), a notorious 'spiritualist' con-artist or cult leader, depending on perspective.

563   William James, *The Meaning of Truth: A Sequel to 'Pragmatism'*, (London: Longmans, Green, and Co., 1909), 215. Sic.

564   James, *Truth*, xvi.

565   A pun based in Johnson's definition: "Meddling; impertinently busy; assuming business without leave or invitation."; "pragmatick," *A Dictionary of the English Language*, by Samuel Johnson. 1773. Accessed February 3, 2025: https://johnsonsdictionaryonline.com/1773/pragmatical_adj.

566   Steel, *Walter Lippmann*, 18.

567   Lippmann, *Preface to Politics*, 200.

568   Stone and Smith, "Human Nature," 698.

political decision making, and derived from William James'
similar *ordo cognoscendi*. "Impulse, it is now agreed, has an
evolutionary history of its own earlier than the history of
those intellectual processes by which it is often directed and
modified."[569] Wallas reduced *all* decision making under the
aegis of impulse or instinct, and dismissed arguments to the
contrary as an intellectual fallacy. As Smith and Stone noted,
drawing from many of Wallas' other works, his cosmology
amounted to something like a soft Darwinian determinism.[570]

Wallas' 'soft' determinism is so called because he
assumed that awareness of the instinct would then allow for
the interpolation of reason.[571] Crucially however, he based his
analysis of instinct in a fundamentally utilitarian estimation
of ends versus means and declared that "...most of the
political opinions of most men are the result, not of reasoning
tested by experience, but of unconscious or half-conscious
inference fixed by habit."[572] With due sympathy for the
myriad of details that reinforce such a conclusion as this –
humanity does so often appear little better than a mass of
prejudiced automatons – such an anthropology inescapably
assumes and requires the existence of a group, a *class*, of
enlightened technicists who know another's mind better than
he himself and Wallas eulogized just such a class "...who are
born to instruct, to guide, and to preserve...."[573] Despite the
delicate and valuable possibility of one assisting another to
improve his own self-awareness, the presumption that the
majority *require* the direction of those who can see the
'unconscious' is definitively elitist. Indeed, Stone and Smith
defined *Human Nature* as having "debunked the liberal myth

---

569   Citing William James, *Principles of Psychology*, vol. II;
      Graham Wallas, *Human Nature in Politics*, (London: Archibald
      Constable and Co Ltd., 1908), 25.
570   Citing Wallas, *Our Partnership*, 1948 "...useless to try to
      make a right-handed boy ambi-dextrous....";   Stone and Smith,
      "Human Nature," 698. Sic.
571   Stone and Smith, "Human Nature," 698, 699.
572   "...means and ends... [based in] survival, in the past, of the
      'fittest'" Wallas, *Human Nature*, 25; 103.
573   Wallas, *Human Nature*, 173 – 177.

of the rational, self-conscious citizen...." based on the presumption of the unconscious mind.[574]

Humorously enough, despite Wallas' carefully constructed elitist-optimism based on fatalistic determinism, he effectively predicted the progression in sentiment that his star pupil – Lippmann – would display in his thinking: from naive idealism to resigned cynicism resulting from experiencing the emotionally driven decision-making of the people.[575] Regarding Wallas' influence on the development of Lippmann's anthropology, especially in reference to the legitimacy of authority, little more can be said than to present the former's thinly veiled seditious scientism from which he justifies, in effect, the realization of Plato's so-called 'noble lie' in the adoption of H.G. Wells' "aristocracy of trained men of science."[576]

> ...our growing knowledge... may be expected to change not only our ideals of political conduct but also the *structure of our political institutions*.

> I have already pointed out that the democratic movement which produced the constitutions under which most civilized nations now live, was inspired by a purely intellectual conception of human nature which is becoming every year more unreal to us. If, it may then be asked, representative democracy was introduced under a mistaken view of the conditions of its working, will not its introduction prove to have been itself a mistake?

> [Analysis requires] considering what are the ends representation is intended to secure....

---

574   Stone and Smith, "Human Nature," 699.
575   Stone and Smith, "Human Nature," 700 – 701.
576   Wallas, *Human Nature*, 201.

> The first end may be roughly indicated by the
> word consent.[577]

Lippmann reduced not only representation, but also
the concept of liberty under Plato's lie. He wrote that Plato's
contribution was to "...formulate the dispositions of men in
the shape of ideals....", and this disposition was to be
"...peculiarly inclined to suppress whatever impugns the
security of that to which we have given our allegiance."[578]
Because of this, in Lippmann's argument "[n]o man has ever
thought out an absolute or universal ideal in politics, for the
simple reason that nobody knows enough, or can know
enough, to do it."[579] Resulting from man's hapless agnostic
groping in Lippmann's view, "[t]he word liberty is a weapon
and an advertisement, but certainly not an ideal which
transcends all special aims."[580]

In a decidedly convoluted manner the relativism of
pragmatism, built on psychology produced by Darwinian
determinism and reinforced with technist elitism, lead
Lippmann directly to the concept of the synthetic production
of 'consent', because consent is the *end goal* of government,
not the foundation. This detail is of paramount importance;
Lippmann's ideal of consent, deriving from Wallas' *inversion*
of consent, is such that the government works to create, to
contrive the necessary and sufficient condition from whence
its just powers arise. Lippmann and Wallas' conception of
government sought to employ its power to legitimize the
existence of its power. This authoritarian Ouroboros is
circularity of such magnitude that its practice wholly
castrates the possibility of legitimate authority as defined by
the Declaration. Authority seeking to contrive consent
produces only an ersatz, inferior, and counterfeit 'consent', a
concept known as 'consent by misrepresentation' or more
simply, deception.[581]

---

577   Wallas, *Human Nature*, 199 – 200. Emphasis added.
578   Walter Lippmann, *Liberty and the News*, (New York:
   Harcourt, Brace and Howe, 1920), 20 – 21.
579   Lippmann, *Liberty*, 22.
580   Lippmann, *Liberty*, 24.
581   Cf. "...sovereignty... belongs to the press... from which
   popular consent is "manufactured.""; John Patrick Diggins, "From

Wallas' political imagination of an evolutionary based 'unconscious', of which only the chosen were aware, reinforced James' reduction of 'truth' to 'whatever works' which he based on the same perverse anthropology. "Pragmatism enabled Lippmann to believe that politics could derive its legitimacy from science."[582] This rather incestuous cosmology resulted in the ideal of manufactured consent, upon which Lippmann's 1922 *Public Opinion* rests. That rather monumental work was not however the origin of Lippmann's technist authoritarianism-by-manipulation as that perspective formed quite early.

> As with James and Dewey, Lippmann turned to science rather than to history, to future consequences rather than to past traditions. Estranged from the Newtonian, mechanistic world of the eighteenth-century framers, Lippmann sought to find a new basis of politics in the ideas of an array of twentieth-century thinkers ranging from Freud to Graham Wallas. But whoever he drew on, Lippmann's pragmatic persuasion meant that the legitimacy of government would be based not on its historical origins but on its subsequent performances.[583]

As with the larger portion of progressives, Lippmann's 1913 *Preface to Politics* and his 1914 *Drift and Mastery* both represent a reaction to neo-feudalism, falsely called 'capitalism,' by positing a 'scientific' elitist oligarchy, best defined as technicism.[584]

Pragmatism to Natural Law: Walter Lippmann's Quest for the Foundations of Legitimacy," *Political Theory* 19, no. 4 (1991): 526.

582   John Patrick Diggins, "From Pragmatism," 523.

583   Diggins, "From Pragmatism," 524.

584   The term itself, rather 'technocracy,' is directly related to Edward Bellamy's (1850 – 1898) 1888 utopian work *Looking Backward* which grained its own following, extant today. Cf. James J. Kopp, "Edward Bellamy and the New Deal: The Revival of Bellamyism in the 1930s." *Utopian Studies*, no. 4 (1991): 10–16; H. G. Wells, *The Shape of Things To Come*, (London: Hutchinson & Co., 1935); https://www.technocracyinc.org/. The proper movement under

Drift and Mastery defined the angst of *fin de siècle* in a similar manner to Patrick Deneen's hedonism masquerading as an existential failing of liberalism: "[l]iberalism suffices our lives and the outstanding fact is the decay of authority."[585] In this quite brief chapter, "The Rock of Ages", Lippmann referenced a thesis that he would reiterate fifteen years later as the central argument of *A Preface to Morals* (1929). Effectively, God is dead because science, modernity, and industrial urbanism killed Him, thusly the experimentation of pragmatism is the only response. "Life has overflowed the little systems of eternity.... We can invoke no monumental creeds, because facts smile ironically upon them.... men have to cast aside the old thickset forms of their thinking for suppler experimental ones."[586] Given such a dim view of spiritual authority, and by extension the possibility of transcendent universal principles, Lippmann argued that "[t]he only possible cohesion now is a loyalty that looks forward." Citing Nietzsche, he declared that "...we should not live for our fatherland, but for our children's land."[587]

This futurist credo is not an admonition to be mindful of one's responsibility to one's children as it may appear, but rather an introduction to the same 'take control of evolution' reasoning that characterized social gospel thinking. Rather than accepting the dictates of the predecessors through tradition, Lippmann calls to dictate to posterity by means of social control – as though there were somehow a practical difference between the two. Lippmann's atheistic version of progress was, in practice, indistinguishable from similar theocratic-based conclusions. "We have to deal with [life] deliberately, devise its social organization, alter its tools,

---

the name is at the fringe of greater currents, it is mentioned for the sake of full disclosure, its ideological provenance, and application to later arguments.

585   Walter Lippmann, *Drift and Mastery: An Attempt to Diagnose the Current Unrest.* (Englewood Cliffs, N.J.: Prentice-Hall, Inc., 1961 [1914]), 116. Cf. Patrick Deneen, *Why Liberalism Failed*, 2018.

586   Lippmann, *Drift and Mastery*, 117.

587   Lippmann, *Drift and Mastery*, 147.

formulate its method, *educate and control it*."[588] Lippmann's
view assumed that evolutionary psychology had unveiled a
'subconscious' that is wholly identical to determinism. In
response, Lippmann advocated 'science' and 'mastery' as the
appropriate progressive response to what amounted to an
animalistic, instinct-driven behavioral dynamic.[589]

Even given the superficial contrast to social gospel
origins, Lippmann quickly found himself walking the same
road, and making the same conclusions. Where Ely and
Commons both claimed there was no limit to the power of
the State, Lippmann stated that "[t]he state may encroach
continuously."[590] In his view, this unlimited encroachment –
one might say *infringement* – was but a utilitarian method to
maximize 'self-government'. He believed that democratic
government was mandated "[t]o create a minimum standard
of life below which no human being can fall…. [because]
You can't build a modern nation out of Georgia crackers,
poverty-stricken negroes, the homeless and helpless of the
great cities. They make a governing class essential."[591]

Adjusted for metaphysical leanings, Lippmann
effectively agreed with the delusion behind Ely's attempt to
force love.[592] Where Ely would employ 'coercive
philanthropy', Lippmann advocated for the effective
revocation of independence as a means of 'coercive self-
government'. Both men advocated this absurd and abusive
psychological paradox as a means of forcing society to
conform to their image; one can no more command self-
government than he can dictate love.[593] It is doubtless that
Ely would have voiced little disagreement with the
anthropology that lead Lippmann to this paradox. Rejecting

---

588   Lippmann, *Drift and Mastery*, 147. Emphasis added.
589   Lippmann, *Drift and Mastery*, 148.
590   Lippmann, *Drift and Mastery*, 71.
591   Lippmann, *Drift and Mastery*, 141 – 142. Sic.
592   Cf. Ely, *Social Aspects*, 88, 89 – 92.
593   A psychological paradox is a statement that defies both logic
    and incorporation such as "I command you not to obey me." When
    employed in concert with authority, such mechanisms produce
    extreme dissonance and subsequent psychological trauma. For
    extensive research and analysis, Cf. Jay Haley, *Strategies of
    Psychotherapy*, (New York: Grune & Stratton, Inc., 1963).

the possibility of virtue, he declared that "[m]en will do
almost anything but govern themselves.... they are looking
for some benevolent guardian, be it a "good man in office" or
a perfect constitution, or the evolution of nature. They want
to be taken in charge."[594]

The inevitable pressures of pragmatism coincided
with Lippmann's anthropology. As men cannot govern
themselves, they must be forced into self-government by
means of a technist elite. Due to this necessity, in Lippmann's
paradigm, the necessary function of authority is to enforce
the 'minimum standard of life' or the 'social-safety-net' as it
would come to be known. It is poignant to note that years
encompassing the Great War and Depression – objective
failures of expertise – did not serve to change this view, but
rather Lippmann appears to have become further ensconced
in his technicism. He wrote in his aforementioned Wallas-
induced *An Inquiry into the Principles of the Good Society*,
1937 regarding the social function of the State:

> It would be mere confusion of mind to argue
> that these are not functions of the liberal state.
> They are inherent in its primary function,
> which is to adjust the social order to the
> economy....Yet it is obvious that these
> functions can be performed only by experts
> using specialized technical procedure.[595]

The reference to experts employing technical
procedure is not coincidentally evocative of Commons'
aforementioned analysis of 'custom' via judicial oligarchy,
but rather a result of it. Lippmann cited Commons' 1924
Legal Foundations of Capitalism to support his expert-
controlled society, and he made the same appeal to judicial
oligarchy as a means of enforcing the power of the
bureaucrat.[596] The necessity of the expert bureaucrat in turn

---

594   Lippmann, *Drift and Mastery*, 108.
595   Walter Lippmann, *An Inquiry into the Principles of The
     Good Society*, (Boston: Little, Brown and Company, 1937), 301.
596   Cf. Shaun P. Hargreaves Heap, and Paul Lewis, "Walter
     Lippmann: An Institutionalist for Our Times?" *Journal of
     Institutional Economics*, 20 (2024): e37, specifically note 20;

derived from the 'complexities' of modern democracy, a perspective originating in Wallas' *The Great Society*.[597]

As Lippmann stated in 1925 "...the problems of the modern world appear and change faster than any set of teachers can grasp them..." being much faster than can be incorporated into a curriculum, and therefore the prerogative of the 'political theorist' who "must not assume that the mass has political genius"; political theorists guided by Wallas' psychology.[598] Given economists in the place of teachers, the pedestal of the expert due to rapid changes aligned perfectly with Commons' position that simply, 'due process takes too long', in addition to reinforcing John Dewey's later analyzed educational paradigm.[599] Simply in Lippmann's perspective, "The problems that vex democracy seem to be unmanageable by democratic methods."[600]

Lippmann presumed that modernity was far too complex for a free people. He declared that "a good conscience" is insufficient for the government of "modern society" because, in his pragmatic view, a universal moral code "...in fact, does not exist...."[601] He cited superficial social problems, conflicting interests, and differing opinions as support for ethical relativism; the exceedingly weak claim that because many ethics appear different, universals are a fantasy. Lippmann presumed the omnipotence of government while rejecting the concept of limited authority under Natural Law. As a result of his rendition of pragmatic-relativism, he

---

Lippmann, *The Good Society*, 301 – 302.

597   Arnold-Forster, "Walter Lippmann," 53.

598   Walter Lippmann, *The Phantom Public*, (New York: Harcourt, Brace and Company, 1925), 27; Cf. Arnold-Forster, "Walter Lippmann," 53.

599   Cf. Commons, *Collective Action*, 231. The idea that 'due process takes too long' has recently again become an issue regarding overtly unconstitutional acts of 'administrative law', relying wholly on judicial oligarchy; Cf. David Risselada, "The Disturbing Possibilities of the Rahimi Ruling," *In Defense of Our Nation*, June 24, 2024, Accessed February 5, 2024: https://defenseofournation.com/uncategorized/the-disturbing-possibilities-of-the-rahimi-ruling/.

600   Lippmann, *Phantom Public*, 189 – 190.

601   Lippmann, *Phantom Public*, 28, 35.

simply could not conceive of any realm beyond the authority of government, or any standard beyond what it might decree.

In his estimation, the 'conflicts' facing modern democracy necessitated the bureaucratic overseer because modern complexity obviated the importance of virtue. "These conflicts of interest are problems. They require solution. But there is no moral pattern available from which the precise nature of the solution can be deduced."[602] It is apparent that Lippmann was either unaware of, or had wholly rejected the ideal that one might circumscribe one's own conduct based entirely on whether or not he would have the same thing done to himself. Lippmann's baseless reasoning is a direct product of his pedantic sophistry fueled by the self-infatuation inherent in modernism. In essence, one might say to Lippmann 'Walter, Walter, you are worried and troubled about many things. But one thing is needed.'[603]

Lippmann's cosmology is apparent in *Drift and Mastery*, but was made more plain in his 1929 *A Preface to Morals*. In *Drift and Mastery* he characterized modern society as having "...exorcised many bogeys and laid many superstitions," and added the self-adulation that technological progress had "ben[t] [reality] to our purposes."[604] Lippmann dramatically expanded his version of the anchor-less society – resulting from the loss of the 'bogeys' – in 1929. "Our forefathers had... religion.... they had no doubt that there was an order in the universe which justified their lives because they were part of it. The acids of modernity have dissolved that order...."[605] In place of this antiquated moral authority, the old order, Lippmann merely substituted his own. *A Preface to Morals* was nothing short of a 'humanist theology' necessitated by the "vacancy" left by the collapse of religious authority.[606]

---

602   Lippmann, *Phantom Public*, 34.
603   Cf. Luke 10:41 – 42.
604   Lippmann, *Drift and Mastery*, 177; cf. "bogeys" 151.
605   Walter Lippmann, *A Preface to Morals*, (London: George Allen & Unwin Ltd. 1942 [1929]), 8.
606   The term 'humanistic' is in reference to universal human supremacy – an atheistic but wholly religious world-view having little to no relation to the humanism one might assume from Petrarch or Erasmus. "vacancy" Lippmann, *Morals*, 3.

Introducing what he termed "The Matrix of Humanism", his substitute theology, Lippmann asserted that the "conception of human nature as developing behavior is, of course, accepted by all modern psychologists."[607] He went on to claim that sufficient scientific knowledge of human nature would "achieve in the humanistic culture that which all theologies have tried to achieve...."[608] Building on this claim, Part III of the work "The Genius of Modernity", may be best described as the overt deification of 'science' as a function of industrialization. Given his ultimately hollow epistemology from William James, it is no surprise that Lippmann defined virtue through a collective lens of habit. He reduced all virtue to effective delayed gratification, but specifically collectivist gratification "to live for ends which are transpersonal."[609] In his view, all virtues are nothing but a function of 'happiness' having created habits. He employed this rendition to claim that many 'virtues' are essentially useless vestiges, though he never offered any definition or example of these "residual and obsolete virtues."[610] Under the weight of such convoluted self-congratulatory sophistry, Lippmann missed that one needed thing. As a result of his wholesale rejection of anything transcendent and universal, of any product of a Creator, Lippmann sought to fill his own feeling of vacancy with what one has chosen to term 'the pragmatick theory of government.'[611]

The pragmatick theory of government is functionally indistinguishable from Plato's 'noble lie' embraced as policy; Lippmann's most well-known work is its manifesto. Where Ely spoke of the 'radical defect in the habitual thinking' of the American, Lippmann rejected foundational principles altogether, in favor of his own brand of utility. As yet another

---

607   Lippmann, *Morals*, 171.
608   Lippmann, *Morals*, 175.
609   Lippmann, *Morals*, 224.
610   Lippmann, *Morals*, 226.
611   This is not a spelling error. Cf. "Meddling; impertinently busy; assuming business without leave or invitation.";
"pragmatick," *A Dictionary of the English Language*, by Samuel Johnson. 1773. Accessed February 3, 2025:
https://johnsonsdictionaryonline.com/1773/pragmatical_adj.

vector in the disease of Progressivism, Charles E. Merriam (1847 – 1953) summarized *Public Opinion* in 1932:

> The central feature of the volume is the belief that the democratic fallacy has been its preoccupation with the origin of government rather than with the process and results. More important than the original consent upon which government is assumed to rest, is the continuing process of government and the means by which consent is created.[612]

Merriam claimed that *Public Opinion* "points the way toward the new politics and the new social science that are now slowly taking shape"; these new things are the authoritarian Ouroboros already defined.[613] The 'democratic fallacy' mentioned by Merriam is in practice identical to the "fallacies of self-government" belittled by Commons, including the repudiation of inalienable rights and the necessity for *pragmatickism* – meddling by the impertinent and the uninvited.[614] The pragmatick theory of government is the rule of the expert class.

---

612   Charles E. Merriam, Review, *International Journal of Ethics* 33, no. 2 (1923): 210; Merriam's career is certainly related to this argument, but omitted for brevity. Merriam "… can be seen in virtually every aspect of modern political science ...Merriam symbolized the scientific, behavioral revolt of the early twenties." Raymond Seidelman and Edward J. Harpham, *Disenchanted Realists: Political Science and the American Crisis, 1884 – 1984*, (Albany: State University of New York Press, 1985), 109; Cf. Merriam's dominance in American academic Political Science via the Chicago School in Gabriel A. Almond, *Ventures in Political Science: Narratives and Reflections*, (Boulder: Lynne Rienner, 2002). Merriam cites Lippmann's *Public Opinion*, 312 "The democratic fallacy has been its preoccupation with the origin of government rather than with the processes and results."

613   Merriam, Review, 212. *Public Opinion* cites Merriam regarding the effect of James' soft determinism on the social sciences; 373.

614   Commons, *Races and Immigration*, 40 – 43. Again, in case the previous footnotes were ignored: "pragmatick" means "Meddling; impertinently busy; assuming business without leave or invitation."

Public Opinion fundamentally assumed modernity, collectivism, and 'democracy' – not representation limited by Natural Law. The concept of a self-sufficient, non-dominating and not-dominated Yeoman is utterly foreign to the principle axioms upon which that work is based. In essence, it would appear that Lippmann simply could not fathom a human being living independently from the busy-bodied oversight of a city council, or perhaps a home owners' association. There was no autonomy in Lippmann's paradigm because he reduced agency to social process. "Lippmann's main source remained William James...."[615]

Citing William James' *Principles of Psychology*, "random irradiations and resettlements of our ideas," Lippmann sought to justify solipsism – what he called "fictions" – because "...the real environment is altogether too big, too complex, and too fleeting for direct acquaintance."[616] He explained these fictions as heuristics by which humanity engages with and incorporates their perceptions, in response to their experiences. "For the most part we do not first see, and then define, we define first and then see."[617] Lippmann defined the heuristics as 'stereotypes', an expansion of James' unconscious decision making, and employed the concept as proof that any given citizen was far too parochial to address his role in an ostensible government by the people. Given the weakness of the people at large, "...the common interests very largely elude public opinion entirely and can be managed only by a specialized class whose personal interests reach beyond the locality."[618] People are too stupid to know reality, only the elite can tell them.

> ...in Lippmann's analysis, sovereignty no longer necessarily resides in the legislature as it had been assumed in both Lockean and classical politics, but now belongs to the press and the media in general, institutions that

---

615   Arnold-Forster, "Public Opinion," 57.
616   Walter Lippmann, *Public Opinion*, (New York: Harcourt, Brace and Company, 1922), 16.
617   Lippmann, *Public Opinion*, 81.
618   Lippmann, *Public Opinion*, 310.

shape the very opinions on which citizens
base their decisions and from which popular
consent is "manufactured." Readers
experience the "news" of the day as "episode,
incidents, eruptions," and to the extent that the
public mind is subjected to the techniques of
communication – stereotyping, image
formation, and prejudice – the
"omnicompetent citizen" so precious to
Jefferson is a lost species.[619]

The so-called "omnicompetent citizen" functioned as
Lippmann's 'paper tiger' or straw-man, and was a perversion
of Jefferson's concept of an enlightened citizenry. He
belittled the idea as something of a naive or quaintly bucolic
image extending from a "village" populated by "men who are
jacks of all trades." This citizen, according to Lippmann,
could function well in isolated settings, but resulted in the
"democratic stereotype" where "men looked at a complicated
civilization and saw an enclosed village."[620] He utterly failed
to recognize the fundamental limits of authority and
therefore, in place of the free man who governs his own life
with a say in public concerns, and a 'public' that refrains
from interfering, Lippmann substituted an 'omnicompetent
expert' who governs everything. Lippmann rejected the
concept of society as related in the principles of the
Declaration because he viewed it as too simplistic and
limited. In viewing the mass of simple interactions as his
object, his view became obscured by complexity – he lost the
trees in the forest. "In short, when more complicated rules are
applied to an economy and society that is also more
complicated, expertise is required."[621] In the pragmatick
theory of government, because society is too complex for the
citizen to understand, "[the expert] takes his place in front of
decision instead of behind it."[622]

---

619   Diggins, "From Pragmatism," 526.
620   Lippmann, *Public Opinion*, 273; Cf. Lippmann belittling
    Jefferson's conception of society, 268 – 269.
621   Hargreaves and Lewis, "Walter Lippmann", no page
    numbers.
622   Lippmann, *Public Opinion*, 375.

According to Lippmann, all other theories of government are deficient. All ideals for reform – education, eugenics, ethics, populism, and socialism – are all flawed because they assume the efficacy of the individual. Only the pragmatick theory of government, being the reign of the expert by means of manipulating the press, is capable of directing a complex society.

> These various remedies… all assume that either the voters are inherently competent to direct the course of affairs or that they are making progress toward such an ideal. I think it is a false ideal. …The ideal of the omnicomptetent, sovereign citizen is, in my opinion, such a false ideal. It is unattainable. The pursuit of it is misleading
>
> The individual man does not have opinions on all public affairs, He does not know how to direct public affairs. He does not know what is happening, why it is happening, what ought to happen.[623]

Lippmann likened himself to a pilot among ignorant sailors who mutiny during an emergency. Because the world is unreasonable, attempting to use reason in it is exceedingly difficult. As a result of this, Lippmann rejected the possibility of voluntary cooperation, convincing arguments, or simply letting to live; society is too complex and too important to leave to the people, public opinion is too confused to inform public policy, and the individual too parochial to understand public affairs. "There is no time during mutiny at sea to make each sailor an expert judge of experts."[624] It is unclear from any of his writing whether or not Lippmann ever considered the implications of the power of the expert who is given the power to decide when he is given power, and he clearly did not consider what is to be done when it was the pilot himself who caused the emergency – precipitating the mutiny. He did

---

623   Lippmann, *Phantom Public*, 39.
624   Lippmann, *Public Opinion*, 413.

not understand that the legitimacy of manufactured consent, whatever its aims or intentions, amounts to the cartoonish image of a man ascending into the sky by climbing on his own knees. Lippmann's ship-of-state intends to cruise by means of blowing its own sail.

Lippmann either forgot or ignored the inescapable fact that the presumption of good-faith, especially regarding men of influence in positions of power, is an act of gross imbecility; expertise does not make for infallibility. No human being – neither supervisor, saint, nor senator – can long be trusted with the ability to effect his will upon another. Man is neither angel nor demon, but the diabolical is far easier than the angelic, and yields its fruit much quicker; consent 'takes too long', tyranny is expedient. Had not the anchor chain been cut by the social gospel the ship would have had no need of Lippmann's pilot. Had the American citizenry not looked to power rather than to virtue to solve their ills, it is unlikely that Lippmann's Ouroboros would have taken hold. An expert does not cease to be human; *errare humanum est, perseverare autem diabolicum.*

More than any other man examined in this argument, Walter Lippmann was responsible for the repudiation of the fundamental basis of legitimacy in American authority. His proximity to power and centrality in journalism, which is to say propaganda, imbues his pragmatick theory of government with permeating aspects that cannot be discounted. Where the historicist would argue that truth is confined to the age wherein it is constructed, the pragmatist abandons a definition altogether to conflate verity with utility. Lippmann's version of pragmatism as applied to a contrived public-government relationship, being the manufacture of consent, is indistinguishable from psychological subjugation. Simple pragmatism asserts that the 'truth' is whatever works. The pragmatick theory of government declares that 'truth' is whatever the expert has decreed it to be, as only the expert is qualified to determine ends, what works to achieve them, and the standards by which one might claim that 'it works'; legitimacy by incest.

To be certain, Lippmann was not alone in his preferred organization for society. Among his pragmatick comrades, including the infamous Oliver Wendell Holmes Jr. treated later, John Dewey stands most noted. Where Lippmann influenced the philosophical underpinning of 'modern' journalism, Dewey stood as the source of the paradigm that would come to dominate American public schooling. As is common among collectivist thinkers, the two men demonstrated substantial agreement by means of disagreement.

The so-called Lippmann-Dewey debate is like Darwin v Lamarck or Commons and Ely v Spencer in that it amounts to much ado about nothing. The 'debate' appeared mostly as differences of interpretation between Lippmann's *Public Opinion* and *Phantom Public*, and Dewey's 1927 *The Public and its Problems*. Tony DeCesare defined the alleged disagreement in 2012 as effectively orbiting the two men's differences of opinion regarding the "problem of knowledge". Lippmann effectively believed that the citizenry was incapable of meaningful participation in modern democracy due to incompetence, whereas Dewey held that the increase of "a different kind of competence" would allow for "a more participatory democratic theory and form of life."[625] Where Lippmann stood for the rule of the expert, Dewey claimed that the public could be educated into a globalized understanding of democracy so as to gauge the value of expertise. These are but mere shades of the same paradigm – the so-called *epistocracy*.[626]

The *epistocracy*, or the rule by those who know, is yet another term for the same thing. As Ned O'Gorman argued in 2024 "Both *The Phantom Public* and *The Public and its Problems* assumed that traditional notions of the democratic public [were obsolete]... and therefore could no longer serve

---

625   Tony DeCesare, "The Lippmann-Dewey "Debate" Revisited: The Problem of Knowledge and the Role of Experts in Modern Democratic Theory," *Philosophical Studies in Education*, 43, (2012): 107 – 108.

626   The term is attributed to Jason Brennan, *Against Democracy*, (Princeton: Princeton University Press, 2016). The work, especially the second chapter regarding the influence of misinformation, is a substantial repeat of Lippmann's *Public Opinion*. The concept itself, with its focus on outcomes, is likely yet another variation of pragmatism.

as legitimate sources for political power and democratic order."[627] Both Lippmann and Dewey claimed that modern society was too complex to leave to the public, and thusly turned to the rule of the scientific elite.[628] In essence, the 'debate' was merely a difference in preferred method for going about enacting the same pragmatick theory of government. Where Lippmann would have employed the press to manipulate consent for the oligarchy, Dewey sought to make use of public education to effectively the same ends.

In yet another slight to Jesus' directive to call no man 'father', John Dewey (1859 – 1952) has been called the "father of Progressive Education."[629] As though this were insufficient, in perfectly modernist self-adulatory fashion he was also anointed 'prophet of an educated democracy' in Phillip B. Moore's 2024 biography.[630] Dewey was not merely a deliberately obtuse philosopher, but also deeply instrumental in the creation of both functional and behavioral psychology, in addition to having held the presidencies of both the American Psychological Association and the American Philosophical Association.[631] All of this was outside of, but wholly intermingled with, his injection of pragmatism into the practice of public education in the United States and elsewhere.[632]

---

627   Ned O'Gorman, "How Liberals Lost the Public: Walter Lippmann, John Dewey, and the Critique of 'Traditional Democratic Theory'" *Quarterly Journal of Speech* 110, no. 3 (2024): 432.

628   Cf. O'Gorman, "Liberals Lost the Public," 433 – 434.

629   Erin A. Hopkins, "John Dewey and Progressive Education," *The Journal of Educational Thought* 50, no. 1 (2017), 60; Hopkins claims that Dewey "did not accept the title… as he knew of the complex origins"; Cf. Matthew 23:9. The capitalization of 'Progressive Education' is in the original, and is telling.

630   Philip B. Moore, *John Dewey: Prophet of an Educated Democracy*, (New York: Rutledge, 2024).

631   Moore, *John Dewey*, 2; Charlotte Nickerson, "John Dewey on Education: Impact & Theory," *Simply Psychology*, February 1, 2024, Accessed February 13, 2025: https://www.simplypsychology.org/john-dewey.html.

632   Numerous scholarly sources regarding Dewey's educational paradigm in foreign nations were encountered – Spain, Italy, Mexico, India, Turkey, Japan, and China. This information is omitted as beyond the scope.

Dewey earned his PhD from John's Hopkins in 1884, and regularly published in *The New Republic* – founded by Lippmann and others in 1914.[633] Dewey's years at Hopkins overlap those of Richard Ely and, while no direct affiliation between these two men is apparent in documentation, Lewis Feuer noted an alignment if not provenance between their paradigms in 1959.[634] It is worthy of note that Dewey's older brother Davis Dewey (1858 – 1942) did study directly under Ely, and Dewey most certainly interacted with Woodrow Wilson, also in attendance.[635] Additionally, Dewey studied under Granville Stanley Hall (1844 – 1924), who worked with Henry W. Beecher for a time, studied in Germany like Ely, and earned the first American Doctorate in Psychology under William James at Harvard.[636] It is sufficient to state that Dewey represented a direct connection between William James' lunacy at Harvard, and Richard Ely's sociopathy at Hopkins.

Prior to proceeding it is reasonable to answer a charge leveled in Moore's biography of his 'prophet.' "[Dewey's] style, public attention, and long career allowed people to see in him what they wanted to see, making the Dewey brand into a kind of shibboleth, where the interpretation of his philosophy reveals something about the

---

633   Hopkins, "John Dewey," 60; Benjamin Wright, "A Brief History of the New Republic: From Lippmann to Peretz to Hughes," *Highbrow Magazine*, August 23, 2013. Accessed February 12, 2025: https://www.highbrowmagazine.com/2737-brief-history-new-republic-lippmann-peretz-hughes.

634   Lewis S. Feuer, "John Dewey and the Back to the People Movement in American Thought," *Journal of the History of Ideas* 20, no. 4 (1959): 568, especially note 87.

635   Clifford F. Thies and Gary M. Pequet, "The Shaping of a Future President's Economic Thought: Richard T. Ely and Woodrow Wilson at "The Hopkins,"" *The Independent Review*, 15, no. 2 (Fall 2010): 263, note 13; Moore, *John Dewey*, 24.

636   Moore, *John Dewey*, 25. Hall was also the first president of the American Psychological Association, and a rabid eugenicist; Cf. Kendra Cherry, "Biography of Psychologist G. Stanley Hall," *Verywellmind*, July 27, 2023, Accessed February 14, 2025: https://www.verywellmind.com/g-stanley-hall-biography-2795507. Hall is central to progressive thinking, but to offer a more thorough treatment would extend this argument considerably.

agenda of the person doing the interpretation."[637] This is always true of every argument and therefore a nonsensical statement, yet its use here revealed much. It is accurate to define a philosopher, especially one in the public eye as was Dewey, as something of a professional explainer; one who seeks to locate and illuminate rational connections such that wisdom might be known – and loved. To deliberately obfuscate is hardly the mark of a 'good' philosopher, despite the reputation that the discipline has earned for itself. While Moore used 'shibboleth' in the commonly used sense of a watchword, it is telling that its origin as such resulted in the deaths of those who did not pronounce it correctly.[638] It is demonstrably elitist – as absurd as venerating a naked emperor – to meet critique with the retort that one 'clearly does not understand' a *deliberately* convoluted argument. This, of course, reveals much about the 'agenda' of one who appears to have endeavored to *not* be understood.

Jesus certainly spoke in parables to deliberately conceal his meaning; to adopt the same rhetorical mechanism necessitates divine pretension.[639] Given the thrust of Lippmann's substantial agreement in *Public Opinion* – that the public was too incompetent to direct the public – it would appear that Moore's self-serving 'shibboleth' could be better defined as a 'dog-whistle' for the epistocracy. Only those in-the-know 'get it', and criticisms only arise from ignorant plebeians. Given Dewey's reputation regarding democratic thought, the irony is delicious; given his alignment with Lippmann, there is no irony at all.

The previously referenced Henry Commager declared that Dewey was "...the guide, the mentor, and the conscience of the American people ... it is scarcely an exaggeration to say that for a generation no major issue was clarified until Dewey had spoken"[640] Disregarding what such a claim might

---

637   Moore, *John Dewey*, 2.
638   Judges 12:6.
639   Cf. Mark 4:10 – 12; II Corinthians 10:5.
640   Commager in Patricia M. Shields, "Rediscovering the Taproot: Is Classical Pragmatism the Route to Renew Public Administration?" *Public Administration Review* 68, no. 2 (Mar, 2008): 205; Cf. Henry S. Commager, *The American Mind An Interpretation of American Thought and Character since the 1880s.*

say of Commager's agenda, Dewey's occluded philosophy hardly clarified much at all – a pun. One would posit that Moore's prophet, as presented by Commager, offered the image of a cryptic guru, an enigmatic sage; the Delphic elite of little practical use. Dewey was, like Deepak Chopra, Kenneth Copeland, Marshall Appelwhite, or L. Ron Hubbard, a flimflam man.

Whatever epithets might be launched in his direction, both Commager and Moore were essentially correct in the broadest thrust of their words. Dewey's 'brand' was effective. As the stand-first to Peter Gibbon's 2019 "Portrait" declared, "[h]is ideas altered the education of children worldwide", and the panegyric that follows claimed that Lyndon Johnson credited Dewey in the creation of his monster society.[641] This is corroborated by Patricia Shields who demonstrated in 2008 that Dewey's pragmatism was fundamental to the creation of administrative law in the United States.[642] This vision of pragmatism is inextricably bound in his pedagogy, and its legacy. "Dewey's ideas on education and his philosophy still influence American thinking and schooling. He sees society, more than family, as the influential educator of character...."[643]

This detail – *society* as the educator of character – represents yet another absurdist tableau of a man pulling himself up by his bootstraps. Virtue or vice, being the substance of character, comprise the atoms from which society is made – much like the group being made of individuals. Society is made of individuals' character, to elevate society in this manner is not only a *non-sequitur*, but is also fundamentally incompatible with the principles of the founding world-view. This is to say Dewey and his pedagogy

(New Haven: Yale University Press, 1950), 100.

641   Peter Gibbon, "John Dewey: Portrait of a Progressive Thinker," *Humanities* 40, no. 2 (Spring 2019). Gibbon used the term 'Great Society', itself deeply reminiscent of both Lippmann and Wallas, evoking images of condescending utopianism.

642   Patricia M. Shields, "Rediscovering the Taproot: Is Classical Pragmatism the Route to Renew Public Administration?" *Public Administration Review* 68, no. 2 (March, 2008): 205-21.

643   Madonna Murphy, "Maritain Explains the Moral Principles of Education to Dewey." *Educational Horizons* 83, no. 4 (2005): 284.

were, outside of any other arguable characterization, fundamentally collectivist.

Dewey's 'brand' of elitism was based on the wholesale rejection of transcendent universals, or indeed even the possibility of such an anchor. His cosmology entirely embraced the thrust of Lippmann's *Preface to Morals*. "Dewey's pragmatism defines truth as a tentative assertion derived from human experience; it rejects metaphysical absolutes. If something works, it is true and useful; if it no longer works, it is no longer true."[644] Obviously, the subjugation of truth to what works betrays the hubris inherent in failing to recognize that it may not have worked for no other reason than that someone simply did it wrong.

The repudiation of transcendent universals is somewhat ironic for the necessity of the vocabulary employed. This argument holds no reference to the briefly fashionable 'transcendentalism' of the mid-nineteenth century; agrarian similarities are mere coincidence because an integral corollary to the independent dignity of the individual is that each will find his own fulfillment – whether that is in the nature of Walden Pond, or elsewhere.[645] The term is necessary in reference to Dewey because Moore placed the beginning of his intellectual development coincident with the decline of transcendentalism as a popular movement.[646]

Specifically, Moore claimed that Dewey's encounter with Huxley's thoroughly Darwinian 1871 *Lessons in Elementary Physiology* focused on "interdependence and interrelation among all things: the organism and the universe." This unitarianism, animism, or monism – depending on preference – easily coincides with some aspects of transcendentalism. Crucially, as Moore noted,

644   Murphy, "Maritain Explains," 283.
645   The peculiarities and extent of transcendentalism are beyond the scope of this argument. Nature is in reference to Ralph Waldo Emerson (1803 - 1882) title of the same name, 1836. Walden Pond is in reference to Henry David Thoreau (1817 – 1862), and one of his most well known works *Walden*, 1854.
646   Moore, "The Last Vermont Trancendentalist (1859 – 1882)", in *John Dewey*, 13 – 22.

Huxley's rendition of this 'one-ness' gave it "immediacy by the promise of scientific thinking."[647]

    The irony in the influence of transcendentalism in Dewey's development is most clearly displayed in Moore's claim that William James "cleared a professional path for Dewey" in seeking to "update transcendentalism by imagining it with the new science of psychology."[648] The 'new science' as later employed by Dewey amounted to an extension of Wallas' soft determinism previously addressed. Dewey stated in his response to Lippmann, *The Public and its Problems*, that "[h]abit is the mainspring of human action, and habits are formed for the most part under the influence of the customs of a group."[649] While certainly written later, the resort to habit created by acclimation to a group is decidedly opposed to the image of self-reliance and individualism for which Thoreau and Emerson have been credited and criticized.[650] One might argue that a core aspect of transcendentalism is the agency of the individual within their interdependency; Wallas and James' anthropology entirely rejected such agency in practice.

    In accordance with the psychology of habituation arising from Darwinism, Dewey came to embrace a constancy of change, and specifically an undirected, blind change.[651] In Dewey's cosmology, life is defined by change, therefore truth and morality are themselves subject to change. As a result, there are no universal principles to be found. In the place of greater transcendent universals as the litmus of what is true or good, Dewey substituted a wholly subjective, somewhat *sapiophillic* deification of human thought. He defined his version of pragmatism as "the formation of a faith in intelligence, as the one and indispensable belief necessary to moral and social life."[652]

---

647   Moore, *John Dewey*, 17.
648   Moore, *John Dewey*, 8.
649   John Dewey, *The Public and its Problems*, (Denver: Alan Swallow, 1927), 159.
650   Cf. Vinayak Sridhar, "Forefathers of Transcendentalism," *Prāgyatā*, February 14, 2025. Accessed: https://pragyata.com/forefathers-of-transcendentalism/.
651   Moore, *John Dewey*, 6.

Dewey based his so exalted 'faith in intelligence' not on the conformity of an individual's notions to things – an objective of truth – but rather on a wholly collectivized subjective rendition. He declared that "...knowledge is a function of association and communication; it depends upon tradition, upon tools and methods socially transmitted, developed and sanctioned."[653] Going far beyond Madison's *lex majoris partis*, Dewey employed something like a historicist-cultural-pragmatism to claim that man's ability to perceive of reality itself was merely a product of grander consensus, as though mass-hysteria was never a thing.

Given this wholesale collectivist epistemology, it is unsurprising that Dewey would argue a total repudiation of "antecedent political rights", Natural Law, and the possibility of an individual human being in the context of his thoughts on commercial activity.[654] Indeed, it would appear that Dewey's faith in intelligence coincided with a clear atheism that he overtly employed as a means of arguing directly against the principles of the Declaration. While the September 1933 issue of *Teacher Magazine* appears not to have been preserved in any identifiable capacity – even in physical catalogs – one particularly clear citation has attended some secondary scholarship of Dewey's world-view.

> Faith in the prayer-hearing God is an
> unproved and outmoded faith. There is no
> God, and there is no soul. Hence, there are no
> needs for the props of traditional religion.
> With dogma and creed excluded, then
> immutable truth is also dead and buried. There
> is no room for fixed, natural law or moral
> absolutes.[655]

---

652   Dewey in Moore, *John Dewey*, 8; citing John Dewey, in Jo Ann Boydston (ed.), *John Dewey: The Later Works, 1925–1953*, Vol. 2, (Carbondale: Southern Illinois University Press, 1985), 21.

653   Dewey, *The Public*, 158.

654   Dewey, *The Public*, 102.

655   John Dewey, "Soul Searching," *Teacher Magazine*, September 1933, 33. Note: This citation was taken from a number of other references, it cannot be independently verified, and so is not

While one may take issue with an unverifiable citation as written, indeed one strongly considered its omission, the content is entirely consistent with Dewey's perspective. Simply put, if the above quote is a fabrication, it is a very good one and neither adds to nor changes any aspect of the man's paradigm. If it is an accurate citation, his declaration that there is no God drove his rejection of Natural Law and all of its attendant implications contained in the Declaration. His rejection of the existence of the soul indelibly taints the whole of his cosmology. If a true reporting, humanity did not exist in Dewey's eyes but only audacious amino acids. This is of course to side-step the obvious questions. If immutable truth is dead, is it immutably true that immutable truth is dead? Is it a fixed moral absolute that there is no room for fixed moral absolutes? One would proffer that this wholesale solipsistic relativism is the seed within American public education that grew into the chocking bramble of nihilism and absurdity that permeates and characterizes that arena in the twenty-first century. If there is no soul, there is nothing to crush and no cause to guard against what would corrode the *anima*.

Dewey developed his collectivized perception extremely early and like Gladden, Ely, et. al, as a direct product of having embraced Darwinism.[656] In 1898, like the aforementioned men, Dewey sought to commingle evolution with ethics in an article of the same name. He expanded some of Huxley's positions by declaring that social shifts were now (meaning, then) intertwined with natural selection.[657] "The conditions with respect to which the term 'fit' must now be used include the existing social structure....the only standard we have of the best is the discovery of that which maintains these conditions in their integrity. The unfit is practically the anti-social."[658] In his estimation, the 'good' in the

included in the bibliography.

656   Cf. Sidney Ratner, "The Evolutionary Naturalism of John Dewey," *Social Research* 18, no. 4 (1951): 435–48, esp. 437.

657   Gladden cites Huxley directly for his conception of the social organism. Gladden, *The Church and the Kingdom*, 6, and throughout.

658   John Dewey, "Evolution and Ethics," *The Monist* 8, no. 3 (1898): 321 – 334; Cf. John Dewey, in Jo Ann Boydston ed., *John*

grandiloquent ethical sense, was only what maintained the prevailing social order (whether or not that order itself was good). The sentiment here strongly invokes Ely's 'social selection' as a function of his organism.[659]

While it is unclear if Dewey ever conceived of the 'social organism' in the same manner as the social gospel, he did employ it in his pedagogy. Additionally, his equation of then-current social demands with 'fitness' coincided very well with both Gladden and Common's subordination of an individual's dignity to whether or not another would hire him.[660] He did not limit this revocation to freedom or protection of law, or place the individual solely under the dominion of an employer, but rather connected social acceptability with fitness for *survival*. Matching Ely's deification of government as the grand delegator of duty beyond rights, Dewey placed his Borg as sovereign over the concept and measurement of right and wrong.[661] Where Gladden declared that the unemployed should be imprisoned, and Commons that they should be bereft of the benefit of law, Dewey subordinated even the right to life under his conception of society.[662] It would seem clear that Dewey did not accept the pithy, and self-evidently true statement that "[i]t is no measure of health to be well adjusted to a

---

Dewey: The Later Works, 1925–1953, (Carbondale: Southern Illinois University Press, 1985), vol. 5, 34 – 54.

659   Cf. Ely, "Social Progress."

660   Dewey used the social organism to explain the purpose of schooling, making correspondence between he and the social-gospel more clear; Cf. Jeremiah Dyehouse, "Theory in the Archives: Fred Newton Scott and John Dewey on Writing the Social Organism," *College English* 76, no. 3 (2014): 248–68; Cf. Gladden, *Social Salvation*, 82; Commons, *Social Reform*, 5 – 6.

661   The 'wrong conception' of government, in Gladden, *The New Idolatry*, 195, 198 – 199.

662   A position wholly encapsulated in Oliver Wendell Holmes Jr.'s majority opinion in *Buck v. Bell* (1927) that upheld the *Virginia Sterilization Act*, 1924, on the grounds of "public welfare". *Buck v. Bell*, 274 U.S. 200 (1927).

profoundly sick society."[663] Indeed, for Dewey it would be insane to oppose the rule of the lunatic in the land of the mad.

Dewey reduced the concept of truth under the extreme vagueries of collectivism. Joseph Betz, effectively an ally of Dewey, distilled the position in 1978, that "truth is public and social," by conflating the necessity of communication with the essential existence of right in and of itself.[664] This position does not attain without first denying the existence of any universal standard. In Betz's estimation, Dewey extended this inverted provenance to ultimately reject the substantial existence of the individual altogether. While he attempted to dissemble the core of his position, Dewey none the less declared that "[t]he real fallacy [in Classical/Lockean Liberalism] lies in the notion that individuals have such a native or original endowment of rights...."[665] Because the 'freedom' of an individual in isolation amounts to very little, Dewey took the view that "[f]reedom is relative to society and a state of being in society rather than opposed to it."[666] Betz defined this rendition of rights as 'transactional' by allegory of the man on the desert island who cannot marry because there is neither possible wife nor witness.[667] Neither he nor Dewey considered that the outcome of this anemic definition of 'rights' was such that, were two on an island and one killed the other for spite, there would have been no murder because there was no society beyond the one to label it so. Dewey's concept of rights is useless.

---

663   Commonly attributed to Jiddu Krishnamurti (1895 – 1986) – the "World Teacher" adopted by the aforementioned Theosophical Society who left that cult in adulthood – quote most probably from Mark Vonnegut, *The Eden Express*, (New York: Seven Stories Press, 1975), 208. Cf. "...there is no salvation in becoming adapted to a world which is crazy." in Henry Miller, *The Colossus of Maroussi*, (New York: New Directions Books, 1941), 58.

664   Joseph Betz, "John Dewey on Human Rights," *Transactions of the Charles S. Peirce Society* 14, no. 1 (1978): 23 – 24. Cf. Dewey, *The Public*, 208.

665   John Dewey, *Philosophy and Civilization*, (New York: G.P. Putnam's Sons, 1931), 281.

666   Betz, "John Dewey," 24.

667   Betz, "John Dewey," 37.

As Dewey declared: "The individual can have these rights only so long as he is a member of his society and his state; there are no such things as individual rights until and unless they are supported and maintained by society, through law."[668] Such a declaration is certainly no surprise as he had earlier declared the definition of 'rights' as "powers to act according to law."[669] One would highlight the clear inversion here; the legitimacy of law does not exist due to its purpose – to secure rights – but rather rights are legitimate only in so far as the law grants them the power to act. Let it be restated that in Dewey's view, rights arise from and are wholly subordinate to law – or in Jefferson's image, *the tyrant's will*.[670] In Dewey's own reasoning, this provenance eviscerates the whole concept of limited government, as well as the possibility of virtue. One cannot do unless he is granted leave, one will not do unless he is commanded.

> As a corollary to the rights which the law confers, it also imposes obligations upon the individual…. This is to say that the law prescribes the scope or range of behavior – *the things a person may do, those he must do,* and those he must not do. Maintenance of social order and the smooth operation of associated living would be impossible without this sort of prescription.[671]

Again, he declared in 1908 that "[t]he only fundamental anarchy is that which regards rights as private monopolies, ignoring their social origin and intent."[672] And like Commons, Dewey elevated the court as the arbiter of all rights, such that he subordinated all natural rights to the

---

668   John Dewey, *Lectures in China: 1919 - 1920*. Robert W. Clopton and Tsuin-Chen Ou Trans. (Honolulu: The University Press of Hawaii, 1973), 151.
669   Betz, "John Dewey," 35; Cf. Dewey, *Lectures in China*, 148.
670   Cf. Jefferson, "to Isaac H. Tiffany, 4 April 1819."
671   Dewey, *Lectures*, 148. Emphasis added.
672   John Dewey and James H. Tufts, *Ethics*, (New York: Henry Holt and Company, 1908), 441.

ability to sue and to be sued.[673] In practice, there is no standard on which these courts are to act, no objective against which to measure their decisions beyond the gossamer estimation of the society that they themselves control. Rights exist only in so far as the courts deign to recognize them – not as a depressing realization of *de facto*, but as a matter of intentional *de jure*. In Dewey's cosmology, because truth is whatever works, there are no limits to or measure of authority beyond what the same has decided to do.

It must be stated given Dewey's influence in public education; one posits that *this* is the origin of the perverse fundamental assumption current in American civilization: that a free people must *first ask permission* of the authorities who are ostensibly their servants, rather than the designed inverse of that state of affairs; that rights come from government, not from God. One who must ask permission is not free, but rather subordinate to the arbitrary will of another. Dewey's ideal of rights and obligations was substantially identical to Locke's State of War – it means nothing if it is one tyrant or one-million.[674] Let it be made abundantly clear: pragmatism and all of its cousins and derivatives, are diametrically opposed to Jeffersonian liberty as defined in the Declaration of Independence. This world-view is the corrosive, *medical* antagonist to the basic foundation of legitimacy as defined by the Declaration.[675]

In a manner wholly agreeing with Gladden's elevation of duty over rights, Dewey declared that inalienable rights simply do not exist. "Absolute rights, if we mean by absolute those not relative to any social order and hence exempt from any social restriction, there are none. But rights correspond even more intrinsically to obligations."[676] There is no right to life unless first a society allows for it *and* enshrines it into law – but there is no safeguard against a

---

673   Elect judges and have access to civil court; Betz, "John Dewey," 36.
674   Locke, *Second Treatise*, III:17.
675   A medical antagonist opposes or blocks biological action of another substance; it is an opponent, aggressive foil, an active enemy.
676   Dewey and Tufts, *Ethics*, 441.

fickle society later revoking that 'right', or a court merely declining to recognize it should it think such to be expedient. Where Lippmann's Ouroboros sought to fabricate its own consent, Dewey's manufactured its own purpose, procedure, and standards of measurement. Because in his cosmology 'truth' does not exist, principles do not exist. Because principles do not exist, it is impossible to accuse a law or a society of doing wrong; if the society (in practice the court or the *party*) does it, it is not illegal. More than any man yet analyzed, it appears that Dewey was the most Orwellian. *Pars non potest peccare; Peritus non potest peccare.*[677]

The baseless, tautological circularity of Dewey's ethics proceeds directly from an identical 'turtles all the way down' reasoning as that of Bury and so many others. Dewey affixed his signature to the first edition of *The Humanist Manifesto* in 1933. Despite both earlier and later interpretations of the term 'humanist', this document overtly declares itself to be a religious tract.[678] First in its fifteen 'articles of faith' is the declaration that "[r]eligious humanists regard the universe as self-existing and not created."[679] Deriving from this, the document builds a self-serving developmental model of history in complete agreement with social gospel historicism before making many of the same references to social control. Other than the overt placement of humanity in the throne of God – it is apparent in the document that the signers intend to literally *worship* their own estimation of humanity – the document makes a demand.

> Fourteenth: The humanists are firmly convinced that existing acquisitive and profit-motivated society has shown itself to be inadequate and that a radical change in methods, controls, and motives must be

677   The party cannot sin; the expert can do no wrong.
678   It has absolutely no relation to Renaissance Humanism, and it is entirely un-secular. It is, in absolute terms, a self-worshiping cult.
679   "Humanist Manifesto I," *American Humanist Association*, Accessed February 18, 2025: https://americanhumanist.org/what-is-humanism/manifesto1/.

instituted. A socialized and cooperative
economic order must be established to the end
that the equitable distribution of the means of
life be possible. The goal of humanism is a
free and universal society in which people
voluntarily and intelligently cooperate for the
common good. Humanists demand a shared
life in a shared world.[680]

Despite the term 'voluntarily,' interspersed with other
unobtrusive language, this cult of the *cognocenti* declared its
desire – demand – to remake the world according to its own
design; it leaves no room for those who do not wish to
participate. This design was based in the idea that "...the
nature of the universe depicted by modern science makes
unacceptable any supernatural or cosmic guarantees of
human values."[681] Simply, there are no transcendent universal
principles, there are no standards apart from what the god-
men might declare by means of 'science'. There is nothing to
pursue beyond social consensus. This is the platform upon
which he based his educational paradigm; the pedagogy of
the pragmatick.

Obviously the timetable is not so linear. Dewey
applied his thinking to education much earlier than the
publication of *The Humanist Manifesto*. In one of his earlier
works, Dewey set the purpose of education, not as an arena
for acquiring knowledge and developing skills, but rather as
an arena for the 'adjustment' of the child to his collectivized
cosmology. "I believe that education is a regulation of the
process of coming to share in the social consciousness; and
that the adjustment of individual activity on the basis of this
social consciousness is the only sure method of social
reconstruction."[682] He does not bother to answer the inherent
question: who decides the 'regulation,' who enforces it? Here
in 1897, Dewey defined education in the context of
assimilation specific to the cause of "social reconstruction."

"The Humanist Manifesto I," 1933.
681   "The Humanist Manifesto I," 1933, "Fifth".
682   John Dewey, *My Pedagogic Creed*, (Chicago: A. Flanagan
   Company, 1897), 16.

School is not for learning, but rather teaching is an agent to precipitate a desired social change. Who designs the reconstruction, according to whose desire? Dewey's first position, under "Article I. What Education Is," asserted a fundamentally collectivized paradigm.

> I believe that all education proceeds by the participation of the individual in the social consciousness of the race....

> I believe that the only true education comes through the stimulation of the child's powers by the demands of the social situations in which he finds himself. Through these demands he is stimulated to act as a member of a unity, to emerge from his original narrowness of action and feeling, and to conceive of himself from the standpoint of the welfare of the group to which he belongs.[683]

From the very beginning, Dewey's pedagogy was entirely encapsulated within the modern semantics of the term 'indoctrination.' Agreement with the ends alleged, or shades that invoke *e pluribus unum* do not alter the fundamental purpose of education as presented: conformity at the expense of individuality. Consistent references to 'uniqueness' and 'individuality' throughout specific teaching methods do not alter the substance of Dewey's foundation; his purpose was to cause the child to internalize a conception of the group as primary to himself. One strenuously asserts that *this* is the root of the rise in school-shootings: the State-enforced pedagogical revocation of individual humanity, the murder of dignity. Dewey does not address the question of what is to be done with the one who does not wish to 'belong' to the group into which arbitrary birth has forced him, nor does he address what is to be done in the case of vicious groups. This paradigm is expanded by his next article, "What the School Is"

---

683   Dewey, *Pedagogic Creed*, 5.

> I believe that the school is primarily a social
> institution. Education being a social process,
> the school is simply that form of community
> life in which all those agencies are
> concentrated that will be most effective in
> bringing the child to share in the inherited
> resources of the race, and to use his own
> powers for social ends.[684]

School is the mechanism by which a student is to become habituated to functioning in society by presenting a miniaturized version of that society; the quality of that society or willingness to participate therein being apparently irrelevant. This microcosm is tasked with presenting the "demands" that will cause the child to act and to think of himself not as an individual, but as an organelle in a larger organism – such that he will "use his own powers for social ends." Like manufactured consent, mandated independence, or coercive philanthropy, the idea of indoctrinated martyrdom – instructed to sacrifice one's self for 'social ends' – is an abusive absurdity. Such paradoxes appear to accompany all collectivist attempts to side-step virtue or to legislate moral character.

The public school system was Dewey's tool to perpetrate *his* ideal of what society ought to be. He declared that "...obviously the first business of the public school is to teach the child to live in the world in which he finds himself, to understand his share in it, and to get a good start in adjusting himself to it."[685] Though he attempted to claim that this *raison d'être* was compatible with individualism, the claim immediately fell flat in its explanation.

> It is duly individual because it recognizes the
> formation of a certain character as the only
> genuine basis of right living. It is socialistic
> because it recognizes that this right character

---

684   Dewey, *Pedagogic Creed*, 8.

685   John and Evelyn Dewey, *Schools of Tomorrow*, (New York: E.P. Dutton & Company, 1915), Chapter VII: 167, Project Gutenberg Ebook #48906. NOTE This edition contains paragraph numbers rather than page numbers.

is not to be formed by merely individual
precept, example, or exhortation, but rather by
the influence of a certain form of institutional
or community life upon the individual, and
*that the social organism through the school,
as its organ, may determine ethical results.*[686]

The appeal to individualism was immediately
rendered impotent by the appeal to ethical standards, a
derivation of applied truth, as defined by means of
consensus. Specifically, *the school* is placed in Moses' seat
so-to-speak, to be the arbitrator of 'ethical results' as an agent
of the organism.[687] Dewey's wording here was certainly
illuminating; he did not state that the school was to inculcate
an understanding of moral principles universally applied, but
rather declared that the organism "may determine ethical
results." Other than this being a 'text-book' example of the
relativism inherent in pragmatism, it effectively deifies the
organism. Where one might disagree with the heavy-handed
imagery of Moses' seat or the claim that he deified the social
organism, the response is simply that Dewey himself used the
same 'theological' justification.

I believe, finally, that the teacher is engaged,
not simply in the training of individuals, but in
the formation of the proper social life.

I believe that every teacher should realize the
dignity of his calling; that he is a social
servant *set apart for the maintenance of*

---

686   Dewey, *Pedagogic Creed*, 16.
687   Cf. Matthew 23:2 – 3. The image of 'Moses' seat' can be
interpreted as a placement of moral judgment, a chair given to a
divinely sanctioned lawgiver, Cf. Steve Siefken, "The Seat of Moses:
What Was It?," *Answereth a Matter*, N.d. Accessed February 19,
2025:
https://answerethamatter.org/biblical_articles/articles/the_seatofmose
s.htm. NOTE. This article cites numerous historical documents, but is
not presented in a traditionally academic manner; the interpretation of
the term is left open to the preference of the reader.

proper social order and the securing of the
right social growth.

I believe that in this way *the teacher always is
the prophet of the true God and the usherer in
of the true kingdom of God.*[688]

It would be quite simple to dismiss Dewey's obvious
social gospel vocabulary here as merely a result of the time
when the work was written, but it has already been
demonstrated that Dewey entertained a different view of the
supernatural than proponents of the social gospel, even if he
advocated for substantially identical ends. Given this
understanding, one would posit that Dewey's construction,
"...prophet of the *true* God ... the *true* kingdom of God" is, at
the very least, a pregnant phrasing. One is compelled to ask,
a bit rhetorically, who he believed was the 'true' god? Given
the substance of his cosmology, and the religion to which he
aligned himself, the answer would seem to be obvious.
Dewey's 'god' was society itself – or more specifically, his
conception of the *proper* social order.

In Dewey's view society was not an emergent
property of individuals going about living their own lives, but
rather the preeminent article. He defined society as "a
number of people held together because they are working
along common lines, in a common spirit, and with reference
to common aims."[689] Again, according to whom? Despite its
utility in smaller, crucially *voluntary* associations, Dewey's
definition was not applied to 'sub-cultures' or what
effectively amount to clubs; he spoke of society as an all-
encompassing whole wherein opting-out was not an option.
He does not describe *a* society, but rather the *entire*
community. The community, or more appropriately the State,
is first in his order of precedence. In his world-view,
individuals do not make society but rather society makes
individuals, and that only to its own ends – despite his

---

688   Dewey, *Pedagogic Creed*, 17. Emphasis added.
689   John Dewey, *The School and Society*, Revised ed., (Chicago:
    Chicago University Press, 1915 [1900]), 11.

anemic claims to the contrary. Dewey's society is wholly a wholistic prison.

Given the question 'which came first, the man or the State?' Locke, Jefferson, Adams, et al. would answer without hesitation 'the man' as they frequently did. Each of the later men so far analyzed, Dewey not the least, answered in the complete opposite. *This* is the core of the Progressive inversion, that the State is primary to the man, that the collective is morally superior to the individual; Progressivism is the Borg. Given this hierarchy, it naturally followed that individuals must needs be inducted and bestowed a position within the greater part; those who do not fit are malfunctioning parts. Who then is to conduct the induction, and who is so elevated to decide the position?

Addressing the utility of History as a discipline in primary education, Dewey stated that "[e]xisting society is both too complex and too close to the child to be studied."[690] This reflected Lippmann's view of society as too complex for the people, and thusly the teacher – Dewey's 'prophet of the true god' – stood as the intermediary, the equivalent of Lippmann's expert manipulators or Commons' administrators. Like Lippmann's experts, Common's administrators, Ely's philanthropists, or any of the others, Dewey's teachers were anointed to produce and to manage a transformation from the founding ideal to a collective. "The desired transformation is not difficult to define in a formal way. It signifies a society in which every person shall be occupied in something which makes the lives of others better worth living…."[691]

Like Locutus of Borg, Dewey cloaked his authoritarianism in the grandiose hubris of seeking to elevate all people, *whether they wanted it or not.* "Why do you resist? We only wish to raise the quality of life, for all species."[692]

---

690 Dewey, *The School*, 155.
691 John Dewey, *Democracy and Education: An Introduction to the Philosophy of Education*, (New York: The Macmillan Company, 1916), 369.
692 Patrick Stewart playing Captain Jean-Luc Picard as Locutus of Borg, "The Best of Both Worlds II" *Star Trek: The Next*

Dewey did not adjust his cosmology after witnessing the drastic horrors of the first half of the twentieth century. Neither the October Revolution, Holodomor, the Great War, the Great Depression, nor the second act of the Great War served to impel him to re-examine his estimation of truth, expertise, education, or social engineering – the latter of which may be cited as at least one common factor among each of the mentioned episodes. Like Lippmann, he only became further entrenched in his own 'western front'.

In 1944 Dewey lamented the effects of the world wars on respect for democracy and education – upon which he bestowed the tile 'faith'. He took the position that these events happened, not because of unscrupulous men with their own designs for society, and the guns and goons to try to force them, but because it was not *his* design that was applied. He demonstrated the promiscuity of his pragmatism in seeking to blame both the idealists who thought that improvement was inevitable (Cf. Spencerian *laissez-faire*), and the 'reactionaries' who sought to 'attack science and technological education' because it interfered with Natural Law.[693]

Simply, 'truth' is whatever works, as long as it was a pragmatist's idea, both executed and evaluated by a pragmatist; standards for measuring what works are apparently irrelevant. "But in practice… it has been denied that man has any responsibility for the consequences that result from what he invents and employs. This denial is implicit in our widespread refusal to engage in large-scale collective planning."[694] To state such a thing after the birth of Sovietism, The New Deal, National Socialism, the Internal Revenue Service, the Social Security Administration, the Federal Reserve System, or any of the other massive central planning behemoths – from which the tragedies of the twentieth century arose – can only be described as either gross incompetence, or deliberate gaslighting.

Generation, Season 4: Episode 1, Aired September 22, 1990.

693   John Dewey, "The Democratic Faith and Education," *The Antioch Review* 4, no. 2 (1944): 274 –283.

694   Dewey, "Democratic Faith," 278.

After blaming the failure of social-engineering on the failure to use *his* social-engineering, Dewey returned back to his deified caricature of 'complex' democracy with the exhortation to his readers to take courage that 'democracy' had worked well in the past. From this, he argued that the world simply needed more social-engineering. If pragmatickism does not work, pragmatick *even harder.*

> But to this courage we must add, if our courage is to be intelligent rather than blind, the fact that successful maintenance of democracy demands the utmost in use of the best available methods to procure a social knowledge that is reasonably commensurate with our physical knowledge, and the invention and use of forms of *social engineering* reasonably commensurate with our technological abilities in physical affairs.[695]

As repeated earlier, it would be simple to dismiss Dewey like the others but for the depth of his influence. His pragmatick pedagogy is continuously referenced in glowing terms, but even among his critics the core weaknesses of his pragmatism – circularity, projection, evasion, elitism, collectivism – upon which his pedagogy was built, are rarely addressed. His paradigm was immediately coupled with overt attempts toward impertinent reform, and formed the core ideology of *The Social Frontier*, a journal established in 1934. This journal declared the death of individualism, and the "new age of collectivist society" with teachers as its builders, and Dewey's ideology as its model.[696] While the journal itself fell apart under the guidance of the very same people who would presume to guide society, *Social Frontier* was affiliated with numerous Progressive organizations and

---

695   Dewey, "Democratic Faith," 282 – 283. Emphasis added.
696   Joseph Edward Rowan, "'The Social Frontier' (1934-1943): Journal of Educational Criticism and Social Reconstruction." (PhD Dissertation, Case Western Reserve University, 1969), 1.

associations, and spawned the John Dewey Society for the Study of Education and Culture in 1936.[697]

The John Dewey Society remains in existence and influence today. The current society devotes itself to "the place and function of education in social change", and seeks to provide "a space for building and sustaining a network of scholars, teachers, and community activists dedicated to democratic social change."[698] One could find no estimation of the size of this network, but the society claims either ownership or substantial affiliation with the journals *Dewey Studies*, *Education and Culture*, *Educational Theory*, and the *Journal of School & Society*, one assumes of rather broad circulation.[699] The society has a clearly zealous bent to its purpose.

In the website header, under a photograph of Dewey's gravestone the caption reads: "The grave of John Dewey on the University of Vermont campus. A quiet place to re-dedicate ourselves to the struggle for a just, democratic, and humane society."[700] It is certain that the overtly religious imagery of the teacher continued from Dewey's 'prophet' through the Society, to its current incarnation, and that Society clearly views Dewey as equivalent to a patron saint and object of pilgrimage. It is exceedingly difficult to gauge the actual extent of influence exerted by the John Dewey Society, but two factors are immediately clear and undeniable. First, the society maintains the perspective of school, specifically public school, as *their* tool to indoctrinate children to bring about *their ideal* for society. Second, and likely most importantly, the John Dewey Society is intimately associated with the largest labor union in the United States, the National Education Association – who like Dewey in 1944, have taken to responding to arguments or

697   C. A. Bowers, "The Social Frontier Journal: A Historical Sketch." *History of Education Quarterly* 4, no. 3 (1964): 167–80.
698   JDS, "Purpose," *John Dewey Society*, N.d. Accessed February 20, 2025: https://www.johndeweysociety.org/.
699   JDS, "Journals."
700   JDS, "Home".

criticisms with cries of 'attack.' – itself indicative of a religious zeal.[701]

Whatever groups or associations exist to maintain and further his paradigm, and there are many, Dewey's influence is far too deeply embedded into the weft of American civilization to be wholly examined in this brief analysis. One has disregarded the specific details of this or that methodology that he advocated in favor of seeking the fundamental world-view upon which he based those arguments. If the ground is sand, it does not matter the quality of wood used to build the house. Contrasting with Lippmann, Dewey targeted something far more primal. Where Lippmann reduced journalism to fetid power-justification-by-deception, Dewey attacked the formative years of the people who would be subject to that propaganda. He deified the State in a more insidious manner than did the others by seeking to indoctrinate the child into conceiving of himself as a mere part of the State – that State who was empowered to presume even to dictate what was true or false, right or wrong. While it is certainly arguable what effects this pragmatick pedagogy has had, another set about seeking to distill those effects:

> Dewey could be considered singularly
> responsible for the dramatic change in schools
> in the twentieth century, from the character-
> promoting mission of American education
> established in colonial days to the current

---

701   Summary, "National Education Association," *Library of Congress*, N.d. Accessed February 20, 2025: https://www.loc.gov/item/lcwaN0002414/; Three articles speak of the 'attacks against public schooling', ex: Mary Ellen Flannery, "Parents and Educators Want the Same Thing," *neaToday*, September 29, 2022. Accessed February 20, 2025: https://www.nea.org/nea-today/all-news-articles/parents-and-educators-want-same-thing; Cf. Review of the JDS's 1953 publication: William J. Codd, "Educational Freedom in an Age of Anxiety: Twelfth Yearbook of the John Dewey Society," *America Magazine: The Jesuit Review of Faith & Culture* 89, no. 2 (April 11, 1953): 53–54; Gordon H. Hullfish, *Educational Freedom in an Age of Anxiety: Twelfth Yearbook of the John Dewey Society*, (New York: Harper & Brothers, 1953).

situation in which violence, unethical
behavior, and disrespect toward others runs
rampant not only in our schools but also in our
society.[702]

Commons effectively created the blueprint to re-
create American civilization on the basis of the 'social-
organism', employing judicial oligarchy as its method of
enforcement and the saprophyte bureaucracy as its
machinery. Lippmann deified the reign of the expert, and
presented journalism as the hallucinogen by which the public
is mesmerized into acquiescing to that necrotrophy. Dewey
conveyed collectivism under the expert into public schooling
at its most basic level, subjugating essential truth and moral
rectitude under the hysteria of the masses as its fundamental
paradigm, making cognitive dissent from the collective an act
of social-deviance. Where before the whole of the matter was
encapsulated in the dignity of the individual, now complexity
had vitiated that individual's capacity to understand, and
obviated his agency in knowing right from wrong.

The epistocrats had 'by the acids of modernity
dissolved that old order' wherein one could seek the truth to
reach for his dignity, to entomb certainty in the sepulcher of
credulity. The elite had made themselves the arbiters of truth
and reality itself; all they lacked was some *imperator* to bring
about *their* kingdom on Earth. The Republic was dead; long
live the Empire.

702 Murphy, "Maritain Explains," 285; citing Dewey, *Democracy and Education*, 411.

Freedom From Fear, Fear of Freedom

No one is more a slave than the man who
thinks himself free, while he is not.[703]

– Johann Wolfgang von Goethe

T he heresy of perfectibility severed America's ancient
and primary cognizance of the origin of rights. Where
man could become gods, it was inevitable that rights
would become mere products of men or, in practice, of the
State. The essential compromise in the patently absurd
amalgam between evolution and Christianity sacralized the
vacuous and unfalsifiable delusions of historicism by
facilitating the self-affirmative 'upward-trend'. The attitude
that truth – 'the correspondence of notions to things' – might
somehow be subject to time, place, or person immediately
allowed for the ascendant to presume to evaluate the truth of
a matter as a mere product of consensus upon curated results.
Where the social gospel cut the anchor chain, and therefore
shattered the cornerstone of the Declaration – inclusive of all
that is built thereon – Pragmatism set the ship on course to
run aground. In the realm of variable 'standards', the
American could no longer find his ancient rights written on
the whole of human nature by Hamilton's sun beam, but
rather was beholden to the epistocrat to deign to explain. The
citizen therefore could know of no northern star to challenge
the broken compass of his power-drunken pilots.

---

703   *"Niemand is mehr Sklave, als der sich für frei hält, ohne es
su sein."* Johann Wolfgang von Goethe, *Elective Affinities: A Novel*
(New York: Henry Holt and Company, 1872), Part II, Chapter 5, 202.
Also rendered as "None are more hopelessly enslaved than those who
falsely believe they are free."

Lippmann's pragmatick theory of government was combined with Dewey's mechanistic indoctrination of wholesale collectivism in public schooling, but the way had been cleared prior to them in the work of yet another apostate descendant of the Second Great Awakening: Francis Julius Bellamy (1855 – 1931). To approach the influence of this man first requires a brief analysis of his cousin, Edward Bellamy (1850 – 1898).

The elder Bellamy wrote *Looking Backward, 2000 – 1887* (1888).[704] Richard T. Ely's 1895 *Socialism*, wherein he credits John R. Commons, declared that "[t]his socialistic work soon attained an enormous circulation, selling for a time at the rate of a thousand copies a day. This was the beginning of the American socialism which has been called nationalism."[705] In a 2019 revisit of the novel, Garrett Nash claimed that "…no cultural work was more responsible for pushing public opinion to the left in the Progressive Era" and cites Dewey (among others) having ranked the work just after Marx's *Das Kapital* (1867) as the most influential works of the then previous fifty years.[706] Donovan E. Smucker credited Edward, alongside Henry George (1839 – 1897) as having influenced the previously mentioned Rauschenbusch's thinking.[707] Edward Bellamy himself

---

704   Edward Bellamy, *Looking Backward: 2000 – 1887*, (New York: Houghton, Mifflin and Company, 1889).

705   Richard T. Ely, *Socialism: An Examination of its Nature, its Strength and Its Weakness, With Suggestions for Social Reform*, (New York: Thomas Y. Crowell & Co, 1895), 69; credits Commons with having assisted with the composition of the work, ix.

706   Garrett Dash Nelson, "The Splendor of Our Public and Common Life," *Places Journal*, (December, 2019), Accessed March 4, 2025: https://placesjournal.org/article/edward-bellamy-urban-planning/; Citing: Erich Fromm, "Introduction to the 1960 edition of Edward Bellamy", *Looking Backward* (New American Library); William Dean Howells, *Literature and Life: Studies*, (Harper & Brothers, 1902), 294; and Elizabeth Sadler, "One Book's Influence: Edward Bellamy's *Looking Backward*," *The New England Quarterly* 17:4 (December 1944), 530.

707   Donovan E. Smucker, "Baptist Cameos," *The Reformed Reader*, n.d. Accessed March 6, 2025: https://www.reformedreader.org/rauschenbusch.htm; Henry George, *Progress and Poverty*, 1879, founder of "Georgism" – a single-tax

described the application of his novel's ideas as something of an accident, produced in part by seeking to apply the mechanisms of the "modern military system… for a national industrial service" meaning, "whole nations organized and manoeuvred as armies."[708] Edward conceived of national-civilian-industrial-armies of a Prussian or Spartan regimented image not at all unlike that later advocated by Richard Ely, as previously analyzed.[709]

This 'industrial army' was characterized according to Catherine Tumber, as "a hierarchical meritocracy of efficiency minded administrators [who] control the state."[710] In Nash's paraphrase, Edward intended this utopian piece to act as "an instruction manual for economic revolution" and it immediately spawned widespread but short lived 'Bellamy Clubs.'[711] The clubs represented what was termed a ""Nationalist" movement that influenced many of the later reforms of the Progressive era."[712] Ely declared that "Important laws can be traced to the agitation of the nationalists."[713]

The term 'nationalist' is of particular importance as Edward selected it deliberately. In his personal correspondence, he explained that while he "…may seem to out-socialize the socialist, yet the word socialist is one I never could well stomach."[714] Thusly as early as the later decade of the nineteenth century, the images 'nationalist' and 'socialist' – or one might say *National Socialism* – were

focused economics paradigm. Cf. Donovan E. Smucker, *The Origins of Walter Rauschenbusch's Social Ethics*, (Montreal: McGill-Queen's University Press, 1994).

708 Edward Bellamy, "How I Came to Write Looking Backward," *Science Fiction Studies* 4, no. 2 (1977): 195; Sic.

709 Cf. Ely, *The World War and Leadership in a Democracy*, 1918.

710 Catherine Tumber, "Edward Bellamy, the Erosion of Public Life, and the Gnostic Revival," *American Literary History* 11, no. 4 (1999): 610.

711 Nelson, "The Splendor".

712 Tumber, "Edward Bellamy," 611.

713 Ely, *Socialism*, 69.

714 Bellamy to Howells, June 17, 1888 in Bowman, Sylvia E. *The Year 2000: A Critical Biography of Edward Bellamy*, (New York: Bowman Associates, 1958).

already intimately connected in a manner both disingenuous for deliberate optics-preferring-semantics, and for the inescapable nature of *militaristic* collectivism inherent therein. So *Looking Backward* became something of a gospel for the creation of widespread, 'big-tent' social organizations that included "[Georgist] single taxers, populists, labor activists, and civil service reformers to theosophists..."[715] Recall the 'theosophy' of William James, and his place in Lippmann's provenance, in addition to the connection between Bellamy's clubs and Graham Wallas whom Ely referred to as a "Fabian" socialist, with Edward Bellamy as "the founder of the school of socialism called nationalism"[716]

The broad membership ensured that whatever ideology was spread by the brief clubs would endure under dozens of names, and in as many policy objectives. One of these names, "Technocracy Incorporated" was founded by Howard Scott (1890 – 1970) in 1919, employing the philosophy of the pragmatist Thorsten Veblen (1857 – 1929) who was at least partially inspired by Edward's novel.[717] Both *Looking Backward* and 'Technocracy Inc' were endorsed by Dewey because they obviously shared a substantially identical worldview, to the extent that Dewey (like many others) bestowed the title 'Great America Prophet' on the elder Bellamy.[718]

It is vital to note that, as of this writing, Technocracy Inc continues to exist as something of a fringe entity but its founders included Marion King Hubbert (1903 – 1989), creator of the Malthusian 'peak oil' zealotry of 1956, and originator of 'environmental sustainability' later

---

715   Tumber, "Edward Bellamy," 611.
716   Ely, *Socialism*, 23 – 24.
717   James J. Kopp, "Edward Bellamy and the New Deal: The Revival of Bellamyism in the 1930s." *Utopian Studies*, no. 4 (1991): 13. Veblen is likely intimately connected with Lippmann, Dewey, Holmes, et. al, but such connections are proximate to this argument, and analyzing them would extend it beyond reason.
718   Kopp, "Edward Bellamy," 11, 13; Cf. John Dewey, "A Great American Prophet," *Common Sense* 3, (1934). Most secondary literature treating the elder Bellamy extensively discuss his 'prophecies', especially regarding technological innovation of the early twentieth-century.

characterized by *authoritarian* policies championed through histrionic adolescent female rampages.[719] Additionally, the current plutocrats of 'Silicon Valley', in concert with further pathogenic hysteria of the 2020's, continue to invoke the 'scientism' of Technocracy as pioneered by Edward Bellamy.[720]

Furthermore, Bellamy inspired Upton Sinclair's (1878 – 1968) "End Poverty in California" (EPIC – 1934), in addition to contributing many aspects to the 'New Deal', that has been characterized as something like a 'Bellamy revival.'[721] Truthfully, an exhaustive analysis of Bellamyism conveyed through Technocracy; connected to Theosophy, "humanism", Pragmatism, scientism, environmentalism, National Socialism, Communism, the New Deal, and curiously *religious* iconography – at the foundation of Progressivism – would contribute greatly to this argument but such an analysis would necessitate an entire book-length treatment on its own.[722] It is sufficient to state that *Looking*

---

719   Lukas Organ, "The Technocracy Movement and Howard Scott," *Mises Wire*, February 18, 2025, Accessed March 4, 2025: https://mises.org/mises-wire/technocracy-movement-and-howard-scott; Cf. M. King Hubbert, " Nuclear Energy and the Fossil Fuels," *Drilling and Production Practice*, Shell Development Company Publication No. 95., American Petroleum Institute, (June 1956): 22 – 27; Greta Thunberg, "United Nations Climate Action Summit," Speech, New York: 2019.

720   Ira Basen, "In Science We Trust," *CBCNews- Radio Canada*, June 28, 2021, Accessed March 4, 2025: https://newsinteractives.cbc.ca/longform/technocracy-incorporated-elon-musk/. While this piece amounts to an attack on the currently infamous Elon Musk, it demonstrates a curious connection between that man and Bellamy via Technocracy, as well as the appeal of technicism among the extremely wealthy in twenty-first century America.

721   Kopp, "Edward Bellamy," 12, 13.

722   Indeed, Bellamy appears even to be connected to esotericism and the occult, not only in Theosophy, but in 'New Age' spiritualism, 'seances,' and something like a neo-Gnosticism. This effective luciferianism or satanism, implies further book-length connections with Anton Lavey (1930 – 1997), Wicca, and neo-paganism of the 1960's – 1990's. Cf. Tumber, "Edward Bellamy". For a complete treatment of Edward Bellamy's place in the creation of authoritarian collectivism in the United States, Cf. Arthur Lipow, *Authoritarian*

Backward primed the pump as it were. Edward gave a deep, almost *metaphysical-religious* justification to the idea that "For utopia, freedom must be eliminated and all choices are made by "experts.""[723]

Edward Bellamy's nationalism was, from its very inception, the total eradication of both individualism and federalism. Ely stated that "Mr. Bellamy contemplates the wiping out of the separate commonwealths as distinct political divisions."[724] This was later expanded by Bill Kaufmann who quoted in 2002 that "state governments would have interfered with the control and discipline of the industrial army."[725] Defining 'nationalism' as "the military model of socialism", Arthur Lipow argued quite forcefully that these clubs pressed an image of the all-encompassing State, the ""Nation" as a mystical community to which the individual had to subordinate his private needs and desires...."[726] This characterization stands in perfect agreement with Common's previously cited 'duty' that one economically martyr one's self for the good of the State, and is a natural and inevitable application of social-organism reasoning.[727]

Most poignant for this argument, Edward Bellamy's Nationalist Clubs served as one primary venue by which his cousin Francis Bellamy spread the deepest and arguably most insidious influence in the metastasization of collective-statism in the United States: the so-called "Pledge of Allegiance."

The younger Bellamy began as a Baptist in the tradition of the Second Great Awakening, but turned to join

---

Socialism in America: Edward Bellamy and the Nationalist Movement, (Berkeley: University of California Press, 1982).

723 Organ, "The Technocracy Movement", sic.
724 Ely, *Socialism*, 87.
725 Bill Kaufmann, "The Bellamy boys pledge allegiance. (Flashback: to know nothing of what happened before you were born is to remain ever a child—Cicero)," *The American Enterprise* 13, no. 7 (2002): 50. NOTE: Kaufmann did not include a source for this quote, it's provenance could not be established.
726 Lipow, *Authoritarian Socialism*, 160.
727 Commons, *Labor and Administration*, 4.

both the Freemasons and Christian Socialism.[728] Additionally, Francis Bellamy participated in the 'public school movement,' stood as a committee chairman of the National Education Association, and was a "Charter member of the First Nationalist Club of Boston."[729]

Francis co-founded The Society of Christian Socialists in 1889 as an outgrowth of Henri de Saint-Simon's (1760 – 1825) proto-technicist-social-gospel "new Christianity." The society, itself connected with the Women's Christian Temperance Union under Francis' direction, sponsored public education courses for discussion of his cousin's famous book among other subjects. At least one of these courses was published in "the Nationalist Club's newspaper, the *Arena*." It is apparent that Francis' broad affiliations lead to his employ at the children's magazine *The Youth's Companion* in 1891, wherein he would launch his public and political lobbying campaign to adopt a nationalist loyalty-oath with the full cooperation of the National Education Association.[730] *The Youth's Companion* was the most broadly circulated weekly in the United States at the time, with a readership of "more than four hundred thousand households in 1888."[731]

His specific motives in the composition of the new oath are debatable, but one easily finds the perspective that he employed. Giving due place to his membership in both the

728   "Francis Bellamy," N.d. *Grand Lodge of British Columbia and Yukon*, Accessed March 5, 2025: https://freemasonry.bcy.ca/biography/bellamy_f/bellamy_f.html.
729   Timothy Kubal, *Cultural Movements and Collective Memory: Christopher Columbus and the Rewriting of the National Origin Myth*, (New York: Palgrave Macmillan, 2008), 14; Kaufmann, "The Bellamy Boys,"; "Francis Bellamy," N.d. *Grand Lodge of British Columbia and Yukon*, Accessed March 5, 2025: https://freemasonry.bcy.ca/biography/bellamy_f/bellamy_f.html.
730   Kubal, *Cultural Movements*, 15.
731   Richard J. Ellis, "Under God: Frances Bellamy and the Origins of the Pledge of Allegiance," *Oregon Humanities*, December 10, 2011, Accessed March 6, 2025: https://www.oregonhumanities.org/rll/magazine/encore-fall-winter-2011/under-god/#:~:text=And%20among%20Bellamy's%20ancestors%20was,Bellamy%20genealogy%20bordered%20on%20fanaticism.%E2%80%9D.

christian socialists and his cousin's Nationalist club among other organizations, Francis wished use the public schooling system to re-create America, and he explicitly wrote of these schemes.

Predicting Dewey's purpose for public schooling, Francis wrote for *The Journal of Education* in 1892 that "[t]rue Americanism is devotion to the highest interests of America…. The public school is the place where this Americanism can be taught. The school master must recognize himself as directly responsible for good citizenship."[732] Where Dewey anointed the public school teacher as a "prophet of the true God" whose holy work was "the formation of the proper social life," Francis elevated that 'prophet's' direct supervisor to the office of steward for the creation of 'good citizens.'[733] It is deeply appropriate that Ely approached the concept of public education – specifically *compulsory* public education – as inherent to and wholly reliant upon the widespread adoption of socialism, and noted it as the *first* objective or demand in yet another socialist organization of the time, the American Federation of Labor, Chicago.[734] In his suggestions for the application of socialism to social reform, Ely consistently spoke of the centrality of compulsory education for the improvement of his social organism.[735]

The connection in Francis Bellamy between socialism, nationalism, and public schooling was not restricted to perverse 'christianity', social gospel or social organism imagery, but also included the expected frequent appeals to racial purity. Francis, in his capacity as the editor of *The Illustrated American* wrote in 1897:

> The hard, inescapable fact is that men are not born equal. Neither are they born free, but all

---

732   Francis Bellamy, "Americanism In The Public Schools," *The Journal of Education* 36, no. 6 (881) (1892): 107.

733   Dewey, *Pedagogic Creed*, 17.

734   Ely, *Socialism*, 164, 70.

735   Ely, *Socialism*, 255, and the whole of Chapter VIII "Other Reforms Calculated to Lessen the Dis-advantages of Private Industry, and Secure some of the Advantages of Socialism", esp. 323, 325, and 378.

in bonds to their ancestors and their environments. Many achieve freedom, but by no means all.

The success of government by the people will depend upon the stuff the people are made of. The people must realize their responsibility to themselves. They must guard, more jealously even than their liberties, the quality of their blood.

A democracy like ours cannot afford to throw itself open to the world where every man is a lawmaker, every dull-witted or fanatical immigrant admitted to our citizenship is a bane to the commonwealth. Where all classes of society merge insensibly into one another every alien immigrant of inferior race may bring corruption to the stock.

There are races, more or less akin to our own, whom we may admit freely, and get nothing but advantage from the infusion of their wholesome blood. But there are other races which we cannot assimilate without a lowering of our racial standard, which should be as sacred to us as the sanctity of our homes.[736]

The specific 'races' of whom he spoke, both in the positive and the negative, were entirely unsurprising. The preferred groups "came from the northern and western nations of Europe, from peoples who were really Americans in spirit before they came." The undesirables hailed from southern and eastern Europe, specifically "expelled [Russian and Polish] Jews who will not labor with their hands, but choose rather to be parasites of tenement houses and

---

736   Francis Bellamy, Ed., *The Illustrated American*, Vol. XXII, no. 9 (August 28, 1897), 258.

worthless vendors."[737] In Francis' view, "America owed its greatness not only to God but also to the superiority of the Anglo-Saxon race."[738]

It must be wholly reiterated that each of the themes thus far analyzed, from perfectibility and eugenics, to the nauseating quantity of 'isms' that all amount to authoritarian collectivism, amalgamated in the Bellamy cousins. The former exercised a vast and likely unknowable *cultural* – social – influence extant today, and the latter conveyed this monstrosity directly to the root of 'the people' in the 'education' of the young under *threat of death* by the State, this being the definition of 'compulsory'.

The specifics and subsequent meaningless controversies surrounding the adoption of Francis' draft of the Pledge of Allegiance are merely proximal to this argument. *The Youth Companion* initiated a campaign to sell American flags to every public school in the country to commemorate the four-hundredth anniversary of Columbus' landing. Francis wrote the original version of the Pledge to accompany a ceremony attending that celebration.[739]

Not contented to restrict the festivities to recitation in concert with raising the flag, Francis also contrived a very familiar *ritual* to attend his oath of loyalty to the State, captured in and described below Figure 1.

---

737   Francis Bellamy speech to the Women's Literary Union, in
        Ellis, "Under God".
738   Ellis, "Under God".
739   Ellis, "Under God".

Figure 1: R.G. Price, "Fascism Part II: The Rise of American Fascism," Rational Revolution, Accessed January 13, 2025: http://www.rationalrevolution.net/ articles/rise_of_american_fascism.htm.
Image in the Public Domain.

Salute to the Flag, by the Pupils.

At a signal from the Principal the pupils, in ordered ranks, hands to the side, face the Flag. Another signal is given; every pupil gives the flag the military salute -- right hand lifted, palm downward, to a line with the forehead and close to it. Standing thus, all repeat together, slowly, "I pledge allegiance to my Flag and the Republic for which it stands; one Nation indivisible, with Liberty and Justice for all." At the words, "to my Flag," the right hand is extended gracefully, palm upward, toward the Flag, and remains in this gesture till the end of the affirmation; whereupon all

hands immediately drop to the side. Then, still
standing, as the instruments strike a chord, all
will sing AMERICA- "My Country, tis of
Thee."[740]

In current (2025) social-dysfunction, this gesture has
lead to much hysteria – especially surrounding the public
antics of one earlier mentioned grandson of a Technocrat –
due to its association with a certain historical figure who died
by his own hand in 1945, and the ideology he ostensibly
founded. That particular dictator was aged only two when
this collectivist performance took hold of the United States,
and it has been wholly demonstrated that nationalism and
socialism – again, *National Socialism* – did not only predate
the birth of the Austrian-born German dictator, but comprised
the essential core of the Progressive Era in the United States
before the turn of the century.

One may well disagree with the conjunction of
'nationalism' and 'socialism' under the Bellamy cousins with
the ideology of National Socialism, but such is an absurdity.
The 'bogey' of current parlance is entirely falsely conflated
with Fascism, that is an *Italian* conflation of *Roman*
symbolism. This symbolism is itself invoked by the *fasces* of
fascism on display behind the podium in the United States
House of Representatives.[741]

The so-called 'Bellamy salute', the 'Nazi salute', or
the 'Roman salute' (entirely dependent on preference) appear
to be accidental correspondences that underlie the *substantial*
agreement between the Bellamyist iteration of National
Socialism, and the *Nationalsozialistische Deutsche
Arbeiterpartei*, known as the NSDAP or more commonly as
the Nazi party. Nationalism was what Ely called the
American branch of Socialism.[742] In perfect agreement with

---

740   "National School Celebration of Columbus Day, The
      Official Programme," *The Youth's Companion*, 65 (September 8,
      1892): 446 – 447. NOTE, there is some controversy regarding
      authorship that is here disregarded.
741 The *fasces* is a bundle of sticks with an axe, bound in leather. It
      originated in Etruscan culture and was adopted by Rome as a symbol
      of *imperium* – absolute authority.
742   Ely, *Socialism*, 69

German National Socialism, probably no accident given it's social gospel and social organism elements and connection to German Historicism from Ely and John's Hopkins, American National Socialism – that being Progressivism – relied on an image of regimented authoritarian collectivism, racial purity, eugenics, the State in place of God, and co-opted Roman iconography. Additionally, these *consanguineous* pathologies exhibit an identical, fanatically zealous obsession with pubic schooling. Whether *The Youth's Companion* and *compulsory* public schooling curriculum under diktat of the State, or *Die Hitlerjungend*, they both first go after the kids.

It is a dangerous and foolhardy thing for anyone, let alone an historian, to make grandiose claims regarding what would or would not 'horrify' the so-called 'founding fathers' (though their familiarity with the Bible would likely cause them to feel irritation with the title 'father'[743]). It is simply a bad idea to claim that Washington, Adams, Jefferson, Mason, and the others would 'roll over in their graves'. Perhaps Hamilton or even Adams would endorse the idea of educating patriotism, but Madison overtly opposed the very idea of public schooling itself as a function of government – stating outright that such a thing "would subvert the very foundations... of the limited government established by the people of America."[744] These being said, one cannot dream of a Jefferson or even a Washington endorsing the idea of extracting an oath of loyalty from young children – an oath to "one Nation indivisible" in direct opposition to the concept of Federalism. Whether it is to the Mad King George III, Emperor Gaius Julius Octavius Caesar Augustus, or merely 'the Republic for which it stands', such an oath – 'pledge' being a weaseler – being *commanded* to *children* under the

---

743 Cf. Matthew 23:9.
744 James Madison, "The Cod Fishery Bill, February 7, 1792," in Jonathan Elliott, ed. *The debates in the several state conventions on the adoption of the federal Constitution, as recommended by the general convention at Philadelphia, in 1787. Together with the Journal of the federal convention, Luther Martin's letter, Yates's minutes, Congressional opinions, Virginia and Kentucky resolutions of '98-'99, and other illustrations of the Constitution ... 2d ed., with considerable additions. Collected and rev. from contemporary publications,* (Washington: 1836), Vol. IV, 429.

authority of the *State* is wholly outside of any rational measure of the design founded on the Declaration.

The argument may arise that this is merely a performance, a meaningless ritual; malarkey. Ritual and ceremony contain intrinsic power, and this understanding was at the foundation of the creation of this particular ritual. If this is an insufficient response, it is also clear from all of his writing, especially regarding 'Americanism,' that Francis Bellamy considered this ritual to be a fundamental *sacrament* in his drive to convert the United States into a National Socialist, Borg collective. One may retort that the children may simply say the words, go through the motions, without any surrender; such a rebuttal is so thoroughly disingenuous as to be dismissed with contempt. Finally, the argument may be made that this was not a State-compelled ceremony and confession of fealty; the legislatures of at least two States and the Supreme Court of the United States did not agree.

Between 1892 and 1940 at the very least both West Virginia and Pennsylvania passed compulsory Pledge laws. At some point between then and 2022, forty-five other states followed suit with the passage of their own requirements.[745] At some time before 1940, the Minersville School District of Pennsylvania expelled two students who refused the ritual on religious grounds.[746] The father of the children then sued on the claim that he was then required to pay for private schooling. After two lower courts found in favor of the father, the Supreme Court under Chief Justice Charles Hughes (1862 – 1948; Chief Justice 1930 – 1941) reversed that finding partially based on the claim that such matters should be decided in public opinion and legislatures, rather than the courts.[747]

---

745   Brad Dress, "Here is a Breakdown of Laws in 47 States that Require Reciting the Pledge of Allegiance," *The Hill*, April 2, 2022, Accessed March 7, 2025: https://thehill.com/homenews/3256719-47-states-require-the-pledge-of-allegiance-be-recited-in-schools-here-is-a-breakdown-of-each-states-laws/.

746   *Minersville School District v. Gobitis*, 310 U.S. 586 (1940), Accessed March 7, 2025: https://www.law.cornell.edu/supremecourt/text/310/586.

747   *Minersville School District v. Gobitis*, 16.

Far more crucial than the cowardly dereliction of the Supreme Court's role in protecting the practice of limited government, Associate Justice Felix Frankfurter (1882 – 1965) wrote that the issue at hand was "the best way to train children for their place in society"[748] This statement was deeply reminiscent of, if not a direct allusion to Dewey's 1897 *Pedagogic Creed.*[749] More illuminating however, Frankfurter went on to justify the punishment by claiming some level of 'victimhood' on behalf of the school district. "What the school authorities are really asserting is the right to awaken in the child's mind considerations as to the significance of the flag *contrary to those implanted by the parent.*"[750] An important detail of National Socialism, or all authoritarian collectivism, is its presumption to insert itself between the parent and the child, *parens patrie in loco parentis.*

The court was not unanimous in this despicable and overtly tyrannical act, as then Associate Justice Harlan Stone (1872 – 1946) dissented:

> Two youths, now fifteen and sixteen years of age, are by the judgment of this Court held liable to expulsion from the public schools and to denial of all publicly supported educational privileges because of their refusal to yield to the compulsion of a law which commands their participation in a school ceremony contrary to their religious convictions.[751]

The decision rendered in *Minersville v. Gobitis* amounted to a perversion of consent, and therefore a repudiation of the basis of the Declaration – and crucially, the court *never measured this*, but rather limited its review on religious grounds. This decision did not hold for long, but

748   Associate Justice Felix Frankfurter in *Minersville School District v. Gobitis*, 13.
749   Dewey, *Pedagogic Creed*, 8, 16, and elsewhere.
750   *Minersville School District v. Gobitis*, 14; Emphasis added.
751   Associate Justice Harlan Stone in *Minersville School District v. Gobitis*, 21.

even when it was overturned three years later by the Harlan
Stone court (1941 – 1946), the legal reasoning employed still
did not approach the fundamental act of government
usurpation.

Emboldened by *Minersville v. Gobitis*, West Virginia
expanded their own compulsory Pledge statute, with the
overt decree that "refusal to salute the Flag be regarded as an
Act of insubordination, and shall be dealt with
accordingly."[752] The measure of "accordingly" was expulsion,
with "[r]eadmission … denied by statute until compliance,"
during which the "the expelled child is 'unlawfully absent',"
with the parents facing fines and imprisonment.[753] It is
illuminating that Justice Jackson noted that by 1943, many
had objected to how closely the *mandated* salute resembled
that of the Nazis, but the requirement remained "the 'stiff-
arm' salute" as though it were any different.[754] Again on
religious grounds children refused, but this time "[o]fficials
threaten to send them to reformatories maintained for
criminally inclined juveniles." Because the parents "have
been prosecuted and are threatened with prosecutions for
causing delinquency", they brought suit.[755]

It must be inserted here that such excuses for
kidnapping children and sending them to 'reformatories' is
substantially related to Gladden's claim that freedom is
forfeit "by their unsocial conduct."[756] While Gladden spoke
of indigence, it is exceedingly clear that especially in matters
of law, the 'slippery slope' is not a fallacy, but rather standard
operating procedure – this being the inescapable reality of
stare decisis. Justice Jackson noted this inevitable fact as he
analyzed the Nationalism behind the pledge, and its coercive

---

752   Associate Justice Robert H. Jackson in *West Virginia State
    Board of Education et al. v. Barnette et al.* (1943) 319 U.S. 624, 2,
    Accessed March 7, 2025:
    https://www.law.cornell.edu/supremecourt/text/319/624.
753   *West Virginia State Board of Education et al. v. Barnette et
    al.*, 4.
754   *West Virginia State Board of Education et al. v. Barnette et
    al.*, 3.
755   *West Virginia State Board of Education et al. v. Barnette et
    al.*, 6.
756   Gladden, *Social Salvation*, 82.

nature.[757] Children who refused to perform a State-mandated ritual, and recite a State-coerced oath of loyalty, were viewed as deviant – as *criminals* – and their parents the same.

The statute was overturned on grounds that it compelled speech. Associate Justice Murphy (1890 – 1949) concurred, stating that "[t]he right of freedom of thought... as guaranteed by the Constitution against State action includes both the right to speak freely and *the right to refrain from speaking at all....*"[758] The court did not recognize that compulsory oaths do not make for a free people, of whom the government is allegedly comprised, and to whom the government is ostensibly accountable; they did not chastise this usurpation by the presumptive legislature. Associate Justice Frankfurter dissented. While he again took the cowardly position that this was a matter for the ballot, he presaged Commons almost verbatim by citing the same dissent from Harlan Stone in *United States v. Butler.* "Not so long ago we were admonished that 'the only check upon our own exercise of power is our own sense of self-restraint.... We have been told that generalities do not decide concrete cases.[759] He did not cite a source for who 'told' the court about generalities, but it is certain that he held similar ideas to Commons' later published *Collective Action.*

Justice Frankfurter's influences may have extended to the pragmatist. In his overly verbose dissent, he made the eminently pragmatic statement that "[o]ur constant preoccupation with the constitutionality of legislation rather than with its wisdom tends to preoccupation of the American mind with a false value."[760] This statement evokes Ely's "radical defect in the habitual thinking of the average American."[761] The 'false value' was to measure law against the Constitution, that being merely the application of the

757   *West Virginia State Board of Education et al. v. Barnette et al.*, 31.
758   Associate Justice William "Frank" Murphy in *West Virginia State Board of Education et al. v. Barnette et al.*, 49; Emphasis added.
759   Associate Justice Frankfurter in *West Virginia State Board of Education et al. v. Barnette et al.*, 53; Cf. Commons, *Collective Action*, 214, 223.
760   Frankfurter in *West Virginia State Board of Education et al. v. Barnette et al.*, 97.

principles of the Declaration. The measure of 'wisdom' in Frankfurter's words appears to have been nothing more complex than 'whatever works', principles or even the Supreme Law notwithstanding.

Not all of the Court was so lost. Justice Jackson finalized his prevailing opinion with at least a rhetorical recognition of the supremacy of principles:

> The very purpose of a Bill of Rights was to withdraw certain subjects from the vicissitudes of political controversy, to place them beyond the reach of majorities and officials and to establish them as legal principles to be applied by the courts. One's right to life, liberty, and property, to free speech, a free press, freedom of worship and assembly, and other fundamental rights may not be submitted to vote; they depend on the outcome of no elections.[762]

Such a grand statement was rendered wholly meaningless by the 1944 decision in *Korematsu v. United States* and others that held 'constitutional' the imprisonment of Japanese-descent American citizens for no other reason than that because they were Japanese, they *might* do something.[763] This was, to be certain, not remotely the only court decision moving forward that entirely nullified the content and context of the Bill of Rights, to say nothing of the principles in the Declaration. The aforementioned practice of *stare decisis* may have been on Jefferson's mind in yet another admonition wherein he wholly predicted that the court would be the creeping worm by which infringement would become precedent.

---

761   Washington Gladden, *The New Idolatry: and Other Discussions*, (New York: McClure, Phillips & Co., 1905), 195, 198 – 199.

762   *West Virginia State Board of Education et al. v. Barnette et al.*, 26.

763   *Korematsu v. United States*, 323 U.S. 214 (1944).

At the establishment of our constitutions, the
judiciary bodies were supposed to be the most
helpless and harmless members of the
government. Experience, however, soon
showed in what way they were to become the
most dangerous; that the insufficiency of the
means provided for their removal gave them a
freehold and irresponsibility in office; that
their decisions, seeming to concern individual
suitors only, pass silent and unheeded by the
public at large; that these decisions,
nevertheless, become law by precedent,
sapping, by little and little, the foundations of
the constitution, and working its change by
construction, before any one has perceived
that that invisible and helpless worm has been
busily employed in consuming its substance.
In truth, man is not made to be trusted for life,
if secured against all liability to account.[764]

Minersville v. Gobitis and its sister case Board of
Education v. Barnette were obviously later than the Bellamy
cousins, but the general trend of 'time dilation' regarding
Supreme Court review, to say nothing of the central issues in
the cases crystallized by the Bellamys, permits the argument
that a 'climate' one describes as American National
Socialism had risen to shade perspectives within the
population. The 'nationalist' representatives elected by this
population passed such reprehensible laws so as to rise to the
Supreme Court.[765] Especially in West Virginia, but certainly
elsewhere, the idea of 'insubordination' commingled with
threats of fines and imprisonment – death threats – appeared
in the first and most clearly present image of State power: the
public school. In the Progressive Era, the manner of the State

---

764   Thomas Jefferson, "From Thomas Jefferson to Adamantios
           Coray, 31 October 1823," Founders Online, National Archives,
           https://founders.archives.gov/documents/Jefferson/98-01-02-3837.
           NOTE The National Archives notes that this is an 'early access / not
           authoritative final version'.
765   Cf. Ely, Socialism, 69.

towards children and their parents was established: believe, obey, comply, *or else.*

Such is the nature of the stage that the Bellamys, Dewey, and Lippmann built, but they were greatly assisted by arguably the most powerful pragmatist up to that point, Oliver Wendell Holmes Jr (1841 – 1935), an Associate Justice of the Supreme Court from 1902 until his retirement in 1932.

Justice Holmes is certainly one of the most famous, most widely cited, and most influential jurists ever to live. Francis Biddle (1886 – 1968), United States Attorney General and one-time personal secretary to Holmes, was inspired by that service to write an exceedingly eulogistic biography.[766] He called Holmes "the most distinguished of all American jurists."[767] To magnify the Justice's reputation, he cited the British Lord Chancellor Haldane (1856 – 1928) "...Holmes was a greater man than John Marshall."[768] Biddle noted that Holmes was a fan of Thomas R. Malthus (1766 – 1834), in addition to having been strongly influenced by Darwin's concept of fitness for survival.[769] More so than Malthusianism and Darwinism, Biddle commented innocently enough on Holmes' Mephistophelianism – the demon to whom the erudite *Faust* sold his soul.[770]

> The old boy had something of Mephistopheles
> in himself — the Mephistopheles who
> summoned Marlowe and Shakespeare,

766   "Francis B. Biddle (1941 – 1945)," *UVA Miller Center*, N.d. Accessed March 11, 2025: https://millercenter.org/president/fdroosevelt/essays/biddle-1941-francis-attorney-general#:~:text=Francis%20B.-,Biddle%20(1941%E2%80%931945),1968%2C%20in%20Wellfleet%2C%20Massachusetts.

767   Morison and Commager in Francis Biddle, *Justice Holmes, Natural Law, and the Supreme Court: The Oliver Wendell Holmes Devise Lectures, 1960,* (New York: The Macmillan Company, 1961), 3.

768   Lord Chancellor Haldane in Biddle, *Justice Holmes*, 3.

769   Biddle, *Justice Holmes*, 7, 8.

770   Cf. Johann Wolfgang von Goethe, *Faust with illustrations by Harry Clarke*, Translated by Bayard Taylor, (New York: Arden Book Company, 1900. [c. 1832]).

Fletcher and Goethe and Thomas Mann; and
who, after giving Dr. Faustus twenty-four
glorious years of youth and love, carried him
off at night between the 23rd and 24th of
October, 1538. In Holmes the
Mephisthophelean attributes were an amused
arrogance, a rebellious iconoclasm — he
would reach out to pull down the sanctities if
they showed signs of interfering with the
earth-born — and a delight in paradoxes....[771]

In response to the first 'red scare' (~1918 – 1920),
Holmes quipped that "[j]udges are apt to be naif, simple-
minded men, and they need something of Mephistopheles."[772]
His precise meaning appears to have been that a jurist ought
not to mistake "what seemed to him to be first principles"
with universal beliefs, even should those "sanctities" be the
foundation of the authority from which he operated – like the
Declaration.[773] It would follow then that he wholly rejected
the idea of Natural Law because the factor of one not wishing
to be murdered apparently gives no indication that murder is
universally wrong – because others might believe differently.

Apparently natural law, for instance, in
addition to existing in the mind of the Creator,
and in the mind of man when he exercised his
reason in order to find it, was conceived as
something with a separate being of its own,
irrespective of divine or human recognition.
Holmes had never experienced it, and, not
believing in revelations which he had not
shared, denied its external validity. The
unwillingness to accept less than being on the
ground floor with God did not impress him
much except as a fact of psychology. The
assumption of a knowledge of ultimate truth

---

771   Biddle, *Justice Holmes*, 12.
772   Biddle, *Justice Holmes*, 12, sic.
773   Biddle, *Justice Holmes*, 11.

implied a kind of arrogance that he
distrusted.[774]

Biddle's characterization of "a knowledge of ultimate
truth" as arrogance stands in strange context. Moreover, the
claim that Holmes had never experienced Natural Law is
flatly dishonest; every living soul knows what is against its
precepts when they have been the target of the act, this being
the origin of irritation, victimization, and outrage – of the
desire for and drive towards Justice itself. One aspect of
Holmes' Mephistophelianism was a "delight in paradoxes," it
is therefore appropriate that Holmes dismissed the concept of
principles – to which all functioning human minds have
access by the utterly simplistic "do you want it done to
you?". Holmes rejected the freely accessible nature of the
Creator's laws, especially as the foundation for the
Declaration, as arrogance. It would appear that Natural Law,
being the equal possession of all men, was too sullied for his
elevated tastes.

> Although Holmes... objected to conservative
> activist decisions striking down progressive
> regulations, Holmes... had no personal
> sympathy for the Progressive movement. An
> aristocratic nihilist who once told his sister
> that he loathed "the thick-fingered clowns we
> call the people," Holmes believed that judges
> should vote to uphold virtually all laws, even
> the ones they hate.[775]

Holmes sought to apply his personal cosmology to all
in his capacity as Associate Justice, contrary to his personal
cosmology: as a first principle. His universal principle of
repudiation of universal principles expressed in a *pragmatic*
deference to legislatures, and matched the general thrust of
Justice Frankfurtur's approach to the Bellamy cases. If the

---

774   Biddle, *Justice Holmes*, 41.
775   Jeffrey Rosen, "Brandeis's Seat, Kagan's Responsibility,"
The New York Times, July 3, 2010. Accessed March 10, 2025:
https://www.nytimes.com/2010/07/04/opinion/04rosen.html?
ref=opinion.

legislature does it, it is not illegal; *rex non potest peccare*.[776]
In Associate Justice Oliver Wendell Holmes Jr.'s view, there
was no limit to what the government might do, and the
people from whom it must derive consent for its just powers
were "thick fingered clowns". In Justice Holmes' personal
and judicial cosmology, Justice did not exist; perfectly
pragmatic.

In equivalent manner to both Dewey and Lippmann,
Holmes' convoluted and self-contradictory ideology was a
direct product of his wholly root-less world-view. As stated,
he criticized Natural Law because in his view, it amounted to
universalizing one's parochial understanding, yet he himself
universalized *this* perspective. This is merely another
rendition of the absolutist claim that there are no absolutes,
or the supremely dissonant position that it is true that there is
no truth. Again, if solipsism is true, it does not matter
because one imagines it to be false. Holmes' fell victim to the
same *stupidity* that always accompanies this self-corrosive
circularity; he rejected the *moral* foundation of rights, as
though these had nothing to do with the inescapable moral
calculus of right and wrong. Rejecting any moral foundation
for rights, this Associate Justice of the Supreme Court
inevitably rejected the Organic Act from whence his
authority derived – the Constitution – relegating it to mere
'construction by consensus' as did all pragmatists.

> The law is full of phraseology drawn from
> morals, and talks about rights and duties,
> malice, intent, and negligence — and nothing
> is easier in legal reasoning than to take these
> words in their moral sense. So we speak of the
> rights of a man meaning to mark the limits of
> interference with individual freedom
> prescribed by conscience, or by our ideal....
> Therefore nothing but confusion can result

776   Cf. Congress.Gov, "Transcript of David Frost's Interview
with Richard Nixon, 1977," *Teaching American History*, Accessed
January 28, 2025:
https://www.congress.gov/116/meeting/house/110331/documents/H
MKP-116-JU00-20191211-SD408.pdf.

from assuming that the rights of man in a
moral sense are equally rights in the sense of
the Constitution and the law.

And that is precisely how he thought of
natural law — a mystic overlaw, not law in
any true sense, theology or morals if you like,
but not law. The demand for the superlative
that we find in all men was at the bottom of
the philosopher's effort to prove that truth was
absolute, and of the jurist's search for criteria
of universal validity which he collects under
the head of natural law. That is why the jurists
who believed in natural law seemed to him to
be "in that naive state of mind that accepts
what has been familiar and accepted by them
and their neighbors as something that must be
accepted by all men everywhere."[777]

Seeking to divest morality from the law, Holmes yet
again contradicted himself. In a manner evocative of
Gladden's biblical caricature of "progress from a lower to a
higher morality", Holmes described the history of law as
moral development. He employed his pragmatism to claim
some incision regarding a difference between the two, but it
would appear that the difference was merely one of preferred
origins, or some inappropriate and artificially constrained
insistence on empiricism.

The law is the witness and external deposit of
our moral life. Its history is the history of the
moral development of the race. The practice
of it, in spite of popular jests, tends to make
good citizens and good men. When I
emphasize the difference between law and
morals I do so with reference to a single end,
that of learning and understanding the law.[778]

---

777   Biddle, *Justice Homes*, 40, 41.
778   Oliver Wendell Holmes, Jr., "The Path of the Law: A Study".
Harvard Review 10, No. 457 (1897), Accessed March 10, 2025:

The popular jest to which he referred was the claim that "you cannot make men good by law" against which Ely wrote his statism-justifying retort the year prior.[779] Neither Ely nor Holmes answered the shouting question of how this is to work in the midst of bad law – or what is the origin of good law if men make the laws, but themselves must first be made good by that law. Biddle argued that Holmes' position was "neither radical – for our day and age – nor disturbing… that men make their own laws; that these laws do not flow from some mysterious omnipresence in the sky…. The justification of any rule of law is that it helps to bring about a desired social end…"[780] And yet again, neither Holmes nor Biddle appear to have addressed the origin and quality of a social end, if it was the law that made them good – but they who made the law. The Ouroboros appears to have been pragmatism's defining detail.

The most succinct summary of Holmes' cosmology was penned as though it were a good thing. Biddle distilled the Justice's perspective – and therefore *judicial philosophy*: "Holmes did not believe in natural law or any other absolute, and said so a good many times without noticeable restraint. He included moralities and religious beliefs in the sweep of his skepticism…."[781] He did not believe in any absolute; he did not believe 'that to secure these Rights governments are instituted among men, deriving their just powers from the consent of the governed' because such is an absolutist appeal to the Laws of nature, and of nature's God. Justice Holmes, by his own position, had no authority under the government founded by the Declaration.

His influence was extensive; he was a member of the esoteric Metaphysical Club and close personal friend of William James.[782] The historical reality of the club, as a club rather than a rhetorical device, is a different matter than the overtones of conspiracy that attend the innocent socializing

---

https://moglen.law.columbia.edu/LCS/palaw.pdf, 2, 3.

779   Ely, *The Social Law*, 186 – 187.

780   Biddle, *Justice Holmes*, 49.

781   Biddle, *Justice Holmes*, 4.

782   David Kenny, *Pragmatism, Law, and Literature*, (Oxon, U.K.: Routledge, 2024), 41.

of philosophers who then go on to become deeply influential in their respective careers. Louis Menand approached the drastic shift in the foundations of dominant American cosmology around the latter decades of the nineteenth century in 2001 by writing what amounts to a history of pragmatism, entitled *The Metaphysical Club*.[783] The work features a pencil drawing by William James as a frontispiece, and narrates the personal and professional histories of William James, John Dewey, Charles S. Peirce (1839 - 1914), and Oliver Wendell Holmes. Introducing this objectively momentous association, Menand stated that "[t]heir ideas changed the way Americans thought – and continue to think – about education, democracy, liberty, justice, and tolerance."[784]

Menand was not wrong, but would have done well to address Lippmann's intellectual decent in this line – rather than quickly passing by him as an acolyte to Holmes' judiciary.[785] It is likely that he did not treat Lippmann because he was effectively a 'next-generation' pragmatist, but this is not a weakness. Holmes, Dewey, and James' influence traveled through the likes of Lippmann, and Menand merely speaks of the origin and nature of that influence. Either way, whatever ideals were hatched or developed by this club immediately began to alter – to *pervert* – American jurisprudence in the person of Holmes.

Contemporaneously to Menand, John Sutton stated that "Holmes recognized that law is, in contemporary terms, socially constructed."[786] He came to this conclusion while seeking to "rethink the intellectual premises of American law" as an attempt "to break formalism's stranglehold on American legal thinking."[787] In Sutton's definition, formalism

---

783   Menand addressed the questionable historicity of an 'official' club, citing Charles Peirce and William James' bother Henry, but concludes that some kind of association was created in January, 1872. Louis Menand. *The Metaphysical Club*, (New York: Farrar, Straus, and Giroux, 2001), 201.

784   Menand. *The Metaphysical Club*, xi.

785   Cf. Menand, *The Metaphysical Club*, 66.

786   John Sutton, *Law/Society: Origins, Interactions, and Change*, (Thousand Oaks, Calif: Pine Forge Press, 2001), 138.

787   Sutton, *Law/Society*, 137.

was the perspective that law was "...an autonomous and self-contained body of knowledge, and rulings should be guided by abstract legal precepts rather than by tradition, sentiment, or shifting public attitudes."[788] Given that Sutton expanded this definition to include a 'get-with-the-times' attitude toward the law – because of economics and technological advance – one interprets "abstract legal precepts" to be the agreed upon function of government according to the Declaration, with allowance for drifting common law precedent set by mistaken interpretations of those principles. In Sutton's view, "[t]o the activists of the Progressive era, the courts were an obstacle to change."[789] Given such an interpretation, 'formalism' seems to be employed as an epithet, and functioned as Holmes' straw-man in his attempt to make law more amenable to 'sentiment' and 'shifting' – hysterical and fickle – 'public attitudes.' Madison speaks again: "Law is defined to be a rule of action; but how can that be a rule, which is little known and less fixed?"[790]

    Whether or not he was a friend to the Progressives, Holmes broke the Court's ability to stand against their policy-objectives.[791] He brought his disdain for 'formalism' and the pragmatism he developed in the Metaphysical Club into his judicial career – and the legal perspective that it spawned. In his 1882 work *The Common Law*, Holmes applied his paradigm to the practice of law. "The life of the law has not been logic: it has been experience.... The law embodies the story of a nation's development..."[792] David Kenny very recently explained this to mean that the things of reason "...are not the reality of the law [but rather] the coat that the law wears; underneath lie the real needs of the society that the law sets out to serve."[793] One can certainly see correspondence between this branch of pragmatism and Justice Frankfurter's 'reasoning' (meaning, rationalization) in

---

788   Sutton, *Law/Society*, 135, 136.
789   Sutton, *Law/Society*, 137.
790   James Madison [Attributed], "The Senate," *Federalist no. 62*, 1788, in *Constitution*, 2012, 534; Emphasis added.
791   Cf. Rosen, "Brandeis's Seat, Kagan's Responsibility."
792   Oliver Wendell Holmes Jr., *The Common Law*, (London: Macmillan & Co., 1882), 1.
793   Kenny, *Pragmatism*, 43.

Board of Education v. Barnette. The commonality being that the constraints of the Declaration are secondary to the 'needs of society' – rather the preferences of the loudest and most influential – to the extent that 'limited government' is more of a loose guideline than a principle. Given Justice Stone's 'limits' of self-restraint, to the court there really were no limits at all.[794]

Holmes' law was nothing more complicated than adolescent relativism, extending from the natural contempt of the arrogantly inexperienced teen for his forebears. "The customs, beliefs, or needs of a primitive time establish a rule or a formula. In the course of centuries the custom, belief, or necessity disappears, but the rule remains."[795] It would seem likely that, then President of Princeton University, Woodrow Wilson was aware of and agreed with Holmes' concept of vestigial rules as he challenged his audience to remake society – in *his* image: "We are not bound to adhere to the doctrines held by the signers of the Declaration of Independence: we are as free as they were to make and unmake governments."[796] Not bound by those doctrines in the least, but to throw them out would be by definition *a revolution*, and the repudiation of the authority descending from those 'doctrines.' No house is 'bound' to stand on its foundation, but no house can well stand without one; Wilson's baby sits crying in a puddle of his own bathwater, beneath the window from which he was thrown. If Justice can be 'miscarried', it can also be 'birthed'; it would seem that Holmes' infant was also so thrown.

Justice Holmes represented the abnegation of the principles from which a Justice's authority is derived, in concert with a variable, almost flighty rendition of law as without limit, subject only to "shifting public attitudes" as defined by unknown, unknowable, unaccountable persons. Holmes' pragmatick theory of law extends from this rootless

---

794   Cf. Frankfurter in *West Virginia v. Barnette*, 53; Commons, *Collective Action*, 214, 223.
795   Holmes, *The Common Law*, 5.
796   Woodrow Wilson, "The Author and Signers of the Declaration of Independence," *The North American Review* 186, no. 622 (1907): 25.

ideal. Again, law in an ostensible 'republic of law' is the measure by which death threats are acceptable or even necessary due to prevailing moral principles. Holmes most certainly knew this, but he rationalized away the substance of such threats because he rejected the possibility of prevailing moral principles.

Holmes wrote *The Path of the Law* in 1897 to expound on his view that the principles, morality, and even motives behind acts of both individuals and legislatures were effectively irrelevant, only the consequences, outcomes, the results were of any value. The content and substance of law meant nothing, rather "[t]he prophecies of what the courts will do in fact, and nothing more pretentious, are what I mean by the law."[797]

Given this thoroughly pragmatic view, Holmes claimed that law must be a profession because "...societies like ours the command of the public force is intrusted to the judges in certain cases, and the whole power of the state will be put forth, if necessary, to carry out their judgments and decrees."[798] Ultimately it would seem that in matters of law, Holmes would agree with Mao Zedong (1893 – 1976) that "political power grows out of the barrel of a gun."[799] This is not a criticism – it is self-evidently true that all government power is ultimately and entirely variations on the use of violence. To place law in the hands of elevated 'experts' not only serves to shift Holmes' legal theory further away from the principle of popular sovereignty, but squarely places it in the same elitism of the previous chapter. The law, and the lawyers, are merely prophecies and prophets of what the courts will do, but no guarantee. In this view, justice became a temple staffed with *priests* to whom the mere plebeians must turn to read the auguries. These 'omens' amount to nebulous, diaphanous, and ultimately vacuous appeals to 'sentiment' or what Holmes meant when he spoke of

---

797   Holmes, "The Path of the Law," 4.
798   Holmes, "The Path of the Law," 1, sic.
799   枪杆子里面出政权; (*Qiang gan zi li mian chu zheng quan*);
         Li Gucheng, ed., *A Glossary of Political Terms of the People's Republic of China*, (Hong Kong: The Chinese University Press, 1995), 325.

'common law.' The law became entirely inscrutable – a
capricious and arbitrary toy for the powerful.

Regarding the opinion of the Supreme Court in the
exceedingly dry question of maritime tort jurisdiction as
decided in *Southern Pacific Co. v. Jensen*, Holmes wrote in
his 1917 dissent: "The common law is not a brooding
omnipresence in the sky, but the articulate voice of some
sovereign or quasi sovereign that can be identified…. It
always is the law of some state..."[800] Holmes used this
premise to argue that the Workman's Compensation law of
New York took precedence over Article III § 2, and Article I
§ 8 of the Constitution, the conjunction of which gave
Congress and the Judiciary power over "admiralty and
maritime jurisdiction." He explained this usurpation the next
year.

Holmes wrote the prevailing opinion in *Towne v.
Eisner* 1918 to decide a question regarding the definition of
'income' arising from the newly delivered devil child of
Wilson: the Income Tax Law of 1913.[801] In his majority
opinion, Holmes declared that "...it is not necessarily true
that income means the same thing in the Constitution and the
Act. A word is not a crystal, transparent and unchanged, it is
the skin of a living thought, and may vary greatly in color
and content according to the circumstances and the time in
which it is used."[802] As already exhaustively demonstrated,
semantics may certainly move over the span of time, but to
make the declaration that the *same word* in a law and the
Supreme Law from which it gains authority do not have the
same definition, by one in authority, is at *best* an abusive act
of gaslighting. There is no barrier to any claim that any word
means something wholly different, at any time. This
particular detail would go on to nullify the Sixth Amendment
words "In all criminal prosecutions…" through the
amalgamation of *Baldwin v. New York* (1970), and *Lewis v.*

---

800   *Southern Pacific Co. v. Jensen*, 244 U.S. 205, 222 (1917),
        Page 244 U.S. 222, Accessed March 13, 2025:
        https://supreme.justia.com/cases/federal/us/244/205/.
801   *Towne v. Eisner*, 245 U.S. 418, 425 (1918), Accessed March
        13, 2025: https://supreme.justia.com/cases/federal/us/245/418/.
802   *Towne v. Eisner*, Page 245 U.S. 425.

United States (1996) that have effectively revoked the right
to a jury *in all* criminal prosecutions.

Holmes' utterly dishonest reasoning in *Towne v. Eisner* extended from the view that The Constitution was a 'living' document. This is not the perspective that it can be amended according to its own provisions, but rather that operative vocabulary – from 'income' to 'all,' or the definition of what 'is, is' – can be altered by mere sorcery of narcissistic-semantics. By this simple trick, 'law' became unpredictable, unknowable, and unreliable for the citizens from whom it ostensibly gains its legitimacy. With these few words, Holmes reduced the law to a plaything and castrated the principle behind the rule of law, not of men. By precedent, the law no longer meant what the law said, it came to mean whatever a court decided it meant, whenever it so desired. Because of this, the citizen must entreat Holmes' 'prophets' to read the entrails on his behalf. Because of this, the citizen is beholden to the arbitrary will of any given magistrate as expressed in his use of semantics. Because of this, the law became incomprehensible.

Holmes amputated the ability of the citizen to know the meaning of law by employing the same historicist, evolution, social-organism reasoning as the men previously analyzed. In his 1914 majority opinion for *Gompers v. United States* Holmes declared "The provisions of the Constitution are not mathematical formulas that have their essence in form, they are organic, living institutions transplanted from English soil. Their significance is vital, not formal; it is to be gathered not simply by taking the words and a dictionary but by considering their origin and the line of their growth."[803] The operative terms of this declaration – organic, origin, and growth – may be lifted directly from the musings of men such as Gladden or Ely as they refer directly to inscrutable historicism and the view of society as an evolving organism. Yet again Holmes' perspective was aligned with Woodrow Wilson whose public campaign excused itself with feigned humility. "All that progressives

---

803   *Gompers v. United States*, 233 U.S. 604, 610 (1914), Page
    233 U.S. 605, Accessed March 13, 2025:
    https://supreme.justia.com/cases/federal/us/233/604/.

ask or desire is permission… to interpret the Constitution according to the Darwinian principle; all they ask is recognition of the fact that a nation is a living thing and not a machine."[804] All that the Progressives ask for or desire is *power.*

Holmes' shifting vocabulary leads directly to the absurdity of claiming that anything is unconstitutional. If the Constitution is a 'living document' that merely reflects a given time's 'consensus', the limitation of government is reduced to little better than self-referential judicial pronouncement on the current state of the Overton window, gaslit by Lippmann's manufactured consent. In 1927 that Overton window allowed for the murder and mutilation of those deemed racially or socially unfit, and Associate Justice Holmes was in complete agreement.

As stated, where Gladden wanted the unemployed imprisoned and Commons called them outlaws, Dewey revoked the right to life in his ideal of society, and Holmes enshrined this despicable view of humanity into the common law. In an uncharacteristically brief majority opinion – there being but one *silent* dissenter – Holmes upheld the *Virginia Eugenical Sterilization Act*, 1924 with the now thoroughly 'politically incorrect' words:

> Carrie Buck is the probably potential parent of socially inadequate offspring… and that her welfare and that of society will be promoted by her sterilization….It is better for all the world if, instead of waiting to execute degenerate offspring for crime or to let them starve for their imbecility, society can prevent those who are manifestly unfit from continuing their kind…. Three generations of imbeciles are enough.[805]

---

804   Woodrow Wilson, *The New Freedom: A Call for the Emancipation of the Generous Energies of a People*, (New York: Doubleday, Page & Co, 1913), Project Gutenberg Ebook #14811, Chapter 2: "What is Progress?".

805   *Buck v. Bell*, 274 U.S. 200 (1927), Page 274 U.S. 207, Accessed March 13, 2025: https://supreme.justia.com/cases/federal/us/274/200/.

Ultimately, the actual circumstances surrounding the case are beside the current argument. It should however be noted that in this case, a human being was denied the championship of the court, and became its victim. A probably average-intelligence twenty-one year old woman who may have been raped was committed to the asylum that condemned her by the relatives of the rapist, to cover up the rape, and the highest court in the United States added grievous insult to that horrific injury.[806] It is obvious from all foregoing analysis that Holmes relied upon the concept of the social organism in his reasoning, and he conveyed Gladden and Ely's policy objectives into law – nullifying the whole dignity of the individual which lie at the heart of the creation of the United States of America.

It is also appropriate here to note that somewhat recently, scholarly engagement with this particular aspect of Holmes' breed of justice has illuminated the previously made connection between Progressivism, eugenics, and *German* National Socialism. Holmes' words in *Buck v. Bell* were cited to defend an accused at the Nuremberg trials for crimes against humanity.[807] The reality of Progressivism as American National Socialism was hardly a trick of conflating 'nationalist' clubs and 'socialist' objectives; in the person of the pragmatist Oliver Wendell Holmes Jr., it was *policy*.

"On the surface, the ideas of [Dewey, Peirce,] Oliver Wendell Holmes Jr., [James, and Jane Addams (1860 – 1935)] seem like like a natural theoretical base for an emerging profession challenged with making government work."[808] That profession was created by auto-apotheosis, driven by the heresy of perfectibility, and justified by the solipsism of pragmatism. Pragmatism, or rather the

---

806   Czarr, ""Three Generations of Imbeciles are Enough" – The Case of Buck v. Bell," *National Archives*, Education Updates, May 2, 2017, Accessed March 13:
https://education.blogs.archives.gov/2017/05/02/buck-v-bell/.

807   Cf. Harry Bruinius, *Better for All the World: The Secret History of Forced Sterilization and America's Quest for Racial Purity*, (New York: Knopf, 2006), 316.

808   Shields, Patricia M. "Rediscovering the Taproot: Is Classical Pragmatism the Route to Renew Public Administration?" *Public Administration Review* 68, no. 2 (Mar, 2008), 205.

Pragmatick Theory of Government – Progressivism or
American National Socialism, is itself the root that grew the
poisoned tree; the deadly fruit of which is the current
undeniable dysfunction within American civilization. It is
supremely ironic that it was Holmes who purloined Jesus'
words to exclude evidence unlawfully obtained, as it is by his
own words that he is condemned:[809]

> Words which, ordinarily and in many places,
> would be within the freedom of speech
> protected by the First Amendment may
> become subject to prohibition when of such a
> nature and used in such circumstances a to
> create a clear and present danger that they will
> bring about the substantive evils which
> Congress has a right to prevent.[810]

Words mean whatever the court decides they mean,
even in contradiction. The principles of the Declaration based
in Natural Law do not exist; the Bill of Rights is no
protection against 'circumstances'. The dignity of the
individual, safety from *mutilation*, must needs be sacrificed
on the altar of the welfare of society. While it is certain that
one may point to any Justice or magistrate and call him a
criminal, the obvious pun here is too appropriate to omit.
Oliver Wendell Holmes Jr. was, as a direct product of his
pragmatism, a *criminal Justice*; he was unapologetically
seditious. It has already been shown that he had a certain
accomplice in his sedition; now it is appropriate to analyze
the treason of Woodrow Wilson, twenty-eighth President of
the United States, Sulla's Scion, and undertaker to the second
Great Republic.

Buck v. Bell was merely one instance wherein Holmes
was fully allied with Wilson. Wilson's contempt for

---

809   *Silverthorne Lumber Co., Inc. v. United States*, 251 U.S. 385
(1920); Cf. *Nardone v. United States*, 308 U.S. 338, 341 (1939); Cf.
Matthew 7:18.

810   *Schenck v. United States*, 249 U.S. 47 (1919), Page 249
U.S. 48, Accessed March 13, 2025:
https://supreme.justia.com/cases/federal/us/249/47/, sic (the typo 'a'
for 'as' is in this citation).

'formalism' as well as his wholly pragmatic approach to policy function stood in substantial parity with Holmes. Additionally, Wilson successfully recruited Bellamyist nationalism in his political goals that were, in all respects, the application of the social gospel. In many aspects Wilson was the culmination of the previously analyzed currents – both from a social and from an intellectual perspective. Where others spread ideals and policy objectives, or in the case of Holmes merely took advantage of opportunities to apply a perverse world-view, Wilson sought out and used power to force his image of the world upon the world, under the ever present Damoclean sword of law-*enforcement*.

Wilson's historicist *bona fides* have already been well established. Richard Ely thought of himself as Wilson's "mid-wife", though he considered Wilson to have been a bit of an empty can.[811] His perspective on the time-dependent conception of truth painted his first book as he immediately began to argue that the foundations of American civilization were no longer relevant. To be certain, he couched his paradigm in positive rhetoric like each of the men previously examined, but the substance of his modernism remained clear.

> ...*Congressional Government* (1885), is still famous for its attack on formalistic readings of the Constitution, for its realism in assessing the workings of American government, for its call for more responsible forms of leadership, and for its openness to alternative governing arrangements that might be more fully attuned to the changing demands of the times[812]

---

811   Paraphrasing Richard Ely, Clifford F. Thies and Gary M. Pequet, "The Shaping of a Future President's Economic Thought: Richard T. Ely and Woodrow Wilson at "The Hopkins,"" *The Independent Review*, 15, no. 2 (Fall 2010): 259. Ely commented on Wilson's speeches in 1939 "[he] could speak beautifully and say nothing." Note 5 in Thies and Pequet, 259. NOTE: Thies and Pequet argue that Wilson only adopted historicism at a later time, having "derided" it earlier in his academic career.

812   Stephen Skowronek, "The Reassociation of Ideas and Purposes: Racism, Liberalism, and the American Political

Time did not change his attitude toward the foundation; years later in his position as President at Princeton, he "...dismissed talk of the inalienable rights of the individual as "nonsense.""[813] He developed this perspective, it would appear, from his appraisal regarding the legacy of Reconstruction, claiming that "it had opened the door to empire." Indeed, he claimed that the time had "...dispelled the conceit that government could be limited and vested rights protected by resort to the old balance of powers."[814] He eventually developed this perspective into what Thies and Pequet termed "his "principle" of ad hoc pragmatism in pursuit of the greater good as he understood it...."[815] His 'greater good' was certainly the previously disregarded utility of John Commons, being a simple outgrowth of social organism that is, the Borg.[816]

Introducing his previously mentioned feigned humility in "all that progressives ask", Wilson invoked both Darwin and the social organism as cause to wholly reject the concept of fixed and unchanging principles – that might be accessed, understood, predicted, relied upon, and employed by all. He spoke of this repudiation of the 'north star' as inarguable fact, equating the separation of powers (the safeguard against tyranny) to a living organism having "its organs offset against each other....":

> The trouble with the theory is that government
> is not a machine, but a living thing. It falls,
> not under the theory of the universe, but under
> the theory of organic life. It is accountable to
> Darwin, not to Newton....Living political

Tradition," *American Political Science Review* 100, no. 3 (2006): 390.

813   Thomas C. Leonard, *Illiberal Reformers : Race, Eugenics, and American Economics in the Progressive Era*, (Princeton: Princeton University Press, 2016), 25.

814   Paraphrasing Wilson, Skowronek, "The Reassociation," 391.

815   Thies and Pequet, "The Shaping," 275.

816   Cf. Commons, *Labor and Administration*, v. This citation, "not so much the law and its abstract rights, as administration and its concrete results" demonstrates a deeper connection between 'utility' and pragmatism.

constitutions must be Darwinian in structure
and in practice. Society is a living organism
and must obey the laws of life, not of
mechanics; it must develop.[817]

In harmony with the other social-gospellers, notably
Gladden and Rauschenbusch, Wilson employed a baseless,
apostate perversion of Christianity as evidence that "he was
one of the elect in the service of God."[818] He reflected the
concept of a 'socialized' Christianity, seeking to redeem
society into the Kingdom, though he conveyed it through the
lens of "individual well-being."[819]

Christianity gave us, in the fullness of time,
the perfect image of right living, the secret of
social and of individual well-being; for the
two are not separable, and the man who
receives and verifies that secret in his own
living has discovered not only the best and
only way to serve the world, but also the one
happy way to satisfy himself.[820]

To employ his retort to the inalienable rights of the
individual: nonsense. His social organism to which he spoke
regarding 'well-being' was the same as Rauschenbusch's:
Teutonic. Wilson made identical historical interpretations to
Rauschenbusch regarding "the early history of the Aryan
race."[821] He lay the origin of the social order of the early
colonials at the same root, claiming that "[the colonists] were
inventing nothing; they were simply letting their race habits
and instincts have natural play.... they rested... upon original

817   Wilson, *The New Freedom*, Chapter 2: "What is Progress?".
Cf. Leonard, *Illiberal Reformers*, 250. Cf. Woodrow Wilson,
Constitutional Government in the United States, (New York:
Columbia University Press, 1908), 56, verbatim.
818   Thies and Pequet, "The Shaping," 275.
819   Cf. Rauschenbusch, *The Social Crisis*, 65; Rauschenbusch,
A Theology, 24.
820   Woodrow Wilson, *When A Man Comes to Himself*, (New
York: Harper and Brothers, 1901), Project Gutenberg Ebok #5078,
section VI.
821   Rauschenbusch, *The Social Order*, 375.

Teutonic principles."[822] This rendition, in Wilson's 1898 *The State*, perfectly matches the reasoning behind Rauschenbusch's "social supremacy of the Aryan race", making identical social-Darwinist arguments.[823] Indeed, the whole work was written from an identical historical fabrication, narrating the development of social order from the same Aryan foundations, employing the same assumptions.[824] As expected, Wilson's perverse corelation of "Teutonic stock" with Christianity appears to side-step the "Semitic" nature and origins of the Bible – drawing ever greater doubt as to what he conceived when he spoke of 'christianity'.[825]

Yet again it must be reiterated that Wilson's currently-unpalatable racial ideology was not simply from 'another time' – that being a supremely ironic rationalization given that he used the same excuse to reject the very origins of Presidential and legal authority. His misanthropy cannot be dismissed by sleight of hand. Wilson's sickly condescension was not just 'theory' to him; it was not simply adjunct to his social programs or conception of government authority. Like Commons' 1907 *Races and Immigration*, the borderline genocidal arguments that Wilson made were *the origin* of his authoritarianism, of his entire world-view. Like Ely, he viewed greater society as merely a resource pool, and for this reason like Ely, he advocated for, approved of, and enabled eugenics.[826]

Like Holmes, Wilson's perspectives quickly found their way to central Europe. Geza von Hoffmann (1885 – 1921), a prominent Austrian eugenicist, specifically cited Wilson's 1913 Presidential address: "the whole nation has awakened to and recognizes the extraordinary importance of the science of human heredity, as well as its application to the

---

822   Woodrow Wilson, *The State: Elements of Historical and Practical Politics*, (Boston: D.C. Heath & Co, 1907 [1898]), 509.
823   Rauschenbusch, *The Social Order*, 376.
824   Cf. Wilson, *The State*, "The Early Forms of Government", Part I.
825   Cf. Wilson, *The State*, I:3 "Semitic and Tauranian Instance," 2.
826   Cf. Ely, *The World War*, 115.

ennoblement of the human family."[827] This was not merely
an endorsement of State-enforced mutilation from the most
powerful man in America, it was an overt declaration that he
would continue to employ the power of his office to
completely disregard the dignity of the individual as he had
when he legalized forcible sterilization as Governor of New
Jersey in 1911.[828]

Relying on this same caste-like perspective, one of
his first acts as President of the United States was to apply
his conception of social-strata directly to his new domain.
Being the first southern Democrat to return to the White
House after the Civil War, Wilson segregated the whole of
the federal government. He did this in response to his view of
the disastrous consequences of Reconstruction resulting from
the "blatant disregard of the child-like state of the Negro and
natural order of life"[829] Additionally, Wilson spoke highly of
the *Klan* and other similar organizations, calling them in
overly romantic terms "knights errant."[830]

In response to the likely retort that forcible mutilation
is not so bad, that segregation was merely from a 'different
time,' or some other absurd attempt to maintain a view of
Wilson's quality, it must be noted that another Nobel laureate
(Wilson was granted the Peace Prize in 1919), and self-
confessed "Humanist" in the Dewey sense, Francis Crick,
FRS (1916 – 2004) made the perspective at the heart of *all*
eugenics abundantly clear: "no newborn infant should be
declared human until it has passed certain tests regarding its
genetic endowment, and that if it fails these tests it forfeits
the right to live."[831] It is not at all unreasonable to conceive of

---

827   Stefan Kühl, *The Nazi Connection: Eugenics, American
Racism, and German National Socialism*, (New York: Oxford
University Press, 1994), 16.

828   Paul Lombardo, "Taking Eugenics Seriously: Three
Generations of ??? Are Enough," *Florida State University Law
Review* 30 no. 2, (2003), 209.

829   Wilson in Skowronek, "The Reassociation," 391.

830   Woodrow Wilson, *A History of the American People in Five
Volumes*, Vol. V, (New York: Harper & Brothers, 1916 [1902]), 60 –
62.

831   Lombardo, "Taking Eugenics Seriously," 209, Note 124;
Francis Crick, "Why I am a Humanist," *Francis Crick Papers, The*

being in a 'child-like state' as grounds for genetic failure. Like Gladden, Ely, Rauschenbusch, et al., 'rights' are and have always been conditional from a Progressive perspective, subject to arbitrary forfeit especially for the 'unfit', and Wilson's world-view was no different.

In an extended discussion regarding the several functions of government – of which he lay heavy into what he called the "ministrant functions" – Wilson subordinated all conception of rights to the State, declaring that "government does now whatever experience permits or the times demand...."[832] In these ministrant functions, Wilson included what he called "Sumptuary laws, such as 'prohibition'" and, crucially *occupational licensing*.[833] His perspective was such that there was no realm in which government authority was inappropriate – including one's personal consumption, or one's freedom to earn a living; *caveat emptor*. The ideal of the pragmatick theory of government seems inadequate to encapsulate the scope of Wilson's meddling. He came upon this view quite early in life. In a now infamous unpublished essay, Wilson destroyed any doubt regarding the nature of 'socialism' and 'democracy' (or the weaseler 'democratic socialism'):

> 'State socialism' is willing to act through state authority as it is at present organized. It proposes that all idea of a limitation of public authority by individual rights be put out of view, and that the State consider itself bound to stop only at what is unwise or futile in its universal superintendence alike of individual and of public interests. The thesis of the state socialist is, that no line can be drawn between private and public affairs which the State may not cross at will; that *omnipotence of*

Wellcome Collection, 1966, Accessed March 19, 2025: https://wellcomecollection.org/works/j6f2tqg2/items?canvas=3; Nobel Prize in Physiology, 1962.

832   Wilson, *The State*, 625.
833   Wilson, *The State*, 614 – 615.

legislation is the first postulate of all just
political theory.

Applied in a democratic state, such doctrine
sounds radical, but not revolutionary. It is only
an acceptance of the extremest logical
conclusions deducible from democratic
principles long ago received as respectable.
For it is very clear that, in fundamental theory,
socialism and democracy are almost, if not
quite, one and the same. They both rest at
bottom upon the absolute right of the
community to determine its own destiny and
that of its members. *Men as communities are*
supreme over men as individuals. Limits of
wisdom and convenience to the public control
there may be: *limits of principle there are,*
upon strict analysis, none.[834]

Wilson declared that government must "lay aside all
timid scruple and boldly make itself an agency for social
reform as well as for political control" and the means by
which this was to be accomplished was yet again,
"administration."[835] The derivation and meaning of that term
has already been exhaustively treated in the self-deification
of the 'expert class'; Wilson took that concept to the
Executive office. The image in Wilson's mind was quite
clear.

The collective is supreme to the individual,
omnipotent legislation is the first premise of 'just'
government, and principles do not, cannot limit that
omnipotence. It is a logical impossibility in Wilson's
conception of society to claim that murder is wrong, provided
fifty-one percent of the electorate approves of the killing –

---

834   Woodrow Wilson, "Socialism and Democracy,"
        Unpublished Essay, 1887. In "Woodrow Wilson on Socialism and
        Democracy," *Progressivism and Liberalism*, The Heritage
        Foundation, Accessed March 17, 2025:
        https://static.heritage.org/CPP/FP_PS19.pdf, Emphasis added.
835   Wilson, "Socialism and Democracy," 5.

perhaps to clean the blood, or because Lippmann told them to believe thus – as he did. One has not found a more thoroughly inverse rendition of the principles of the Declaration of Independence than this statement by then-future-President Woodrow Wilson. A totally unlimited government is, without the possibility of rational objection, a Total State. This perspective is, in so many ways, far worse than anything even fantasized by George III. Recall that Wilson repudiated the separation of powers – there were not three branches to him, but one 'organism'. To Wilson, the Executive and the Legislative branches were one; to declare government to be omnipotent is not rhetoric, it is *insane*.

Wilson's insanity was the fruit of the poisoned tree that sprang from the social gospel and Bellamyist National Socialism. In his particular case, it expressed as another branch of perverse Calvinism. Malcom Magee addressed Wilson's 'Calvinist' presbyterianism as the foundation of his thinking. Deeply connected to the delusional view of America as the literal Kingdom of God, perfection and 'post-millennial' theology, Magee analyzed the reciprocity between the Bellamy brother's National Socialism and perfection theology. He noted the religiously-fueled collectivizing climate of the end of the nineteenth century. "For many political leaders the religious optimism of the late 19th century was background noise. For Wilson, however, it was more fundamental to his thought and action."[836]

Wilson was driven by his self conception, and by the climate in which he found himself, to combine the pragmatick theory of government with both the social gospel and Bellamyism. In two separate speeches given in 1915, he betrayed his approach to government and to society. He stated his 'ad-hoc pragmatism' when he declared that "[t]he only legitimate object of organization is efficiency," and linked his social gospel to National Socialism by asserting that "[p]atriotism in its redeeming quality resembles Christianity."[837] In Magee's generously apologetic treatment,

---

836   Malcolm Magee, "Woodrow Wilson, Wilsonianism, and the Idealism of Faith," *The Review of Faith & International Affairs* 9 no. 4 (2011): 30.
837   Wilson in Magee, "Wilsonianism," 31, 34.

"[w]orld events conspired to create in Wilson a view of himself as not only a man on a divine mission but a man on the mission of his generation, the savior of his world."[838]

In Wilson, as with all men, zealotry quickly degenerated to madness. He appears to have believed that motives grant immunity from fallibility and exemption from criticism; a shade of utility, but ultimately an expression of pragmatism given intended results – that is, machiavellianism. In essence, Wilson's pragmatism in concert with his social gospel precipitated a sickly rationalized utilitarianism – if the ends are the redemption of the world, the means were of no consequence.

> Wilson remained convinced that America, by acting on God's behalf, was above the venal politics of this present age. Thus it could remain "neutral" even as it used its military and economic power to produce the righteous outcome. American troops could invade and occupy Mexican territory, but America was not an occupier. The United States could violate all the accepted standards of neutrality as spelled out by international law and still be neutral by a higher law. The United States was on God's side, not that of any political entity.[839]

It would seem strange that one has not yet found the obvious correlation; in reference to an out-dated bumper-sticker-criticism of George W. Bush's foreign policy as "yea-haw!", it is strongly apparent that Wilson's administration drove itself with the ancient slogan *Deus Vult*! There are none more destructive than the man with both a righteous cause, and the power to impose it on others. Wilson disregarded the admonitions that accompanied the documents from which he derived his authority, precisely because his cause was just, and the men who issued those warnings were unevolved egotists:

---

838   Magee, "Wilsonianism," 34.
839   Magee, "Wilsonianism," 33 – 34.

> It was once fashionable—and that not a very
> long time ago—to speak of political society
> with a certain distaste, as a necessary evil, an
> irritating but inevitable restriction upon the
> "natural" sovereignty and entire self-
> government of the individual. That was the
> dream of the egotist.[840]

It is not rational to dismiss Wilson's rhetoric –
whether in his ridicule of the founders, seething, murderous
hatred for the 'unfit,' or lavish praise of the *Ku Klux Klan*. As
Magee argued due to his homiletic upbringing, "[f]or Wilson,
words, be they treaty or scripture, were substance."[841] It is not
rational to dismiss his rhetoric, but it would also be ill-
advised to focus on his words to the exclusion of his actions.

Wilson was by no means the first President to engage
in 'imperial' tendencies, but his recruitment of Christianity,
to say nothing of his posturing around the League of Nations,
stand in stark contrast to his military adventurism in Mexico
1913, Haiti 1915, and in the Dominican Republic in 1916.
Conversely, his supposed ministrant functions of government
inevitably raise the question of funding, to which he gave
answer in the form of the Federal Reserve System and the
Income Tax act of 1913, the former of which simply
disregarded Article 1§8.5 of the Constitution, the latter
requiring an amendment to end-run Article 1§1.1.[842]

His support for prohibition (sumptuary laws) not only
lead to the immediately imbecilic eighteenth amendment, but
effectively precipitated organized crime, the horrifically
cancerous 'War on Drugs', and the resultant militarized
conception of police powers with its attendant perverse
repudiation of the majority of the Bill of Rights. It is an
assertion to be certain, but Wilson's 'sumptuary' laws, being
nothing more complicated than the legislation of peevish,

---

840   Wilson, *When a Man*, VI.
841   Magee, "Wilsonianism," 30.
842   The Income Tax Act is called the 'Tariff Reduction Act', or
the Underwood Simmons Tariff, but was wholly characterized by its
imposition of the income tax, and lead directly to the Internal
Revenue Service 1953. Cf. Frank Chodorov, *The Income Tax: Root
of All Evil*, (New York: The Devin-Adair Company, 1954).

self-righteous moralism, erased the distinction between public and private in accordance with his designs, and placed the sword of the State into the hands of the aforementioned 'moral busybodies.' This sword was not merely rationalized by means of the self-righteous delusions of those who believed themselves to be, or becoming gods, but now it was to be funded by theft of the labor of those so enslaved.

Wilson's 'domestic agenda' draws a comparison of the direct election of senators and separation of powers, against Edward Bellamy seeking to erase federalism.[843] Wilson championed the seventeenth amendment in his campaign, and effectively nullified the animating purpose behind the bicameral legislature – that being *the prevention of demagoguery*.[844] Given Wilson's method of acquiring and exercising power, there is a strong argument to be made that he found no disagreement with demagoguery *per se*. He is only surpassed in quantity of the 'Executive Order' by Franklin Roosevelt – crucially as applied to *citizens*, rather than merely public servants under his direct authority.

By means of executive order, Wilson dictated the necessity and regulation of the passport, with an unqualified and unexplained Bellamyist requirement that "[t]he applicant must take the oath of allegiance to the United States."[845] It

---

843   Ely, *Socialism*, 87.
844   Wilson, *The New Freedom*, Chapter 10 "The Way to Resume is to Resume"; The purpose of the Senate was to represent *States*, the purpose of the House was to represent *People*; this was to act as a prophylactic against "democratic licentiousness" and "encroachments of the Executive who will be apt to form combinations with the demagogues of the popular branch." Cf. Edmund Randolph (1753 – 1813) in Paul Eidelberg, "The Philosophy of the American Constitution: A Reinterpretation of the Intentions of the Founding Fathers." PhD Diss. *University of Chicago*, 1966, 111 – 112; Roger Sherman 8 December, 1787, no addressee, draft in "A Citizen of New Haven," *Connecticut Courant*, 7 in *The Documentary History of the Ratification of the Constitution Digital Edition*, ed. John P. Kaminski, Gaspare J. Saladino, Richard Leffler, Charles H. Schoenleber and Margaret A. Hogan. (Charlottesville: University of Virginia Press, 2009).
845   Executive Order no. 2119-A (1915), Enclosure 1: "Rules Governing the Granting and Issuing of Passports in the United States," *Office of the Historian*, Item 4, Accessed March 21, 2025:

would appear that the devout Presbyterian Wilson simply ignored Jesus' prohibition of oaths.[846] He then made passports mandatory in order to leave the country, specifically mandating that *anyone* who attempted to leave the United States "must inform the Department of State...."[847] Passports could then be seized at will, effectively imprisoning those who wished to leave.[848] It would seem that in Wilson's time, the United States officially took possession of its citizens – as property – to dictate where and when these might travel, by decree of the President. The ostensible sovereign of the country must now ask permission of the government he allegedly ruled if he wished to leave.

By executive order, Wilson seized *all* radio stations, closing those found to be unnecessary for the war effort.[849] By diktat, he established the "Committee on Public Information" to induce positive public opinion regarding United States participation in the Great War, as well as seeking to censor what was considered to be seditious anti-war propaganda.[850] This act was a direct product of Walter Lippmann's meddling, and operated in full accord with his rendition of manipulative 'consent'.[851]

> It has been said that in the United States during 1917 – 18 nearly every right guaranteed under the Constitution was either abridged or nullified, especially freedom of the press and freedom of speech.... At the national level a combination of federal statutes

---

https://history.state.gov/historicaldocuments/frus1915Supp/d1279.

846   Matthew 5:32 – 37.
847   Executive Order no. 2285 (1915).
848   Executive Order no. 2341 (1916).
849   Executive Order no. 2585 (1917).
850   Executive Order no. 2594 (1917).
851   Stephen Vaughn, *Holding Fast the Inner Lines: Democracy, Nationalism, and the Committee on Public Information*, (Chapel Hill: The University of North Carolina Press, 1980), 6. This work exhaustively treats the CPI and its role in manufacturing consent for American participation in the Great War, as well as the demonization of the German people – in addition to government – as the war progressed.

and executive orders sharply limited freedom of expression.[852]

These abridgments and nullifications – usurpations – were mostly by decree, but not entirely; the executive order acted in concert with perverse legislation. Stephen Vaughn briefly narrated the Espionage Act (1917), the Sedition Act (1918), and most importantly, the Trading-with-the-Enemy Act of 1917 that would later empower one of Franklin Roosevelt's most infamous, and obviously treasonous executive orders. Most appropriately, Vaughn addressed the broadband blame for these things – demagogues cannot arise without willing fools; tyrants without their goons are merely noise. Vaughn analyzed the reality that these things were empowered by a *climate*.[853] The irony of the prevalent sentiment at the time was objectively that in order to protect the Constitution, the Constitution had to be suspended; to save America, America had to be killed – wholly presaging any number of repulsive acts of the twentieth and twenty-first centuries. The contention of this argument is that the climate so mentioned was American National Socialism; the sentiment that allowed this absurdity, of which there are many historic analogs, was Progressivism. Progressivism was the hysteria that produced a demagogue and, like all such men, he was a madman.

This author is not the first to view Wilson as a madman, among them it would seem is counted none other than Sigmund Freud (1856 – 1939) who, with Ambassador William C. Bullitt (1891 – 1967), Wilson's special envoy to Vladimir Lenin in 1919, wrote the book on Wilson's neurosis.[854] While one thinks of this as something like a pot-and-kettle situation, with little regard for psychoanalytics, it is none the less an obligatory mention. In a 2023 revisit of that work, Patrick Wile cited Frank C. Waldrop (1905 – 1997):

---

852   Vaughn, *Holding Fast*, 215.
853   Vaughn, *Holding Fast*, 215 – 216.
854   Sigmund Freud and William C. Bullitt, *Woodrow Wilson: A Psychological Study*, (New Brunswick: Transaction Publishers, 1999 [1966]). The work was widely condemned.

It was not Wilson's idealism, but those springs
in his nature which drove his pursuits, that
weighted most in the world while he lived,
and which weighted most, even yet. Not
protestations, but acts, are what we must
consider in choosing among those who would
lead us, whether a Wilson, a Hitler, a Stalin, or
a Mao.[855]

Given this, one is compelled to examine Wilson's
'protestations': "I don't want a smug lot of experts to sit
down behind closed doors in Washington and play
Providence to me."[856] He made this claim in his 1913 bid to
become President, wherein he would immediately appoint
experts to sit behind closed doors and decide what money is
worth, how much interest would be paid, how much inflation
is ideal, and how much of one's labor one ought to be
allowed to keep. The man whose successful campaign
feigned that "Freemen Need no Guardians" immediately
employed the power of his office to enact the "science of
administration."[857] It is by his acts that one may interpret his
meaning when he speaks of the *Darwinian* principle. By his
deeds one understands his meaning behind 'freedom':

Without the watchful interference, the resolute
interference, of the government, there can be
no fair play between individuals and such
powerful institutions as the trusts. Freedom today is something more than being let alone.
The program of a government of freedom
must in these days be positive, not negative
merely.[858]

855   Frank C. Waldrop in Patrick Weil, *The Madman in the White
House : Sigmund Freud, Ambassador Bullitt, and the Lost
Psychobiography of Woodrow Wilson*, (Cambridge: Harvard
University Press, 2023), 297.
856   Wilson, *The New Freedom*, Chapter 3 "Freemen Need no
Guardians".
857   Cf. Woodrow Wilson, "The Study of Administration,"
Political Science Quarterly, Vol. 2, no. 2 (June, 1887): 198 – 222.
858   Wilson, *The New Freedom*, Chapter 12 "The Liberation of a
People's Vital Energies".

The substance of Wilson's presidency appears in two exceedingly appropriate, and quite ancient sources. First, replete with delicious irony, the ancient nation of Israel had similar experiences that lead to similar outcomes – and Wilson probably read these very words at least once, but he disregarded Samuel's admonitions as easily as those of the founders.

> And he said, This will be the manner of the king that shall reign over you: He will take your sons, and appoint them for himself, ... And he will appoint him captains over thousands, and captains over fifties; and will set them to ear his ground, and to reap his harvest, and to make his instruments of war, and instruments of his chariots. And he will take your daughters.... And he will take your fields... even the best of them, and give them to his servants. And he will take the tenth of your seed... and give to his officers, and to his servants. And he will take... your goodliest young men... and put them to his work. ...and ye shall be his servants. And ye shall cry out in that day because of your king which ye shall have chosen you; and the Lord will not hear you in that day. Nevertheless the people refused to obey the voice of Samuel; and they said, Nay; but we will have a king over us....[859]

Second as previously mentioned, Woodrow Wilson may easily be characterized as Sulla's scion; where Lucius Cornelius Sulla (138 – 78 BC) stood as the 'prototype princeps' who very effectively paved the way for Augustus, so too Wilson was the man who broke ground for the Imperial Presidency.[860] This is not a simple poetic insertion, the parallels are curious to say the least.

859   I Samuel 8:11 – 19.
860   Regarding the 'prototype princeps', Cf. Spencer D. Miles, *Gaius Orwellian Caesar*, April 14, 2020, Article Preprint: http://dx.doi.org/10.13140/RG.2.2.12366.16966.

The renowned Plutarch described Sulla as "...of very uneven character, and at variance with himself...."[861] Robin Waterfield's introduction to his 1999 translation of the same text stated that "Sulla, a champion of order and tradition, brought chaos and revolution such as Rome had never seen."[862] Plutarch wrote:

> At the slightest pretext he might have a man crucified, but on another occasion would make light of the most appalling crimes; or he might happily forgive the most unpardonable offenses and then punish trivial, insignificant misdemeanors with death and the confiscation of property.[863]

Wilson, a champion of freedom and principle, brought domination and unpredictability such as America had never seen. Whether in search of an oedipal father-enemy as Freud would argue, or merely lost in his own grandiosity as this argument contends, Wilson was most certainly of uneven character and at odds with himself. One of his many biographers wrote of him in an almost Plutarchian voice:

> Those who held office under him lived in fear of his disfavor – they repressed their criticisms....
>
> Stern and impassive, yet emotional; calm and patient, yet quick-tempered and impulsive; forgetful of those who had served him, yet devoted to many who had rendered but minor service; unforgiving and fierce in his contempt for some who had dared to disagree with him, yet generous with others even to the extent of

861   Plutarch, "The Life of Sulla". *The Parallel Lives* Vol. IV. Loeb Classical Library Edition, 1916. Accessed March 21, 2025: http://penelope.uchicago.edu/Thayer/E/Roman/Texts/Plutarch/Lives/Sulla*.html, 343.
862   Robin Waterfield in Plutarch, *Roman Lives*, Translation by Robin Waterfield, (Oxford University Press, 1999), 169.
863   Plutarch, *Roman Lives*, Waterfield, 181.

> appointing them to high office; precise and
> business-like, and yet, upon occasion, illogical
> without more reason than intuition itself;
> seclusive, yet a crusader for democracy – thus
> might his characteristic contradictions be
> grouped incoherently in a series of paradoxes.

> And even these are not all the attributes of the
> strange personality of Woodrow Wilson. The
> author knew Woodrow Wilson for eighteen
> years, stood at close range through the rise
> and fall of his eventful career....[864]

Wilson was the embodiment of Jefferson's moralist who had been fully lead astray by artificial rules. He was positively enamored of 'modern' scholarship and 'modern science'; he completely swallowed the ridiculous idea that the sorcery of time had developed humanity beyond the capacity for tyranny – *his* tyranny. Woodrow Wilson honestly believed himself to be God's instrument to bring about some image of His Kingdom on earth – in a literal sense – by force of law.

The history of power is the tale of heaping power upon the most polished sociopath of any given age. Whether he was neurotic in a Freudian sense, or merely driven mad by messianism and power is irrelevant. Whether or not Wilson could be 'diagnosed' with "Antisocial Personality Disorder", or sociopathy, the general description of that 'diagnosis' is most appropriate. "Antisocial Personality Disorder is a pattern of disregard for, and violation of, the rights of others."[865] Grandiose rationalizations for motives are conspicuously absent from that description – likely deliberately. One will note that psychiatric 'diagnosis' of anyone, let alone dead historical figures, is at the very best of

---

864   Frank Lawrence, *The True Story of Woodrow Wilson*, (New York: George H. Doran Company, 1924), 13.

865   American Psychiatric Association, *Diagnostic and Statistical Manual of Mental Disorders*, Fourth edition, Text Revision, (DSM-IV-TR), (Washington D.C.: American Psychiatric Association, 2000), 685.

times a self-referential *opinion* and little more. It is none the less a curious correspondence that 'sociopathy' is directly tied to the disregard for the rights – the dignity and value – of others, and this detail fundamentally characterizes the inescapable nature of all of progressivism, to say nothing of an imperial presidency.

As Sulla's dictatorship effectively killed the Roman Republic, leaving an interregnum before the proper rise of the Principate, so too did the American Republic give up the ghost around or about 1913, with an analogous delay before the ascension of Franklin Delano Augustus. It is wholly relevant – but merely the introduction of some other larger work – to state that in a manner of speaking after the American Civil War, the *first Southern Democrat to sit the Presidency killed the Republic that killed his Confederacy.* This is not an inappropriate 'partisan' comment – Wilson himself made such an allusion in the concluding remarks to his *New Freedom*: "...we Democrats would not have endured this long burden of exile if we had not seen a vision."[866] What a curious thing to say, democrats in exile after the Civil War. Quite the 'vision' it appears to have been. Driven by messianism, misanthropy, and hubris, it would seem that one may count *vengeance* among Wilson's motives.

Whatever doubts may arise regarding Wilson's motives, the nature of his acts as compared against the very clear design of the founding leave no rational possibility for argument. Woodrow Wilson was the very man against whom the admonitions had been written. A madman, a demagogue, a tyrant – these are useless terms as they are so easily thrown about. Woodrow Wilson was the embodiment and application of the previously analyzed factors – pragmatism, delusional auto-apotheosis, murderous misanthropy. His presidency was the last of the Republic.

Many will take issue with such a declaration as that above, but between just two of his many crimes he shattered the basis for practicable liberty in the United States. Between the creation of the Federal Reserve, and the grandiosity behind his 'sumptuary' laws, Wilson created *the two*

866   Wilson, *The New Freedom*, Chapter 12 "The Liberation of a People's Vital Energies".

monstrosities of which the founders warned the most: a central bank leading to the robbery of posterity by indenture, and the *gendarmerie* leading directly to the castration of *all* alleged 'rights' in favor of 'officer safety,' 'protecting the State,' and 'national security.' The former of these immediately demonstrated the reason behind the warnings; the latter has become the whole substance of power in America.

> And I sincerely believe with you, that banking establishments are more dangerous than standing armies; & that the principle of spending money to be paid by posterity, under the name of funding, is but swindling futurity on a large scale[867]

To speak of a central bank in the same breath as a standing army contains more poignant meaning than can be conveyed in this work; the Progressives fully established both. These two establishments – force over the substance of money, and control of the body as the tool of the State – constitute the twin mechanisms created by Wilson that fully empowered America's first emperor, Wilson's Assistant Secretary of the Navy, Franklin Delano Roosevelt (1882 – 1945). It may be said that Roosevelt sought to fix the disasters that Wilson caused, by doing what Wilson did – only *harder.*

To be absolutely certain, the causes of the Great Depression or the 'War on Drugs' and its resultant anomie as domestic policy are items for impotent debate among persons with far more prestigious credentials than this author. As with most things, it is not so simple as to toss blame at any particular door. Regarding the Depression in particular, one will have no trouble locating arguments regarding the downturn, analysis of securities mania, or comparisons with previous banking panics. What stands out most clearly in this sea of speculation regarding the influence of speculation

---

867   Thomas Jefferson, "Thomas Jefferson to John Taylor, 28 May 1816," *Founders Online*, National Archives, https://founders.archives.gov/documents/Jefferson/03-10-02-0053.

however is the fact that, long after responsibility was rendered meaningless, then Governor of the Federal Reserve Ben Bernanke flatly accepted institutional responsibility for that event.[868] While the causes of the Depression and Prohibition are debated, the effects, especially regarding the power they lent to Roosevelt and his goons are inarguable.

Given that those two details served as some seeds of his power, it is reasonable to keep with the theme of this argument in offering an analysis of Roosevelt's 'political philosophy' – if indeed it can be said to be anything other than power-lust. Roosevelt is different from all other men thus far examined; he was not an intellectual, he left neither treatise nor tract to analyze. Roosevelt's thinking is displayed almost entirely by his behavior.

In response to a question regarding the origin of his perspective, Roosevelt described himself as "a Christian and a Democrat."[869] As with the previous men, his 'christian' is at best dubious as he clearly ignored the reality that no man can serve two masters.[870] To throw a bone to the unlikely reviewer of this work, one will state quite succinctly that according to Jesus, one can be *either* a Christian *or* a Democrat, Whig, Federalist, Republican, Socialist, Nationalist, Conservative, Progressive, etc; My kingdom is not of this world.[871] Positions are far easier to take than principles are to maintain; this is to say that one who claims a title – especially one beginning with 'christian and...' – is posturing, not elucidating; it is as lazy as it is dishonest. Whatever his commingling, Roosevelt's 'christianity' was the social gospel, his worldview was pragmatism, and his politics were simply power.

There is a glut of secondary literature regarding Gaius Octavian Roosevelt, much of it written by his compatriots

---

868 "Remarks by Governor Ben S. Bernanke At the Conference to Honor Milton Friedman, University of Chicago, Chicago, Illinois," November 8, 2002, Accessed March 31, 2025: https://www.federalreserve.gov/boarddocs/speeches/2002/20021108/.

869 John F. Woolverton, with James D. Bratt, *A Christian and a Democrat: A Religious Biography of Franklin D. Roosevelt*, (Grand Rapids: Eerdmans, 2019), 1.

870 Cf. Matthew 6:24.

871 John 18:36.

and party functionaries – by his goons. William Leuchtenburg (1922 – 2025; *Franklin D. Roosevelt and the New Deal*, 1963), James MacGregor Burns (1918 – 2014; *Roosevelt: The Lion and the Fox*, 1956), and Arthur M. Schlesinger (1917 – 2007; *The Coming of the New Deal*, 1958) have been greatly honored for their histories, are in many respects responsible for whatever 'consensus' might be claimed regarding the quality of Roosevelt's presidency, and all worked directly for Roosevelt's machine. His later Virgils, Eric Rauchway (*The Money Makers*, 2015), David Kennedy (*Freedom from Fear*, 1999) and Ira Katznelson (*Fear Itself*, 2013) merely continued to polish the image of the Caesar, and were similarly honored. Of these men, none sought to analyze the world-view that drove him, let alone address the clear crimes he commit.[872]

John Woolverton (1926 – 2014) sought to fill part of this gap in his religious biography of Roosevelt, completed and posthumously published by James Bratt in 2019. The work was introduced with the strangest of endorsements – a foreword penned by former FBI Director James Comey. Strange inclusions in this curious foreword, in concert with clear references in James Bratt's preface, leave absolutely no doubt as to the nakedly biased narrative under which the work was undertaken. Bratt introduced the subject with either appalling ignorance or deliberate projection regarding the nature of the social gospel as he decries the "white evangelical Protestantism [that] has overwhelmingly endorsed... the most forthright pagan ever to occupy the

---

872   James MacGregor Burns, *Roosevelt: The Lion and the Fox*, (New York: Harcourt Brace, 1956); Ira Katznelson, *Fear Itself: The New Deal and the Origins of our Time*, (New York: Liveright, 2013); David Kennedy, *Freedom from Fear: The American People in Depression and War, 1929-1945*, (New York: Oxford University Press, 1999); William E. Leuchtenburg, *Franklin D. Roosevelt and the New Deal, 1932 – 1940*, (New York: Harper and Brothers, 1963); Eric Rauchway, *The Money Makers: How Roosevelt and Keynes Ended the Depression, Defeated Fascism, and Secured a Prosperous Peace*, (New York: Basic Books, 2015); Arthur Schlesinger, *The Coming of the New Deal: The Age of Roosevelt, 1933 – 1935*, (Boston: Houghton Mifflin, 1958).

Oval Office...."[873] Humorously enough, given such obvious histrionic pandering for an introduction, Woolverton devoted the first third of his work to champion the influence of the social gospel over Roosevelt – the same social gospel wholly rooted in the "social supremacy of the Aryan race"[874]

While it may be decried as an inappropriate insertion, or at the very least unwelcome editorializing, it must be stated that to endorse a work that eulogizes the social gospel while lamenting "white evangelical Protestantism" requires that either one has not the slightest understanding of the fundamentally bigoted reality of the social gospel – making that one incompetent – or the one merely hopes that audiences are too stupid, or too ignorant to make the connection – an act of malice. Whether or not Donald Trump is a pagan, forthright or otherwise, is irrelevant to the inescapable 'white supremacist,' eugenic, self-worshiping authoritarian core of the social gospel, which Woolverton credits as the wellspring of Roosevelt's goodness, and Bratt wholeheartedly endorsed as "...the better heritage of Christian social witness in American history...."[875]

There is a deep level of irony that runs throughout Woolverton and Bratt's work. Among the many who sought to paint Roosevelt as America's hero, worthy of his gaudy likeness enormously set in bronze someplace, *A Christian and a Democrat* decided to focus on the supremely elitist, superbly privileged, eminently condescending, and wholly cloistered Groton prep-school that embraced the social gospel as its guiding principle under its founder, and foremost mentor for the young Roosevelt, Endicott Peabody (1857 – 1944). Woolverton and Bratt employed this exceedingly elitist training academy, operating on a sickly self-aggrandizing perversion of christianity, to attempt to portray Roosevelt as a pious, equality-minded champion of the little people. The tableau is the very image of sleaze.

The authors of *A Christian and a Democrat* had no excuse; they were aware of the inherently bigoted world-view at the heart of the social gospel. They introduce the

---

873   James Bratt in Woolverton, *A Christian and a Democrat*, xi.
874   Rauschenbusch, *The Social Order*, 376.
875   James Bratt in Woolverton, *A Christian and a Democrat*, xi.

concept much in the same manner as this argument – with a citation of both Darwinism and Gladden's 'higher criticism', but they stop short of anything that might be called a rational inquiry into what, exactly, those two terms encompassed and advocated.[876] An appropriately weak investigation to be endorsed by a former Director of the Federal Bureau of *Investigation*s. Had they given at least a cursory examination into both paradigms, the viciously racist foundations of higher criticism and direct lineage of Darwinism in eugenics, they may have refrained from crediting Rauschenbusch – that man who based his 'gospel' on the aforementioned "Aryan social supremacy."[877] Either way, in the apparent rush to polish the already shining symbol, these Virgils commit a ridiculous *faux pas* in presenting the social gospel as though it were a good thing, neither apparently aware that it was in all respects the polar opposite of the class-less society they clearly believe is the ideal for American civilization.[878]

With even greater irony, Comey's foreword cites Woolverton, who in-turn cites Roosevelt's transparently obvious projection regarding the danger of demagoguery. Woolverton claimed that it was the direct influence of the "liberal theological and Social Gospel atmosphere to which the young Roosevelt was exposed" that lead him to speak against "the eternal trick of the demagogue."

> ...who espouses 'doctrines that set group against group, faith against faith, race against race, class against class, fanning the fires of hatred in men.'" As he writes here, that demagoguery is toxic for the church, the state, and the world. But it is not new. And in that

---

876   Woolverton, *A Christian and a Democrat*, 37.
877   Woolverton, *A Christian and a Democrat*, 38, Note 21; Cf.
        Rauschenbusch, *The Social Order*, 376.
878   "It meant diminishing class distinctions and acknowledging
        all people as children of God." Woolverton, *A Christian and a
        Democrat*, 38. To make such a statement regarding the social gospel
        is absurd; to make it in the context of the *supremely* elitist Groton
        prep-school is despicable.

familiarity lies a certain comfort. We have
been here before. We know what to do.[879]

Comey's wholly obvious infantile jab at the President
who fired him is an excellent example of *tu quoque* wrapped
in projection, concealed in gaslighting. As with all things in
analysis, it is appropriate to return *ad fontes* for
understanding and application. Samuel Johnson defined the
demagogue as "A ringleader of the rabble; a populous and
factious orator."[880] Far more recent definitions remain
curiously similar, but add shades including "false claims and
promises",[881] rising to power by means of "exciting the
emotions of ordinary people,"[882] and effectively employing
the substance of *democracy* to transform society.[883] One who
does not understand the horrific irony in that last definition
after having read this far in this argument will not understand
any further attempt to expand it; the United States was not
supposed to be a *democracy* for very good reasons.[884]

Roosevelt was not simply an obvious 'text-book'
example of a demagogue who employed the fear of
demagoguery as a mechanism for his own demagoguery, he
perfected the use of 'democracy' as a battle cry of
demagoguery in the political party that he lead. His version
of 'christianity' was then, as it is now, nothing more than
transparent pandering. "We call what we have been doing

---

879   James Comey in Woolverton, *A Christian and a Democrat*,
viii; Roosevelt, Radio Address, February 1936, in Woolverton, 110.
880   "demagogue," *A Dictionary of the English Language*, by
Samuel Johnson. 1773. Accessed April 2, 2025:
https://johnsonsdictionaryonline.com/1773/demagogue_ns.
881   "demagogue," *Merriam-Webster*, Accessed April 2, 2025:
https://www.merriam-webster.com/dictionary/demagogue.
882   "demagogue," *Cambridge Dictionary*, Accessed April 2,
2025:
https://dictionary.cambridge.org/us/dictionary/english/demagogue.
883   Cf. Martin Ostwald, *From Popular Sovereignty to the
Sovereignty of Law: Law, Society, and Politics in Fifth-Century
Athens*, (Berkeley: University of California Press, 1986), 201.
884   For further reading, and even greater examples of partisan
projection, Cf. Michael Singer, *Demagogue: The Fight to Save
Democracy from its Worst Enemies*, (New York: Palgrave Macmillan,
2009); Cf. United States Constitution Article IV § 4.

'human security' and 'social justice.' In the last analysis all of those terms can be described by one word; and that is 'Christianity.'"[885] One need not cite Franklin's impotent words regarding the exchange of freedom for security; the term 'social justice' itself, being *only* a mask for tyranny, would require a book-length treatment – say, by someone like Thomas Sowell.[886]

Not to be limited to wholly vacuous promises by the Patrician's Patrician regarding 'security' and 'social justice', Roosevelt's first inaugural address employed the very 'class against class, fanning the fires of hatred in men' that he decried.[887] Given the year – 1933 – it is no surprise that his platform was entirely built on the Depression; given his unscrupulous pragmatism, it is obvious why he chose to speak of the 'money changers'.[888]

> Primarily this is because the rulers of the exchange of mankind's goods have failed, through their own stubbornness and their own incompetence, have admitted their failure, and abdicated. Practices of the unscrupulous money changers stand indicted in the court of public opinion, rejected by the hearts and minds of men.... The money changers have fled from their high seats in the temple of our civilization. We may now restore that temple to the ancient truths. The measure of the

885   Roosevelt in Woolverton, *A Christian and a Democrat*, 110.
886   Cf. Thomas Sowell, *Social Justice Fallacies*, (New York: Basic Books, 2023).
887   Woolverton frequently references Roosevelt's "blue blood" and even one of Roosevelt's clearest Virgils spoke of him as "The Patrician as Opportunist" – a fitting title to bestow on a clear parallel to Augustus. Richard Hofstadter, *The American Political Tradition and the Men Who Made It*, (New York: Vintage Books, 1948), Chapter XII; Cited in Clarke A. Chambers, "FDR, Pragmatist-Idealist: An Essay in Historiography," *The Pacific Northwest Quarterly* 52, no. 2 (1961): 52.
888   Regarding Roosevelt's pragmatism, especially the New Deal, Cf. Clarke A. Chambers, "FDR, Pragmatist-Idealist: An Essay in Historiography,; Richard Hofstadter, *The Age of Reform: From Bryan to F.D.R.*, (New York: Alfred A. Knopf, 1955), 314 – 323.

restoration lies in the extent to which we apply
social values more noble than mere monetary
profit…. Happiness lies not in the mere
possession of money….[889]

That last bit – coming from the powerful wealthy
scion of a powerful rich family who suffered nothing from
the Depression – was merely an insult bordering on
psychopathy. The substance of Roosevelt's first inaugural
address was to assume the posture of 'savior' of the people
from the ravages of the 'money changers.'

Who, one asks with unconcealed contempt, were the
'money changers' after Wilson's Federal Reserve Act of
1913? In his description of the problem he sought the power
to solve, Roosevelt decried that "[v]alues have shrunken to
fantastic levels; taxes have risen; our ability to pay has fallen;
government of all kinds is faced by serious curtailment of
income…."[890] But, to be most certain, this had nothing to do
with Wilson's science of administration or the Underwood
Tariff – Income Tax – Act, also of 1913.[891]

In perfect form, Roosevelt cast the failures of the
pragmatick theory of government as the faults of others, and
breathlessly orated the emergency requiring immediate
action; action that necessitated ever more pragmatick
government. As it was the pilot who ran the ship aground, it
was clear that only that same pilot could respond to the very
emergency he caused. "It can be helped by national planning
for and supervision of all forms of transportation and of
communications and other utilities…."[892] There could be no
time for deliberation or dissent from *national control of
movement and communication*. "This Nation asks for action,
and action now…. It can be accomplished in part by direct
recruiting by the Government itself, treating the task as we

---

889   Franklin D. Roosevelt, "First Inaugural Address of Franklin
     D. Roosevelt," Saturday, March 4, 1933, *Yale Law School, The
     Avalon Project*, Accessed April 2, 2025:
     https://avalon.law.yale.edu/20th_century/froos1.asp.
890   Roosevelt, "First Inaugural."
891   Cf. Woodrow Wilson, "The Study of Administration,"
     Political Science Quarterly, Vol. 2, no. 2 (June, 1887): 198 – 222.
892   Roosevelt, "First Inaugural."

would treat the emergency of a war...."[893] And, because this was clearly a national emergency, as apparent and deadly as *war*, Roosevelt would humbly ask and accept the mantle of extraordinary powers.

> It is to be hoped that the normal balance of executive and legislative authority may be wholly adequate to meet the unprecedented task before us. *But it may be that an unprecedented demand and need for undelayed action may call for temporary departure from that normal balance of public procedure.* But in the event that the Congress shall fail to take one of these two courses, and in the event that the national emergency is still critical, I shall not evade the clear course of duty that will then confront me. I shall ask the Congress for the one remaining instrument to meet the crisis--*broad Executive power to wage a war against the emergency,* as great as the power that would be given to me if we were in fact invaded by a foreign foe.[894]

The emergency caused by government's impudent meddling where it had no business was apparently so immediate as to necessitate a threat to Congress; so dire that no Congressional objection to this overt usurpation was apparent. There are parallels to this factor – not merely in the young Augustus to whom Roosevelt is herein compared, but also to another much closer in time.

A mere nineteen days after Roosevelt's first inaugural address, a second speech was given whose parallels are many. This speech was also concerned with unemployment, especially in agriculture, and cited unused surplus. This speech also conceived of a national army to respond to a similar economic crisis, a national army that would take advantage of "[t]he organizational capabilities of our people", such that "every worker shall be utilized in the

---

893   Roosevelt, "First Inaugural."
894   Roosevelt, "First Inaugural." Spelling sic, emphasis added.

service of the public." Parallel to Roosevelt's claim that
"[o]ur greatest primary task is to put people to work", so this
world leader declared that "it is perfectly clear to the national
government that the removal of the distress in both
agricultural and urban economy is contingent upon the
integration of the army of unemployed in the process of
production." The people must "move as a trained and loyal
army willing to sacrifice for the good of a common
discipline, because without such discipline no progress is
made, no leadership becomes effective."

One speech stated that "[a]s a matter of principle, the
Government will avoid currency experiments;" the other that
"there must be provision for an adequate but sound
currency." The one expressed hope that "[a]ction in this
image and to this end is feasible under the form of
government which we have inherited from our ancestors."
The other declared that government's aim "must be to design
a constitution which ties the will of the people to the
authority of a genuine leadership." One man humbly
accepted "unhesitatingly the leadership of this great army of
our people dedicated to a disciplined attack upon our
common problems." The other man spoke of the importance
of christianity, promising that "the government is creating
and securing the requirements for a genuinely profound
return to religious life."

One of these leaders based his whole platform in the
good of the nation, as a noble sacrifice, stating that "[n]ot the
individual but the people as a whole must be the focal point
of legislative efforts." The other ended his grand oration with
a wondrous call to faith: "We face the arduous days that lie
before us in the warm courage of the national unity; with the
clear consciousness of seeking old and precious moral
values; with the clean satisfaction that comes from the stern
performance of duty by old and young alike. We aim at the
assurance of a rounded and permanent national life."

It is left to the reader to discern between the words of
Franklin Delano Roosevelt in his first inaugural address – the
one that claimed no fear but fear itself – and those of Adolf

Hitler in his 1933 Enabling Act address to the Reichstag.[895] It
is left to the reader to distinguish the words of these
contemporaneously powerful men, and to decide – blindly –
which are the words of the murderous dictator, and which are
those of the democrat savior of America. Thereafter, it is left
to the reader to measure whether or not Roosevelt knew, or
knew, the "eternal trick of the demagogue."

From here, the reader is asked to consider that even as
the District of Columbia burned – when the United States
were *actually* invaded by a foreign foe in 1814 – then
President James Madison wholly refrained from taking upon
himself 'broad Executive power'. This comparison –
Madison against Roosevelt, the *actual* war of 1812 against
the *manufactured consequences* of the Depression – is by far
the most critical, most stark contrast between principled and
pragmatick leadership. The nature of Roosevelt's pragmatism
in application brings to the surface the most poignant and
most clearly ignored question to arise from that perverse
ideology of 'truth' being what works: works *for whom*? To do
what, precisely? The answer to both is terribly mundane:
power.

In his 2003 analysis of the New Deal, Jim Powell
effectively exposed the reality of the situation with an in-
depth treatment of Treasury Secretary Henry Morgenthau Jr.
(1891 – 1967), the very man who wrote the Federal Housing
Authority (FHA) into existence.[896] It is crucial to recognize
that Morgenthau was every bit Roosevelt's man – even
helping to nullify Roosevelt's hand-wringing over the high
taxes of the Depression by "leading the charge for sky-
rocketing taxes to finance the war effort."[897] He was also

---

895   Adolf Hitler, "Official Speech on the Enabling Act to the
    Reichstag," Berlin, March 23, 1933. *World Future Fund*. Accessed
    April 2, 2025:
    https://www.worldfuturefund.org/reports2013/hitlerenablingact.htm.
    One will note the *extreme* irony of this speech being published by the
    "World Future Fund", a self-styled 'democratic-socialist /
    Progressive" organization.
896   Jim Powell, *FDR's Folly: How Roosevelt and his New Deal
    Prolonged the Great Depression*, (New York: Crown Forum, 2003),
    18.

among the earliest to condemn his opponents as 'fascists'.[898]
In a committee meeting, he stated outright in 1938 that "after
eight years of this Administration we have just as much
unemployment as when we started", then added "And an
enormous debt to boot! We are just sitting here and fiddling
and I am just wearing myself out and getting sick."[899]

Morgenthau, in his diaries and in Powell's treatment
of him, demonstrated the inarguable fact that Roosevelt's
complaint about taxes in his first inaugural address was an
absolute lie. Further, he proved by his very support of
Roosevelt, that the New Deal was an unmitigated failure
regarding employment – again painting the inaugural a lie –
but adding the horrors of poverty caused by debt-induced
inflation.

A contemporary to Roosevelt, Journalist John T.
Flynn (1882 – 1964), exposed two further lies. First, he cited
Arthur Schlesinger – the foremost Virgil – who gleefully
celebrated Roosevelt's utilitarian duplicity. "If he was going
to induce the people to move at all… he had no choice but to
trick them into acting for what he conceived to be their best
interests."[900] The tricks lauded by Schlesinger were manifold,
but the deception of which Flynn spoke was the entry of the
United States into the Second World War.

Flynn noted that war fever had overtaken the people,
to the point that "[critics of Roosevelt's duplicity]… were
denounced as fascists and Hitler-lovers." He contrasted this
against the (then) "new kind of apology"; citing Thomas
Bailey's 1948 *The Man in the Street* that Schlesinger had

897   Powell, *FDR's Folly*, 9. Morgenthau's diaries contain
extensive demands and suggestions that taxes, all manner of taxes, be
consistently increased.
898   Powell, *FDR's Folly*, 82.
899   Henry Morgenthau Jr., House Ways and Means Committee
transcript, "Diary Book 189, May 9 – May 15, 1939," *Diaries of
Henry Morgenthau Jr.*, Franklin D. Roosevelt Presidential Library,
Accessed April 3, 2025:
http://www.fdrlibrary.marist.edu/_resources/images/morg/md0249.pd
f, 42.
900   Schlesinger in John T. Flynn, *The Roosevelt Myth*, (New
York: The Devin-Adair Company, 1948), 298; citing a *New York
Times* Book Review of Thomas A. Bailey (1902 – 1983), *The Man in
the Street*, May 9, 1948.

given a glowing review: "Roosevelt repeatedly deceived the American people during the period before Pearl Harbor."[901] One will reiterate yet again that consent cannot be derived of deceit despite what Lippmann and his posterity might claim.

Bailey, Flynn, and Schlesinger were probably unaware of the extent of that deception. Franklin Delano Roosevelt did not merely deceive the American people regarding jobs and taxes during the period before Pearl Harbor. Robert B. Stinnett, a veteran of the War in the Pacific conclusively proved that the President of the United States was fully aware of the impending attack on Hawaii, ordered that *nothing be done* to prepare, and indeed not only provoked the attack, but deliberately ordered the fleet to be assembled in the harbor – and dismissed the Fleet Commander Admiral who protested that derelict act.[902] The attack pleased him, empowered him, and constituted an overt act of treason. Franklin Delano Roosevelt *facilitated*, and may even have deliberately caused the Japanese attack on Pearl Harbor.

As each analysis of Stinnett's work cites, Roosevelt was re-elected for his third term on the promise that "While I am talking to you fathers and mothers, I give you one more assurance. I have said this before, but I shall say it again and again; your boys are not going to be sent into any foreign wars." While this 'promise' was uttered in October 1940, Eleanor Roosevelt (1884 – 1962) wished it to be clarified. She wrote in November of 1941 that her husband had said in another speech, October 23, 1940, "We will not participate in foreign wars, and we will not send our Army, naval or air forces to fight in foreign lands outside of the Americas, except in case of attack."[903] This additional verbiage was certainly not part of the first speech, and her dissembling only serves to add an overtly Orwellian flavor to that ret-conned promise.[904] It is most appropriate that Mr. and Mrs. Roosevelt should stand as the model American couple – to

---

901   Flynn, *The Roosevelt Myth*, 297.
902   Robert B. Stinnett, *Day of Deceit: The Truth About FDR and Pearl Harbor*, (London: Constable. 2000), 10, 11.
903   Eleanor Roosevelt, "If You Ask Me," *Ladies Home Journal*, vol. 58 (November 1941).

match the young Augustus and his wife Livia Drusilla (59 BC – AD 29).

The timing of Livia Roosevelt's dissembling could not have been any more fortunate for the Traitor. Her words were published less than a month before the necessary attack. Given the incontrovertible proof that Stinnett uncovered, Emperor Roosevelt was hoping for a Japanese attack to facilitate his designs as early as October of 1940.[905] It would strain credulity to simply dismiss the *strong* likelihood that Mrs. Roosevelt was privy to Mr. Roosevelt's duplicity, and that she gave this transparent 'out' as a result. Whether she was a co-conspirator or not, the timing and substance of this treason coincidentally matches that of Wilson's 1916 campaign slogan "he kept us out of the war" that he immediately repudiated the very next year.[906]

False promises are among the factors that define the demagogue. Despite the cynical 'grown-up' attitude of simply winking at campaign promises in contemporary society, these two demagogues – Wilson and Roosevelt – uttered their lies in direct connection to both world wars. This is not a small matter.

Where Wilson was a traitor to the substance of the Declaration, Roosevelt commit a direct violation of Article III §3.1 of the United States Constitution in assembling the fleet at Pearl Harbor, making no preparations for an attack that he was deliberately provoking, and dismissing the Fleet Commander who protested. Roosevelt deliberately gave "Aid and Comfort" to the Empire of Japan in his design to *deceive* the people, to *manufacture consent* for America's participation in the Second World War. Machiavellian 'necessity' cannot excuse treason.

There is much that can be heaped upon the grave of the first American Emperor. He used Wilson's Trading with

---

904   From *Animal Farm*, "No animal shall kill any other animal *without cause*" – added after the murder of an opponent.
905   Stinnett, *Day of Deceit*, 10.
906   John Milton Cooper Jr. *Woodrow Wilson: A Biography* (New York: Vintage Books, 2011), 342. It is important to note that "he kept us out of the war" was the *entire* platform for Wilson's second election.

the Enemy Act of 1917 as justification to rob Americans of
their gold – under threat of fines and imprisonment.[907]
Justifications for this act do not compare against the words of
Madison, the President who refrained from using real crisis
to empower himself. "As a man is said to have a right in his
property, he may equally be said to have a property in his
rights. *Where an excess of power prevails, property of no sort
is duly respected.* No man is safe in his opinions, his person,
his faculties, or his possessions."[908] Roosevelt's diktat lead
directly to the repudiation of contract by the facile Supreme
Court in *Nortz v. United States*.[909]

It is well-known that Roosevelt forcibly imprisoned a
vast number of American citizens without charge and without
process under the exceedingly weak claim that they had been
"deemed a threat to national security." It is not as well known
that this was a *military act* "by virtue of the authority vested
in me as President of the United States, and Commander in
Chief of the Army and Navy..."[910] A military act in direct
violation of the so-called *Posse Comitatus Act* of 1878 that
was supposed to prohibit the domestic use of the military.[911]
Again, the castrated Supreme Court served only to justify
these overt crimes of the *gendarmerie* against the people –
the very same Court in which Associate Justice Robert H.
Jackson had spoken so highly of the Bill of Rights regarding
the Bellamyist oath and ritual salute.[912]

---

907   Executive Order no. 6102 (1933)
908   James Madison, "For the *National Gazette*, 27 March
1792," *Founders Online*, National Archives,
https://founders.archives.gov/documents/Madison/01-14-02-0238;
Emphasis added.
909   *Nortz v. United States*, 294 U.S. 317 (1935).
910   Executive Order no. 9066 (1942).
911   18 U.S.C. § 1385.
912   Korematsu v. United States, 323 U.S. 214 (1944);
Hirabayashi v. United States, 320 U.S. 81 (1943); and Yasui v. United
States, 320 U.S. 115 (1943), aforementioned Associate Justice Felix
Frankfurter concurring in all three; Chief Justice Harlan Stone
concurred in the first two, and remained "officially" silent on the
third. Cf. *West Virginia State Board of Education et al. v. Barnette et
al.* (1943) 319 U.S. 624, 26. Associate Justice Jackson dissented in all
three cases.

More than merely employing the military to march against and imprison American citizens without cause, charge, or process, few recognize that Roosevelt's clear act of tyrannical abuse was a direct product of his social gospel – in perfect accord with Rauschenbusch's Aryan supremacy. David Beito recently published his analysis of Roosevelt's 'civil rights' record, and he revealed two items pertinent to the subject at hand. First, Roosevelt ascribed to the same nakedly bigoted rot as did all social gospellers – speaking of the "most unfortunate results" of the miscegenation between "Asiatic blood with European or American blood...."[913] Second, Roosevelt did not think of Japanese internment as 'internment', he thought of it in a substantially similar manner to his German counterpart. Roosevelt conceived of and executed both an 'Enemies of the State' list, and the *concentration camp* as his own solution, as early as 1936 – a few months after Germany passed the Nuremberg Laws.

> ...every Japanese citizen or non-citizen on the Island of Oahu who meets these Japanese ships or has any connection with their officers or men should be secretly but definitely identified and his or her name placed on a special list of those who would be the first to be placed in a concentration camp.[914]

One has not found an historian, nor even an ethicist who has wrestled with Roosevelt's part in the firebombing of Dresden, a mere two months before his death in 1945. To be certain, there is much ink spilled around the 'ethics' of indiscriminate bombing of civilian populations, and the use of incendiary weapons in general, but precious little thought appears to have been given to such a gross act of sociopathy done by, or under the auspices of, the ostensible social-gospel-driven-christian-and-democrat savior of America.

---

913   Roosevelt in David T. Beito, *The New Deal's War on the Bill of Rights: The Untold Story of FDR's Concentration Camps, Censorship, and Mass Surveillance*, (Oakland: Independent Institute, 2023), 166.

914   Roosevelt in Beito, *The New Deal's War on the Bill of Rights*, 166.

Woolverton did not bother to compare the firebombing of Dresden against the sickly pious image of a man that he sought to bestow upon Roosevelt. None of Roosevelt's champions speak of Dresden; no Virgil would ever commit *carmen et error* like a wayward Ovid.[915]

Much could be said regarding the Social Security Act of 1935 – John R. Common's creature – that amounts to little more than *Cura annonae*, or the grain dole of the Roman Principate. One of the many vestiges of the New Deal (that was a total failure), this creature has grown to be a monster consuming twenty-two percent of the entire federal budget as of 2024.[916] Moreover, this one act is administered by *force* of the IRS, and accounts for an unavoidable "Self Employment Tax" of fifteen and three tenths percent (as of 2024) on any income over four-hundred dollars – a tax "primarily for individuals who work for themselves."[917] To address what this does to the Yeomanry, how it impacts independence and therefore *freedom* – to say nothing of *taking a man's money by force*, on the excuse that it will somehow help him avoid poverty – would require yet another full-length treatment.

Even more could be said regarding the Emergency Banking Act of 1933 that gave the Federal Reserve the power to print 'money' in direct violation of Article I §8.5 of the Constitution, and the legacy that this has bequeathed to subsequent generations. Indeed, the 'money' used in the United States, is currently worth eight-*hundredths* of what it was before this Act.[918] Much could be, and is said regarding

915   "a poem and a mistake," the mysterious reason Ovid – Publius Ovidius Naso (43 BC – AD 17) was exiled by Augustus.

916   USAFacts, "How Much Does the US Spend on Social Security? Is it Sustainable?" *USAFacts*, Updated August 1, 2024, Accessed April 3, 2025: https://usafacts.org/articles/how-much-does-the-us-spend-on-social-security-is-it-sustainable/.

917   IRS, "Self-employment tax (Social Security and Medicare taxes)" *IRS*, nd. Accessed April 3, 2025: https://www.irs.gov/businesses/small-businesses-self-employed/self-employment-tax-social-security-and-medicare-taxes.

918   "US Dollar Devaluation," *United States Gold Bureau*, nd. Accessed April 3, 2025: https://www.usgoldbureau.com/news/post/us-dollar-devaluation-since-1913. Note: This is a commercial website, but the same statistic is cited universally.

how this compares to 'coin-clipping,' currency devastation, devaluation, and the Crisis of the Third Century that began with Augustus.[919]

To address the modern *Praetorian* guard – that behemoth once directed by James Comey, and founded by none other than the grand-nephew of Napoleon Bonaparte, the *progressive* Secretary of the Navy and Attorney General Charles J. Bonaparte (1851 – 1921) would require *volumes* to expose. This ever expanding Bureau was employed in force by both Wilson and Roosevelt, among many others, and maintains a consistently criminal record regarding the Bill of Rights, to say nothing of the principles of the Declaration. Much could be said, but this argument draws to a close.

No, the last of Roosevelt's Intolerable Acts to be examined in the conclusion to this long saga is both another lie, and the beginning of understanding the true extent of Wilson's sumptuary laws.

Roosevelt introduced his third inaugural address with a wonderfully reminiscent phrase. "Eight years ago, when the life of this Republic seemed frozen by a fatalistic terror, we proved that this is not true. We were in the midst of shock-- but we acted. We acted quickly, boldly, decisively."[920] According to his own Treasury Secretary Morgenthau, that eight years had been an unmitigated failure and, combined with the debt produced by Roosevelt's quick, bold, decisive action, an unrelenting failure. While this certainly cast the entire speech as an act of gaslighting, this is not the lie in reference to sumptuary legislation.

In 1941 Roosevelt spoke in highest praise of himself. He declared that all of his critics were wrong, that his demagoguery had not destroyed 'democracy'. "For action has been taken within the three-way framework of

---

919   David Serrano Ordozgoiti, "It Didn't Begin with FDR: Currency Devaluation in the Third Century Roman Empire," *Mises Wire*, November 7, 2022, Accessed April 3, 2025: https://mises.org/mises-wire/it-didnt-begin-fdr-currency-devaluation-third-century-roman-empire.

920   Franklin D. Roosevelt, "Third Inaugural Address of Franklin D. Roosevelt," Monday, January 20, 1941, *Yale Law School, The Avalon Project*, Accessed April 7, 2025: https://avalon.law.yale.edu/20th_century/froos3.asp.

the Constitution of the United States. The coordinate branches of the Government continue freely to function. The Bill of Rights remains inviolate…. Prophets of the downfall of American democracy have seen their dire predictions come to naught."[921] Owing to nothing further than his wholly unlawful confiscation of American gold, the claim that 'the Bill of Rights remains inviolate' would be a cruel insult, but again this is not the lie arising from Wilson's attempt to moralize America by force.

Prohibition, among other similar Acts, precipitated and facilitated the birth of organized crime. This is not a controversial opinion. Roosevelt then employed the widespread hatred of the eighteenth amendment as a campaign stump.[922] Organized crime lead directly to numerous events such as the St. Valentine's Day Massacre in 1929, to which the Congress responded under Roosevelt's approval with the National Firearms Act of 1934. This act was deliberately crafted to both "curtail if not prohibit" possession of firearms, and to disallow firearms to *those who could not afford the tax* as a transparent work around to the primordial right to self-defense.[923] It requires the hubris of pragmatism, or the delusional self-worship of the social gospel to choke down the vacuous claim that this is not 'infringement' of the right of the people to keep and bear arms. Indeed, Samuel Johnson made it very clear that 'to infringe' is "To violate; break laws or contracts… To destroy; *to hinder.*"[924]

---

921   Roosevelt, "Third Inaugural."
922   Hparkins, "Prohibition and the Rise of the American Gangster," *National Archives, Pieces of History*, January 17, 2012, Accessed April 7, 2025: https://prologue.blogs.archives.gov/2012/01/17/prohibition-and-the-rise-of-the-american-gangster/.
923   ATF, "National Firearms Act," *Bureau of Alcohol, Tobacco, Firearms, and Explosives*, Reviewed March 14, 2025, Accessed April 7, 2025: https://www.atf.gov/rules-and-regulations/laws-alcohol-tobacco-firearms-and-explosives/national-firearms-act.
924   "infringe," *A Dictionary of the English Language*, by Samuel Johnson. 1773. Accessed April 7, 2025: https://johnsonsdictionaryonline.com/1773/infringe_va.

290 Part II: The American Aeneid

Like any good demagogue, Roosevelt claimed that the Bill of Rights remained inviolate, against clear violations of the Bill of Rights, excused as a necessary response to conditions *created by Wilson*. He made this transparent lie against a cruel reference.

> The destiny of America was proclaimed in words of prophecy spoken by our first President in his first inaugural in 1789--words almost directed, it would seem, to this year of 1941: "The preservation of the sacred fire of liberty and the destiny of the republican model of government are justly considered ... deeply, ... finally, staked on the experiment intrusted to the hands of the American people."[925]

He was correct, the words of 1789 from the President who *did not* empower himself with crisis *were* directed at 1941: "The right of the people to keep and bear arms shall not be infringed; a well armed, and well regulated militia being the best security of a free country...."[926]

It is likely an unexpected benefit to the manner and content of this argument that one who would make the vacuous retort regarding the 'militia' has not read this far. There is, therefore little need to cite George Mason declaring what the militia is – and how it necessitates that *the people* have the prerequisite right, not the members of the militia.[927] It was absolutely clear to the founders that a free people must be armed – individually, wholly – because only an armed people can be free: "Before a standing army can rule, the people must be disarmed; as they are in almost every kingdom in Europe.... for [the people] will possess the

925   Roosevelt, "Third Inaugural," sic.
926   James Madison, "Amendments to the Constitution, [8 June] 1789," *Founders Online*, National Archives, https://founders.archives.gov/documents/Madison/01-12-02-0126.
927   The people *are* the militia. George Mason, "Debate in Virginia Ratifying Convention," June 14, 1788, Document 9, Article 4, Section 4. Accessed April 7, 2025: University of Chicago https://press-pubs.uchicago.edu/founders/documents/a4_4s9.html.

power, and jealousy will instantly inspire the *inclination*, to resist...."[928]

Few things were made as clear, as frequently, as the reason behind codifying the *already extant* individual right to keep and bear arms – it was *never about hunting*:

> And what country can preserve its liberties if
> their rulers are not warned from time to time
> that their people preserve the spirit of
> resistance? Let them take arms. The remedy is
> to set them right as to facts, pardon and pacify
> them. What signify a few lives lost in a
> century or two? The tree of liberty must be
> refreshed from time to time with the blood of
> patriots and tyrants. It is its natural manure.[929]

The people did not take up arms in response to the National Firearms Act. They did not take arms against Executive Orders 9066 or 6102, The New Deal, Prohibition, *Wickard v. Filburn*, or the pragmatick theory of pedagogy, government, and law. They did not take arms against the rule of the expert class. They did not take arms, and so have gotten what was chief among fears in the admonitions: the tyranny of the Total State.

The people accepted a standing army – a *gendarmerie*. They accepted greater and more police in response to Prohibition, and when this meddling created ever more opportunistic and sophisticated criminals, the people cried out for – or merely meekly accepted – ever more variations of standing armies, ever more excuses to disregard the substance of their ancient rights.

---

928   Noah Webster, "An Examination into the Leading Principles of the Federal Constitution: Philadelphia, October 17, 1787," in *The Constitution of the United States of America and Selected Writings of the Founding Fathers*, (New York: Barnes & Nobel, 2012), 687. Emphasis in original.

929   Thomas Jefferson, "From Thomas Jefferson to William Stephens Smith, 13 November 1787," Founders Online, National Archives, https://founders.archives.gov/documents/Jefferson/01-12-02-0348.

The people accepted eugenics. They accepted State enforced mutilation and categorization of their members into those who were fit, and those who had 'forfeit' their rights. They accepted ever growing agencies and offices who would 'play providence' to them from behind closed doors. They accepted State mandated 'education'; the authorities' over whom they ostensibly held sovereignty dictating to their children what was and was not true, good, or acceptable. They permit the State to direct their children to perform a ritual of fealty in clear opposition to the substance of freedom, under threat of imprisonment. They accepted the solutions offered by the very people who caused the problems they claimed to wish to solve; they ignored the obvious reality – that each 'solution' was only ever more power, and led only to ever more problems requiring more power in the hands of the psychotic few.

The people accepted the manipulation of 'public opinion' and the simple, easily understood meaning of words in law. They accepted patently obvious dissembling and transparent dishonesty as a means of flouting, side-stepping, ignoring, and rendering impotent the clear and easily understood principles of the Declaration of Independence and its derivative documents.

The people accepted an obvious demagogue, whose biographers would brag about his deception a few years after his death. The people accepted "By Order of the President" as though it were at all different than "By Order of Caesar." Disregarding the provenance of the citation, it is wholly clear that the people proved entirely incapable of keeping their Republic.[930]

---

930   Famous phrase attributed to Benjamin Franklin, 1787.

Epilogue: By Their Fruits

When you see that in order to produce, you
need to obtain permission from men who
produce nothing - When you see that money is
flowing to those who deal, not in goods, but in
favors - When you see that men get richer by
graft and by pull [rather] than by work, and
your laws don't protect you against them, but
protect them against you - When you see
corruption being rewarded and honesty
becoming a self-sacrifice - You may know that
your society is doomed.[931]

– Ayn Rand, *Atlas Shrugged*

P rogressive *Republican* Congressman for New York,
Hamilton Fish III (1888 – 1991) hailed Roosevelt's
election as "an American dictatorship based on the
consent of the governed without any violation of individual
liberty or human rights."[932] This is, to be certain, an extreme
non-sequitur. It is incompetent in the best possible
interpretation to claim that 'dictatorship' can be coupled with
'consent' – these are diametrically opposed. Further than this,
Roosevelt's administration was *defined* by violations of
liberty and rights; while Fish said this at the beginning, the
absurdity inherent in the statement does not allow him to be
pardoned by innocence through ignorance.

---

931   Ayn Rand, *Atlas Shrugged*, (New York: Signet, 1992
        [1957]), 383.
932   Congressman Hamilton Fish (1888 – 1991) in Tim Weiner,
        Enemies: A History of the FBI. (New York: Random House, 2012),
        68, Cf. Schlesinger *The Age of Roosevelt: The Coming of the New
        Deal* (Boston: Houghton Mifflin, 1957), vi.

What a claim it is to couple dictatorship with consent
– as ridiculous as the thought may be, it demonstrates that
this author has not made a great leap in defining Roosevelt as
the first American Emperor. Like Augustus before him,
Roosevelt's *dictatorship* and *duplicity* were hailed as good
things by his contemporaries – one will tolerate no
gaslighting to retcon *that* detail.

The previous criticisms of the people for having not
taken arms against the sea of troubles may well be criticized
as histrionic, overly rhetorical, dramatic, or even
sophomoric. Indeed, it is the greatest mark of how far
America has degraded that in certain contexts, because of
Justice Oliver Wendell Holmes Jr in *Schenck v. United States*,
the sentiments that underlie the Founding are not only
rejected by derision, but greeted with contempt and
lawfare.[933] Only the 'anti-government extremist' cites the
Declaration's prescribed duty regarding "a long train of
abuses and usurpations." What is it now, in light of the clear
comparison, to cite Alexander Hamilton? In some contexts,
this paragraph is *illegal* to cite, and it contains within it the
very reasons as to why:

> If the representatives of the people betray their
> constituents, there is then no resource left but
> in the exertion of that *original right of self-
> defense which is paramount to all positive
> forms of government,* and which against the
> usurpations of the national rulers, may be
> exerted with infinitely better prospect of
> success than against those of the rulers of an
> individual state. In a single state, if the
> persons intrusted with supreme power become
> usurpers, the different parcels, subdivisions, or
> districts of which it consists, having no
> distinct government in each, can take no
> regular measures for defense. *The citizens
> must rush tumultuously to arms, without
> concert, without system, without resource;*

---

933   *Schenck v. United States*, 249 U.S. 47 (1919), 'shouting fire
in a crowded theater.'

*except in their courage and despair. The
usurpers, clothed with the forms of legal
authority, can too often crush the opposition
in embryo....*

The obstacles to usurpation and the facilities
of resistance increase with the increased
extend of the State, *provided the citizens
understand their rights and are disposed to
defend them.*[934]

Because of Dewey, the NEA, Lippmann, and
narrative crafting via media, the citizens do not understand
their rights; because of dependence on government for
subsistence, they are not disposed to defend them. The
'original right of self-defense' is inherent in the right to life,
this can by no rational argument be termed a controversial
statement – let those who disagree argue with the grizzly bear
that he has no right to defend himself, or to keep and to eat
his fish. Hamilton and so many others placed this right as
primary and superior to the whole existence of government,
overriding all legitimate authority. So primary is this right
that it comprises the basis upon which all government is
built, yet American government has degenerated so far as to
presume itself superior even to this.

Congressman Fish is poignant in comparison to
Hamilton's words for his more well-known part in the 1930
'Fish Committee' – one of the earlier American political
witch-hunts – and substantial alignment with the infamous
Praetorian J. Edgar Hoover (1895 – 1972), or the American
equivalent to Lucius Aelius Sejanus (~20BC – AD 31).[935]
Simply, under the guise of fighting Communism (or poverty,
drugs, terrorism, fascism, discrimination, racism, climate

934   Alexander Hamilton [Attributed,] "The Federalist, No.
   XXVIII," in *The Constitution of the United States of America And
   Selected Writings of the Founding Fathers*, (New York: Barnes &
   Nobel, 2012), 371. Spelling sic, emphasis Added.
935   Cf. Weiner, *Enemies*, 2012. Sejanus was the Prefect of the
   Praetorian Guard under Tiberius, the man who turned Augustus'
   bodyguard into its own intelligence 'fourth-branch', that would
   eventually select, depose, and assassinate emperors.

change, disinformation, misinformation, the pandemic, etc
ad nauseam), 'the usurpers, clothed with the forms of legal
authority, regularly seek to crush opposition in embryo.' Let
the one who would scoff at that statement examine the
evidence and history offered by John Whitehead (*Battlefield
America*, 2015), Ivan Greenberg (*The Dangers of Dissent*,
2010), and Bryan Burrough (*Public Enemies*, 2009).[936]

Rand's fictional words are a perfect summation of the
current lived reality of American civilization. It would, to be
certain, require volumes to narrate each hairline fracture in
the shattering of the so-called 'palladia of freedom' of which
Webster spoke.[937] It is the author's contention that the bulk of
these usurpations became procedure as a result of the
'Progressive Era', and that the legacy of these has not only
been ever more encroachments, but a *progressive*
degeneration of the ability to conceive of a life independent
of the meddling by the State. The author does not 'blame the
Progressive Era', but rather sought to juxtapose an analysis
of that worldview as compared against the very clear design
of the Founding. The juxtaposition is stark and inarguable;
the legacy resulting from that very clear departure may be
argued in detail, but not in substance.

Item for item the admonitions of the Founders have
been consistently disregarded with the smug, arrogantly
adolescent dismissal of the past. Line upon line, the
principles of the Declaration were explained away by means
of self-worshiping presentism. Very simply, with sublime
poetry only available to the Divinely inspired, the
Progressive Era is the praxis of Paul's words to the Romans:
"Professing to be wise, they became fools...."[938]

One need not resort to Scripture to condemn, nor cite
an Apostle for prophesy; John Adams' famous quote is

---

936   John W. Whitehead, *Battlefield America: The War on the
American People*, (New York: Select Books Inc. 2015); Ivan
Greenberg, *The Dangers of Dissent: The FBI and Civil Liberties
since 1965*, (Lanham, MD: Lexington Books, 2010); Bryan
Burrough, *Public Enemies: America's Greatest Crime Wave and the
Birth of the FBI, 1933-34*, (New York: Penguin Books, 2009).
937   Noah Webster, "An Examination into the Leading Principles
of the Federal Constitution," in *Constitution*, 2012, 689.
938   Romans 1:22.

prefaced with the same warning. Avarice, ambition, revenge, gallantry, and notorious hypocritical duplicity *define* American civilization both at home and abroad. It is no marvel. The religion of self-worship has no morality beyond self-aggrandizement; self-aggrandizement has no principle beyond a lust for power. One who believes himself a god can by no means be called 'religious'; neither can the moralizer by any guise be termed moral.

> But should the People of America, once become capable of that deep simulation towards one another and towards foreign nations, which assumes the Language of Justice and moderation while it is practicing Iniquity and Extravagance; and displays in the most captivating manner the charming Pictures of Candour frankness & sincerity while it is rioting in rapine and Insolence: this Country will be the most miserable Habitation in the World. Because We have no Government armed with Power capable of contending with human Passions unbridled by morality and Religion. Avarice, Ambition, Revenge or Gallantry, would break the strongest Cords of our Constitution as a Whale goes through a Net. Our Constitution was made only for a moral and religious People. It is wholly inadequate to the government of any other[939]

Among the many wholly clear items to cite from the eighteenth century, few are as clear as the purpose of government "...to secure these rights Governments are instituted among Men...."[940] American government does not exist to 'order liberty,' to 'administer society', or to 'provide safety,' but rather to "...secure the Blessings of Liberty to

939   John Adams, "From John Adams to Massachusetts Militia, 11 October 1798," *Founders Online*, National Archives, https://founders.archives.gov/documents/Adams/99-02-02-3102, sic.
940   United States Declaration of Independence.

ourselves and our Posterity...."[941] Regarding the security of
these rights, of these blessings, let it be proved yet again, in
the words of the President who did not use crisis to empower
himself:

> The internal effects of a mutable policy are
> still more calamitous. It poisons the blessing
> of liberty itself. It will be of little avail to the
> people that the laws are made by men of their
> own choice, if the laws be so voluminous that
> they cannot be read, or so incoherent that they
> cannot be understood; if they be repealed or
> revised before they are promulgated, or
> undergo such incessant changes that no man
> who knows what the law is today can guess
> what it will be tomorrow. Law is defined to be
> a rule of action; but how can that be a rule,
> which is little known and less fixed?[942]

Compare that sublime wisdom against the United
States Tax Code that monopolizes and dictates the entire
subsistence of the United States Citizen.

There is not room enough in any monograph to
narrate the objectively *schizophrenic* nature of law as it
currently exists in America; *no one* understands, let alone can
predict it. The very detail that one is regularly advised to hire
a lawyer to *ensure compliance* – not to defend from an
accusation, but to preemptively seek permission – this is
enough. The Declaration and Constitution are simple enough
that any youth of twelve can comprehend its meaning and
application; it is the convoluted *dissembling* falsely called
'law' that necessitates a *Juris Doctorate* to navigate. The glee
of the expert attorney in narrating how the public just does
not understand the law, and therefore must hire him, is proof
enough. Natural Law is apparent to *toddlers*, one must
ascend the steps of the Supreme Court or the Ivy League to
uncover all the 'reasons' why it is actually a 'social

---

941   United States Constitution, Preamble.
942   James Madison [Attributed], "The Senate," *Federalist no.
62*, 1788, in *Constitution*, 2012, 534; Emphasis added.

construction.' If any randomly selected citizen cannot comprehensively understand and apply *every* law, the law is itself a tyranny; 'expertise' in law is despotism.

> If Congress can employ money indefinitely, for the general welfare, and are the sole and supreme judges of the general welfare, they may take the care of religion into their own hands; they may appoint teachers in every state, county, and parish, and pay them out of the public treasury; they may take into their own hands the education of children, the establishing in like manner schools throughout the union; they may assume the provision of the poor.... Were the power of Congress to be established in the latitude contended for, *it would subvert the very foundations, and transmute the very nature of the limited government established by the people of America.*[943]

Public schools *are not supposed to exist* in the United States because they subvert the very foundations, and transmute the very nature of limited government. They convert nascent citizens into pliant slaves. One whose 'education' is at the behest and direction of the State can by no means grow to hold that State to account. There is a very good, and very evil reason why all authoritarianism seeks to direct education; there is a very solid reason to state that all attempts to direct education are fundamentally authoritarian. Madison knew, and said as much; Limited Government is impossible in such a climate.

---

[943]   James Madison, "The Cod Fishery Bill, February 7, 1792," in Jonathan Elliott, ed. *The debates in the several state conventions on the adoption of the federal Constitution, as recommended by the general convention at Philadelphia, in 1787. Together with the Journal of the federal convention, Luther Martin's letter, Yates's minutes, Congressional opinions, Virginia and Kentucky resolutions of '98-'99, and other illustrations of the Constitution ... 2d ed., with considerable additions. Collected and rev. from contemporary publications,* (Washington: 1836), Vol. IV, 429. Emphasis added.

Welfare, in its bastardized modern sentiment as an entitlement for 'free' stuff, is not a benefit, it is a trap. To receive one's subsistence at the hands of government – without regard to the organization or rationalization of the bureaucrat – is no different than *loansharking*. Dependence upon government for subsistence is slavery.

Whether convinced by fear of the Gauls, or of Baby Face Nelson, to 'be protected' is to be subject to the arbitrary will of the 'protector' – it is the state of being *cattle*. Whether it is a deliberate conspiracy for power or not is irrelevant, every demagogue and despot is aware of this. The progressives used the problems they caused as an emergent excuse to seize and contrive ever more power for themselves, and the people were befuddled enough to buy it. Whether or not it was a vicious plot, the true legacy of the Progressive Era is *slavery*, but of such a nature that the slaves love their chains, and cry out for more.

The American citizen is supposed to be the Yeoman, living an independent life derived of private, productive land-ownership. This has become functionally impossible for any but the wealthy – for whom it is no necessity. Zoning and property taxes; permitting and certificates of occupancy; occupational licensing; commerce-licensing and the sequester of fallow land into parks, preserves, and 'BLM'; commercial development for the connected and wealthy; and especially the 'aggregation principle' of *Wickard v. Filburn* have rendered the Yeoman an outlaw – bereft of the benefit of law.

To pursue an independent life, the citizen must continually ask permission, and perpetually pay for the *privilege*: dependence by definition. To 'legally' live as the Yeoman, the yeomanry must submit to tenancy. This is to say nothing of indenture of the mortgage for the un-farmable, indefensible suburban 'home,' (wherein it is normally illegal to cultivate or to keep livestock) or the fundamentally dependent transience of the rental. The vast majority of American civilization has become nothing more sophisticated than moldering wood made pretty with a thin veneer of latex – both the homes, and the serfs who inhabit them.

Why in God's name are the quality of milk and beef a suitable excuse to exercise *law-enforcement raids?*[944] It is clear that the citizen, in the view of government, is incapable of measuring the quality of his food for himself. If the citizen cannot measure his milk, it is no wonder he is not trusted with actual policy – to say nothing of possessing equivalent weaponry to his 'protectors' who are supposed to be his servants.[945]

This is all, of course, to say nothing of the blithering cowardice and rank dereliction demonstrated by the *entire* Uvalde Texas police department who, in 2022, facilitated the murder of 19 children and both arrested and tasered the parents who attempted to rescue their children when the police refused.[946] The Uvalde Police Department commit accessory to murder, with little done in the way of judicial response.

Government has usurped the definition of right and wrong, and as expected quickly declared that it is wrong,

944   Tom Venesky, "Raid on Farm Sparks Debate Over Raw Milk Oversight and Government Overreach," *Lancaster Farming*, April 17, 2025, Accessed April 17, 2025: https://www.lancasterfarming.com/farming-news/dairy/raid-on-farm-sparks-debate-over-raw-milk-oversight-and-government-overreach/article_002d5ebc-ba30-11ee-8f53-6f93227a52c2.html; Patrick Carroll, "Amish Farmer Faces Fines, Prison Time for Refusing to Comply with USDA Regulations," *Foundation for Economic Education*, August 23, 2022, Accessed April 17, 2025: https://fee.org/articles/amish-farmer-faces-fines-prison-time-for-refusing-to-comply-with-usda-regulations/.

945   The Courts have overtly, consistently, and wholly disavowed *any* duty for law-enforcement to protect, or *any* right of the citizen to protection, yet law consistently exempts law enforcement from weapons restrictions. Cf. *Town of Castle Rock Colorado v. Gonzales*, 545 U.S. 748 (2005); *Deshaney v. Winnebago County*, 489 U.S. 189 (1989); *Warren v. District of Columbia*, 444 A.2d. 1, D.C. Ct. of Ap. 1981; *Lozito v. City of New York*, 283 AD 2d 251 – NY: Appellate Div., 1st Dept. (2001).

946   News Desk, "Cops Handcuffed Mother, Tasered Parent While Gunman Killed Children in Uvalde School," *News 18*, May 28, 2022, Accessed April 21, 2025: https://www.news18.com/news/world/cops-handcuffed-mother-tasered-parent-while-gunman-killed-children-in-uvalde-school-5262991.html.

dangerous, and hateful to oppose anything that government might do.[947] This is the applied meaning of *rex non potest peccare* and its despicable weaseler 'qualified immunity.' The conflation of moral quality with legislation has wholly castrated Virtue.

Virtue is the voluntary, consistent, balanced moral excellence in seeking one's purpose; it is the essential quality that allows for a man to be free. This quality cannot be delegated or 'outsourced,' one cannot say 'but another told me thus.' Men cannot be made good by law because law is made by fallible man; to presume the inverse is the delusion of auto-apotheosis. God Himself asked for *voluntary* compliance; behavior is the outward expression of inward *belief.* To seek to *make* men anything is paramount to the presumption to dictate both substance and belief. It is not merely that a vicious people will necessitate more laws, but that one who seeks to make men good by means of more laws seeks to dictate the thoughts, beliefs, and opinions of others – a total violation.[948] This is a supremely arrogant

---

947   "far-right extremists" defined as "reverent of individual liberty"; Department of Homeland Security, "The Organizational Dynamics of Far-Right Hate Groups in the United States: Comparing Violent to Non-Violent Organizations; Final Report to Human Factors/Behavioral Sciences Division, Science and Technology Directorate, U.S. Department of Homeland Security," December 2011, Accessed April 21, 2025: https://www.dhs.gov/sites/default/files/publications/944_OPSR_TEV US_Comparing-Violent-Nonviolent-Far-Right-Hate-Groups_Dec2011-508.pdf. Cf. James Bovard, "A Billion Dollars of Federally Funded Paranoia," *Mises Wire*, February 6, 2017, Accessed April 21, 2025: https://mises.org/mises-wire/billion-dollars-federally-funded-paranoia.

948   Cf. Benjamin Franklin, "To Messrs. The Abbés Chalut and Arnaud," April 17, 1787, in: Jared Sparks, ed., *The Works of Benjamin Franklin; containing several political and historical tracts not included in any former edition, and many lettersm official and private, not hitherto published; with notes and a life of the author,* Vol. X, (Boston: Hillard, Gray, 1840), 297; Thomas Jefferson,"82. A Bill for Establishing Religious Freedom, 18 June 1779," *Founders Online*, National Archives, https://founders.archives.gov/documents/Jefferson/01-02-02-0132-0004-0082, sic; Cf. Witherspoon, *Annotated Edition of Lectures on Moral Philosophy*; Belief cannot be compelled, John Locke, *A Letter*

delusion of deification and, like all such things, merely initiates a recursive cycle of usurpation. Who would presume to 'make men good' has already exceeded any possible limit to his power; he has assumed both infallibility and omnipotence; presumed to re-create the universe itself; presumed to be God Himself.

By design, the whole of American authority is subordinate to Natural Law; this far, and no farther. A government who interprets its own limitations is by no means limited. This is an identical circumstance to the opponent in a debate who changes the definitions of key terms mid-sentence, but combined with the ability to murder with impunity. An authority who has presumed to originate or define rights, that being the wellspring of authority itself, has *already* usurped the function of law and repudiated the possibility of legitimacy. A variable standard is an elastic scale, a rubber-rule. Government who rejects Natural Law *cannot* meet its purpose, and cannot be limited by any rational measure – it has disavowed the existence of rational measure.

Ignorance of the law is supposed to be no excuse because the law is properly rooted in Natural Law, of which all are intimately and wholly aware. To repudiate Natural Law is to repudiate the concept of law itself. One knows murder, theft, assault, trespass, and the rest to be wrong because he does not want it done to him or his. This is a distant thing from the inscrutable minefield of legislation and regulation for which one may be prosecuted, impoverished, and imprisoned, but no person would know was illegal if not previously told. If the law is not a *simple* reflection of Natural Law, there is no validity in the claim that anyone has an obligation to know and to follow the law; Jefferson said as much when he subordinated *all* law to "the limits drawn around us by the equal rights of others...."[949] It is inarguable that Holmes Jr. and Wilson both wholly amputated lady Justice's legs with perverse definitions and 'omnipotent'

Concerning Toleration, ed. J. Brook, (Yorkshire: Huddersfield, 1796 [1689]), 12-13.

949   Jefferson, Thomas. "Thomas Jefferson to Isaac H. Tiffany, 4 April 1819." Emphasis added.

legislature. They were enabled to do so by an extension of Beecher, Gladden, and Ely's historicism – the transparent prevaricating equivocation inherent in 'what this *really* means....'

The rule of the expert, the 'science of administration' is a perverse theocracy. In truth the Master, in the universal metaphysical sense, is God as expressed through the innate, universal, approachable, obvious, and personal understanding of Natural Law, not by diktat of the arrogant esoteric priestly *cognocenti*. In the particular, the physical master is 'We the People' – all of them. The people do not ask the government, but rather the government must ask the people; a freeman does not ask, seek, nor require permission. The ruler – the citizen – does not beg of the servant – the government.[950] But even this true ruler is neither unlimited nor omnipotent.

The people as a whole cannot command any more than might any one man of their number. The 'community' by no means has an "absolute right... to determine its own destiny and that of its members;" the 'community' is decidedly not "supreme over men as individuals."[951] *Lex majoris partis* is also subject to limitation; all sovereignty, all right acts, all authority is subordinate to Natural Law.[952] The whole does not have more right to act than the one, because the right of the whole derives solely of the consent of the one.[953]

Consent is the application of human dignity, the antonym of enslavement. This is the practicable, identifiable praxis of equality. Equality is the soul of the Declaration as a

---

950   Benjamin Franklin, *The Political Thought of Benjamin Franklin*, ed. Ralph Ketchum, (Indianapolis: Hackett Publishing Company, 1965), 398; Cf. *Virginia Declaration*, Section 2.

951   Woodrow Wilson, "Socialism and Democracy," *Unpublished Essay*, 1887. In "Woodrow Wilson on Socialism and Democracy," *Progressivism and Liberalism*, The Heritage Foundation, Accessed March 17, 2025: https://static.heritage.org/CPP/FP_PS19.pdf, Emphasis added.

952   James Madison, "Essay on Sovereignty", December, 1835. *Founders Early Access*. Accessed September 25, 2024: https://rotunda.upress.virginia.edu/founders/default.xqy?keys=FOEA-print-02-02-02-3188.

953   Locke, *Second Treatise*, IV:23, VIII:96.

direct product of all having been created and endowed with inalienable rights by their Creator. The Declaration is the anima of the Constitution, the latter is merely the procedural application of the former.[954] The whole of legitimate power in the United States of America derives entirely from the Declaration of Independence – *rule number one* of American law.[955]

The validity of legitimacy in the Declaration derives of consent, and the fundamental purpose of authority in that same document is a direct paraphrase of Locke. To secure the inalienable rights given by God is not merely the whole purpose, it is the self-dissolving *sine qua non*: "Where there is no longer the administration of justice, for the securing of men's rights… there certainly is no government left."[956] Authority that alienates the inalienable is not merely illegitimate, it is criminal; bad government is so bad that it is the polar-opposite of government. A lawmaker who ignores his own laws is a worse than senseless thing. The whole purpose is liberty; to neither dominate, nor be dominated; neither by others, nor by one's own passions.

What is just need rarely be *justified*, what is rational is never *rationalized*. The moral quality of an act is inversely proportional to the effort required to excuse it; the effort required to explain or to excuse is itself the most damning evidence that it is inexplicable and inexcusable. State the case to the plowman; good, right, just, and moral do not submit to the lawyer, leader, technocrat, epistocrat, or expert pragmatick administrator.

And so the matter returns to originalism; that dismissive red-herring that, like 'formalism,' serves only to obfuscate the eminently simple. It is self-evident that only the illiterate or the power-mad can read either the Declaration or

---

954   James Wilson, "Remarks of James Wilson in the Pennsylvania Convention to Ratify the Constitution of the United States, 1787," in *Collected Works of James Wilson*, Vol. 1, Eds. Kermit L. Hall and Mark David Hall. (Indianapolis: Liberty Fund, 2007); Cf. Justice David Brewer citing *Yick Wo v. Hopkins,* 118 U.S. 356 (1886) in *Gulf, Colorado & Santa Fe Railway Co. v. Ellis*, 165 U.S. 150 (1897).

955   1 U.S.C. § 1 (2012).

956   Locke, *Second Treatise*, XIX:219.

the Constitution and come away with pretensions of supreme
authority, collective omnipotence, 'democracy', epistocracy,
or sovereign immunity. All such positions are soundly and
completely rejected by the Organic Acts that birthed
American civilization, yet to hold these Acts in their rational
content is dismissed as merely one mode of interpretation –
the worthless appellation 'originalism.' Principles transcend
even paradigms and 'schools-of-thought;' they are
fundamental axioms whose value is usually found, with deep
irony, when disregarded. Only the thirsty know the flavor of
water; only the hopeless understand the value and nature of
Hope. Abandoning the axioms of the Declaration has
produced *exactly* what the Declaration was written to reject,
and the Revolution fought to eradicate in this land.

Many times this author has referenced *rex non potest
pecarre* – "the king cannot sin" – many times, because this
attitude utterly vitiates any possibility of an accountable
authority. The paradigm of Sovereign Immunity, 'qualified
immunity', is the position that if the president, legislature,
court, or law enforcement does it, it is not illegal. It is wholly
lawless government. Let this be stated again: *the doctrine of
immunity is lawless government*; it is the policy of piracy.
This policy is, and has been, the *modus operandi* of
American power structures since Wilson deluded himself
with messianic pretensions.

Sovereign immunity is the medical antagonist to
limited government; the acid to all human liberty, yet it is the
presumed prerogative of American government at every
level.[957] Wholly military units, called "SWAT" but entirely
gendarmerie, have been and are given absolute license to
enter and destroy homes – even when that home has
absolutely no relation to the crime (supposed or real) that
provokes the *invasion*. The Courts have, by cowardice of
declining *certiorari*, and by *overt decision*, given total license
to this extreme abuse.[958]

---

957   Erwin Chemerinsky, "Against Sovereign Immunity,"
Stanford Law Review Vol. 53, (May, 2001): 1201 – 1224.
958   The Rutherford Institute, "Supreme Court Protects Rogue
SWAT Leader Who Raided Wrong Home," *The Free Thought
Project*, March 9, 2025, Accessed April 22, 2025:

The Courts have declined to prosecute police officers who dropped an *explosive* in a toddler's crib.[959] The Courts ignore the wanton murder of a completely uninvolved man by Police Officers so incompetent as to execute a search warrant at the wrong address.[960] A SWAT Team completely destroyed an entirely uninvolved family home, rendering it uninhabitable, and the Federal Appeals Court declared no liability – no aid, no redress, no compensation – then the Supreme Court declined to hear the case, letting this violent robbery stand unopposed – *stare decisis*.[961] There are *literally hundreds* of similar and even identical instances – especially the horrifically incompetent murder and destruction at the *wrong address* for a warrant – covering every level of jurisdiction, in nearly every State of the Union, as well as Federal agencies.

Courts and legislatures completely ignore the enabling basis for 'Swatting' – or the malicious use of SWAT by means of false reporting. No authority in the United

---

https://thefreethoughtproject.com/cop-watch/supreme-court-protects-rogue-swat-leader-who-raided-wrong-home.

959 Eliott C. McLaughlin, "No Indictments for Georgia SWAT Team that Burned Baby with Stun Grenade," *CNN.com*, October 7, 2014, Accessed April 22, 2025: https://www.cnn.com/2014/10/07/us/georgia-toddler-stun-grenade-no-indictment/index.html.

960 Lauren Minor, "Neighbors: Police Killed Man after Serving Warrant to Wrong Home," *Lex18.com*, December 30, 2024, Accessed April 22, 2025: https://www.lex18.com/news/covering-kentucky/neighbors-police-killed-man-after-serving-warrant-to-wrong-home.

961 Elise Schmelzer, "A SWAT Team Destroyed a Greenwood Village Family's Home. Now, a Federal Appeals Court Says Police Don't Have to Pay for the Damage," *The Denver Post*, October 30, 2019, Accessed April 22, 2025: https://www.denverpost.com/2019/10/30/swat-team-destroyed-greenwood-village-familys-home-police-dont-have-to-pay-for-damages/#:~:text=A%20SWAT%20team%20destroyed%20a%20Greenwood%20Village%20family's%20home.,to%20pay%20for%20the%20damage. Cf. Institute for Justice, "Lech v. City of Greenwood Village," *Institute for Justice*, N.d. Accessed April 22, 2025: *https://ij.org/case/lech-v-city-of-greenwood/#:~:text=But%20a%20three%2Djudge%20panel,overturned%20in%20a%20future%20case.*

States, as of this writing, appears to question why or how it is so very simple to send the *gestapo* to a rival's house *with nothing but a false claim over a phone-call*; none question why procedure has totally failed to prevent such obvious abuses of such clearly unlawful power. In the simplest terms, a mere unannotated bibliography of the abuses and crimes of law-enforcement from say, 1913, would easily exceed five-hundred pages, single spaced. Yet all of these are excused, ignored, and even *vindicated* by means of THE KING CANNOT SIN. To maintain the delusion of limited government in contemporary America requires only one variable: deliberate ignorance.

The Courts have done much more than use 'sovereign immunity' or 'qualified immunity' to excuse murder, robbery, theft, assault, mutilation, kidnapping, and *even rape*.[962] The courts have also simply declared – outright – that the Bill of Rights has no application, that it does not exist. A Federal Judge simply stated that there is no second amendment right to purchase a firearm.[963] Another judge went further to declare that the Second Amendment *simply does not exist* in *her courtroom*, and sentenced a man to a decade in prison for perfectly legal acts.[964] The Supreme Court of Hawaii nullified

---

962   Lynette Christmas, "A Bad Cop Secually Assaulted Me. Qualified Immunity Protected him and his Boss," *USA Today*, September 19, 2021, Accessed April 22, 2025: https://www.usatoday.com/story/opinion/voices/2021/09/19/qualified-immunity-cop-sexual-assault-lynette-christmas/8240249002/. Cf. Training Division, "Second Circuit Finds Qualified Immunity Applies to Prison Guard Sexual Abuse Lawsuit," *Defender Services Office*, December 29, 2020, Accessed April 22, 2025: https://www.fd.org/news/second-circuit-finds-qualified-immunity-applies-prison-guard-sexual-abuse-lawsuit; *Tangreti v. Bachmann*, No. 19-03712 (2d Cir. Dec. 28, 2020).

963   Institute for Legislative Action, "Federal Judge in Colorado Insists There is No Second Amendment Right to Buy a Gun," *NRA-ILA*, November 20, 2023, Accessed April 22, 2025: https://www.nraila.org/articles/20231120/federal-judge-in-colorado-insists-there-is-no-second-amendment-right-to-buy-a-gun.

964   News Staff, "Gunsmith Sentenced to Prison for Legal Firearm Told: "The Second Amendment Doesn't Exist in My Courtroom," by New York Judge," *WNY News Now*, May 20, 2024, Accessed April 22, 2025: https://wnynewsnow.com/2024/05/20/gunsmith-sentenced-to-prison-

the Supreme Court of the United States *and* both their State Constitution and the Constitution of the United States with an overt reference to sorcery, that they termed 'the spirit of Aloha.'[965] The police and the courts are for all intents and purposes, wholly unlimited – even and especially by the very documents from which they ostensibly derive their authority, and for which they allegedly swear an oath to support, defend, and uphold. American law is wholly *lawless*.[966]

It is no surprise that in a psychotic society, madmen should rule – and this is nothing new. America's ruling class is utterly degenerate in an eerily similar manner to the other Republic-cum-Empire. An unprosecuted act of sodomy, having taken place in the Senate Judiciary Committee Chambers, was *filmed and published*, and it was… *mundane*.[967] One cannot be faulted for being reminded of Nero and Sporus.[968] This is to say nothing of the rampant *stupidity* exemplified by the still-sitting Congressman who expressed concern that the island of Guam might capsize due to a Marine base on one side.[969] One can say little of the overgrown child-Congressman who pulled a fire alarm to delay a vote – who was only censured due to *party*

for-legal-firearm-told-the-second-amendment-doesnt-exist-in-my-courtroom-by-new-york-judge/.

965   Amy E. Swearer, "Hawaii Supreme Court Rejects Bruen as Inconsistent With "Aloha Spirit"," *The Federalist Society*, August 1, 2024, Accessed April 22, 2025: https://fedsoc.org/scdw/hawaii-supreme-court-rejects-bruen-as-inconsistent-with-aloha-spirit.

966   For an extensive analysis of the sickness endemic to 'process', Cf. Prentice L. White, "Absolute Immunity: A License to Rape Justice at Will," *Washington and Lee Journal of Civil Rights and Social Justice*, 17, no. 2 (2011): 333 – 383.

967   Armstrong Williams, "Sodomy in the Halls of Congress," *Creators.com*, December 21, 2023, Accessed April 22, 2025: https://www.creators.com/read/armstrong-williams/12/23/sodomy-in-the-halls-of-congress.

968   Nero Claudius Caesar Augustus Germanicus (AD 37 – 68) who castrated then 'married' the slave Sporus (d. AD 69).

969   Stephanie Condon, "Hank Johnson Worries Guam Could "Capsize" After Marine Buildup," *CBS News*, April 1, 2010, Accessed April 22, 2025: https://www.cbsnews.com/news/hank-johnson-worries-guam-could-capsize-after-marine-buildup/.

allegiance having a slight majority.[970] It would be a waste of breath to narrate and cite the wealthy and somewhat popular Congresswoman who faked Native American ancestry for 'diversity points,' or the other who told her supporters and constituents to attack and harass anyone who voted for someone she did not like – both of whom are still lawmakers. It is an horrific and inarguable state of affairs that nearly all members of Congress become obscenely wealthy – far beyond their legal pay, and totally outside of any explanation beyond obvious corruption – while their people struggle with depreciating currency and exponential costs caused by incessant meddling.

It is clear that the Congress is wholly corrupt by any standard, and this is no surprise anymore so than the viciously authoritarian agencies being facilitated by the delusional Courts. The championed 'oath' of office to support and defend the Constitution is a meaningless performance; the forsworn are not seen as traitors nor even criminals. The 'oaths' mean nothing; they are worthless. Hawaii will not be reprimanded, Judges will not be punished, Law-Enforcement is immune, and Congress is above them all. Whoever happens to be President amounts to less than nothing.

The common theme between the current state of affairs and the Progressive Era is self-obsession, narcissism. This is also the common theme among the men and the ideologies analyzed. From Gladden and Beecher, Dewey and Lippmann, to Holmes and Wilson, whether the social gospel and historicism, or 'humanism' and pragmatism, they all see themselves as gods – above the petty concerns of the lowly and the unfit; immune to the seductions of power and corruption. While there are thousands of names and dozens of ideologies, they all amount to men claiming to be God and because they are gods, they substitute their ersatz moralism in place of transcendent principles.

The principles of the Declaration are internally consistent; the musings of the progressives, self-

---

970 Justin Papp, "House Censures Rep. Jamaal Bowman for Pulling Fire Alarm," *Roll Call*, December 7, 2023, Accessed April 22, 2025: https://rollcall.com/2023/12/07/house-censures-rep-jamaal-bowman-for-pulling-fire-alarm/.

contradictory. The position that rights are the free and universal grant of God leads to dignity and freedom; the perversity that rights descend from government leads only to dependence and degradation. America has become a rapidly oscillating feverish cesspool because it repudiated the primacy of principles. Both the death of the Republic, and the immanent collapse of the Empire are the direct result of the delusion that drove the Progressive Era.

The greatest irony of this analysis has been to find that the feverish rush to re-make American society was not merely the total repudiation of the principles of the foundation excused by circumstance and necessity, but that item for item it was an abject failure. Owing to the sociopolitical climate wherein this argument is written, it is disheartening to view ever more histrionic escapades against 'oligarchy' – when the angered are trying to protest *plutocracy* – and it would seem that none of these understand that only Natural Law distinguishes them both from the designed Republic of laws.

Banks, corporations, 'government contracts,' and effective monopolism define the United States to a far greater degree now than they did in the late nineteenth century. No sane person who interacts with any level of American government today would elect to use the term 'efficient' as anything other than a sarcastic epithet. Bureaucracy is synonymous with two things: industrialized inefficiency taken to the level of cartoonish stupidity, and Progressivism.

Efficiency is an excuse – and a hollow one. Parasitic industries, favor trading by the wealthy, rich union bosses, untouchable 'trusts', depressed wages, increased costs, devalued currency, unemployment, and rent-based living are the standard of current American life. Warmongering, financial-manipulation, and military adventurism define American foreign policy. Demands of evermore *donativa* and an ever higher grain dole characterize domestic organization – the largest single employer in the United States is the Federal Government.[971]

---

971   The *donativa* were gifts, meaning bribes, given from the treasury by the various Caesars to officials, usually the army and Praetorian Guard, to secure and ensure power. Office of Disability

John Dewey and the NEA have bequeathed horrendous education standards. Effectively, most young Americans are functionally illiterate and innumerate.[972] This goes far beyond basic skills, future 'job' prospects, or arbitrary test scores. Any randomly selected American – whether civilian or official – is likely to be wholly ignorant of the principles, the practice, or the place of the Declaration, to say nothing of the history around these items – though many of them will likely enthusiastically endorse the rhetoric. Few understand that the battles of Lexington and Concord – that began this country – were fought to *reject gun control*.[973] Let this fact stand against the charge that this author has lain overmuch on 'second amendment' arguments. Benjamin Rush may have been a prodigy for having completed Princeton at 14, but Madison's extensive study – *proficiency* – in the broad range of disciplines from History and Mathematics to Hebrew and Agronomy was *normal* for a university graduate of the tender age of twenty. The absolute best graduates of the best institutions of today, barely make par.

It is little wonder then that Americans today – those who are not lost in the narcissism of self-worship – cannot truly comprehend the extent of the comparison between the Roman and American Empires. The crisis of the third-century, barbarian invasions, inept leadership, currency devaluation, and the resultant millennium of 'dark ages' all

---

Employment Policy, "Federal Employers," *U.S. Department of Labor*, N.d., Accessed April 21, 2025: https://www.dol.gov/agencies/odep/program-areas/employers/federal-employment.

972   Literacy Network, "The Issue," *Reading is Fundamental*, N.d. Accessed April 22, 2025: https://www.rif.org/literacy-network/the-issue; Wylie Communications, "What's the Latest U.S. Numeracy Rate?" N.d., Accessed April 22, 2025: https://www.wyliecomm.com/2021/11/whats-the-latest-u-s-numeracy-rate/#:~:text=U.S.%20adults%20have%20basic%20numeracy,%2C%20or%20basic%2C%20numeracy%20skills.

973   David B. Kopel, "How the British Gun Control Program Precipitated the American Revolution," *Charleston Law Review*, 38, no. 283 (2012).

extended from somewhere. While this work is not a treatment of the Roman Principate, one would assert that the degradation that the west experienced from *somewhere* around 140 BC until *somewhere* around 1600 was a result of the repudiation of principles – punctuated by the Roman *Aeneid*. How long the destruction from 1913 will last would be a question for a man from *somewhere* around AD 3000, if such a question is possible – punctuated by the American Aeneid; that is, the social gospel and its Progressive Era.

The dissolute political shenanigans as of this current writing are no more complex or sophisticated than infantile arguments around who should be in command of powers that are not supposed to exist. As it is absurd to honor Trajan or venerate Aurelius as one abhors Caligula or Nero, so too it is rank insanity to eulogize Kennedy or emulate Reagan while rejecting Johnson and criticizing Nixon. An imperial presidency is an affront to the principles of the Declaration without regard to the man by whom it happens to be wielded. A corrupted chair cannot be sanctified by the saintly ass what sits it. The 'moderate' of today is indistinguishable from the 'radical' of the New Deal; the 'conservative' serves only to conserve those policies – which time has made no less treasonous. An enlightened dictator is no less a dictator, a kindly tyrant is no less tyrannical; dictatorship by 'consent' is nonsense.

To look in feigned horror upon the Praetorian Guard as the apparatus of domination in the Roman Principate, and fail to recognize the same apparatus – spread among 'agencies' – in the United States is a dereliction. It is the very image of despair to frequently witness the impotent Spartan 'second amendment' slogan ΜΟΛΩΝ ΛΑΒΕ (*molon labe* – 'come, take') in concert with "Back the Blue" – as the fervently patriotic soul is entirely unclear who it is who will come and do the taking. And he who takes finds no dissonance between his 'oath' to support and defend "the right of the people to keep and bear arms" and his own act of infringement. Yet again, a tyrant without his goons, whatever uniform they wear, is mere noise. In the manufactured rush to back the blue against 'defund the police' and 'ACAB', the patriot utterly fails perceive that under the next administration, that same 'blue' will take new orders. Increased powers are perennially perilous, and always a treason to the Declaration. The essence is transparently clear; what power can be abused *will* be abused: 'back the blue, until it happens to you.' Simply, if there were any 'good cops', there would be *no* bad cops.

Who is it who would fight 'fascism' then make a great showing of the 'Pledge of Allegiance'? He knows nothing of either fascism or the Pledge. By reciting the oath of American National Socialism, he affirms in deed what he opposes in word. Who would declare a thing to be 'the LAW' can rarely specify the chapter, let alone the section – and never whether it is Civil, Criminal, Statutory, Constitutional, Case, or 'Administrative'. The one who declares the 'LAW' never takes pause to understand that it is all meaningless without a magistrate to agree, and there are no guarantees in this. Without competent understanding there can be no consent; without consent there can be no legitimacy. Authority bereft of legitimacy is wholly reduced to power – that is, *do as I say, or else.*

To speak of the imperial presidency and make no mention of the festering mass of appalling stupidity, feral hysterics, perpetual histrionics, and corruption-as-procedure that is the Congress would be a dereliction. As the Roman Senate was no guard to the wholly unlawful incarnation of *Senatus Publique Romanus* in the Person of Augustus, so too have the various Legislatures utterly failed in all respects to insist upon the principles of the Declaration in practice – indeed, being too often the midwife of usurpation. It is far too tempting to lay blame at some practice, lobby, or 'special interest', but reality is far less sophisticated.

No human being can long be entrusted with the ability to enforce his will upon others. To allow a man with the power to tax to decide what and how much to tax, allows and encourages him to use that revenue to grant bribes from the treasury, favors to his supporters, and promises to solve the very problems that he created with his solutions to previous problems. Such an arrangement leaves that man only ever granting himself more power with each recursion;

this is the worst possible safeguard to limited government by principle.

A man elected on a promise to solve a social ill has a clear and vested interest in the perpetuation and magnification of that social ill, simply to secure his incumbency. Evil is terribly mundane, terribly banal; entropy is the default process, and it is always the path of least resistance. In the absence of overt and threatening vigilance, extending from a deep and organic understanding of *principles*, the decay to tyranny is the natural and unavoidable path.

To seek the protection of the Supreme Court is an act of gross negligence. To be certain, the Court may deign to recognize rights as opposed to wrongs, but it is not and never was the originator nor granter of any right. If the court were the arbiter of rights, it would also be the arbiter of wrongs – the judge of ethics or morality itself. Law is not equivalent to morality; evil men cannot make good laws. To view the court in such a light does not merely exalt it to the status of a demigod, it rejects the very first clause of Jefferson's famous preamble. Men were not endowed by their government with certain inalienable rights; God originated rights in both the moral *and* the legal sense; Natural Law is the only basis of *all* law. Only God is qualified to make such grand decrees; the Court can either apply these self-evident Forms, or it can dissemble. The courts can either recognize that the Constitution is *procedure* written to secure *principles*, or it can repudiate the foundations of its own authority. The 'justices' are able to either act as guarantor to the *preexisting rights* and ratified limitations of the Constitution, or they can presume to dictate the very meaning of words – of thought and reality itself – say, *man and woman* for instance.

The great stupidity behind viewing government, society, the Constitution, or the Declaration as 'living,' and therefore subject to change and development, was the self-obsession-induced failure to understand that the adaptations of living creatures act *in accordance with unchanging and immutable* principles. It is supreme imbecility to see an adaptation to improve survivability, and then to use this observation to claim that the principle of survivability itself ought to change. So it is with the principles upon which the Declaration is written, from which the Constitution is derived. The principles do not change, and though the society or civilization may, it ought to do so only to better reflect or to better achieve those static, transcendent, redoubtable Forms.

Pursuing justice by changing the definition of Justice is an act of absolute madness; presuming to *provide* general welfare, when told to *promote* it, is an act of enslavement. Quibbling over semantics in Civil Asset Forfeiture, 'No Knock' raids, and the right to trial by jury in *all* criminal prosecutions is an act of abuse. Conflating the infringement of the right *of the people* with the regulation of the militia is an act of tyranny.

Good men do not seek the ability to effect their will upon others; good men do not seek power. Without regard to the rhetorical or to the sincere motives, it is inescapable that only evil men seek to reduce another under their arbitrary will because to do such a thing is a fundamentally evil act – without regard to the nature of that will. Even the most selfless, the most saintly man becomes a devil the moment he seeks to impose his will. Lust for power is the seduction of Satan; it is the very means by which the son of the morning became the father of lies. As one may ignore one's health, but not the consequences of ignoring one's health, so too might one disregard the substance of an act in favor of its justification – but one cannot ignore the resultant degradation, tyranny, and enslavement of that act. Motives determine flavor; motives do not determine facts.

Whoever seeks to impose their will upon another has declared war against that person; there can be no good faith in such a state. There can be no honest debate where one party to that debate has predetermined to control the other. Absent the mutual recognition of universal principles, one opponent will invariably seek to deceive, coerce, manipulate, or force the other to acquiesce. Like the pigeon who will wipe clean the chessboard, then strut about as though victorious, so too the conduct of every solipsist under any name. To whom reality is subjective, and truth a construction, only one principle exists: *POWER*.

The man who would presume to dictate reality itself is so mad as to presume anything at all, he is only a danger and unworthy of any trust. Simply put, the Progressive is, and has always been, *hostis humani generis* – the enemy of all mankind – as he has from his earliest thought presumed to dictate, to reduce all others under his will. Any attempt to reduce another under one's will is inherently evil. Any compromise is a total compromise; to treat with evil is to become evil, to negotiate with evil is to permit evil. There is and can be no fellowship between light and dark; there are no 'half' slaves.

There can be no agreement without a thorough understanding of both its nature and possible consequences. In the absence of agreement, freely acquiesced without the shade of threats, duplicity, manipulation, or deceit – with total freedom to decline without repercussion – there can be no consent. Where there is no possibility of the 'no', any 'yes' is meaningless. Without consent there can be no legitimacy, and therefore no authority. The power of government within the United States of America is illegitimate according to its own definition of the term, and has been for more than a century. According to the Declaration of Independence, the current powers wield great force, but lack *any* legitimate authority.

It was a long death, likely began somewhere around Lincoln, and it cannot be wholly attributed to any single man or ideology. The *res publica* is not such a simple thing whose demise can be lain at any small number. As stated, a tyrant without goons is little more than noise; tyranny necessitates complicity, and complicity breeds tyranny. Were the people not so credulous as to buy the social gospel, so cowardly as to accept the promise of safety, so weak as to tolerate the intolerable acts, so stupid as to swallow the obvious charms of such clear psychopaths – there might have remained an American Republic. Would-be tyrants could simply be ignored to death.

Whatever the cause, upon whomever the blame may fall, it is wholly self-evident that no American citizen living today has ever experienced life in the civilization they so readily champion. By exception upon exception, circumstance upon compromise, 'the people' ate what poisoned fruit they were offered as they fell for the oldest lie ever told: "Ye shall not surely die… ye shall be as gods, knowing good and evil."[974] What troubles plague the United States of America today are no more complex than the vapors of decay.

The Declaration of Independence represents the shining jewel of the Enlightenment; the recognition of first-things – principles – as the basis for social cooperation lie at the root of all rational measurement. By elevating rights to a universal grant of God, limiting authority by clear lines, the sentiments of the eighteenth century allowed for an end to the perpetual piracy of power. Progressivism and its precipitant social gospel end-ran that sublime provenance to reduce the dignity of a man to impotent talking points – toys for madmen who would be gods. American freedom was to be lived; by means of hubris, it has been reduced to the mere dressing of a lie.

---

974   Genesis 3:4 – 5.

Coda

But a Constitution of Government once
changed from Freedom, can never be restored.
Liberty once lost is lost forever. When the
People once surrender their share in the
Legislature, and the Right of defending the
Limitations upon the Government, and of
resisting every Encroachment upon them, they
can never regain it.

– John Adams, 1775

Many of the early reviewers of my work have noted
the pessimistic tone; some have suggested some
'call to action' or other attempt to end on a more
positive note. I very much wish that I were able to do so.

It is not that I do not have ideas in this regard – a so
called 'Restoration Act' in a manner of speaking – but rather
that I have seen far too much of sweeping reforms in my
study of history. I was very young when first I noticed in a
history book that once I saw the words "he instituted
sweeping reforms", the collapse and demise of that
civilization had already begun. It can't be fixed.

As I write this, the 'government' is enduring another 'shut-down' for some ridiculousness or another, and one major concern clogging up the inter-webs is the hysterical fear and machinations surrounding SNAP benefits – the old grain dole. Some go so far as to predict widespread mayhem as soon as the EBT cards stop working. Maybe it will happen like that, or maybe it is yet more juvenalia… probably both. Imagine the chaos should government actually try to confine themselves to Natural Law, freedom, and the Principles of the Declaration – the serfs would utterly lose it, and you know it.

What is clear is that belief cannot be compelled. It is impossible to free a people who have come to love their slavery. American civilization is thoroughly, and likely irreparably institutionalized. Democracies can vote themselves into a dictatorship – as they have *always* done – but for some reason, they cannot re-vote themselves into freedom… *gee, I wonder why.*

One of my reviewers in my dissertation defense expressed concern that my work would be merely a polemic, that it could serve as the impetus for violence. That is certainly a possibility, but to use my work to excuse some bloody episode would be to fail to understand my work.

This is the reality of the scholar's burden – we make all sorts of screwy arguments, and then people run off half-cocked and start killing each other because of what we have written. That is the essence of my criticism against Gladden, Beecher, Ely, and their ilk. Scholarship is not a harmless hobby, and historic writing is not masturbation.

The truth of the philosopher or the historian is that 'success' for them takes one of two forms: either eighth-graders hate them three-hundred years after their death because of the boring assignments based on grand ideals that amount to very little, or legions of people start killing each other over their ideas. It's gross, but that's the way of things.

If people start trying to impose their will on others because of my work, they did not understand a damn thing in my work. This is not a polemic or some kind of 'manifesto', it is the most honest comparative analysis that I could write – it is the most reasonable, most complete image America that I could formulate, given what I have found. If that is too pessimistic, reality is often disappointing.

I will say to the imagined 'partisan', the 'patriot', or the 'freedom fighter' who might take my work as an excuse: be careful. There is a weird fascination with the 'subversive' in American culture, but only by those who do not know what that word means. In the life of the subversive, there is no time for fishing trips or barbecues, no room for prom night or ice-cream socials, no real possibility of laughing with delight as your daughter hands you your third grand-child. If you choose to be a subversive, that is *all* you get to do. Revolutionaries never reach utopia.

Don't use my arguments as an excuse for vice because if you do, you only prove that you did not understand my arguments.

What then?

Probably the apocalypse. I cannot predict the End – nobody can, and anyone who tries is a moron – but I can discern the face of the sky. Western civilization as a whole is irreparably moribund. We've messed it up so badly that it cannot be fixed by any human means. The cure would kill the patient.

So what then!?

Why did I write as I have, if I believe that there is effectively nothing that can be done about it? Truth is its own value. The fearless search for Truth is, in my opinion, an imperative of virtue. Not that I am virtuous mind you, far from it, but I cannot feel comfort or honesty with anything less. Some people claim I've got ass-burgers; I do not agree.

But what then, therefore what!?!

My best answer to the practical application of what I believe I have uncovered is to re-dedicate one's self to the search for Truth – the attempt to find and define the Principles to which I so frequently refer, and to disengage.

I have learned through much pain that good faith is impotent in the face of such reckless solipsism. One cannot argue with a child, a drunk, or a madman, and anyone who swallows the idea that reality is subjective is likely all three. Do not attempt, in any way, to debate the delusional – the

Bible has much to say about this, but I will only say that to do so is self-destructive. Disengage.

Now, that's not very positive, nor is it satisfying.

Fine. Do this as well: Act justly, love mercy, and walk humbly with your God. Measure your own beliefs, your own conduct. Love your people in deed, not in word, and do what you can to avoid and mitigate the influence of the madness on your life. Refrain from any attempt to impose your will on anyone.

Oh, and quit fetishizing 'America', the Constitution, Ludwig von Mises, 'MAGA', or the accursed GOP. Stand on your own damned principles. If you disagree with Locke or Jefferson that's cool – just don't take the coward's way out of basing that disagreement on the slavish worship of Hegel, Marx, or Gloria Fu**ing Steinem.

For me, this means cultivating as much reflection, self-evaluation, and self-discipline as I can so that I don't harm my wife and daughters because of my own stupidity – that, and hoping that I either win the lotto jackpot or sell a gajillion copies of this book so I can buy a farm and live something like a pseudo-yeoman's life away from the increasingly nasty cities of my country. I really want a tractor, some mini-moos, and an Edwardian inspired gentleman's library; what good is a freaking PhD without Phineas Fogg's laboratory?

I have written what I have written, and I have done so as honestly as I can. What you do with my words is your problem.

Select Bibliography

Please note that, in order to avoid unnecessary duplication, bibliographic entries are given only in the fist section in which they are cited.

Unless otherwise noted, all scripture references are taken from the King James Bible.

Prologue

The Holy Bible, New King James Version (NKJV): Thomas Nelson, 1982.

Primary Sources:

Adams, John. "Letter to the Massachusetts Militia, October 11, 1798." *Founders Online*, National Archives. https://founders.archives.gov/documents/Adams/99-02-02-3102.

Jefferson, Thomas. "Letter to John Jay, Paris". August 23, 1785. *The Letters of Thomas Jefferson*, Yale Law School, https://avalon.law.yale.edu/18th_century/let32.asp.

Secondary Sources:

Monographs:

Leuchtenburg, William E. *Franklin D. Roosevelt and the New Deal, 1932 – 1940*. New York: Harper and Brothers, 1963.

Rakove, Jack N. *Original Meanings : Politics and Ideas in the Making of the Constitution*. New York: Vintage Books, 2013 [1996].

Articles:

Calo, Adam. "The Yeoman Myth: A Troubling Foundation of
the Beginning Farmer Movement," *Gastronomia: The
Journal for Food Studies* 20, no. 2 (2020): 12 – 29.

Diner, Steven J. "Linking Politics and People: The
Historiography of the Progressive Era." *Magazine of
History* 13, no. 3 (Spring, 1999): 5,
https://go.openathens.net/redirector/liberty.edu?
url=https://www.proquest.com/scholarly-journals/
linking-politics-people-historiography/docview/
213741201/se-2.

Part I: The Design

Primary Sources:

Adams, John. "VI. "A Dissertation on the Canon and the
Feudal Law," No. 4, 21 October 1765," *Founders
Online*, National Archives.
https://founders.archives.gov/documents/Adams/06-
01-02-0052-0007.

Adams, John. "III. Reply of the House to Hutchinson's
Second Message, 2 March 1773," *Founders
Online*, National Archives.
https://founders.archives.gov/documents/Adams/06-
01-02-0097-0004.

Adams, John. "John Adams to Abigail Adams, 7 July
1775," *Founders Online*, National Archives.
https://founders.archives.gov/documents/Adams/04-
01-02-0160.

Adams, John. "From John Adams to Massachusetts Militia,
11 October 1798," *Founders Online*, National
Archives.
https://founders.archives.gov/documents/Adams/99-
02-02-3102.

Adams, John, and Johnathan Sewall. *Novanglus, and Massachusetts; or Political Essays*. Boston: Hews & Goss, 1819 [1775]. Gutenberg Ebook #45205.

Adams, John. Letter to the Massachusetts Militia. October 11, 1798, https://founders.archives.gov/documents/Adams/99-02-02-3102.

Adams, John. *Papers of John Adams*. Vol. 2. Cambridge: Harvard University Press, 1977.

Adams, John. *Works of John Adams, Second President of the United States: with a Life of the Author, Notes and Illustrations*. Edited by Charles Francis Adams. 10 vols. Boston: Little, Brown and Co., 1850 – 1856. https://oll.libertyfund.org/titles/adams-the-works-of-john-adams-10-vols.

Aristotle. *The Basic Works of Aristotle*. Edited by Richard McKeon. New York: The Modern Library, 2001. [1941].

Augustine. *Confessions*. Translated by R.S. Pine-Coffin. New York: Dorset Press, 1961 [c. AD 398].

Cicero. *De Re Publica, De Legibus*. Vol. 16, *Cicero in Twenty-Eight Volumes*. Translated by Clinton Walker Keyes, Ph.D. Cambridge: Harvard University Press, 1970.

Farrand, Max. ed. *The Records of the Federal Convention of 1787*. Revised ed. 4 vols. London: Yale University Press, 1937.

Fitzpatrick, John C. ed. *The Writings of George Washington*. Washington D. C.: U. S. Government Printing Office, 1939.

Franklin, Benjamin. "Constitutional Convention Address on
        Prayer." June 28, 1787. *American Rhetoric: Online
        Speech Bank*. Accessed September 12, 2024:
        https://www.americanrhetoric.com/speeches/benfrank
        lin.htm.

Franklin, Benjamin. *The Political Thought of Benjamin
        Franklin*. Edited by Ralph Ketchum. Indianapolis:
        Hackett Publishing Company, 1965.

Franklin, Benjamin. *The Complete Works of Benjamin
        Franklin*, Vol. V, 1772-1775. John Bigelow, ed. New
        Yok: G.P. Putnam's Sons, 1887.

Franklin, Benjamin "Positions to be Examined, 4 April
        1769." *Founders Online*, National Archives,
        https://founders.archives.gov/documents/Franklin/01-
        16-02-0048.

Hamilton, Alexander. "*The Farmer Refuted*, &c., [23
        February] 1775," *Founders Online*, National
        Archives,
        https://founders.archives.gov/documents/Hamilton/01
        -01-02-0057.

Hamilton, Alexander [Attributed]. "The Same Subject
        Continued: The Idea of Restraining the Legislative
        Authority in Regard to the Common Defense
        Considered." *Federalist No. 28*, 1787. *Library of
        Congress*. Accessed September 19:
        https://guides.loc.gov/federalist-papers/text-21-30#s-
        lg-box-wrapper-25493341.

Hartley, L.P. *The Go-Between*. London: Penguin Books,
        1953.

Henry, Patrick. "Give me liberty or give me death". March
        23, 1775. *Yale Law School*.
        https://avalon.law.yale.edu/18th_century/patrick.asp.

Jefferson, Thomas. *The Works of Thomas Jefferson*. Edited by Paul Leicester Ford. 12 vols. New York: G.P. Putnam's Sons, 1904 – 05. https://oll.libertyfund.org/titles/ford-the-works-of-thomas-jefferson-12-vols.

Jefferson, Thomas. "82. A Bill for Establishing Religious Freedom, 18 June 1779." *Founders Online*, National Archives. https://founders.archives.gov/documents/Jefferson/01-02-02-0132-0004-0082.

Jefferson, Thomas "From Thomas Jefferson to John Jay, 23 August 1785." *Founders Online*, National Archives. https://founders.archives.gov/documents/Jefferson/01-08-02-0333.

Jefferson, Thomas. "From Thomas Jefferson to Chastellux, with Enclosure, 2 September 1785." *Founders Online*, National Archives, https://founders.archives.gov/documents/Jefferson/01-08-02-0362.

Jefferson, Thomas. *Notes on the State of Virginia : An Annotated Edition*. New Haven: Yale University Press, 2022 [1785].

Jefferson, Thomas. "From Thomas Jefferson to Peter Carr, with Enclosure, 10 August 1787," *Founders Online*, National Archives. https://founders.archives.gov/documents/Jefferson/01-12-02-0021.

Jefferson, Thomas. "From Thomas Jefferson to William Stephens Smith, 13 November 1787," *Founders Online*, National Archives. https://founders.archives.gov/documents/Jefferson/01-12-02-0348.

Jefferson, Thomas. "To James Madison from Thomas Jefferson, 20 December 1787," *Founders*

Online, National Archives.
https://founders.archives.gov/documents/Madison/01-10-02-0210.

Jefferson, Thomas. "From Thomas Jefferson to John Trumbull, 15 February 1789," *Founders Online*, National Archives.
https://founders.archives.gov/documents/Jefferson/01-14-02-0321.

Jefferson, Thomas "From Thomas Jefferson to James Madison, 28 August 1789," *Founders Online*, National Archives,
https://founders.archives.gov/documents/Jefferson/01-15-02-0354.

Jefferson, Thomas. "To James Madison from Thomas Jefferson, 6 September 1789," *Founders Online*, National Archives.
https://founders.archives.gov/documents/Madison/01-12-02-0248.

Jefferson, Thomas. "IV. Opinion on the Treaties with France, 28 April 1793." *Founders Online,* National Archives.
https://founders.archives.gov/documents/Jefferson/01-25-02-0562-0005.

Jefferson, Thomas. "Resolutions Relative to the Alien and Sedition Acts." November 10, 1798. In "The Founders' Constitution." Volume 1, Chapter 8, Document 41. *The University of Chicago Press*, Accessed October 1, 2024: http://press-pubs.uchicago.edu/founders/documents/v1ch8s41.html.

Jefferson, Thomas. "Thomas Jefferson to James Fishback (Final State), 27 September 1809." *Founders Online*, National Archives.
https://founders.archives.gov/documents/Jefferson/03-01-02-0437-0003.

Jefferson, Thomas. "Thomas Jefferson to Miles King, 26 September 1814," *Founders Online*, National Archives. https://founders.archives.gov/documents/Jefferson/03 -07-02-0495.

Jefferson, Thomas. "Thomas Jefferson to Benjamin Austin, 9 January 1816," *Founders Online*, National Archives, https://founders.archives.gov/documents/Jefferson/03 -09-02-0213.

Jefferson, Thomas. "Proposals to Revise the Virginia Constitution: I. Thomas Jefferson to "Henry Tompkinson" (Samuel Kercheval), 12 July 1816." *Founders Online*, National Archives, https://founders.archives.gov/documents/Jefferson/03 -10-02-0128-0002.

Jefferson, Thomas. "Thomas Jefferson to William Plumer, 21 July 1816." *Founders Online*, National Archives, https://founders.archives.gov/documents/Jefferson/03 -10-02-0152.

Jefferson, Thomas. "Thomas Jefferson to Isaac H. Tiffany, 4 April 1819." *Founders Online*, National Archives, https://founders.archives.gov/documents/Jefferson/03 -14-02-0191.

Jefferson, Thomas. "Thomas Jefferson to John Adams, 10 December 1819," *Founders Online*. National Archives, https://founders.archives.gov/documents/Jefferson/03 -15-02-0240.

Jefferson, Thomas. "From Thomas Jefferson to Henry Lee, 8 May 1825," *Founders Online*, National Archives, https://founders.archives.gov/documents/Jefferson/98 -01-02-5212.

Johnson, Samuel. *Johnson's Dictionary Online*. 1755, 1773. https://johnsonsdictionaryonline.com/.

Koch, A. and W. Peden. eds. *The Selected Writings of John and John Quincy Adams.* New York: Knopf, 1946.

Locke, John. *Second Treatise of Government.* 1690. Reprint, London: A. Millar et. al., 1764. Project Gutenberg Ebook #7370.

Locke, John. *An Essay Concerning Human Understanding.* in *Great Books of the Western World*, Vol. 35. Edited by Robert Maynard Hutchins. Chicago: Encyclopædia Britannica, Inc., 1952 [1689].

Locke, John. *A Letter Concerning Toleration.* Edited by J. Brook. Yorkshire: Huddersfield, 1796 [1689].

Madison, James. *The Writings of James Madison.* Edited by Gaillard Hunt. 9 vols. New York: G.P. Putnam's Sons, 1900 – 10. https://oll.libertyfund.org/titles/madison-the-writings-of-james-madison-9-vols.

Madison, James. "Madison Debates," July 11, 1787. *Yale Law School.* Accessed September 14, 2024: https://avalon.law.yale.edu/18th_century/debates_711.asp.

Madison, James [Attributed]. "Method of Guarding Against the Encroachments of Any One Department of Government by Appealing to the People Through a Convention." *Federalist no. 49*, February 5, 1788. Accessed September 18, 2024: https://guides.loc.gov/federalist-papers/text-41-50.

Madison, James. "Judicial Powers of the National Government, [20 June] 1788," *Founders Online,* National Archives. https://founders.archives.gov/documents/Madison/01-11-02-0101.

Madison, James. "Amendments to the Constitution, [8 June] 1789," *Founders Online*, National Archives.

https://founders.archives.gov/documents/Madison/01-12-02-0126.

Madison, James. "Essay on Sovereignty" December, 1835. *Founders Early Access*. Accessed September 25, 2024: https://rotunda.upress.virginia.edu/founders/default.xqy?keys=FOEA-print-02-02-02-3188.

Mason, George. "The Virginia Declaration of Rights." June 12, 1776. *National Archives: America's Founding Documents*. https://www.archives.gov/founding-docs/virginia-declaration-of-rights.

Rush, Benjamin "Thoughts Upon The Mode of Education Proper in a Republic." 1786. in *Essays, Literary, Moral and Philosophical.* Philadelphia: Thomas and William Bradford, 1806.

Sparks, Jared. ed. *The Works of Benjamin Franklin; containing several political and historical tracts not included in any former edition, and many lettersm official and private, not hitherto published; with notes and a life of the author.* Vol. X. Boston: Hillard, Gray, 1840.

Tansil. Charles C. ed. *Documents Illustrative of the Formation of the Union of the American States.* Washington: Government Printing Office, 1927.

The Papers of Daniel Webster Digital Edition. Edited by Charles M. Wiltse. The University of Virginia Press. https://rotunda.upress.virginia.edu/founders/WBST.html.

The American Republic: Primary Sources. Edited by Bruce Frohnen. Indianapolis: Liberty Fund, 2002.

The Constitution of the United States of America and Selected Writings of the Founding Fathers. New York: Barnes & Noble, 2012.

The Works of James Wilson. Robert G. McCloskey, ed. 2 vols. Cambridge: Harvard University Press, 1967.

The Papers of Thomas Jefferson. Vol. 1, 1760-1776. Ed. Julian P. Boyd. Princeton: Princeton University Press, 1950.

Wells, William V. *The Life and Public Service of Samuel Adams*. Boston: Little, Brown, & Co., 1865.

Wilson, James. *Collected Works of James Wilson*, Vol. 1. Eds. Kermit L. Hall and Mark David Hall. Indianapolis: Liberty Fund, 2007.

Witherspoon, John. "Thoughts on American Liberty." 1774. from *The Works of John Witherspoon*, 9 vols. Edinburgh, 1804, 9:73-77. Accessed September 11, 2024: https://www.njstatelib.org/wp-content/uploads/slic_fil es/imported/NJ_Information/Digital_Collections/ NJInTheAmericanRevolution1763-1783/ ThoughtsOnAmericanLiberty.pdf.

Witherspoon, John. *Annotated Edition of Lectures on Moral Philosophy*, edited by Jack Scott. Newark: University of Delaware Press, 1982.

Secondary Sources:

Monographs:

Commager, Henry Steel. *The Search for a Usable Past, and Other Essays in Historiography*. New York: Alfred A. Knopf, 1967.

Deneen, Patrick J. *Why Liberalism Failed*. 1st ed. New Haven: Yale University Press, 2018.

Eicholz, Hans L. *Harmonizing Sentiments: The Declaration of Independence and the Jeffersonian Idea of Self-Government*. Masterworks in the Western Tradition. Edited by Nicholas Capaldi and Stuard D. Warner. Vol. 4. New York: Peter Lang, 2001.

Eidelberg, Paul. "The Philosophy of the American Constitution: A Reinterpretation of the Intentions of the Founding Fathers." PhD Dissertation. *University of Chicago*. 1966.

Eidelberg, Paul. *The Philosophy of the American Constitution: A Reinterpretation of the Intentions of the Founding Fathers*. New York: The Free Press, 1968.

Eidelberg, Paul. *On the Silence of the Declaration of Independence*. Amherst: University of Massachusetts Press, 1976.

Hofstadter, Richard. *The Age of Reform: From Bryan to F.D.R.* New York: Alfred A. Knopf, 1955.

Maier, Pauline. *American Scripture: Making the Declaration of Independence*. New York: Alfred A. Knopf. 1997.

Morrison, Jeffry H. "The Political Thought of John Witherspoon, 1768-1794." PhD Dissertation., Georgetown University, 1999.

Morrison, Jeffry H. *John Witherspoon and the Founding of the American Republic*. Indiana: University of Notre Dame Press, 2005.

Pei, Mario. *The Story of Language*, Revised ed. New York: New American Library, 1984 [1949].

Rakove, Jack N. *Original Meanings : Politics and Ideas in the Making of the Constitution*. 1st Vintage books ed. New York: Vintage Books, 2013 [1997].

Urmson, J.O. *The Greek Philosophical Vocabulary.* Great
Britain: Duckworth, 2001 [1990].

Waldron, Jeremy. *God, Locke, and Equality: Christian
Foundations in Locke's Political Thought,*
Cambridge: Cambridge University Press, 2002.

Articles:

"Benjamin Rush." *Princeton University, Art Museum.* n.d.
Accessed October 8, 2024:
https://artmuseum.princeton.edu/collections/objects/4
5169.

De Witte, Melissa. "When Thomas Jefferson penned 'all men
are created equal,' he did not mean individual
equality, says Stanford scholar." *Stanford Report*, July
1, 2020.
https://news.stanford.edu/stories/2020/07/meaning-
declaration-independence-changed-time.

Duschinsky, Robert. "'Tabula Rasa' and Human Nature."
Philosophy 87, no. 342 (2012): 509–29.

Fawbush, Joseph. "Marbury v. Madison Case Summary:
What You Need to Know." *FindLaw.* March 24, 2023.
Accessed October 1, 2024:
https://supreme.findlaw.com/supreme-court-
insights/marbury-v—madison-case-summary--what-
you-need-to-know.html.

Homer, Harlan H. "The American Flag." *Proceedings of the
New York State Historical Association* 14. (1915):
108–21.

James Madison Montpelier. "The Life of James Madison".
n.d. Accessed September 10, 2024:
https://www.montpelier.org/learn/the-life-of-james-
madison/.

"Jon Jay, 1789-1795." *Supreme Court Historical Society*. n.d. Accessed September 25, 2024: https://supremecourthistory.org/chief-justices/john-jay-1789-1795/.

Knudson, Jerry W. "The Jeffersonian Assault on the Federalist Judiciary, 1802-1805; Political Forces and Press Reaction." *The American Journal of Legal History* 14, no. 1 (1970): 55–75.

Krall, Lisi. "Thomas Jefferson's Agrarian Vision and the Changing Nature of Property." *Journal of Economic Issues* 36, no. 1 (2002): 131–50.

Laconte, Joseph. "1776: A Lockean Revolution" *The Heritage Foundation*. July 7, 2021 https://www.heritage.org/american-history/commentary/1776-lockean-revolution.

Maier, Pauline. "The Strange History of "All Men Are Created Equal"." *Washington and Lee Law Review* 56, issue 3 (Summer 6-1-1999): 873 – 888. https://scholarlycommons.law.wlu.edu/cgi/viewcontent.cgi?article=1547&context=wlulr.

"Marbury v. Madison: Primary Documents in American History." *Library of Congress*. n.d. Accessed October 1, 2024: https://guides.loc.gov/marbury-v-madison#:~:text=The%20U.S. %20Supreme%20Court%20case,by%20Chief%20Justice%20John%20Marshall.

Miles, Spencer D., "Path To Pardon: Ending the Abuse of Perpetual Criminal Sanctions", Article Preprint: http://dx.doi.org/10.13140/RG.2.2.33957.22249.

Nash, George H. "John Witherspoon: Educating for Liberty". *Religion & Liberty* 34, no. 1 (February 19, 2024): https://www.acton.org/religion-liberty/volume-34-number-1/john-witherspoon-educating-

liberty#:~:text=Good%20Calvinist%20that%20he%2
0was,make%20man%20perfect%20or%20perfectible.

Obituary. "Professor J.O. Urmson." March 16, 2012. *The Times.* Accessed October 9, 2024:
https://www.thetimes.com/article/professor-j-o-urmson-lq5c8wwtt3h.

The Lehrman Institute. "The Founders, Farms, and Facts." n.d. Accessed October 16, 2024:
https://lehrmaninstitute.org/history/founders-farms-facts.html.

Thompson, D. F. "The Education of a Founding Father: The Reading List for John Witherspoon's Course in Political Theory, as Taken by James Madison". *Political Theory* 4, no. 4 (1976): 523-529.
https://doi.org/10.1177/009059177600400414.

USHistory.org. "James Wilson," *Independence Hall Association,* n.d., Accessed September 17, 2024:
https://www.ushistory.org/declaration/signers/wilson.html.

The Heresy of Perfectibility

Primary Sources:

Adams, John. "From John Adams to Boston Patriot, 4 August 1809," *Founders Online*, National Archives,
https://founders.archives.gov/documents/Adams/99-02-02-5405.

Beecher, Henry Ward. *Evolution and Religion.* London: James Clarke & Co., 1885.

Ely, Richard T. *The Past and the Present of Political Economy.* Baltimore: N. Murray, 1884.

Ely, Richard T. *Social Aspects of Christianity, and Other Essays*. New York: Thomas Y. Crowell & Company, 1889.

Ely, Richard. *Introduction to Political Economy*. New York: Chautauqua Press, 1889.

Ely, Richard T. *The Social Law of Service*. New York: Eaton & Mains, 1896.

Ely, Richard T. "Social Progress." *The Cosmopolitan* 31, no.1. (1901): 61– 64.

Ely, Richard T. *Studies in the Evolution of Industrial Society*. New York: Chautauqua Press, 1903.

Ely, Richard T. *Property and Contract in their Relations to the Distribution of Wealth*, Vol. I Dallas: Kennikat Publishing Co., 1971 [1914].

Ely, Richard T. *The World War and Leadership in a Democracy*. New York: Macmillan Co. 1918.

Ely, Richard T."The Price of Progress." *Administration* 3, no.6. (1922): 657-663.

Farrand, Max, ed. *The Records of the Federal Convention of 1787*, vol. 3. New Haven: Yale University Press, 1911.

Gladden, Washington. *The Christian Way: Whither it Leads and How to Go On*. New York: Dodd, Mead & Company, 1877.

Gladden, Washington. *The Lord's Prayer: Seven Homilies*. Boston: Houghton Mifflin & Co, 1880.

Gladden, Washington. *Who Wrote the Bible?: A Book for the People*. Boston: Houghton, Mifflin, & Company, 1891. Project Gutenberg Ebook #6928.

Gladden, Washington. *The Church and the Kingdom*, New York: Fleming H. Revell Co., 1894.

Gladden, Washington. *Social Salvation*. Boston: Houghton Mifflin, 1902.

Gladden, Washington. *The New Idolatry: and Other Discussions*. New York: McClure, Phillips & Co., 1905.

Gladden, Washington. *Recollections*. London: Houghton Mifflin Company, 1909.

Hegel, Georg Wilhelm Friedrich. *The Philosophy of History*. Translated by J. Sibree. New York: Dover Publications, Inc., 1956 [1831].

Jefferson, Thomas. "82. A Bill for Establishing Religious Freedom, 18 June 1779." *Founders Online*, National Archives. https://founders.archives.gov/documents/Jefferson/01-02-02-0132-0004-0082.

Jefferson, Thomas. "From Thomas Jefferson to Bishop James Madison, 31 January 1800," *Founders Online*, National Archives, https://founders.archives.gov/documents/Jefferson/01-31-02-0297.

Jefferson, Thomas. "V. To the Danbury Baptist Association, 1 January 1802." *Founders Online*, National Archives, Accessed October 2, 2024: https://founders.archives.gov/documents/Jefferson/01-36-02-0152-0006.

Jefferson, Thomas. "Thomas Jefferson to Isaac H. Tiffany, 4 April 1819." *Founders Online*, National Archives, https://founders.archives.gov/documents/Jefferson/03-14-02-0191.

Jefferson, Thomas. "Thomas Jefferson to Nathaniel Macon, 23 November 1821." *Founders Online*, National Archives. https://founders.archives.gov/documents/Jefferson/03-17-02-0549.

Madison, Bishop James. *Manifestations of the Beneficence of Divine Providence Towards America; a Discourse, Delivered on Thursday the 19th of February, 1795, Being the Day Recommended by the President of the United States, for General Thank giving and Prayer.* Richmond: Thomas Nicolson, 1795. Accessed November 6, 2024: https://quod.lib.umich.edu/e/evans/N22012.0001.001/1:2?rgn=div1;view=fulltext.

Madison, James. "The Cod Fishery Bill, February 7, 1792," in Jonathan Elliott, ed. *The debates in the several state conventions on the adoption of the federal Constitution, as recommended by the general convention at Philadelphia, in 1787. Together with the Journal of the federal convention, Luther Martin's letter, Yates's minutes, Congressional opinions, Virginia and Kentucky resolutions of '98-'99, and other illustrations of the Constitution ... 2d ed., with considerable additions. Collected and rev. from contemporary publications,* Washington: 1836, Vol. IV.

Mencken, H.L. *Minority Report: H.L. Mencken's Notebooks.* New York: Alfred A. Knopf, 1956.

Rauschenbusch, Walter. *Christianity and the Social Crisis.* New York: The Macmillan Company, 1907.

Rauschenbusch, Walter. *Christianizing the Social Order.* New York: The Macmillan Company, 1912.

Rauschenbusch, Walter. *The Social Principles of Jesus.* New York: Grosset & Dunlap, 1916.

Rauschenbusch, Walter. *A Theology for the Social Gospel.* New York: The Macmillan Company, 1917.

Tassin, Algernon. "The Magazine in America." *The Bookman*, Vol 42. (September, 1915 – February, 1916): 396 – 412. New York: Dodd, Mead and Company, 1916.

Virgil. *The Aeneid of Virgil.* Translated by J.W. Mackail. London: Macmillan and Co., 1885 [c. 25 BC], Project Gutenberg Ebook #22456.

Winthrop, John. "A Model of Christian Charity." 1630. *Gilder Lehrman Institute of American History.* 2012. Accessed November 6, 2024: https://www.gilderlehrman.org/sites/default/files/inline-pdfs/A%20Model%20of%20Christian%20Charity_Full%20Text.pdf.

Secondary Sources:

Monographs:

Brodrecht, Grant R. *Our Country: Northern Evangelicals and the Union during the Civil War Era.* New York: Fordham University Press, 2018.

Clark, J.C.D. *The Language of Liberty, 1660-1832: Political Discourse and Social Dynamics in the Anglo-American World.* New York: Cambridge University Press, 1994.

Dorn, Jacob Henry. *Washington Gladden: Prophet of the Social Gospel.* Columbus: Ohio State University Press, 1967.

Eidelberg, Paul. "The Philosophy of the American Constitution: A Reinterpretation of the Intentions of the Founding Fathers." PhD Dissertation. *University of Chicago.* 1966.

Heimert, Alan. *Religion and the American Mind: From the Great Awakening to the Revolution*. London: Oxford University Press, 1966.

Holowchak, M. Andrew. *Thomas Jefferson's Philosophy of Education: A Utopian Dream*. London: Routledge, 2014.

Howe, Daniel Walker. *What Hath God Wrought: the Transformation of America, 1815-1848*. New York: Oxford University Press, 2007.

Lewis, C.S. *God in the Dock: Essays on Theology and Ethics*. Edited by Walter Hooper. Grand Rapids: William B. Eerdmans Publishing Company, 1970.

Leonard, Thomas C. *Illiberal Reformers: Race, Eugenics & American Economics in the Progressive Era*. Princeton: Princeton University Press, 2016.

Mazlish, Bruce. ed. P*sychoanalysis and History*, revised ed. New York: Grosset & Dunlap, 1971.

Miller, Perry. *Errand into the Wilderness*. Cambridge: Belknap Press of Harvard University Press, 1956.

Moorhead, James H. *American Apocalypse: Yankee Protestants and the Civil War, 1860-1869*. New Haven: Yale University Press, 1978.

Rable, George C. *God's Almost Chosen Peoples: A Religious History of the American Civil War*. Chapel Hill: University of North Carolina Press, 2010.

The Constitution of the United States of America and Selected Writings of the Founding Fathers. New York: Barnes & Noble, 2012.

Van Engen, Abram C. *City on a Hill : A History of American Exceptionalism.* New Haven: Yale University Press, 2020.

Watson, Bradley C. S. *Progressivism : The Strange History of a Radical Idea.* Notre Dame: University of Notre Dame Press, 2020.

Articles:

Boyer, Paul. "An Ohio Leader of the Social Gospel Movement: Reassessing Washington Gladden." *Ohio History* 116, no. 1 (2009): 88-100.

Bureau of Justice Statistics. "Recidivism of Prisoners Released in 24 States in 2008: A 10-Year Follow-Up Period (2008 – 2018)." *U.S. Department of Justice, Office of Justice Progarams.* September 2021. Accessed November 19, 2024: https://bjs.ojp.gov/sites/g/files/xyckuh236/files/media /document/rpr24s0810yfup0818_sum.pdf.

Clark, Clifford E. "The Changing Nature of Protestantism in Mid-Nineteenth Century America: Henry Ward Beecher's Seven Lectures to Young Men." *The Journal of American History* 57, no. 4 (1971): 832–46.

Crowe, Charles. "Bishop James Madison and the Republic of Virtue." The Journal of Southern History 30, no. 1 (1964): 58–70.

Gilens, Martin, and Benjamin I. Page. "Testing Theories of American Politics: Elites, Interest Groups, and Average Citizens." *Perspectives on Politics* 12, no. 3 (2014): 564–81.

Grebe, Sabine. "Augustus' Divine Authority and Vergil's "Aeneid"". *Vergilius* 50, (2004): 35 – 62.

Howerth, I. W. "Natural Selection and the Survival of the Fittest." *The Scientific Monthly* 5, no. 3 (1917): 253–57.

Jensen, Howard E. "The Social Gospel in America, 1870 – 1920: Washington Gladden, Richard T. Ely, and Walter Rauschenbusch, Edited by Robert T. Handy," Review in *Social Forces*, 45, no. 4 (June, 1967): 612.

Jones Miller, Tiffany. "Richard T. Ely, The German Historical School of Economics, And the "Socio-Teleological" Aspiration of the New Deal Planners." *Social Philosophy & Policy* 38, no. 1 (Summer, 2021): 52-84.

Moorhead, James H. "Between Progress and Apocalypse: A Reassessment of Millennialism in American Religious Thought, 1800-1880." *The Journal of American History* 71, no. 3 (1984): 524–42.

Pratt, Julius W. "The Origin of 'Manifest Destiny.'" *The American Historical Review* 32, no. 4 (1927): 795–98.

Roberts, Robert R. "The Social Gospel and the Trust-Busters." *Church History* 25, no. 3 (1956): 239–57.

Simon, Walter M. "Herbert Spencer and the 'Social Organism.'" *Journal of the History of Ideas* 21, no. 2 (1960): 294–99.

Souders, Michael. "'Truthing It in Love': Henry Ward Beecher's Homiletic Theories of Truth, Beauty, Love, and the Christian Faith." *Rhetoric Society Quarterly* 41, no. 4 (2011): 316–39.

Thies, Clifford F. and Gary M. Pecquet. "The Shaping of a Future President's Economic Thought: Richard T. Ely and Woodrow Wilson at "the Hopkins"." *The Independent Review* 15, no. 2 (Fall, 2010): 257-77.

Thies, Clifford F. and Ryan Daza. "Richard T. Ely: The Confederate Flag of the AEA?" *Econ Journal Watch* 8, no. 2 (May, 2011): 147 – 156.

van Wyhe, John. "Why there was no 'Darwin's bulldog.'" *The Linnean Society of London.* July 1, 2019. Accessed November 12, 2024: https://www.linnean.org/news/2019/07/01/1st-july-2019-why-there-was-no-darwins-bulldog.

Auto-Apotheosis

Primary Sources:

"Agricultural Adjustment." 73rd Congress, Session I, Chapter 25, May 12, 1933. Pub. L. 73-10. Accessed January 27, 2025: https://govtrackus.s3.amazonaws.com/legislink/pdf/stat/48/STATUTE-48-Pg31.pdf.

Boydston, Jo Ann ed. *John Dewey: The Later Works, 1925–1953.* Carbondale: Southern Illinois University Press, 1985.

Bury, J.B. *A History of Freedom of Thought.* Cambridge: Henry Holt and Company, 1913. Project Gutenberg Ebook #10684.

Bury, J.B. *The Idea of Progress: An Inquiry into its Origin and Growth.* London, 1920. Project Gutenberg Ebook #4557.

Commons, John R. *Social Reform and The Church, With an Introduction by Prof. Richard T. Ely.* New York: Thomas Y. Crowell & Company, 1894.

Commons, John R. *Races and Immigrants in America.* London: The Macmillan Company, 1907.

Commons, John R. *Labor and Administration*. New York: The Macmillan Company, 1913.

Commons, John R. *The Economics of Collective Action*. New York: The Macmillan Company, 1951.

Dewey, John. *My Pedagogic Creed*. Chicago: A. Flanagan Company, 1897.

Dewey, John. "Evolution and Ethics." *The Monist* 8, no. 3 (1898): 321 – 334.

Dewey, John. *The School and Society*. Revised ed. Chicago: Chicago University Press, 1915 [1900].

Dewey, John, and James H. Tufts. *Ethics*. New York: Henry Holt and Company, 1908.
Dewey, John and Evelyn. *Schools of Tomorrow*. New York: E.P. Dutton & Company, 1915. Project Gutenberg Ebook #48906.

Dewey John, *Democracy and Education: An Introduction to the Philosophy of Education*. New York: The Macmillan Company, 1916.

Dewey, John. *The Public and its Problems*. Denver: Alan Swallow, 1927.

Dewey, John. *Philosophy and Civilization*. New York: G.P. Putnam's Sons, 1931.

Dewey, John. *Lectures in China: 1919 - 1920*. Robert W. Clopton and Tsuin-Chen Ou Trans. Honolulu: The University Press of Hawaii, 1973.

Dewey, John. "The Democratic Faith and Education." *The Antioch Review* 4, no. 2 (1944): 274 –283.

Haley, Jay. *Strategies of Psychotherapy*. New York: Grune & Stratton, Inc., 1963.

Hullfish, Gordon H. *Educational Freedom in an Age of Anxiety: Twelfth Yearbook of the John Dewey Society.* New York: Harper & Brothers, 1953.

"Humanist Manifesto I," *American Humanist Association,* Accessed January 16, 2025: https://americanhumanist.org/what-is-humanism/manifesto1/.

James, William. *The Meaning of Truth: A Sequel to 'Pragmatism'.* London: Longman's, Green, and Co., 1909.

Gibbon, Edward. *The Decline and Fall of the Roman Empire: An Abridgement by D.M. Low.* New York: Harcourt Brace and Company, 1960 [1776].

Lippmann, Walter. *A Preface to Politics.* New York: Mitchell Kennerley, 1913.

Lippmann, Walter. *Drift and Mastery: An Attempt to Diagnose the Current Unrest.* Englewood Cliffs, N.J.: Prentice-Hall, Inc., 1961 [1914].

Lippmann, Walter. *Liberty and the News.* New York: Harcourt, Brace and Howe, 1920.

Lippmann, Walter. *Public Opinion.* New York: Harcourt, Brace and Company, 1922.

Lippmann, Walter. *The Phantom Public.* New York: Harcourt, Brace and Company, 1925.

Lippmann, Walter. *A Preface to Morals.* London: George Allen & Unwin Ltd. 1942 [1929].

Lippmann, Walter. *An Inquiry into the Principles of The Good Society.* Boston: Little, Brown and Company, 1937.

Miller, Henry. *The Colossus of Maroussi*. New York: New
    Directions Books, 1941.

Vonnegut, Mark. *The Eden Express*. New York: Seven Stories
    Press, 1975.

Wallas, Graham. *Human Nature in Politics*. London:
    Archibald Constable and Co Ltd., 1908.

Wells, H. G. *The Shape of Things To Come*. London:
Hutchinson & Co., 1935.

Secondary Sources:

Monographs:

Almond, Gabriel, A. *Ventures in Political Science:
    Narratives and Reflections*. Boulder: Lynne Rienner,
    2002.

Brennan, Jason. *Against Democracy*. Princeton: Princeton
    University Press, 2016.

Chasse, John Dennis. *A Worker's Economist: John R.
    Commons and His Legacy from Progressivism to the
    War on Poverty*. New York: Taylor & Francis, 2018
    [2017].

Commager, Henry S. *The American Mind An Interpretation
    of American Thought and Character since the 1880s*.
    New Haven: Yale University Press, 1950.

McNulty, Paul, J. *The Origins and Development of Labor
    Economics: A Chapter in the History of Social
    Thought*. Cambridge: The MIT Press, 1980.

Moore, Philip B. *John Dewey: Prophet of an Educated
    Democracy*. New York: Rutledge, 2024.

Rowan, Joseph Edward. "'The Social Frontier' (1934-1943): Journal of Educational Criticism and Social Reconstruction." PhD Dissertation, Case Western Reserve University, 1969, ProQuest Dissertations & Theses Global.

Seidelman, Raymond, and Edward J. Harpham. *Disenchanted Realists: Political Science and the American Crisis, 1884 – 1984*. Albany: State University of New York Press, 1985.

Steel, Ronald. *Walter Lippmann and the American Century*. Boston: Little Brown, 1980.

Articles:

Arnold-Forster, Tom. "Walter Lippmann and Public Opinion." *American Journalism* 40, no. 1 (2023): 51–79.

Betz, Joseph. "John Dewey on Human Rights." *Transactions of the Charles S. Peirce Society* 14, no. 1 (1978): 18-41.

Blumenthal, Sidney "Walter Lippmann and American Journalism Today." *Open Democracy*. October 31, 2007. Accessed February 3, 2025: https://www.opendemocracy.net/en/walter_lippmann_and_american_journalism_today/.

Bowers, C. A. "The Social Frontier Journal: A Historical Sketch." *History of Education Quarterly* 4, no. 3 (1964): 167–80.

Cherry, Kendra. "Biography of Psychologist G. Stanley Hall." *Verywellmind*. July 27, 2023. Accessed February 14, 2025: https://www.verywellmind.com/g-stanley-hall-biography-2795507.

Codd, William J. "Educational Freedom in an Age of Anxiety: Twelfth Yearbook of the John Dewey Society." *America Magazine: The Jesuit Review of Faith & Culture* 89, no. 2 (April 11, 1953): 53–54.

Coleman, Aaron N. "Anti-Federalists and the Roots of Judicial Oligarchy." *Law and Liberty.* August 5, 2020, https://lawliberty.org/anti-federalists-and-the-roots-of-judicial-oligarchy/.

Congress.Gov. "Transcript of David Frost's Interview with Richard Nixon, 1977." *Teaching American History.* Accessed January 28, 2025: https://www.congress.gov/116/meeting/house/110331 /documents/HMKP-116-JU00-20191211-SD408.pdf.

DeCesare, Tony. "The Lippmann-Dewey "Debate" Revisited: The Problem of Knowledge and the Role of Experts in Modern Democratic Theory." *Philosophical Studies in Education* 43, (2012): 106 – 116.

Diggins, John Patrick. "From Pragmatism to Natural Law: Walter Lippmann's Quest for the Foundations of Legitimacy." *Political Theory* 19, no. 4 (1991): 519–38.

Dillon, Bekah "Psyography: William James." Archive accessed February 2, 2025: https://web.archive.org/web/20141124184737/http://f aculty.frostburg.edu/mbradley/psyography/ williamjames.html.

Dyehouse, Jeremiah. "Theory in the Archives: Fred Newton Scott and John Dewey on Writing the Social Organism." *College English* 76, no. 3 (2014): 248–68.

Feuer, Lewis S. "John Dewey and the Back to the People Movement in American Thought." *Journal of the History of Ideas* 20, no. 4 (1959): 545–68.

Flannery, Mary Ellen. "Parents and Educators Want the Same Thing." *NEAToday*, September 29, 2022. Accessed February 20, 2025: https://www.nea.org/nea-today/all-news-articles/parents-and-educators-want-same-thing.

Gibbon, Peter. "John Dewey: Portrait of a Progressive Thinker." *Humanities* 40, no. 2 (Spring 2019).

Hargreaves Heap, Shaun P., and Paul Lewis. "Walter Lippmann: An Institutionalist for Our Times?" *Journal of Institutional Economics*, 20 (2024): e37.

Harris, Abram L. "John R. Commons and the Welfare State." *Southern Economic Journal* 19, no. 2 (1952): 222–33.

Henretta, James A. "Charles Evans Hughes and the Strange Death of Liberal America." *Law and History Review* 24, no. 1 (2006): 115–71.

Hopkins, Erin A. "John Dewey and Progressive Education." *The Journal of Educational Thought* 50, no. 1 (2017): 59–68.

Kopp, James J. "Edward Bellamy and the New Deal: The Revival of Bellamyism in the 1930s." *Utopian Studies*, no. 4 (1991): 10–16.

Leonard, Thomas C. ""More Merciful and Not Less Effective": Eugenics and American Economics in the Progressive Era." *History of Political Economy*, 35 no. 4, (2003). 687 – 712.

Manhattan Rare Book Company. "Lippmann, Walter. Public Opinion." Accessed February 3, 2025: https://www.manhattanrarebooks.com/pages/books/2869/walter-lippmann/public-opinion.

Merriam, Charles E. *International Journal of Ethics* 33, no. 2 (1923): 210–12.

Murphy, Madonna. "Maritain Explains the Moral Principles of Education to Dewey." *Educational Horizons* 83, no. 4 (2005): 282–91.

Nickerson, Charlotte. "John Dewey on Education: Impact & Theory." *Simply Psychology*, February 1, 2024. Accessed February 13, 2025: https://www.simplypsychology.org/john-dewey.html.

O'Gorman, Ned. "How Liberals Lost the Public: Walter Lippmann, John Dewey, and the Critique of 'Traditional Democratic Theory.'" *Quarterly Journal of Speech* 110, no. 3 (2024): 419–41.

Ratner, Sidney. "The Evolutionary Naturalism of John Dewey." *Social Research* 18, no. 4 (1951): 435–48.

Risselada, David. "The Disturbing Possibilities of the Rahimi Ruling." *In Defense of Our Nation*, June 24, 2024, Accessed February 5, 2024: https://defenseofournation.com/uncategorized /the-disturbing-possibilities-of-the-rahimi-ruling/.

Saunders, Harry David. "Civil Death – A New Look at an Ancient Doctrine." *William & Mary Law Review* 11, no. 4, (May 1970): 898 – 1003.

Shields, Patricia M. "Rediscovering the Taproot: Is Classical Pragmatism the Route to Renew Public Administration?" *Public Administration Review* 68, no. 2 (Mar, 2008): 205-21.

Siefken, Steve "The Seat of Moses: What Was It?." *Answereth a Matter.* N.d. Accessed February 19, 2025: https://answerethamatter.org/biblical_articles/articles/the_seatofmoses.htm.

Sridhar, Vinayak. "Forefathers of Transcendentalism." *Prāgyatā*, February 14, 2025. Accessed:

https://pragyata.com/forefathers-of-transcendentalism/.

Stone, William F., and David C. Smith. "Human Nature in Politics: Graham Wallas and the Fabians." *Political Psychology* 4, no. 4 (1983): 693–712.

Storm, Jason Ānanda Josephson. "A Theosophical Discipline: Revisiting the History of Religious Studies," *Journal of the American Academy of Religion* 89, no. 4, (December 2021): 1153–1163.

Summary, "National Education Association," *Library of Congress*, N.d. Accessed February 20, 2025: https://www.loc.gov/item/lcwaN0002414/.

Thies Clifford F. and Gary M. Pequet, "The Shaping of a Future President's Economic Thought: Richard T. Ely and Woodrow Wilson at "The Hopkins,"" *The Independent Review*, 15, no. 2 (Fall 2010): 257 – 277.

Wright, Benjamin. "A Brief History of the New Republic: From Lippmann to Peretz to Hughes." *Highbrow Magazine*. August 23, 2013. Accessed February 12, 2025: https://www.highbrowmagazine.com/2737-brief-history-new-republic-lippmann-peretz-hughes.

Freedom from Fear, Fear of Freedom

Primary Sources:

Bellamy, Edward. *Looking Backward: 2000 – 1887*. New York: Houghton, Mifflin and Company, 1889.

Bellamy, Edward. "How I Came to Write Looking Backward." *Science Fiction Studies* 4, no. 2 (1977): 194–95.

Bellamy, Francis. "Americanism In The Public Schools." *The Journal of Education* 36, no. 6 (881) (1892): 107.

Bellamy, Francis. Ed. *The Illustrated American*. Vol. XXII, no. 9. (August 28, 1897).

Crick, Francis. "Why I am a Humanist." *Francis Crick Papers, The Wellcome Collection*. 1966, Accessed March 19, 2025: https://wellcomecollection.org/works/j6f2tqg2/items? canvas=3.

Ely, Richard T. *Socialism: An Examination of its Nature, its Strength and Its Weakness, With Suggestions for Social Reform*. New York: Thomas Y. Crowell & Co, 1895.

Goethe, Johann Wolfgang von. *Faust with illustrations by Harry Clarke*. Translated by Bayard Taylor. New York: Arden Book Company, 1900. [c. 1832].

Goethe, Johann Wolfgang von. *Elective Affinities: A Novel*. New York: Henry Holt and Company, 1872.

Hitler, Adolf. "Official Speech on the Enabling Act to the Reichstag" Berlin, March 23, 1933. *World Future Fund*. Accessed April 2, 2025: https://www.worldfuturefund.org/reports2013/hitleren ablingact.htm.

Holmes, Oliver Wendell Jr. *The Common Law*. London: Macmillan & Co., 1882.

Holmes, Oliver Wendell Jr. "The Path of the Law: A Study". *Harvard Review* 10, No. 457 (1897). Accessed March 10, 2025: https://moglen.law.columbia.edu/LCS/palaw.pdf.

Jefferson, Thomas. "From Thomas Jefferson to William Stephens Smith, 13 November 1787." *Founders Online*. National Archives. https://founders.archives.gov/documents/Jefferson/01 -12-02-0348.

Jefferson, Thomas. "Thomas Jefferson to John Taylor, 28 May 1816." *Founders Online*. National Archives. https://founders.archives.gov/documents/Jefferson/03 -10-02-0053.

Jefferson, Thomas. "From Thomas Jefferson to Adamantios Coray, 31 October 1823." *Founders Online*, National Archives. https://founders.archives.gov/documents/Jefferson/98 -01-02-3837.

John Dewey. "A Great American Prophet." *Common Sense* 3 (1934).

Madison, James. "Amendments to the Constitution, [8 June] 1789." *Founders Online*, National Archives. https://founders.archives.gov/documents/Madison/01- 12-02-0126.

Madison, James. "For the *National Gazette*, 27 March 1792." *Founders Online*, National Archives. https://founders.archives.gov/documents/Madison/01- 14-02-0238.

Mason, George. "Debate in Virginia Ratifying Convention." June 14, 1788. Document 9, Article 4, Section 4. Accessed April 7, 2025: University of Chicago https://press-pubs.uchicago.edu/founders/documents/a 4_4s9.html.

Morgenthau, Henry Jr. House Ways and Means Committee transcript. "Diary: Book 189, May 9 – May 15, 1939." *Diaries of Henry Morgenthau Jr.* Franklin D. Roosevelt Presidential Library. Accessed April 3, 2025: http://www.fdrlibrary.marist.edu/_resources/images/m org/md0249.pdf, 42.

"National School Celebration of Columbus Day, The Official Programme," *The Youth's Companion*, 65 (September 8, 1892): 446 – 447.

Plutarch. "The Life of Sulla" in *The Parallel Lives* Vol. IV. Loeb Classical Library Edition, 1916. Accessed March 21, 2025: http://penelope.uchicago.edu/Thayer/E/Roman/Texts/ Plutarch/Lives/Sulla*.html, 343.

Plutarch. *Roman Lives*. Trans. Robin Waterfield. Oxford: Oxford University Press, 1999.

Roosevelt, Franklin D. "First Inaugural Address of Franklin D. Roosevelt." Saturday, March 4, 1933. *Yale Law School, The Avalon Project*. Accessed April 2, 2025: https://avalon.law.yale.edu/20th_century/froos1.asp.

Roosevelt, Eleanor. "If You Ask Me," *Ladies Home Journal*. vol. 58 (November 1941).

Roosevelt, Franklin D. "Third Inaugural Address of Franklin D. Roosevelt." Monday, January 20, 1941. *Yale Law School, The Avalon Project*. Accessed April 3, 2025: https://avalon.law.yale.edu/20th_century/froos3.asp.

Sherman, Roger. 8 December, 1787. "A Citizen of New Haven," *Connecticut Courant*, 7 in *The Documentary History of the Ratification of the Constitution Digital Edition*. ed. John P. Kaminski, Gaspare J. Saladino, Richard Leffler, Charles H. Schoenleber and Margaret A. Hogan. Charlottesville: University of Virginia Press, 2009.

Webster, Noah. "An Examination into the Leading Principles of the Federal Constitution: Philadelphia, October 17, 1787." in *The Constitution of the United States of America and Selected Writings of the Founding Fathers*. New York: Barnes & Nobel, 2012.

Wilson, Woodrow. "The Study of Administration." *Political Science Quarterly*, Vol. 2, no. 2 (June, 1887): 198 – 222.

Wilson, Woodrow. "Socialism and Democracy," *Unpublished Essay*, 1887. In "Woodrow Wilson on Socialism and Democracy," *Progressivism and Liberalism*, The Heritage Foundation, Accessed March 17, 2025: https://static.heritage.org/CPP/FP_PS19.pdf.

Wilson, Woodrow. *Constitutional Government in the United States*. New York: Columbia University Press, 1908.

Wilson, Woodrow. *The State: Elements of Historical and Practical Politics*. Boston: D.C. Heath & Co, 1907 [1898].

Wilson, Woodrow. *When a Man Comes to Himself.* New York: Harper and Brothers, 1901. Project Gutenberg Ebook #5078.

Wilson, Woodrow. *A History of the American People in Five Volumes*. Vol. V. New York: Harper & Brothers, 1916 [1902].

Wilson, Woodrow. "The Author and Signers of the Declaration of Independence." *The North American Review* 186, no. 622 (1907): 22–33.

Wilson, Woodrow. *The New Freedom: A Call for the Emancipation of the Generous Energies of a People*. New York: Doubleday, Page & Co, 1913, Project Gutenberg Ebook #14811.

Secondary Sources:

Monographs:

Beito, David T. *The New Deal's War on the Bill of Rights : The Untold Story of FDR's Concentration Camps,*

    Censorship, and Mass Surveillance. Oakland:
    Independent Institute, 2023.

Biddle, Francis. *Justice Holmes, Natural Law, and the
    Supreme Court: The Oliver Wendell Holmes Devise
    Lectures, 1960.* New York: The Macmillan Company,
    1961.

Bowman, Sylvia E. *The Year 2000: A Critical Biography of
    Edward Bellamy.* New York: Bowman Associates,
    1958.

Bruinius, Harry. *Better for All the World: The Secret History
    of Forced Sterilization and America's Quest for
    Racial Purity.* New York: Knopf, 2006.

Burns, James MacGregor. *Roosevelt: The Lion and the Fox.*
    New York: Harcourt Brace. 1956.

Chodorov, Frank. *The Income Tax: Root of All Evil.* New
    York: The Devin-Adair Company, 1954.

Cooper, John Milton Jr. *Woodrow Wilson: A Biography.* New
    York: Vintage Books. 2011.

Eidelberg, Paul. "The Philosophy of the American
    Constitution: A Reinterpretation of the Intentions of
    the Founding Fathers." PhD Dissertation. *University
    of Chicago.* 1966.

Flynn, John T. *The Roosevelt Myth.* New York: The Devin-
    Adair Company. 1948.

Freud, Sigmund, and William C. Bullitt. *Woodrow Wilson: A
    Psychological Study.* New Brunswick: Transaction
    Publishers, 1999 [1966].

Gucheng, Li, ed. *A Glossary of Political Terms of the
    People's Republic of China.* Hong Kong: The Chinese
    University Press, 1995.

Hofstadter, Richard. *The American Political Tradition and the Men Who Made It*. New York: Vintage Books, 1948.

Hofstadter, Richard. *The Age of Reform: From Bryan to F.D.R.* New York: Alfred A. Knopf, 1955.

Katznelson, Ira. *Fear Itself: The New Deal and the Origins of our Time*. New York: Liveright, 2013.

Kennedy, David. *Freedom from Fear: The American People in Depression and War, 1929-1945*. New York: Oxford University Press, 1999.

Kenny, David. *Pragmatism, Law, and Literature*. Oxon, U.K.: Routledge, 2024.

Kubal, Timothy. *Cultural Movements and Collective Memory: Christopher Columbus and the Rewriting of the National Origin Myth*. New York: Palgrave Macmillan, 2008.

Kühl, Stefan. *The Nazi Connection: Eugenics, American Racism, and German National Socialism*. New York: Oxford University Press, 1994.

Lawrence, Frank. *The True Story of Woodrow Wilson*. New York: George H. Doran Company, 1924.

Leonard, Thomas C. *Illiberal Reformers: Race, Eugenics, and American Economics in the Progressive Era*. Princeton: Princeton University Press, 2016,

Leuchtenburg, William E. *Franklin D. Roosevelt and the New Deal, 1932 – 1940*. New York: Harper and Brothers, 1963.

Lipow, Arthur. *Authoritarian Socialism in America: Edward Bellamy and the Nationalist Movement*. Berkeley: University of California Press, 1982.

Menand, Louis. *The Metaphysical Club*. New York: Farrar, Straus and Giroux, 2001.

Ostwald, Martin. *From Popular Sovereignty to the Sovereignty of Law: Law, Society, and Politics in Fifth-Century Athens*. Berkeley: University of California Press, 1986.

Powell, Jim. *FDR's Folly: How Roosevelt and his New Deal Prolonged the Great Depression*. New York: Crown Forum, 2003.

Rauchway, Eric. *The Money Makers: How Roosevelt and Keynes Ended the Depression, Defeated Fascism, and Secured a Prosperous Peace*. New York: Basic Books, 2015.

Schlesinger, Arthur M. *The Coming of the New Deal: The Age of Roosevelt, 1933 – 1935*. Boston: Houghton Mifflin, 1958.

Singer, Michael. *Demagogue: The Fight to Save Democracy from its Worst Enemies*. New York: Palgrave Macmillan, 2009.

Smucker, Donovan E. *The Origins of Walter Rauschenbusch's Social Ethics*. Montreal: McGill-Queen's University Press, 1994.

Sowell, Thomas. *Social Justice Fallacies*. New York: Basic Books, 2023.

Stinnett, Robert B. *Day of Deceit: The Truth About FDR and Pearl Harbor*. London: Constable. 2000.

Sutton, John R. *Law/Society: Origins, Interactions, and Change*. Thousand Oaks, Ca.: Pine Forge Press, 2001.

UVA Miller Center. "Francis B. Biddle (1941 – 1945)." N.d. Accessed March 11, 2025: https://millercenter.org/president/fdroosevelt/essays/b

iddle-1941-francis-attorney-general#:~:text=Francis%20B.-,Biddle%20(1941%E2%80%931945),1968%2C%20in%20Wellfleet%2C%20Massachusetts.

Vaughn, Stephen. *Holding Fast the Inner Lines: Democracy, Nationalism, and the Committee on Public Information*. Chapel Hill: The University of North Carolina Press, 1980.

Weil, Patrick. *The Madman in the White House : Sigmund Freud, Ambassador Bullitt, and the Lost Psychobiography of Woodrow Wilson*. Cambridge: Harvard University Press, 2023.

Woolverton, John F. with James D. Bratt. *A Christian and a Democrat: A Religious Biography of Franklin D. Roosevelt*. Grand Rapids: Eerdmans, 2019.

Articles:

ATF. "National Firearms Act." *Bureau of Alcohol, Tobacco, Firearms, and Explosives*. Reviewed March 14, 2025. Accessed April 7, 2025: https://www.atf.gov/rules-and-regulations/laws-alcohol-tobacco-firearms-and-explosives/national-firearms-act.

Basen, Ira. "In Science We Trust." *CBCNews- Radio Canada*. June 28, 2021. Accessed March 4, 2025: https://newsinteractives.cbc.ca/longform/technocracy-incorporated-elon-musk/.

Bernanke, Ben. "Remarks by Governor Ben S. Bernanke At the Conference to Honor Milton Friedman, University of Chicago, Chicago, Illinois." November 8, 2002. Accessed March 31, 2025: https://www.federalreserve.gov/boarddocs/speeches/2002/20021108/.

Chambers, Clarke A. "FDR, Pragmatist-Idealist: An Essay in Historiography." *The Pacific Northwest Quarterly* 52, no. 2 (1961): 50–55.

Czarr. ""Three Generations of Imbeciles are Enough" – The Case of Buck v. Bell." *National Archives*. Education Updates. May 2, 2017. Accessed March 13: https://education.blogs.archives.gov/2017/05/02/buck -v-bell/.

Dress, Brad "Here is a Breakdown of Laws in 47 States that Require Reciting the Pledge of Allegiance." *The Hill*. April 2, 2022, Accessed March 7, 2025: https://thehill.com/homenews/3256719-47-states- require-the-pledge-of-allegiance-be-recited-in- schools-here-is-a-breakdown-of-each-states-laws/.

Ellis, Richard J. "Under God: Frances Bellamy and the Origins of the Pledge of Allegiance." *Oregon Humanities*. December 10, 2011. Accessed March 6, 2025: https://www.oregonhumanities.org/rll/magazine/encor e-fall-winter-2011/under-god/ #:~:text=And%20among%20Bellamy's%20ancestors %20was,Bellamy%20genealogy%20bordered%20on %20fanaticism.%E2%80%9D.

"Francis Bellamy." N.d. *Grand Lodge of British Columbia and Yukon*. Accessed March 5, 2025: https://freemasonry.bcy.ca/biography/bellamy_f/bella my_f.html.

Hubbert, M. King. "Nuclear Energy and the Fossil Fuels." *Drilling and Production Practice*, Shell Development Company Publication No. 95. American Petroleum Institute. (June 1956): 22 – 27.

Hparkins. "Prohibition and the Rise of the American Gangster." *National Archives, Pieces of History*. (January 17, 2012). Accessed April 7, 2025:

https://prologue.blogs.archives.gov/2012/01/17/prohi
bition-and-the-rise-of-the-american-gangster/.

IRS. "Self-employment tax (Social Security and Medicare
taxes)" *IRS*. nd. Accessed April 3, 2025:
https://www.irs.gov/businesses/small-businesses-self-
employed/self-employment-tax-social-security-and-
medicare-taxes.

Kaufmann, Bill. "The Bellamy boys pledge allegiance.
(Flashback: to know nothing of what happened before
you were born is to remain ever a child--Cicero)."
The American Enterprise 13, no. 7 (2002): 50.

Kopp, James J. "Edward Bellamy and the New Deal: The
Revival of Bellamyism in the 1930s." *Utopian
Studies*, no. 4 (1991): 10–16.

Lombardo, Paul. "Taking Eugenics Seriously: Three
Generations of ??? Are Enough." F*lorida State
University Law Review* 30 no. 2, (2003): 191– 219.

Malcolm Magee, "Woodrow Wilson, Wilsonianism, and the
Idealism of Faith," *The Review of Faith &
International Affairs* 9 no. 4 (2011): 29–38.

Nelson, Garrett Dash. "The Splendor of Our Public and
Common Life." *Places Journal*. (December, 2019).
Accessed March 4, 2025:
https://placesjournal.org/article/edward-bellamy-
urban-planning/.

Ordozgoiti, David Serrano. "It Didn't Begin with FDR:
Currency Devaluation in the Third Century Roman
Empire." *Mises Wire*. November 7, 2022. Accessed
April 3, 2025: https://mises.org/mises-wire/it-didnt-
begin-fdr-currency-devaluation-third-century-roman-
empire.

Organ, Lukas. "The Technocracy Movement and Howard
Scott." *Mises Wire*. February 18, 2025, Accessed

March 4, 2025: https://mises.org/mises-wire/technocracy-movement-and-howard-scott.

Rosen, Jeffrey. "Brandeis's Seat, Kagan's Responsibility." *The New York Times*, July 3, 2010. Accessed March 10, 2025: https://www.nytimes.com/2010/07/04/opinion/04rosen.html?ref=opinion.

Shields, Patricia M. "Rediscovering the Taproot: Is Classical Pragmatism the Route to Renew Public Administration?" *Public Administration Review* 68, no. 2 (Mar, 2008): 205-21.

Skowronek, Stephen. "The Reassociation of Ideas and Purposes: Racism, Liberalism, and the American Political Tradition." *American Political Science Review* 100, no. 3 (2006): 385–401.

Smucker, Donovan E. "Baptist Cameos." *The Reformed Reader.* n.d. Accessed March 6, 2025: https://www.reformedreader.org/rauschenbusch.htm.

Thies, Clifford F. and Gary M. Pequet. "The Shaping of a Future President's Economic Thought: Richard T. Ely and Woodrow Wilson at "The Hopkins."" *The Independent Review*, 15, no. 2 (Fall 2010): 257 – 277.

Tumber, Catherine. "Edward Bellamy, the Erosion of Public Life, and the Gnostic Revival." *American Literary History* 11, no. 4 (1999): 610–41.

USAFacts. "How Much Does the US Spend on Social Security? Is it Sustainable?" *USAFacts*, Updated August 1, 2024. Accessed April 3, 2025: https://usafacts.org/articles/how-much-does-the-us-spend-on-social-security-is-it-sustainable/.

"US Dollar Devaluation," *United States Gold Bureau*, nd. Accessed April 3, 2025:

https://www.usgoldbureau.com/news/post/us-dollar-
devaluation-since-1913.

Images:

Price, R.G. "Fascism Part II: The Rise of American
Fascism," *Rational Revolution*, Accessed January 13,
2025:
http://www.rationalrevolution.net/articles/rise_of_am
erican _fascism.htm.

Epilogue: By Their Fruits

Primary Sources:

Department of Homeland Security. "The Organizational
Dynamics of Far-Right Hate Groups in the United
States: Comparing Violent to Non-Violent
Organizations; Final Report to Human
Factors/Behavioral Sciences Division, Science and
Technology Directorate, U.S. Department of
Homeland Security." December 2011. Accessed April
21, 2025:
https://www.dhs.gov/sites/default/files/publications/9
44_OPSR_TEVUS_Comparing-Violent-Nonviolent-
Far-Right-Hate-Groups_Dec2011-508.pdf.

Hamilton, Alexander [Attributed]. "The Federalist, No.
XXVIII," in *The Constitution of the United States of
America And Selected Writings of the Founding
Fathers*. New York: Barnes & Nobel, 2012 [1787].

Secondary Sources:

Monographs:

Burrough, Bryan. *Public Enemies: America's Greatest Crime
Wave and the Birth of the FBI, 1933-34*. New York:
Penguin Books, 2009.

Greenberg, Ivan. *The Dangers of Dissent: The FBI and Civil Liberties since 1965*. 1st ed. Lanham, MD: Lexington Books, 2010.

Rand, Ayn. *Atlas Shrugged*. New York: Signet, 1992 [1957].

Schlesinger, Aurthur. *The Age of Roosevelt: The Coming of the New Deal*. Boston: Houghton Mifflin, 1957.

Weiner, Tim. *Enemies: A History of the FBI*. New York: Random House, 2012.

Whitehead, John W. *Battlefield America: The War on the American People*. New York: Select Books Inc. 2015.

Articles:

Bovard, James. "A Billion Dollars of Federally Funded Paranoia." *Mises Wire*. February 6, 2017. Accessed April 21, 2025: https://mises.org/mises-wire/billion-dollars-federally-funded-paranoia.

Carroll, Patrick. "Amish Farmer Faces Fines, Prison Time for Refusing to Comply with USDA Regulations." *Foundation for Economic Education*. August 23, 2022, Accessed April 17, 2025: https://fee.org/articles/amish-farmer-faces-fines-prison-time-for-refusing-to-comply-with-usda-regulations/.

Condon, Stephanie. "Hank Johnson Worries Guam Could "Capsize" After Marine Buildup." *CBS News*. April 1, 2010. Accessed April 22, 2025: https://www.cbsnews.com/news/hank-johnson-worries-guam-could-capsize-after-marine-buildup/.

Chemerinsky, Erwin. "Against Sovereign Immunity," *Stanford Law Review* Vol. 53. (May, 2001): 1201 – 1224.

Christmas, Lynette. "A Bad Cop Secually Assaulted Me.
     Qualified Immunity Protected him and his Boss."
     USA Today. September 19, 2021. Accessed April 22,
     2025:
     https://www.usatoday.com/story/opinion/voices/2021/
     09/19/qualified-immunity-cop-sexual-assault-lynette-
     christmas/8240249002/.

Institute for Justice. "Lech v. City of Greenwood Village."
     Institute for Justice. N.d. Accessed April 22, 2025:
     https://ij.org/case/lech-v-city-of-greenwood
     /#:~:text=But%20a%20three%2Djudge%20panel,ov
     erturned%20in%20a%20future%20case.

Institute for Legislative Action. "Federal Judge in Colorado
     Insists There is No Second Amendment Right to Buy
     a Gun." NRA-ILA. November 20, 2023. Accessed
     April 22, 2025:
     https://www.nraila.org/articles/20231120/federal-
     judge-in-colorado-insists-there-is-no-second-
     amendment-right-to-buy-a-gun.

Kopel, David B. "How the British Gun Control Program
     Precipitated the American Revolution." *Charleston
     Law Review.* 38, no. 283 (2012).

Literacy Network. "The Issue," *Reading is Fundamental.*
     N.d. Accessed April 22, 2025:
     https://www.rif.org/literacy-network/the-issue.

McLaughlin, Eliott C. "No Indictments for Georgia SWAT
     Team that Burned Baby with Stun Grenade."
     CNN.com. October 7, 2014. Accessed April 22, 2025:
     https://www.cnn.com/2014/10/07/us/georgia-toddler-
     stun-grenade-no-indictment/index.html.

Minor, Lauren. "Neighbors: Police Killed Man after Serving
     Warrant to Wrong Home." *Lex18.com.* December 30,
     2024, Accessed April 22, 2025:
     https://www.lex18.com/news/covering-kentucky/neig

hbors-police-killed-man-after-serving-warrant-to-wrong-home.

News Desk. "Cops Handcuffed Mother, Tasered Parent While Gunman Killed Children in Uvalde School." *News 18*. May 28, 2022. Accessed April 21, 2025: https://www.news18.com/news/world/cops-handcuffed-mother-tasered-parent-while-gunman-killed-children-in-uvalde-school-5262991.html.

News Staff. "Gunsmith Sentenced to Prison for Legal Firearm Told: "The Second Amendment Doesn't Exist in My Courtroom," by New York Judge." *WNY News Now*. May 20, 2024. Accessed April 22, 2025: https://wnynewsnow.com/2024/05/20/gunsmith-sentenced-to-prison-for-legal-firearm-told-the-second-amendment-doesnt-exist-in-my-courtroom-by-new-york-judge/.

Office of Disability Employment Policy. "Federal Employers." *U.S. Department of Labor*. N.d. Accessed April 21, 2025: https://www.dol.gov/agencies/odep/program-areas/employers/federal-employment.

Papp, Justin. "House Censures Rep. Jamaal Bowman for Pulling Fire Alarm." *Roll Call*. December 7, 2023. Accessed April 22, 2025: https://rollcall.com/2023/12/07/house-censures-rep-jamaal-bowman-for-pulling-fire-alarm/.

The Rutherford Institute. "Supreme Court Protects Rogue SWAT Leader Who Raided Wrong Home." *The Free Thought Project*. March 9, 2025. Accessed April 22, 2025: https://thefreethoughtproject.com/cop-watch/supreme-court-protects-rogue-swat-leader-who-raided-wrong-home.

Schmelzer, Elise. "A SWAT Team Destroyed a Greenwood Village Family's Home. Now, a Federal Appeals

Court Says Police Don't Have to Pay for the
Damage." *The Denver Post*, October 30, 2019,
Accessed April 22, 2025:
https://www.denverpost.com/2019/10/30/swat-team-
destroyed-greenwood-village-familys-home-police-
dont-have-to-pay-for-damages/
#:~:text=A%20SWAT%20team%20destroyed%20a%
20Greenwood%20Village%20family's%20home.,to%
20pay%20for%20the%20damage.

Swearer, Amy E. "Hawaii Supreme Court Rejects Bruen as
Inconsistent With "Aloha Spirit"." *The Federalist
Society*. August 1, 2024. Accessed April 22, 2025:
https://fedsoc.org/scdw/hawaii-supreme-court-rejects-
bruen-as-inconsistent-with-aloha-spirit.

Training Division. "Second Circuit Finds Qualified Immunity
Applies to Prison Guard Sexual Abuse Lawsuit."
Defender Services Office. December 29, 2020.
Accessed April 22, 2025:
https://www.fd.org/news/second-circuit-finds-
qualified-immunity-applies-prison-guard-sexual-
abuse-lawsuit.

Venesky, Tom. "Raid on Farm Sparks Debate Over Raw Milk
Oversight and Government Overreach." *Lancaster
Farming*. April 17, 2025, Accessed April 17, 2025:
https://www.lancasterfarming.com/farming-news/dair
y/raid-on-farm-sparks-debate-over-raw-milk-
oversight-and-government-overreach/
article_002d5ebc-ba30-11ee-8f53-
6f93227a52c2.html.

White, Prentice L. "Absolute Immunity: A License to Rape
Justice at Will." *Washington and Lee Journal of Civil
Rights and Social Justice*. 17, no. 2 (2011): 333 –
383.

Williams, Armstrong. "Sodomy in the Halls of Congress."
Creators.com. December 21, 2023. Accessed April

22, 2025: https://www.creators.com/read/armstrong-williams /12/23/sodomy-in-the-halls-of-congress.

Wylie Communications. "What's the Latest U.S. Numeracy Rate?" N.d. Accessed April 22, 2025: https://www.wyliecomm.com/2021/11/whats-the-latest-u-s-numeracy-rate/#:~:text=U.S. %20adults%20have%20basic%20numeracy, %2C%20or%20basic%2C%20numeracy%20skills.

Historiographical Survey

Monographs:

Aaron, Daniel. *Men of Good Hope: A Story of American Progressives*. New York: Oxford University Press, 1951.

Burns, James MacGregor. *Roosevelt: The Lion and the Fox*. New York: Harcourt Brace. 1956.

Bury, J.B. *The Idea of Progress: An Inquiry into its Origin and Growth*. London, 1920.

Carey, John. *The Intellectuals and the Masses: Pride and Prejudice among the Literary Intelligentsia, 1880 – 1939*. London: Faber and Faber, 1992.

Commager, Henry Steele. *The American Mind: An Interpretation of American Thought and Character since the 1880's*. New Haven: Yale University Press, 1950.

Deneen, Patrick J. *Why Liberalism Failed*. 1st ed. New Haven: Yale University Press, 2018.

Epstein, Richard A. *How Progressives Rewrote the Constitution*. Cato Institute, 2007.

Flew, R. Newton. *The Idea of Perfection in Christian Theology*. New York: Oxford University Press, 1934.

Flynn, John T. *The Roosevelt Myth*. New York: The Devin-Adair Company, 1956.

Gasman, Daniel. *The Scientific Origins of National Socialism*. New Brunswick: Transaction Publishers, 2004.

Hartz, Louis. *The Liberal Tradition in America: An Interpretation of American Political Thought since the Revolution*. New York: Harcourt, Brace and Company, 1955.

Hatch, Nathan O. *The Democratization of American Christianity*. New Haven: Yale University Press, 1989.

Hawkins, Mike. *Social Darwinism in European and American Thought, 1860–1945: Nature as Model and Nature as Threat*. Cambridge: Cambridge University Press, 1997.

Hayek, Friedrich A. *The Road To Serfdom with The Intellectuals and Socialism*. Norwich: The Institute of Economic Affairs, 2005. [1945].

Herring, Pendleton. *The Impact of War: Our American Democracy under Arms*. New York: Farrar and Rinehart, 1941.

Hofstadter, Richard. *The Age of Reform: From Bryan to F.D.R.* New York: Alfred A. Knopf, 1955.

Hofstadter, Richard. *Anti-Intellectualism in American Life*. New York: Knopf, 1962.

Howe, Daniel Walker. *What Hath God Wrought: the Transformation of America, 1815-1848*. New York: Oxford University Press, 2007.

Johnson, Walter. *William Allen White's America*. New York: Henry Holt and Company. 1947.

Kazin, Michael. *A Godly Hero: The Life of William Jennings Bryan*. New York: Knopf, 2006.

Lasch, Christopher. *The Culture of Narcissism: American Life in an Age of Diminishing Expectations*. 1st ed. New York: Norton, 1978.

Lasch, Christopher. *The Revolt of the Elites: And the Betrayal of Democracy*. 1st ed. New York: W.W. Norton, 1995.

Leonard, Thomas C. *Illiberal Reformers: Race, Eugenics, and American Economics in the Progressive Era*. Princeton: Princeton University Press, 2016.

Leuchtenburg, William E. *The Perils of Prosperity, 1914-1932*, 2nd Edition. University of Chicago Press, 1993.

Lilienthal, David E. TVA: *Democracy on the March*. New York: Harper and Brothers, 1944.

Mandelbaum, Maurice. *History, Man, & Reason A Study in Nineteenth-Century Thought*. Open access edition. Baltimore, Maryland: Johns Hopkins University Press, 2019. [1971].

Passmore, John. *The Perfectibility of Man*. London: Duckworth, 1970.

Pestritto, Ronald J. *Woodrow Wilson and the Roots of Modern Liberalism*. Lanham, MD: Rowman & Littlefield, 2005.

Pestritto, Ronald J. "Making the State into a God: American Progressivism and the Social Gospel." In *Progressive Challenges to the American Constitution: A New Republic*. edited by Bradley C. S. Watson.

Cambridge: Cambridge University Press, 2017, 144–
59.

Pestritto, Ronald J. *America Transformed: The Rise and Legacy of American Progressivism*. New York: Encounter, 2023.

Postell, Joseph, and Johnathan G. O'Neill, eds. *Toward an American Conservatism: Constitutional Conservatism During the Progressive Era*. New York, New York: Palgrave Macmillan, 2013.

Rable, George C. *God's Almost Chosen Peoples: a Religious History of the American Civil War*. Chapel Hill: University of North Carolina Press, 2010.

Robinson, Edgar. *The Roosevelt Leadership*. Philadelphia: J.B. Lippincott Company, 1955.

Schlesinger, Arthur M. *The Coming of the New Deal: The Age of Roosevelt, 1933 – 1935*. Boston: Houghton Mifflin, 1958.

Schlesinger, Arthur M. Jr. *The Vital Center: The Politics of Freedom with a New Introduction by the Author*. Sentry Edition. Boston: Houghton Mifflin Company, 1962 [1949].

Watson, Bradley C.S. *Progressivism: The Strange History of a Radical Idea*. University of Notre Dame Press, 2020.

Articles:

Aubrey, Edwin Ewart. "Review of *Christian Perfection: In This World?*, by R. Newton Flew". *The Journal of Religion* 15, no. 1 (1935): 106–8. http://www.jstor.org/stable/1195834.

Cunningham, Joseph W. "The Methodist Doctrine of Christian Perfection: Charles Wesley's Contribution

Contextualized." *Wesley and Methodist Studies*, 2
(2012): 25 – 44,
http://www.jstor.org/stable/42909783.

Hofstadter, Richard. "The Myth of the Happy Yeoman."
American Heritage 7 no. 3. (April 1956):
https://www.americanheritage.com/myth-happy-
yeoman.

Miller, Perry. "The Garden of Eden and the Deacon's
Meadow." *American Heritage* 7 no. 1. (December
1955).

Moorhead, James H. "Between Progress and Apocalypse: A
Reassessment of Millennialism in American
Religious Thought, 1800-1880." *The Journal of
American History* 71, no. 3 (1984): 524–42.
https://doi.org/10.2307/1887470.

Dissertations:

Schearer, Michael. "Our Enemy, the State: Liberty versus
Power on the American Home Front during the First
World War." PhD diss., Liberty University, 2004.

Appendix to Part I

Email Conversation with Dr. Jack N. Rakove; edited for privacy, author 'Super Guy'.

> Dissertation: Please clarify
> 5 messages
> Super Guy
> Mon, Sep 9, 2024 at 11:01 AM
> To: Jack N. Rakove
> Dr. Rakove,
>
> I am performing dissertation research and I am attempting to verify and clarify the substance of your statement to Melissa De Witte (Stanford Report, July 1, 2020):
>
> When Jefferson wrote "all men are created equal" in the preamble to the Declaration, he was not talking about individual equality.
>
> I have the context, as relating to your work Original Meanings, but I have not found any corroboration to the statement that equality of creation was a wholly collectivist ideal to Jefferson - or Madison, upon whom your work focuses.
>
> Will you please clarify, specifically what is the basis for your claim that Jefferson "...was not talking about individual equality", especially in answer to the image of a 'natural aristocracy' - a purely Lockean meritocratic ideal predicated upon such individual equality - of which Gordon Wood spoke (Wood, Gordon. "Thomas Jefferson and the Idea of Equality". Speech. American Enterprise Institute. January 9, 1995. https://www.aei.org/research-products/speech/thomas-jefferson-and-the-idea-of-equality/.)
>
> Thank you.

Jack N Rakove
Mon, Sep 9, 2024 at 11:37 AM

To: Super Guy <spencersclassemail@gmail.com>
Dear Super,

This is mostly derived from my first book on the Continental Congress and a few other essays on TJ I have written over the years, though I did not really spend too much time on the Declaration in Beginnings.

The basic argument is that the form of equality the opening of the Declaration was concerned with was the collective right of the American people, having suffered a long train of abuses, to institute new governments, open relations with other nations, renounce their loyalty to the Crown (and G) etc. The delegates were not sitting around Philadelphia discussing theories of individual equality. Not that they were renouncing them either; only that the context of political action had other, more specific ends.

But over time, and certainly by the 1790s, the Declaration becomes susceptible to other readings, and the emphasis on individual equality has become its most powerful legacy.

Good luck with your dissertation!
j.r.

Super Guy
Mon, Sep 9, 2024 at 11:56 AM
To: Jack N Rakove
Thank you for such a prompt reply!

I am curious, Wood claimed that:

"Equality for Jefferson was related to the personal independence of each citizen, which was essential for Republicanism. .... He and the other revolutionary leaders shared the liberal premises of Lockean sensationalism; that is, that all men were born equal and that only the environment working on their senses made them different." (AEI; 1-9-1995)

And Jefferson:

"the rights of the whole can be no more than the sum of the rights of the individuals." (To Madison, 9-6-1789)

Whereas your statement makes an overt claim regarding equality among groups alone. In such a climate the ideal that a 'nobody' might by merit arise beyond arbitrary distinction would be impossible, thereby invalidating the entire premise of Jefferson's republicanism, of which he and Wood spoke at length.

Perhaps you might offer some specific instance wherein Jefferson subordinated the individual to the collective, beyond the Lockean circumscriptions inherent in his definition of liberty?

Jack N Rakove
Mon, Sep 9, 2024 at 1:36 PM
To: Super Guy
Well, I am certainly not claiming that Jefferson did not speak in egalitarian terms elsewhere (sorry for the double negative). See my Jefferson chapter in Revolutionaries and also the opening chapter in Beyond Belief. Again, what I was discussing is simply the context within which the Declaration was written.

Super Guy
Mon, Sep 9, 2024 at 2:13 PM
To: Jack N Rakove
Thank you.

Historiographical Survey

Removed from the Prologue because nobody cares about the literature survey, but they are still required in every dissertation. Placed here for anyone masochistic enough to want to read it – and to irritate the snooty academics.

While the present work focused on the shift in American perspectives regarding the scope and purpose of authority, few recent scholars have explored the multi-thematic nature of the development of this inverted worldview. The intersect of intellectual currents in the development of 'progress' as a perspective, and the social influence of self-affirming heresy in 'christian perfectibility' necessitated analysis of some works that were only related in part. These scholars, while not focused on the wholistic inversion of individualism, served to illustrate some of the primary themes required by the subject matter. Among these themes one has selected perfectibility, elitism, and collectivism for a more focused survey.

Heretical perfectibility displays the perversion of the central Christian eschatological culmination of Christ's Kingdom by means of presuming a gradual, democratically self-directed improvement or ascension of society. This fantasy of auto-apotheosis serves to betray American society, subsequent to the Progressive Era, as a counterfeit, ersatz, inferior kingdom of God.

As will be shown, the elitist so-called 'expert-class' oligarchy was a direct product of self-congratulatory presumption resulting from the previously mentioned scientific and industrial achievements of the previous decades. The result of this development is that American society retains some of the trappings of a republic, but none of the essential quality or *anima* – in essence, the Republic became an Empire.

Collective paradigms appeared in a number of fields; they are distinguished by consistent reference to variations of 'the greater good', with little to no reflection on the concept of individual liberty or limited government. Prior to granular, thematic historiographical analysis however, it was reasonable to address some few scholars whose work is nearest in purpose and scope to the current argument.

Michael Shearer Ph.D. argued in his 2024 doctoral dissertation "Our Enemy, the State" for a substantially similar interpretation of early twentieth century American society. His thesis differs from this work in some key details. Schearer places the substance of America's conversion in the transformation of social voluntarism to state-power resulting from domestic policy enacted around America's brief participation in the Great War. He identified a series of 'states' that, when taken as a whole, demonstrate the creation of the *apparatus* of the authoritarian monster; entities such as 'The Regulatory State', 'The Propaganda State' and 'The Class Warfare State'.[975] Schearer's voluminous argument touches many related themes, especially in his tenth and final chapter, but focuses exclusively on warfare as the flag under which authoritarianism was introduced into the United States, primarily from a public policy perspective. He does not analyze the worldviews *behind* this apparatus as much as its development.

The substance of Part I of this work will most certainly draw parallels to the legal paradigm called 'originalism,' but to make such a comparison would be to miss the point entirely. Falling to the seduction of that misdirect, Emeritus Professor of Political Science at Stanford, Jack N. Rakove Ph.D. was bestowed the Pulitzer for his 1996 *Original Meanings: Politics and Ideas in the Making of the Constitution*. This work employed a substantially post-modern legerdemain to conceal interpretation in the robes of sophistry – using current presumptions to 'analyze' past contexts. To be certain, the book is very well researched and makes a reasonable attempt to maintain a reasonable approach, but the narrowness of its treatment by necessity rejected the necessity of its topic. In seeking to address the myriad of complicated details in the

---

975 Chapters six, seven, and nine respectively in Michael Schearer, "Our Enemy, the State: Liberty versus Power on the American Home Front during the First World War," (PhD diss., Liberty University, 2024).

history of the drafting and ratification of the Constitution, Rakove substantially missed the point – that it was mere procedure to pursue the principles of the Declaration. As an unfortunate result of a myopic focus on the context of ratification, Rakove fell victim to the red-herring represented by his title, and so failed to grasp the timelessness of concepts that underlie vocabulary.

Dean of Hillsdale Graduate School and Professor of Politics, Ronald J. Pestritto Ph.D. in many ways represents a mirror image of Rakove. He is an exceedingly prolific scholar of the Progressive Era and the themes contained therein – most especially historicism. One of his earlier works, *Woodrow Wilson and the Roots of Modern Liberalism* (2005), analyzed the extensive influence exercised by Georg W.F. Hegel (1770 – 1831) over the development of Wilson's political philosophy, and especially his contempt for the thought of universal, transcendent principles.[976] His latest work *America Transformed* (2023), lay heavy into the Central European origins of historicism seeking to highlight its extensive infection of American public policy primarily through Roosevelt the First, and Woodrow Wilson among others.[977] Additionally, Pestritto's contribution to Watson's compilation, *Progressive Challenges to the American Constitution* (2017) offered a fertile clue into the origins of the zealotry that characterized the Progressive Era.[978] Pestritto has in many ways assembled many of the pieces of the argument of this work, but he does not compile them into a cohesive analysis of two divergent worldviews.

Economic historian Thomas C. Leonard contended that the Progressives opposed the concept of individualism altogether and viewed *society* as a single organism, against which the 'cells' – individuals – could have no rights at all. The Progressives, as Leonard argues in his 2016 *Illiberal*

---

976   Ronald J. Pestritto, *Woodrow Wilson and the Roots of Modern Liberalism*, (Lanham, MD: Rowman & Littlefield, 2005).

977   Ronald J. Pestritto, *America Transformed: The Rise and Legacy of American Progressivism*, (New York: Encounter, 2023).

978   Ronald J. Pestritto, "Making the State into a God: American Progressivism and the Social Gospel," In *Progressive Challenges to the American Constitution: A New Republic*, edited by Bradley C. S. Watson, (Cambridge: Cambridge University Press, 2017), 144–59.

Reformers: Race, Eugenics and American Economics in the Progressive Era, sought to create a powerful centralized government of experts.[979] Leonard lay hard into the racially motivated genocidal elitism that characterized the time. He exposed the deliberate, almost conspiratorial drive to abolish the ideal of individual liberty in American society. His work focused on a vital aspect of Progressivism, but did not address the manner by which it served to invert American worldviews, or how this has invalidated legitimacy itself.

As a companion to Leonard's 2016 work, Bradley Watson's 2020 *Progressivism: The Strange History of a Radical Idea* placed the intellectual grounding of Progressivism squarely at the feet of Darwinian nihilism masquerading as pragmatism.[980] This view repudiated any ideal of a fixed point or first principles that might act as something against which the (then) present might be compared, and replaced it with a universalized external ideal of adaptation: society was evolving, and must therefore evolve under the authority of the expert. He attacked the positions of some notable Progressive Historians such as Henry Steele Commager *The American Mind*, 1950, who cast the Federal government as a "social welfare agency". Watson also opposed Richard Hofstadter's 1955 *The Age of Reform* who defined Progressivism as an essentially reactionary appeasement that sought to address the fundamentally Marxist ideal of 'middle-class [bourgeois] status anxiety'.

Watson's primary thesis was that the Progressive Era represented the repudiation of Constitutionalism focused on the principle of Natural Law. He argued that historians have effectively failed to make this connection, and that the vital recognition of the essential character of the progressive paradigm has come instead from disciplines outside of History. This work is a direct if unintentional response to that challenge.

---

979   Thomas C. Leonard, *Illiberal Reformers: Race, Eugenics, and American Economics in the Progressive Era*, (Princeton: Princeton University Press, 2016).

980   Bradley C.S. Watson, *Progressivism: The Strange History of a Radical Idea*, (University of Notre Dame Press, 2020).

Henry Steele Commager's 1950 *The American Mind* presented a similar comparative analysis as this work in that he compared the 'mind' of the nineteenth century American against that of the twentieth century. He employed Watson's Darwinian pragmatism to characterize a shift in American society during a very similar time-frame (1890's to the 1950's), but argued, contrary to this author's contention, that the essential character of the American remained effectively unchanged – a dynamic that he lamented similarly to his contemporaries Daniel Aaron and James Burns, analyzed below.[981]

An exception to Watson's claim that historians have not addressed the fundamental shift in constitutionalism, Legal history scholar Richard A. Epstein makes a forceful argument in his 2006 *How Progressives Rewrote the Constitution*. He directly attacked the Progressive Era in a similar manner to that intended by this work and analyzed both Progressive ideology and the methods it employed as a means of subverting or side-stepping constraints on authority. Specific to his career as a legal scholar, Epstein consulted numerous legal opinions and the historical context in which these arose to ultimately conclude that the Progressive Era was a pseudo-scientific, tyrannical, and elitist autocracy that ultimately failed.[982] Epstein did not venture into the deep socio-intellectual repercussions of his topic, nor its impact on legitimacy of authority as intended for this present work.

Narrowing focus from overall similar arguments to the aforementioned individual themes, the historiography of

---

981   Henry Steele Commager, *The American Mind: An Interpretation of American Thought and Character since the 1880's*, (New Haven: Yale University Press, 1950).

982   Richard A. Epstein, *How Progressives Rewrote the Constitution*, (Cato Institute, 2007). Cf. Edgar Robinson, *The Roosevelt Leadership*, (Philadelphia: J.B. Lippincott Company, 1955); and John T. Flynn, *The Roosevelt Myth*, (New York: The Devin-Adair Company, 1956); Mirroring Epstein, but far more partisan, Joseph Postell, and Johnathan G. O'Neill, eds., *Toward an American Conservatism: Constitutional Conservatism During the Progressive Era*, (New York: Palgrave Macmillan, 2013). For a counterpoint to Epstein, cf. William Leuchtenberg, *The Perils of Prosperity,1914 – 1932*, 2nd Edition, (Chicago: University of Chicago Press, 1992 [1958]).

the inversion of individualism to collectivism, and its attendant implications on legitimate authority became more subject specific. This portion of the analysis began with religious history and the heresy of perfectibility.

As notable religious historian Perry Miller stated in 1955, "The Old Testament is truly so omnipresent in the American culture of 1800 or 1820 that historians have as much difficulty taking cognizance of it as of the air people breathed."[983] It is by no means limited to that specific time frame. The essential nature of the metaphysical image of 'Americanism', today reflected in 'exceptionalism', is wholly festooned with biblical, Christian, and Puritan imagery. Simply stated, any examination of American worldviews that fails to address religious themes is as incomplete as failing to address the role of oxygen in cellular respiration. This fundamentally religious – metaphysical, cosmologic – flavor to the topic surrounds and permeates the Progressive Era, but in many ways extends from the very founding of the Republic.

In taking cognizance of this air, Daniel W. Howe Ph.D. analyzed the social effects of the 'Second Great-Awakening' in his 2007 *What Hath God Wrought*. Broadly engaging with primary sources chiefly from the Jacksonian Era, Howe used the public ministries of Lyman Beecher (1775 – 1863) and Charles Finney (1792 – 1875), in addition to Methodist revivalism and the ecumenicism of the Evangelical United Front, to demonstrate a powerful religious motivation for social reform, usually by means of political maneuvering.[984] While such characterizations are somewhat incidental to Howe's thesis, this spiritually infused

---

983   Perry Miller, "The Garden of Eden and the Deacon's Meadow," *American Heritage* 7 no. 1, (December 1955).

984   Daniel Walker Howe, *What Hath God Wrought: the Transformation of America, 1815-1848*, (New York: Oxford University Press, 2007). Cf. Jama Lazerow, *Religion and the Working Class in Antebellum America*, (Washington: Smithsonian Institution Press, 1995). Regarding the Methodist doctrine of Perfectibility, cf. Joseph W. Cunningham, "The Methodist Doctrine of Christian Perfection: Charles Wesley's Contribution Contextualized," *Wesley and Methodist Studies* 2 (2012): 25 – 44, http://www.jstor.org/stable/42909783.

zealotry served to explain a vital aspect of the history into which Howe did not venture.

George C. Rable Ph.D. examined Howe's climate as it fared the Civil War in his 2010 *God's Almost Chosen People*. He employed primary source literature – especially periodicals – to demonstrate the overtly religious interpretation of the war by both sides in the conflict. Crucially, the work demonstrated the manner by which doctrine and belief were recruited to rationalize and justify behavior in favor of given objectives – making religion the hand-maid of power in a manner of speaking.[985] With Howe, Rable concluded his argument prior to the apex of civil-religion sublimated into policy-activism, and thusly did not reach the level intended in this work.

Directly addressing the concept of perfectibility, historian of philosophy John Passmore's 1970 *The Perfectibility of Man* presented an expansive, nearly exhaustive narration of the concept that man might become like God. Beginning with the Greeks and ending with hippies, Passmore's work employed exceedingly technical vocabulary relying on obscure theological concepts.[986] Most poignantly however, he also analyzed the concept from a secular perspective, demonstrating that such a doctrine can

---

985   George C. Rable, *God's Almost Chosen Peoples: a Religious History of the American Civil War*, (Chapel Hill: University of North Carolina Press, 2010). For more analysis regarding the recruitment of religion in social and political causes, cf. James H. Moorhead, "Between Progress and Apocalypse: A Reassessment of Millennialism in American Religious Thought, 1800 – 1880," *The Journal of American History* 71, no 3 (1984) 524 – 42, https://doi.org/10.2307/1887470; Nathan O. Hatch, *The Democratization of American Christianity*, (New Haven: Yale University Press, 1989). An exceedingly partisan portrayal: Michael Kazin, *A Godly Hero: The Life of William Jennings Bryan*, (New York: Knopf, 2006); For similar agenda-driven 'hero-worship' or self-promotion, cf. Walter Johnson, *William White's America*, (New York: Henry Holt and Company, 1947); David E. Lilienthal, *TVA: Democracy on the March*, (New York: Harper and Brothers, 1944); Pendleton Herring, *The Impact of War: Our American Democracy under Arms*, (New York: Farrar and Rinehart, 1941).

986   John Passmore, *The Perfectibility of Man*, (London: Duckworth, 1970).

be, and was, adopted by ideologies without an overtly religious dimension. Crucially, Passmore confronted the imaginary mechanism inherent in the materialist perspective that the lack of perfection in society is caused by institutional structures, therefore making their abolition and replacement the key to the perfection of society, and thereby the species. The scope of his work is admirable, but did not approach the inversion caused by its application in the Progressive Era.

Preceding Passmore, R. Newton Flew's 1934 *The Idea of Perfection in Christian Theology* examined the semantic shadings of the operative term as it was employed from the earliest Apostolic Church to the early American Church. The analysis was chiefly theological from later (after Christ) thinkers; the argument concluded that perfection can only be achieved after death. As it was written around the height of the progressive reform impulse in 1934, it demonstrated one perspective regarding perfectibility that was defined then as one of the "Recent reactions to the liberal movement in theology…."[987] Passmore and Flew provided access to the theological concept itself including its variety of shading and intent, in addition to the state of discourse regarding perfectibility during the Long Progressive Era.

Heretical eschatology around the upward destiny of humanity was not the sole motivation to employ political force for social agenda, but it was certainly a prime-mover in that direction. Where religious ideals provided a moralizing impetus or rationalization for social movement, intellectual developments and their attendant self-affirmations provided both substance to the fantasy, and an ostensible pathway to achieve the imagined ascended society.

J. B. Bury, FBA (1861 – 1927) offered vital details in the research for this argument. His 1920 philosophical work *The Idea of Progress: An Inquiry into Its Origin and Growth* narrated a grandiose shift in perspective central to the Progressive Era. Where in prior ages the cosmological

---

987   R. Newton Flew, *The Idea of Perfection in Christian Theology*, (New York: Oxford University Press, 1934). Edwin Ewart Aubrey, "Review of *Christian Perfection: In This World?*, by R. Newton Flew," *The Journal of Religion* 15, no. 1 (1935): 106.

'Golden Age' had been in the past, scientific and technological developments of the sixteenth to nineteenth centuries inverted that cosmology into 'progress'; mankind was improving – *evolving*. The ideal of forward improvement of the species as a whole was a child of European Enlightenment but this perspective in America created the ideal of science as a mechanism for moral improvement; crucially as an exclusively anthropogenic phenomenon that set history as the key to human development. While certainly not the origin of such a self-aggrandizing teleology, 'modernism', or the idea that 'today' was better than 'yesterday', and 'tomorrow' was better than 'today' would quickly find wide acceptance for the rationalization of elitism that it represents. The idea of progress is more appropriately defined as a self-declared and self-induced apotheosis.[988] The scope of the current work is beyond both Bury's methodology and his time, but the cosmology he presented gave a direct connection between socio-religious activism of Reconstruction and the so-called Gilded Age, and both the motives for and effects of the Progressive Era.

Expanding on Bury's 1920 work by means of a far more focused treatment, John Carey's 1992 *The Intellectuals and the Masses: Pride and Prejudice among the Literary Intelligentsia, 1880 – 1939* drove to the heart of the fundamentally misanthropic nature of modernism. He addressed an extremely broad variety of themes – almost all in a Malthusian vein: elitism, social and actual Darwinism, eugenics, anti-natalism, antisemitism, presentism (at the time), obscurantism, and fascist leanings. His attack on elitism is comparable to Christopher Lasch in general and complimented some of the social commentary made famous

---

988   J.B. Bury, *The Idea of Progress: An Inquiry into its Origin and Growth*, (London, 1920). For the rise of pseudo-scientific elitism, eugenics, etc. in the Progressive Era, cf. Maurice Mandelbaum, *History, Man & Reason: A Study in Nineteenth-Century Thought*, (Baltimore: Johns Hopkins University Press, 2019 [1971]); Daniel Gasman, *The Scientific Origins of National Socialism*, (New Brunswick: Transaction Publishers, 2004); Mike Hawkins, *Social Darwinism in European and American Thought, 1860 – 1945: Nature as Model and Nature as Threat*, (Cambridge: Cambridge University Press, 1997); etc.

by Orwell and Huxley.[989] Carey's interpretation of *fin de siècle* historiography regarding broader elitist bigotry may well be debatable, but it was a suitable mine for its citations that speak to the proclivities of the individuals by whom they were written.

The haughty elitism produced by scientific and industrial advancement commingled with some offshoots of nineteenth century idealism in such a manner as to prompt a managerial or top-down perspective regarding society. This perspective viewed masses of individuals, rather than the individual himself, and recruited a form of the Bentham branch of utility with a decidedly aristocratic determinism. The most appropriate definition for this amorphous amalgam of à la carte philosophies is collectivism. The appropriate term for the socio-political appearance of collectivism is Progressivism.

Steven J. Diner Ph.D. is a notable scholar of the Progressive Era from a social history perspective. His 1999 historiographic review "Linking Politics and People: The Historiography of the Progressive Era" gave a broad overview of the manner by which social history came to dominate the time of so much government intrusion into social arenas.[990] Critically, Diner demonstrated that the Progressive era was the origin of a change in the social character of the Republic – vital to this argument – from individualism to collectivism.

Addressing collectivist approaches is an exercise in attempting to comprehend the absurd. Each collectivist scholar appears more partisan than the last, with each subsequent work contriving more rationalizations for authoritarianism based on increasingly strange, exotic, or flatly delusional presuppositions. Some of these retain varying levels of self-awareness, yet most compose their

---

989   John Carey, *The Intellectuals and the Masses: Pride and Prejudice among the Literary Intelligentsia, 1880 – 1939*, (London: Faber and Faber, 1992). Cf. Christopher Lasch, *The Revolt of the Elites: And the Betrayal of Democracy*, (New York: W.W. Norton, 1995); *The Culture of Narcissism: American Life in an Age of Diminishing Expectations*, (New York: Norton, 1978). Neither Orwell nor Huxley require introduction.

990   *Magazine of History* 13, no. 3. (Spring).

arguments as though it were physically impossible to disagree with their assumptions – presaging the ersatz moralism that would result from their ascendancy in the Progressive Era.

Arthur M. Schlesinger Jr. (1917 – 2007) is mandatory in any examination of collectivist paradigms in twentieth century America. His works *The Vital Center*, (1949) and *The Coming of the New Deal*, (1958) display exactly what may be expected of an historian who overtly functioned as a political operative. The first work [re]defines 'liberalism' as effectively anything that Franklin Roosevelt sought to accomplish; the second work argues that "... the only hope was a federal program" regarding the Depression, extolling Roosevelt's repudiation of constitutionalism and ignoring Progressivism's role in creating that crisis.[991] Most of Schlesinger's work praises Roosevelt, his few criticisms were limited to the New Deal having not gone far enough for his liking.

Weaknesses notwithstanding, Schlesinger directly addressed the perfectibility of man in his introductory remarks to *The Vital Center*. He made a curious (and false) claim that liberalism "had long been almost inextricably linked with a picture of man as perfectible", that Soviet Communism and Fascism had reminded man of his fallibility, but the New Deal had renewed hope in liberalism.[992] Schlesinger clearly had *neo*-liberalism in mind as he equated it with the New Deal without recognition that Liberalism extends from Natural Law, not a 'brain trust.' Schlesinger's strange caricature was by no means isolated; many if not most of his contemporaries adopted a similarly *apologetic* approach, and if nothing else demonstrate the vital need for a glossary.

James Burns' 1956 *Roosevelt: The Lion and the Fox* cast the New Deal as the 'broker state'. He sought to excuse

---

991   Arthur M. Schlesinger, *The Coming of the New Deal: The Age of Roosevelt, 1933 – 1935*, (Boston: Houghton Mifflin 1958), 260.
992   Arthur M. Schlesinger Jr. *The Vital Center: The Politics of Freedom with a New Introduction by the Author*, Sentry Edition, (Boston: Houghton Mifflin Company, 1962 [1949]), xxii – xxiii.

the authoritarian bent of his apparent hero by claiming that
Roosevelt was forced leftward by an obstructing Supreme
Court, showing the rationalizing blame-casting inherent in
collectivism.[993] This position presaged William Leuchtenburg
who repeated and expanded Burns' 'broker state' justification
in his 1963 *Franklin D. Roosevelt and the New Deal*. The
position pioneered by Burns repeated that the president was
'forced' into several programs that Schlesinger, Leuchtenburg
and Richard Hofstadter (1916 – 1970) all correctly defined as
a revolution. Leuchtenburg's criticisms of Roosevelt betrayed
his bias perhaps more than any other aspect of his work. Like
Schlesinger, Leuchtenburg claimed that the scope of this
revolution was insufficiently revolutionary – it did not go far
enough.

　　　The advocacy inherent in these works created the
elements of the American Aeneid: a mandate from heaven to
employ democracy to bring America into the new *modern*
golden age. Yet another advocate, Pendleton Herring's 1941
The Impact of War championed the total abandonment of the
overt prohibition on standing armies, ignoring both civil
liberties and limited government.[994] He was instrumental in
the origin of Eisenhower's 'Military Industrial Complex'. Like
Schlesinger the Democrat Party speech writer, Herring took
part in both the drafting and the passage of the 1947 National
Security Act. While later than the traditional Progressive Era,
Herring, Leuchtenburg, Schlesinger et al. wholly adopted the
collectivist paradigm as their own and sought to employ their
histories as legitimizing literature for the new *imperium*.

　　　These 'Virgils' crafted a deliberate narrative of the
Progressive Era and New Deal, including an almost mythic
hero, but they were not unopposed in their messianic image
of Roosevelt. Freidrich Hayek's *Road to Serfdom* was re-
published as a *Reader's Digest* condensed version the very
same month and year of the president's death (April, 1945).
Hayek wrote it during the height of Roosevelt's power.[995]
Additionally, Edgar Robinson's 1955 *The Roosevelt*

993　　　James MacGregor Burns, *Roosevelt: The Lion and the Fox*.
(New York: Harcourt Brace. 1956).
994　　　Pendleton Herring, *The Impact of War: Our American
Democracy under Arms*, (New York: Farrar and Rinehart, 1941).

Leadership attacked Roosevelt's fundamental alteration of the system of government in the United States.[996] Robinson argued that Roosevelt severely weakened constitutionalism, imperiled national security, decreased American morale, corroded political morality, and stressed the national economy. In Robinson's view, FDR was simply a demagogue and the New Deal is effectively the consummation of Progressive (collectivist) ideologies. This argument invalidates Richard Hofstadter's delusional claim that the Great War killed the Progressive party.

Richard Hofstadter's 1955 *Age of Reform: From Bryan to F.D.R.* presented the 'agrarian myth' (vis. Jefferson's yeoman) as a national fiction.[997] His 1956 "The Myth of the Happy Yeoman" in *American Heritage*, as well as his 1962 *Anti-Intellectualism in American Life* further expanded his patently elitist, and easily disproved caricature of both the American, and the ideal of American society.[998] Hofstadter summarized his elitist approach thusly: "The agrarian myth represents a kind of homage that Americans have paid to the fancied innocence of their origins."[999] His work serves as a late example of an important detail in the analysis of the Progressive Era, and represents a convenient exemplar of many of the wacky presumptions that characterize nearly all collectivist arguments.

These types of arguments and positions appear under a variety of names. Defunct political parties called by the names notwithstanding, there is little consensus regarding the difference between what is called 'Populist' and what is called 'Progressive' in works that examined them. Michael Kazin narrated a conversion of the populists into the progressives,

---

995   Friedrich A. Hayek, *The Road To Serfdom with The Intellectuals and Socialism*, (Norwich: The Institute of Economic Affairs, 2005. [1945]).

996   Edgar Robinson, *The Roosevelt Leadership*, (Philadelphia: J.B. Lippincott Company, 1955).

997   Richard Hofstadter, *The Age of Reform: From Bryan to F.D.R.*, (New York: Alfred A. Knopf, 1955).

998   Richard Hofstadter, "The Myth of the Happy Yeoman," *American Heritage* 7 no. 3, (April 1956); Richard Hofstadter, *Anti-Intellectualism in American Life*, (New York: Knopf, 1962).

999   Hofstadter, *The Age of Reform*, 24.

but Hofstadter distinguished populism from progressivism by
stating "Populism was the first modern political movement of
practical importance... the federal government has some
responsibility for the common weal...."[1000]. It would seem
that his 'myth' was the basis for the populists, but his
definition of populism strikes as identical to the general
thrust of the progressive.

Similar to the previous, Daniel Aaron also took the
position that Theodore Roosevelt and Woodrow Wilson did
not go far enough in their remaking society. His 1951 *Men of
Good Hope: A Story of American Progressives* employed a
position like that of Hofstadter in complicating times and
terms.[1001] This curiosity is not a fatal flaw however as Aaron
both offers and keeps to a definition, and this definition
demonstrated the religious motivation that undergirded the
drive to employ political force for social agenda – without
regard to the terminology under which all such activities
have fallen.

The difficulties in terminology are not adjunct to the
topic of collectivism versus individualism or classical
liberalism opposed to progressivism; the terminology and
arguments thereon are central. For the purposes of this
argument, collectivism was defined as, quite generally,
Bentham's utility writ large: the greatest number as decided
by the elite few. Individualism is a general reverse, but
focused on Natural Law not hedonism. That vital caveat
underlies many of the arguments regarding liberalism –
whether classical or *neo*.

To address Liberalism, the 'Classical' being assumed,
one can do no better than the general sources: Locke,
Madison, Adams, and Jefferson. Such a declaration is
however insufficient for an historiographical survey, and
these men cannot be expected to address the eventual course
of a worldview to which they each contributed a part.

Political scientist Patrick Deneen's 2018 *Why
Liberalism Failed* harnessed some Hegelian methodology in

1000   Kazin, *A Godly Hero*, 2006; Hofstadter, *The Age of Reform*,
    61.
1001   Daniel Aaron, *Men of Good Hope: A Story of American
    Progressives*, (New York: Oxford University Press, 1951).

his argument that the seeds of liberalism's demise are contained within its very essence.[1002] Deneen claimed that social atomization or fragmentation into effectively isolated individuals is a direct product of liberalism's individualist preference. He makes a compelling case to support his mechanism in recognizing the existential isolation – a void – of a life lived without membership in or reference to something greater and more transcendent than the individual. He quite correctly credits this emptiness as the germ that metastasizes into totalitarian power; those without local belonging do indeed go about seeking participation in grander, more distant and more abstract institutions. Deneen analyzes liberalism from the perspective of internal contradictions to ultimately advocate in favor of something resembling a *polis* or a city-state. While such an image does mesh well with the ideal of a republic, his argument fails in one crucial regard that shifts the substance of its direction: he mistook hedonism for individualism, and did not enfold the concept of a moral, voluntary citizenry for whom belonging is a happy side-effect. This oversight does not preclude Deneen's utility for this work rather, he lent a vital focus to understanding the substance of vocabulary in worldview.

Understanding the worldview upon which America was founded is certainly of chief importance – being a primary pillar of this argument. Another scholar critiques the individualism found in Alexis de Tocqueville's famous American ethnography in a similar manner to Deneen, though with a different purpose to a different argument.[1003]

Louis Hartz (1919 – 1986) was a political scientist like Deneen, but also an historian. His 1955 *The Liberal Tradition in America* credits the Lockean atomistic individual personal freedom celebrated in Tocqueville, rather than cites it as a failing.[1004] Extending from Tocqueville, Hartz traced

---

1002   Patrick J. Deneen, *Why Liberalism Failed*, (New Haven: Yale University Press, 2018).

1003   Alexis de Tocqueville (1805 – 1859), *De la Démocratie en Amérique*, 1835, 1840.

1004   Louis Hartz, *The Liberal Tradition in America: An Interpretation of American Political Thought since the Revolution*, (New York: Harcourt, Brace and Company, 1955).

this individualism to the lack of a feudal past on the American continent. Hartz's thesis was that America had only variations of Lockean liberalism for ideology. This, and its freedom from a legacy of feudalism made it effectively immune to socialism. As with the aforementioned centrality of terminology, one may categorically disagree with Hartz on both counts because the Progressive Era effectively nullified that Lockean tradition to an extent that Hartz failed to recognize, and recent trends indicate that socialism is alive and well in America.

About The Author

S pencer D. Miles earned his BA in Philosophy and MA in History from the University of Colorado at Colorado Springs, and his Doctorate in History from Liberty University. He holds a Graduate Certificate of Criminal Justice from UCCS, and works to complete his MS in that discipline by May 2026.

Dr. Miles spent nearly two decades in a variety of industrial trades before completing his academic studies. He has taught Adult Literacy, Languages, Music Theory, and GED Preparation courses in addition to his independent research in fields ranging from Theology and Archaeology, to Chemistry and Mechanical Engineering.

He lives with his wife and three daughters in Colorado; with a glut of creative pursuits, and an overabundance of vegetative and animal friends – of both the fuzzy and scaly variety. He might be a little weird, but you are too!

www.ingramcontent.com/pod-product-compliance
Lightning Source LLC
Chambersburg PA
CBHW031040110426
42740CB00047B/762